A CONCISE DICTIONARY OF
new
WORDS

B.A. Phythian
Completed by Richard Cox

TEACH YOURSELF BOOKS

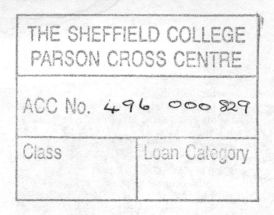
Long-renowned as the authoritative source for self-guided learning – with more than 30 million copies sold worldwide – the *Teach Yourself* series includes over 200 titles in the fields of languages, crafts, hobbies, sports, and other leisure activities.

Library of Congress Catalog Card Number: on file.

First published in UK 1996 by Hodder & Stoughton Educational, a division of Hodder Headline Plc, 338 Euston Road, London NW1 3BH

A catalogue record for this title is available from the British Library.

First published in US 1997 by NTC Publishing Group, 4255 West Touhy Avenue, Lincolnwood (Chicago), Illinois 60646 – 19975 U.S.A.

The 'Teach Yourself' name and logo are registered trade marks of Hodder & Stoughton Ltd in the UK.

Typeset by Wearset, Boldon, Tyne and Wear
Printed in Great Britain by Cox & Wyman Ltd, Reading, Berks.

Impression number 10 9 8 7 6 5 4 3 2 1
Year   1999 1998 1997 1996

TEACH YOURSELF BOOKS

A CONCISE DICTIONARY OF
new
WORDS

Preface

This book is intended both to interest and inform. It will help readers to differentiate between DINKIES, NIMBIES, WRINKLIES and WANNABES, or to distinguish between those who describe themselves or others as PRO-LIFE, PRO-CHOICE, or PRO-DEATH (and why). It will allow you to check on your use of such Americanisms as (TAKE A) RAIN CHECK (often misused in the UK), OUT IN THE LEFT FIELD or IN-YOUR-FACE.

The way it is set out is largely self-explanatory. Each entry begins with a headword printed **bold**, and when variant forms of the headword occur later in an entry they too are printed in **bold**. Later uses of the headword are in *italics* as are other words that are associated or analogous, unless they have entries in their own right elsewhere in the dictionary, in which case they are printed in SMALL CAPITALS, which will help the reader to follow up particular references and interests.

After the headword we give the part of speech (or else record that it is an abbreviation or an acronym). There then normally follows a 'dictionary definition' before any more general comment or history of first usage is given. In a minority of cases, however, we chose to begin with a more general comment or explanation, and it will be seen that such comments begin with an initial capital letter, whereas the dictionary definitions do not – the difference will be seen by comparing **abled**, which is followed by a definition, with **environment**, where a comment was preferred.

We have used the term 'acronym' for those abbreviations which are spoken as words, as for example EFTPOS or AIDS, rather than the letters being recited separately as they are for BSE or CJD, which we label 'abbreviations'. A noun is said to be used 'attributively' when its function is to stand before another noun and define it as an adjective does, e.g. *donor* card or *designer* drug.

We include the date when a word is thought (or known) to have first been used. Sometimes the year of a coinage is known, but more often the listing of a particular year can give a false impression of exactitude, as the word may well have been in spoken use, perhaps among a limited group of specialists or as slang, for many years before the first written record. Sometimes we give '(eighties)' or '(late eighties)' rather than a particular year. If you want the fullest possible account of the meanings and development of a particular word you cannot do better than turn to the twenty-volume second edition of the *Oxford English Dictionary* (published 1989) where you will find the first recorded uses and subsequent developments illustrated by examples.

There were many more words jostling to get in than we could possibly include if this was to remain a *Concise* dictionary. We took the sixties as a starting point, and only included a few key words from the fifties – words that seemed to be important for later coinages and explanations, such as BEATNIK and SPUTNIK. There are also some words whose first recorded use (often in the US) is from the late fifties, but which became familiar to UK users much later, or where the meaning has shifted over the years, as with JET SET, for example.

We hope that you will enjoy dipping into and browsing through this book and that the way it is set out will allow you to follow up leads and particular interests. For example, if military euphemisms such as *collateral damage* or *incontinent ordnance* interest you, then DOUBLE SPEAK could lead on to BODY BAG and FRIENDLY FIRE. Similarly, it is possible to trace shifts in ideas and changing attitudes over the last thirty years, from the SWINGING SIXTIES and WOMEN'S LIBERATION (see MS and CHAIR as well as POST-FEMINIST) to THATCHERISM (see the FALKLANDS FACTOR, YUPPIE and the ENTERPRISE CULTURE) and to more recent preoccupations with DOWNSIZING and OUTSOURCING (or OUTPLACEMENT). ENVIRONMENT, GREEN and ECO- show the comparatively recent surge in interest in ecology, while POLITICAL CORRECTNESS shows how a wholly justified effort to rid our language of gender bias and other prejudices has generated a resistance to what some feel to be dishonest jargon or insensitive coercion: see ABLED, ABLEISM or CHALLENGED. Thus new initiatives and old inertias both play a part in shaping the way we speak and write, and we hope this *Concise Dictionary* will aid your exploration of the shifting scene.

It has been a special pleasure for me to be able to complete the book that Brian Phythian was working on at the time of his death, and of which he had completed the first draft. Many years ago Brian was my Head of Department at Manchester Grammar School, where we both taught English, and in the many initiatives and projects he pursued so energetically he always showed an infectious enthusiasm for words and their histories – an enthusiasm he has demonstrated in earlier volumes in this series (*A Concise Dictionary of English Idioms, A Concise Dictionary of Phrase and Fable* and *A Concise Dictionary of English Slang*).

RICHARD COX

abled   *adj.* (of person) not disabled, able-bodied. A back-formation from *disabled*, **abled** was coined in the US in the early eighties, and used mainly by disabled people to refer to the able-bodied. The word is most familiar in combination with a preceding adverb, especially **differently abled**, as a euphemistic substitute for *disabled*. This combination, and others such as **otherly** or **uniquely abled**, originated in the US in the mid eighties, but though they are known in the UK their serious use is largely restricted to those professionally engaged with people with handicaps. **Differently abled**, like the other combinations, is widely objected to as, though its intentions are good, its sense is not – it is meant to avoid the negative connotations that are thought to attach to *disabled* and *handicapped*, but fudges the issue by appearing to make an unprovable and often unfounded claim to other compensating abilities. See CHALLENGED.

ableism   *noun* discrimination in favour of people who are able-bodied. Coined in the US in the early eighties and found in the UK c.1986. The word has been ridiculed, but is useful in defining, for example, that unthinking prejudice that prevents the employment of a handicapped person who is just as capable of doing a particular job as an able-bodied person, or the unthinking assumption that it is only necessary to cater for the **abled** (in terms of access etc.). Compare AGEISM.

ABM   see ANTI-BALLISTIC MISSILE.

abortuary   *noun* a clinic where abortions are performed. This polemical coinage reflects the bitterness between anti-abortion and pro-choice lobbies in the US. It dates from the end of the eighties and is a blending of *abortion* and *mortuary*.

ABS   (abbreviation for) anti-lock braking system. The term has become familiar since the early eighties, when the system was marketed on private cars, though anti-lock systems (designed to prevent wheels from locking when brakes are strongly applied) had existed previously on heavy goods vehicles and, before that, on aircraft.

absurd   see THEATRE OF THE ABSURD.

abuse   *noun* (of alcohol, drugs or other substances) illegal or dangerous use; (of people, especially children) physical ill-treatment or sexual interference. The word has long signified 'misuse, incorrect or improper use', though commonly applied to abstractions, as in *abuse of trust*, its increasing application to drugs and other substances in the sixties led to the familiarisation of such combinations as DRUG ABUSE, SOLVENT ABUSE and *amphetamine abuse*, and a little later we find CHILD ABUSE and *sexual abuse*.

access   *verb* to gain access to. This use of a much older noun as a verb dates from the early sixties when it was adopted by computer jargon to mean 'to retrieve information from or place it into a computer system, or to gain access to the system itself.' More recently the meaning has been extended so that one may be said to *access* (gain access to) *a market*, for example. The noun **access** is used attributively in a number of comparatively recent compounds, such as **access broadcasting/television**, which gives members of the public and special interest groups access to broadcasting time so that they can put forward a particular point of view (1973). An **Access Course** is an educational course enabling those without traditional qualifications to become eligible for higher education.

AC/DC   *adj.* bisexual. Slang, sometimes humorously employed, based on the technical description of certain electrical appliances on being **AC/DC**, i.e. adaptable for use on both alternating current and direct current. The expression has been used in the UK since the sixties, but originated in the US, where its spoken use goes back to the Second World War.

ace   *adj.* (slang, especially young people's) excellent. In some card games the ace is the most powerful card and this is how the word became associated with excellence. During the First World War, for example, outstandingly successful pilots were known as *aces*; the usage originated with the French, who applied their word *as* (ace) to a pilot who had shot down ten enemy planes. From subsequent association with other sorts of expertise the word has most recently (1980s) entered young people's slang as a term of general approbation, and an exclamation of enthusiasm.

acid   *noun* (shortening of) lysergic acid diethylamide (commonly known as LSD). Originally US slang dating from the early sixties' illegal use of this compound as a popular hallucinogenic drug. See also ACID HEAD, ACID ROCK and ACID TRIP.

acid head or **freak**   *noun* a person addicted to (and often mentally affected by) LSD. Mid sixties US slang terms based on the slightly earlier ACID and the much earlier *head* (drug-addict); see also FREAK.

Acid House   *noun* **1** loud, synthesised, popular, disco-type music with rapid beat, few lyrics and hypnotic effects. A type of HOUSE music originating in Chicago in the mid eighties. It was exported (c.1988) to the UK where it became a youth cult associated with the hallucinogenic drug ECSTASY and very large, all-night **acid house parties** held at often remote venues which were kept secret to avoid police raids and forestall objections on the grounds of nuisance, trespass etc. The use of *acid* in the name is said to have nothing to do with ACID in the sense of LSD. It may be from the adoption of *acid* as a slang term for ECSTASY, or from Chicago slang where the term *acid burning* (for theft) suggested the notion of *acid* music (electronically mixing and modifying passages of recorded music 'borrowed' from other works). For *House* see WAREHOUSE PARTY. **2.** the youth cult and culture associated with the music and movement described above.

acid rain   *noun* rain containing pollutant chemicals from the burning of fossil fuels by factories, cars, etc., and thus liable to destroy crops, trees, etc. The term is not new, the phenomenon of acid rain having been commented on in mid-Victorian times (the OED records a use from 1859), but it did not come to general knowledge and use until the early 1970s, when the Swedes and others expressed a mounting concern. It is now in everyday use as a result of much greater public awareness of widespread environmental damage caused by our industrialised societies, especially to forests and lakes in Northern Europe and America.

acid rock   *noun* a form of **rock** music with strange instrumental effects, electronically amplified and often repeated, with a heavy beat. Popular in the late sixties and early seventies, this was thought to be the musical equivalent of an **acid trip**, and both words and music reflected PSYCHEDELIC preoccupations. It was pioneered in the USA and popularised in the UK when it was taken up by the Beatles on their *Sergeant Pepper* album (1967).

acid trip   *noun* a hallucinatory experience induced by taking LSD. See ACID and TRIP.

act, to get one's act together   (colloquial phrase) to reorganise one's life or affairs more effectively. Originally US (1976); the act referred to being the familiar short theatrical act as in a music hall performance, as also in the earlier (forties) phrase, *to get in on the act*.

action, the   *noun* exciting or profitable activity. The modern colloquialisms **a piece of the action** (1966, involvement in an activity; a share in the profits from a transaction) and **where the action is** (1964, the centre of activity, usually social; the place to be) are developments from thirties underworld slang in the USA, where *the action* meant 'a money making activity', usually in gambling and later in drug trafficking.

action   *verb* to take action on (something), to put into effect. As in 'to action a request'; business and similar jargon (1962).

action replay   *noun* the re-running of a short section of television tape, usually of a sporting event and often in slow motion, to permit closer examination. Common since 1973 as a result of advances in broadcasting technology, the term is now applied more generally to any event which closely resembles or replicates a previous one, thus giving a sense of a duplicated experience as in an action replay.

active   *adj.* (of software in computerised devices) capable of responding to different circumstances or performing a variety of functions. From the vocabulary of microelectronics and ARTIFICIAL INTELLIGENCE, this sense of **active** came increasingly into use in the late eighties, especially in such compounds as **active card** (a smart card accessing banking information and transactions) or **active suspension**, a computerised suspension system for cars, which reads the road and adjusts the suspension to it. See also SMART and INTELLIGENT.

acupressure   *noun* same as SHIATSU. The word has been known in this sense since c.1977 (though it existed earlier with a quite different meaning). It is formed by combining *acupuncture* and *pressure*: the technique uses pressure with the hands instead of puncturing with a needle, despite the retention of *acu* (Latin 'with a needle') in its name. See also SHIATSU, for which **acupressure** is now the normal term.

additive   *noun* a substance added during manufacture to improve a product; especially a chemical food additive. *Additive* has a long history as an adjective, and was not used as a noun until the immediate post-war period. Since the seventies it has been widely used as a short form of *food additive*, a normally artificial substance, added to improve the colour, flavour, appearance or other non-nutritional properties of food. In the eighties there was increasing unease among many consumers, who feared the possible consequences of long-term ingestion of unnecessary chemicals, so that from the mid eighties some manufacturers began to label their food as *free from artificial additives* or else **additive-free**.

adult *adj.* pornographic. A euphemism first recorded in 1958, and commonly found in such compounds as *adult books* or *adult videos*.

advance directive *noun* (same as) LIVING WILL. The preferred British term, used for example by the British Voluntary Euthanasia Society. It has been generally known since c.1990, though the media appear to prefer the more vivid US term LIVING WILL. It is hard to believe that *directive* will catch on, because of the word's bureaucratic associations with EC rulings about such things as the correct shape for bananas.

advertorial *noun* advertising material in a newspaper or magazine, written and printed in such a way that it seems at first sight to be journalism. Such material may be headed 'Advertisement Feature' but it will be deliberately designed to look as though it is not, as for example a 'good food guide' which looks as if it has been compiled by a specialist food-writer but which actually consists of paragraphs contributed and paid for by the restaurateurs themselves. The word is a blend of *advertisement* and *editorial*, the latter designating material contributed by an editor or journalist and therefore supposedly objective and disinterested. Although known in the US since the sixties, the word – and the technique – were not familiar in the UK until the eighties.

aerobics *noun* a fitness routine which seeks to increase oxygen intake to stimulate heart and lung activity. Aerobics was a spin-off from the US space programme, originating as a fitness routine for astronauts; but in the health conscious eighties it became a fitness craze, spreading from California to the UK and beyond and associated with rhythmic dance movements which were performed to music at an *aerobics class*.

aerosol *noun* a small metal container dispensing a substance (e.g. insecticide, perfume, polish) using a propellant under pressure; the substance dispensed in this manner. *Aerosols* became familiar in domestic use during the fifties, (though the technology had been developed during the Second World War) and they remained common until the eighties when the use of CFCS as propellants was alleged to be causing damage to the OZONE LAYER.

affinity card *noun* a form of CREDIT CARD, the acceptance and subsequent use of which results in payments to a designated charity by the card company. The idea originated in the USA, where *affinity group* has been the name (since c.1970) for any group or association of people with an affinity, i.e. a common purpose or interest. *Affinity cards* were first issued to such groups in the late seventies as long as the groups were non-profit-making; the card entitled the members to certain financial benefits. However, payments to a designated charity were substituted for self-interest when affinity cards were introduced in Britain in 1987.

affluenza *noun* a demotivating psychiatric condition among wealthy people and particularly children who will inherit wealth. *Affluenza*, formed by a telescoping of *affluence* and *influenza*, is not as might appear, a facetious coinage but a diagnosable psychiatric disorder, identified in California in the mid eighties and characterised by feelings of guilt, boredom and lack of motivation.

African American *noun* a Black inhabitant of the USA. **African**, as a noun, with this same meaning, was in use in the USA three centuries ago, but fell out of general use by the twentieth century. *African American* is now used by some as a preferred term to Black, perhaps in part as a result of a general anxiety for POLITICAL CORRECTNESS.

Afro *noun* a hairstyle, originally among Black Americans, where the hair is brushed out around the head. Popularised in the mid sixties, initially in the USA, and often considered as a badge of Black liberation and the Black consciousness movement; the *Afro* was thought to be more genuinely African than earlier styles that often involved hair straightening.

ageism *noun* discrimination against people on the grounds of their being elderly. Also *adjective* **ageist** prejudiced in this way. When the word first started to circulate, both the neologism and the concern it represented were looked at askance by many as examples of spurious do-goodery. This reaction did not last, and the word has passed rapidly into Standard English as more people have come to recognise the new problems posed by increased longevity in the population and the equally unfamiliar and frustrating personal difficulties caused by premature retirement or redundancy in many workforces. The word was coined in 1969 by an American specialist in geriatrics, and has been familiar in the UK since the late seventies.

agg (a further abbreviation of) AGGRO.

aggro *noun* violent trouble-making, especially by a gang of youths; aggressive behaviour; a source of irritation. British euphemistic slang, late sixties, from *aggravation*, which is usually understood as a mild word meaning 'annoyance' or 'irritation' – a far cry from the SKINHEAD thuggery, football hooliganism and revolutionary violence which their exponents originally called *aggro*. As time has passed, the word has entered more general colloquial use with the gentler meaning of 'inconvenience', 'bother', etc.

AI (abbreviation for) ARTIFICIAL INTELLIGENCE.

(-)Aid, (-)aid tacked on to numerous words since the eighties to denote an event (or sometimes an organisation) that raises money for a charitable cause. The origin is **Band Aid**, the name of a rock group (i.e. *band*) formed by Bob Geldof in 1984 to raise money (*aid*) for Ethiopian famine relief. *Band Aid* was a double pun as it is the well known tradename of a brand of sticking-plaster used for first aid. The success of the Ethiopian appeal led to the widespread adoption of *(-)Aid* formations in the names of later appeals e.g. *Live Aid*, *Sport Aid*, *Water Aid* etc.

Aids or AIDS (acronym for) Acquired Immune Deficiency Syndrome (or Acquired Immunodeficiency Syndrome). This name was officially adopted in 1982, though the condition it describes was first noticed by American doctors c.1978 and originally given other names. The condition is complex and has given rise to a complex vocabulary which mixes emerging scientific knowledge, a certain amount of prejudice, and some journalistic looseness: see, for example, PWA and PLA, PLWA. Strictly speaking, Aids is a *syndrome* (a set of symptoms running together), not a disease, and therefore cannot be communicated. It is caused – or thought to be caused – by a virus (see HIV) which destroys certain blood cells, resulting in the loss (*deficiency*) of the body's normal ability to protect itself against disease (*immunity*). No cure has yet been found, though hopes have been raised for more effective management of the condition.

airbag *noun* a safety device fixed to the dashboard or steering-wheel area of a car, consisting of a bag that inflates automatically in the event of a collision, preventing the passengers from being projected forwards and injured. First developed in the early seventies, though not available in standard production models until the nineties. The word had previously been used with other meanings.

Airbus *noun* trademark of passenger aircraft built by consortium of European firms. So called (1960) because it was intended for short-range journeys at frequent intervals.

airhead *noun* a stupid person. *Airhead* emerged in North America in the early eighties as a slang term most often aimed at an attractive but empty-headed (young) woman, though it can be applied to any age and either sex. It reached the UK in the late eighties. See DICKHEAD and MEATHEAD.

air miss *noun* the near collision of two aircraft in flight. *Air miss* has been in use among pilots and the aviation authorities since at least 1960 to mean a near miss in the air, but it did not come into more general usage until the late eighties when the media publicised a number of air misses.

airside *noun* that part of an airport to which only passengers (and staff) are admitted. *Airside*, the *side* of an airport which is nearest the *air*craft, is separated off by customs, passport control, etc., and is not open to the non-travelling public. The word has been in the jargon of civil aviation since the late fifties, but has become more familiar since the late eighties, following the greater concern, post-Lockerbie, for airport, and particularly *airside*, security. Its opposite is **landside**.

aleatoric *adj.* (of music) having elements chosen at random by the performer (1961). From an earlier but rare adjective *aleatory* (dependent on chance) which has its origins in a Latin word for 'dice-player'.

Algol *noun* (in computing) a high-level programming language suitable for use in advanced mathematics and technology. An acronym from 'algorithmic language' (1959), it was developed in Europe.

aliterate *adj.* able to read but not inclined to do so. Also *noun*, a person who can read but prefers non-written sources of information, entertainment, etc. Like *illiterate*, which means 'unable to read and write', *aliterate* consists of *literate* plus a prefix (*a-* means 'without') and so could be taken to mean something similar to *illiterate*, but is in fact understood to imply unwillingness to read and not inability. *Aliterate*, though coined in the sixties, did not become familiar until the eighties, by which time there was worrying evidence, particularly in the US, that reading (and writing) skills were in decline as a result of a widespread dependence on television, computers and other graphic media as sources of information. It is not yet a widely used word, though it may become so if modern technology continues to marginalise reading or make it appear too difficult.

all systems go *familiar phrase* everything is ready for imminent action. The catchphrase became popular during the 1960s as a result of broadcast commentaries on the launches of US spacecraft from 1958 onwards. The phrase was originally part of the jargon of mission-controllers, whose voices were heard during the broadcasts, and signified that all of a missile's components were working. *Go* here has the unEnglish meaning of 'functioning normally'. As interest in the US space programme has waned, the catchphrase has become rather dated, but it is still frequently heard, though often in the sense of 'everything is working well' i.e. without any sense of readiness for imminent action.

alpha test *noun* the preliminary test of a new or modified product, especially and originally computer software, carried out in-house by the designer or manufacturer, or by members of the same organisation. Also *verb*, to test in these circumstances. Computerese since the early eighties. After an *alpha test*, a product is passed to an outside specialist or organisation for BETA TESTING before it is regarded as fully developed and ready for general marketing. *Alpha* and *beta*, the first two letters of the Greek alphabet, are sometimes used to signify 'first' and 'second' in a series.

alternative *adj.* different from, and believed by its adherents to be preferable to, what is generally found in contemporary society; *especially* reflecting the values of the COUNTER CULTURE. This sense developed around the *alternative society* or COUNTER CULTURE of the late sixties, when those with hippie values rejected what they took to be the materialistic culture of conventional society for a range of beliefs and life-styles that seemed to offer a truly alternative approach. Some of these ideas, supported at the time by the **alternative press**, may now be dated, but others came back into fashion in the health conscious, ecologically aware eighties, and *alternative* is found in a number of combinations in the sense of 'less conventional or materialistic; more in touch with what is natural'. **Alternative medicine** or **therapy** often avoids the use of drugs, and uses methods such as acupuncture, osteopathy, homeopathy, hypnosis, etc., which are not seen as mainstream treatments. **Alternative energy** (c.1975) is that derived from natural sources (sun, wind, tides etc.) in ways that do not deplete the earth's resources or damage the environment. **Alternative technology** is designed to achieve this. In **alternative comedy** the sense is perhaps rather different; though such comedy eschews the conventional and risks the outrageous in its need to break new ground.

anabolic steroids   *noun* organic compounds, specifically synthetic male sex hormones, that stimulate tissue growth. Although both words have long been used in medical science (*anabolic* means promoting tissue growth), they did not come together until c.1960, but have become commonly known because of the notorious use of anabolic steroids by some athletes to improve muscle and performance, contrary to the regulations of their sports.

anal   *adj.* fussy, obsessive, emotionally constipated. The anal is one of Freud's categories of childhood development, a stage lasting from about eighteen months to three years if all goes well and the individual grows beyond it, but leading to excessive orderliness, obsessive behaviour and tight-fistedness if the individual remains fixated at this stage. **Anal** and **anal retentive** have had a long use as specialist terms in psychoanalysis and its literature, but from the eighties onwards *anal* was being used more generally and often informally to describe anyone who was fussy, nit-picking or obsessed with orderliness.

anchor, anchorman   *noun* a person who introduces and compères a television or radio programme consisting of various components, and who links contributions from outside broadcasts, recorded materials, interviews, etc. This meaning emerged in the 1950s, when television first became a popular entertainment, from earlier use of the word to denote the specially vital person at the end of a tug-of-war or climbing rope. *Anchor* is the non-sexist form, though it is not generally employed.

angel dust   *noun* the hallucinogenic drug PCP. The name is drug user's slang, originally of the sixties and chiefly in the US. *Dust* refers to the drug's powdered form; *angel* may indicate the character of its effects or simply be a reference to its original use and distribution by HELL'S ANGELS.

animal-free   *adj.* not using or containing any product derived from animals. First recorded in 1965, and increasingly used as vegetarianism and animal rights have advanced.

animal liberation   *noun* the act of freeing animals from human exploitation (1973) (e.g. when held for scientific experimentation); a movement that proposes and supports such activity e.g. the Animal Liberation Front (1978). There is also a *noun* **animal liberationist** (1983).

animalist   *noun* a campaigner for ANIMAL RIGHTS. This term derives from the US and the mid eighties, but it is not much used in British English. Perhaps one reason for its failure to catch on is the possibility for confusion that exists because, by analogy with racist or sexist, animalist might seem to denote someone prone to SPECIESISM, or *specism*, that is a *specist*. More important is the well established meaning for *animalism* of 'the creed or practice of sensuality' and thus of the rarer *animalist* as 'sensualist'.

animal rights   *noun* the rights of animals to live free from exploitation, abuse, confinement, etc. by humans. This term based on the expression *human rights* has been generally known only since the seventies, although it was coined much earlier. Its increased use was partly as a result of environmental concerns, partly because of the committed and sometimes violent activities of people opposed to the use of animals in scientific research and to the export of live cattle. The expression is often used attributively, as in *animal rights movement*.

ankle-biter   *noun* a child, especially a toddler. Affectionate slang, originally Australian but later spreading to the UK, from the 1970s.

anorak, an   *noun* a nerdish person. A recent development (early nineties) whereby the garment thought by the smart and snobbish to characterise all that they are glad not to be (e.g. a trainspotter) has become the name for those who wear it.

answering machine   *noun* a machine for receiving incoming telephone calls, relaying a recorded message to the caller and recording a message in reply from them (c.1961).

answerphone   *noun* an ANSWERING MACHINE. This term is now often used in place of *answering machine*, perhaps because of its comparative brevity and perhaps influenced by the proprietary name *Ansafone* (1963).

anti-ballistic missile   *noun* a missile for shooting down a ballistic missile. Developed by the USA and the Soviet Union in the 1960s. Sometimes abbreviated to ABM.

anti-chic   *noun* the fashion for dressing in a deliberately unfashionable or slummocky way (mid eighties). See GRUNGE.

anti-choice   *adj.* opposed to abortion. This coinage stems from the bitter abortion debate in the US. Those who believe that a developing foetus has the right to life and who therefore oppose a woman's right to choose abortion prefer to be called PRO-LIFE. *Anti-choice* is a derogatory coinage of the late seventies which is couched negatively (i.e. using *anti-* instead of *pro-*) to stress that pro-lifers are actually denying a woman's right to choose for herself. The pro-lifers have retaliated against this coinage by labelling their opponents PRO-DEATH (*adj.*) and *prodeathers* (*noun*). See ABORTUARY and PRO-CHOICE.

anti-lock braking system   see ABS.

anti-novel   *noun* a novel which dispenses with traditional structures and characteristics (1958). This type of novel, developed chiefly in France in the 1960s, rejected the orderly presentation of such elements as plot and characters as not being in conformity with the reality of experience. In place of an interpretation of events in psychological, social or moral terms, the *anti-novel* concentrated on prosaic descriptions of things, allowing the reader to understand the mental state of the people in the book who experienced or saw them. Also called NOUVEAU ROMAN.

A-OK or **A-okay**   *abbreviation* in perfect working order. An abbreviation of '*all (systems) OK*'. The expression leapt to sudden prominence when it was used repeatedly in a broadcast of a US astronaut radioing from his space craft to mission-control in 1961. Newspaper reports also reported it, and it has remained current ever since, though still chiefly in the US. It is not known whether the expression was peculiar to the individual astronaut or (more likely) part of the space industry's private jargon that was not generally known until the 1961 flight.

APEX, Apex   *noun* the system whereby airline tickets for scheduled flights are booked at a reduced fare on certain conditions, which usually include payment a specified number of days in advance, and a specified interval between the outward and return journeys. Acronym from **A**dvanced **P**urchase **Ex**cursion. The term, initiated by airlines in the early seventies, is now sometimes used of booking-arrangements for other forms of long-distance travel, particularly by rail.

aquaplane   *verb* (of a motor vehicle) to slide uncontrollably on a wet road because a combination of the high speed of the vehicle and the pressure of a layer of water between the road surface and the moving tyres causes the tyres to lose contact with the road. The phenomenon was first called by this name in 1963, though the word had been applied to a similar problem with an aircraft two years earlier. The term, however, is much older, and was originally used of a sort of water-skiing using a single board.

aquarobics   *noun* a form of **aerobics** performed in a swimming pool. Also **aquaerobics**. Invented in the US in 1980 and known in the UK by the end of the decade. The word, based on *aerobics*, is often spelt with a capital A, as it is a trademark.

architecture   *noun* (in computing) the design of the lay-out and interconnections of a microprocessor and the computer system it controls (mid eighties).

aromatherapy   *noun* the use of oils or creams containing plant extracts to promote health, beauty and well-being. An ALTERNATIVE or COMPLEMENTARY therapy used especially to promote relaxation and relieve stress. The noun, which is based on the therapy's use of aromatic oils, has been generally known in the UK since the seventies, though the technique and term are based on French ideas of the 1930s.

artificial intelligence   *noun* the (projected) capacity of computers to simulate human mental functions. Although the term was in use in the mid fifties, it has only been generally known since the seventies and the development of EXPERT SYSTEMS. Such programs depend on human input, however, and the development of machines able to 'think' for themselves remains in the future.

A-side   *noun* the side of a gramophone record, usually a pop record, that is thought likely to be the more popular and commercially successful (1962).

assertiveness training *noun* a series of techniques and approaches by which unassertive people (and others) are trained to be more assured in their behaviour. Originally American, from the mid seventies, it stresses the value of self worth and is often used in the training of business people and by women's groups.

asset stripping *noun* the practice of taking over a company in order to sell off its assets at a profit. This is legal but is widely regarded with disfavour because it is thought to smack of opportunism, the purpose being to dismantle for quick profit rather than to develop. The term has been known in the US since the early seventies, and in the UK soon afterwards, though the activity itself is older. See UNBUNDLING.

Astroturf, astroturf *noun* an artificial grass surface. So called because it was first used in the Astrodome indoor stadium in Houston, Texas, in 1966. Strictly speaking, the word is a trademark (hence the capital letter) but it has become so familiar that it seems to be on the way to being used as a familiar common noun, rather as *hoover* is.

-athon or **-thon** *suffix* an event, often one that raises funds for charity and that usually requires some degree of athleticism and/or endurance. Based on the pattern of *marathon*, the long distance race (see TELETHON), many are nonce words and most self-explanatory as *bikeathon* or *pedalathon* (both 1986) *readathon* and *swimathon*.

ATM (abbreviation for) automated teller machine, a computerised machine which carries out various banking transactions on receiving the customer's bank card; a cash machine. Such machines came into general use in the UK from the mid eighties. The abbreviation ATM has been widely used in the US since the mid seventies, but it has never caught on with the general public in the UK, where CASHPOINT, *cash machine*, or CASH DISPENSER remain the common names, despite the fact that ATMs are now capable of displaying statements and registering deposits as well as dispensing cash.

attitude *noun* an assertive approach to life and other people; a self-validating response. Originally US, colloquial, an eighties development from the established sense of *attitude*: 'settled behaviour that represents one's feelings or opinions'. A person with *attitude* is someone who refuses to be put down, who is unmoved if someone (in authority) does not like their attitude. It is celebrated in the name of the HIP-HOP group *Niggers with Attitude* and is a strong term of commendation.

auteur *noun* a film director who exercises strong creative control in film-making. This French word, meaning 'author', began to be generally recognised in this new sense from c.1960 when it spread beyond its previously restricted readership in serious French critical writing about the cinema. It refers to a particular style of film-making by directors – largely though not exclusively French – who insisted on exercising exceptional artistic control over every aspect of a film so that they could reasonably be described as distinctive *authors* rather than coordinators of the work of others. **Auteur**

cinema and **auteur theory** (sometimes called **auteurism**) were important and influential in their time, and **auteur** remains in use to denote a style of film-direction.

author *verb* to create or originate (something). *Author* was used as a verb in this sense in the seventeenth century, but fell out of common use in the UK during the following three hundred years, though still used in the US for writing a book or originating a comment. Recently it has come back into common use, influenced perhaps by its use in computing.

autocross *noun* a form of motor sport in which (often dilapidated) cars race over a circuit of rough land. A blending of *auto* and *cross-country* (1965) based on the earlier *motocross*. See also RALLYCROSS.

auto-destructive *adj.* self-destroying or self-destructive. The word was first applied to an artistic movement of the late fifties and sixties which regarded the destruction and decay of objects as an artistic process, but in the seventies came to be used in a more general sense and (with the intransitive verb **autodestruct** – which came into being by back formation from it) was widely used in the eighties, particularly of politicians and parties whose policies and actions seemed calculated to bring about their own destruction.

autogenic training *noun* a relaxation technique that uses mental exercises and self-hypnosis to reduce stress. Also called **autogenics**. The term is a translation from the German, as the technique was invented in Germany in the first half of the twentieth century, though it was not generally known outside that country until the seventies. *Autogenic* means 'self-produced', a reference to the self-hypnosis and other methods of self-control used to produce physical relaxation. The technique has been particularly used by athletes.

aversion therapy *noun* (in psychiatry) a technique to break a patient's habit or addiction (e.g. to drugs, smoking, alcohol, sexual deviance) by associating something unpleasant, such as an electric shock, with enjoyment of the habit (1956).

AWACS, Awacs *noun* an airborne radar system for diverting aircraft and missiles (especially low-flying ones, not readily detectable by ground-based radar), and directing weapons against them. An acronym from **A**irborne **W**arning **a**nd **C**ontrol **S**ystem, developed in the USA from the mid sixties.

awesome *adj.* excellent. Now a term of general approbation and enthusiastic approval in US young people's slang, *awesome* had already undergone a weakening from 'awe-inspiring, dreadful' (its standard, non-slang meaning earlier this century) to something like 'amazing, remarkable' in the slang usage of the seventies. In the eighties it became a much used word of enthusiastic if general approval, especially among young people, but it is not much used in the UK. *Awesome*'s progress from 'dreadful' to 'marvellous' mirrors that of other words such as BAD and WICKED.

ayatollah *noun* Iranian Shiite religious leader. A modern coinage (from the Arabic meaning 'God's miraculous sign (or gift)') which became generally known at the time of the establishment of an Islamic republic in Iran (1979) under Ayatollah Khomeini as absolute ruler.

baby boomer   *noun* a person born during the twenty years immediately following the Second World War, when there was a marked increase in the birth-rate. This colloquialism, largely US, came into popular use only c.1974, though **baby boom** goes back to the early 1940s. Any temporary increase in the birth-rate is known as a *baby-boom* in the US – the equivalent British term is *bulge* – but a *baby-boomer* is specifically a person born between 1945 and the mid sixties. By the late eighties this generation was recognised as a significant group – President Clinton, for example, was proclaimed in 1992 as the first *baby-boomer* to be elected President – and the abbreviation **boomer** became very common. There is a term **buster**, short for *baby buster*, for those born in a period of low birth-rate, i.e. from the late sixties onwards (just as *bust* is likely to follow *boom* in economic terms).

back burner, on the   *phrase* temporarily relegated or postponed. A mid sixties US colloquialism, now common in Britain, based on the image of moving a saucepan from a fast to a slow gas-ring so that it can simmer until needed.

backhander   *noun* a surreptitious tip or bribe; underhand payment. Slang (c.1960) from the action of turning the back of the hand outward to conceal payment. The derivation is probably influenced by 'underhand' rather than by earlier meanings of *backhander* (blow with the back of the hand; a backhanded stroke in some sports).

back up   *verb* (in computing) to copy a file from one disc onto a second (the **back-up** copy) to prevent the data being lost or damaged in the system. There is a long-standing verb to *back up*, meaning to support, but the noun *back-up*, a reinforcement or support, dates only from the fifties, originally in the US. The use of *back up* in computer terminology dates from the early eighties.

bad   *adj.* very good. Also **baddest** superlatively good. Slang, mainly among the young, originating in Black US jazz language, where reverse adjectives were often used to describe a performance. This oddity is also found in older US Black colloquialism and is thought to have originated among speakers of Black English during the period of slavery. Just as the language of some negro spirituals is ambiguous (e.g. yearning for freedom being sometimes expressed as a yearning for religious salvation) so some Black English expressed a subversive attitude to the language of the slave-drivers by employing certain words in a sense opposite to their conventional meaning. *Bad* became popular in the US during the early seventies and common among young people in the eighties; it is often pronounced in a drawling manner, with a long *a*, to distinguish it from *bad* in the conventional sense. It reached the UK in the late eighties, spreading in both Black and White youth slang.

bad-mouth   *verb* to speak slightingly about a person or thing; to rubbish them. Originally US slang, especially in the Black community. It was well established by the sixties (and it was probably in spoken use much earlier). It spread to the UK during the seventies, and is now widely used and accepted as a colloquial expression.

bad news   *noun* a person or thing regarded as undesirable. A slang adaptation, c.1970, of a phrase previously applied only to worrying or upsetting information: e.g. 'She's bad news'.

bag lady or **woman**   *noun* a female tramp. From the plastic shopping bags in which such women often carry about some or all of their possessions. Originally a US euphemism of the early seventies, later common in the UK from the mid eighties. The origin may be the Australian English *bagman* (a male tramp who carries his possessions in a bag). The forms **bag person** and **bag people** have come into existence since *bag lady* was coined.

bail-out or **bailout**   *noun* the rescue of an unsuccessful business by financial help given by a bank, the Government etc. A figurative application (1970s) of the familiar verb *bail out*, to secure the release (of a person) from custody by providing security (i.e. *bail*).

Baker day   *noun* any one of the five days devoted each school year to the in-service training of teachers. They were introduced by the 1988 Education Act and named after the then Secretary of State for Education, Kenneth Baker. They were resented by some teachers as an imposition, especially as the giving up of time which had previously been voluntary was now made contractual.

ball-breaker   *noun* a dominating woman who destroys a man's self-confidence. Originally US slang (recorded 1954), the word has been current in the UK from at least the mid seventies. There is an alternative form, *ball-buster*, with a similar history and meaning.

balance of terror   *phrase* an equilibrium between nations based on their mutual possession of nuclear weapons or other weapons of mass terror. A Cold War term. The expression, a refinement of *balance of power*, is said to have been coined by the prime minister of Canada, Lester Pearson, in 1955. The concept of MAD, mutually assured destruction, is similar: if both sides have sufficient OVERKILL to be confident of destroying each other, come what may, neither will be able to act.

ball game, different or **a whole new**   *phrase* a fresh state of affairs. An informal metaphorical adaptation (originally North American late sixties, but now general) of a popular phrase from broadcast commentaries when a change of fortune during a game of baseball (or football) produced a 'different ball game'. Literally, *ball game* is the North American term where the British say 'match' or 'game'. This metaphorical expression is now near-cliché.

balloon   SEE LEAD BALLOON.

ballpark figure   *noun* a rough estimate (usually of a financial amount). *Ballpark* is the usual North American term for a baseball stadium. One explanation for the sense of 'a rough estimate' is that, as the playing area is large, so a ballpark figure is likewise not a narrowly defined one; perhaps likelier is that it derives from the common practice of estimating the crowd attendance at a game. The term (c.1967) is informal rather than slang.

bankable *adj.* having qualities that will ensure commercial success. Originally used of film stars, this term from the vocabulary of film production in early sixties Hollywood suggests that you can *bank on* that star attracting audiences that will ensure that you all have something to bank at the end of the day – the star can be banked on to provide something *bankable*. Nowadays the term is not confined to film production – it could be a sports star, an author or a project that is considered *bankable*.

bank rate see MINIMUM LENDING RATE.

bar code *noun* a machine-readable arrangement of parallel lines (*bars*) of varying widths printed on a package, book, etc. as a *code*. The code can be electronically scanned at a checkout to register the price, pass information to a computer for stock-control etc. Invented in the early sixties, bar codes are used by libraries to register books issued and returned; since the eighties they have been common on supermarket products and in other sorts of shops. Most recently they have been used to programme video recorders. Also a transitive verb, meaning 'to label with a *bar code*'. See also EPOS.

bargaining chip *noun* an advantage or material asset used by one side in a negotiation in order to gain an agreement, compromise or concession – i.e. offered for surrender in a trade off. This dates from mid sixties US diplomatic usage and appears to be an adaptation of *gambling chip*. In poker or similar gambling games it is an obvious advantage to have a substantial supply of such assets when bluffing or bidding against other players. In the arms limitation talks between the USA and the USSR, where this term came to prominence, the bargaining chips were *assets* in the Pentagon's sense of that word: military hardware and weapons delivery systems. See SALT.

base-jumping *noun* the practice of parachuting from the top of a high building or other fixed point (as distinct from balloons or aircraft). It came to notice c.1991 as the result of a number of fatal accidents. *Base* is an acronym from **b**uildings, **a**ntennae, **s**pans (i.e. bridges) and **e**arth (e.g. cliffs). The aim of the activity appears to be to chase excitement by risking death; the opening of the parachute is delayed for as long as possible after jumping.

base (abbreviation of) FREEBASE. British drug users' slang, late 1980s.

base rate see MINIMUM LENDING RATE.

bash *noun* a temporary and improvised shelter for those sleeping out, such as the constructions of cardboard and polythene sheeting under which the homeless of CARDBOARD CITY sleep. Perhaps ultimately from *basha*, Assamese for a bamboo hut thatched with leaves, and passed on through army slang.

BASIC (acronym for) a high-level computer-programming language designed for use by learners as well as more generally. Acronym for **B**eginners **A**ll-purpose **S**ymbolic **I**nstruction **C**ode, *BASIC* was developed in the USA in 1964 for educational use and was designed to be easy to learn; students could input programs a line at a time, and the computer would check each one before accepting the next.

basket case *noun* a person, organisation or country unable to function properly, in a state of hopeless dependency. This term originated in the jargon of US military hospitals at the end of the First World War, and refers to a soldier so badly crippled (by the loss of all four limbs) that he is confined to and carried in a basket-like construction. In slang use it came to mean a nervous wreck or someone behaving insanely, but most recently the sense of helplessness has revived and it is commonly applied to a firm that is on the ropes (such a firm might also be called a *stranded whale*) or a country that is unable to service its debts or feed its people.

basket of currencies *noun* a group or collection of currencies used for calculating values in certain international financial transactions. Familiar economic jargon (from the early seventies) since Britain joined the European Community. The image may be from the use of a shopping basket to hold a collection of similar things.

baton round *noun* (official name for) a rubber or plastic bullet. In the UK the term first surfaced c.1972 in military circles in Northern Ireland. Some suspected that *round* was no more than a euphemism for the emotive (though inaccurate) word *bullet* as in *rubber bullet*, used in riot control; but it is likely that *baton round* was simply jargon, taken over from the Hong Kong police. The latter had used wooden *baton projectiles* fired from *baton guns* in riot control in the late sixties – presumably the name came from the resemblance, physically and functionally, between the projectile and the wooden truncheons (batons) used by the police. The RUBBER BULLET and the slightly later *plastic* one were direct borrowings of this idea by the British authorities.

battered (baby, child, wife etc.) *noun* one suffering from repeated injury by a parent, husband, etc. Adapted from the slightly more technical *battered baby syndrome* first identified by social workers in the early 1960s, battered was chosen as stronger than 'beaten', 'assaulted' etc. *Battered wife* and *woman* are both first recorded in 1973.

beach buggy *noun* a low car, often open, with wide tyres, used for driving on sand. Devised in the USA c.1961. *Buggy* is earlier US slang for a car, based on much earlier Standard English for a light horse-drawn vehicle.

bean-bag or **beanbag (chair)** *noun* a large cushion used as an informal low seat (1969). The name comes from the small bag filled with dried beans which has been used in children's games since the 19th C. The seat, a product of sixties informality, originally in the USA, was of course much bigger and usually filled with foam rubber or pellets of polystyrene so that it moulded itself comfortably to the sitter's shape.

beat *noun* short for BEATNIK. In the sense of 'a follower of the Beat Generation', the word is said to have been invented by Jack Kerouac and first used in print in JC Holmes' novel *Go* in 1952. In the UK, where the word became popular during the sixties, *beats* were young, liberal and bohemian people, of the sort later known as HIPPIES.

beatbox *noun* an electronic device that produces percussion effects, a drum machine. This is an electronic device (*box*) that provides percussion effects (the *beat*) for HOUSE and other popular music. The term comes from the early eighties, when synthesised sound became popular, especially for the performance of RAP and HIP-HOP.

Beat Generation *noun* a group of young people, mainly writers, artists and their followers, in San Francisco in the 1950s; later similar groups elsewhere. Their outward signs were unconventional dress and behaviour as a means of self-expression and of protest against Western social and political values – authoritarianism, middle-class moves, puritanism, regular employment, private property, etc. Artistically they tended towards the experimental and improvisational; spiritually they interested themselves in Buddhism and other Eastern religions. Their title appears to be from *beat* (i.e. *beaten*) or *beat up*, in the sense of 'worn out, exhausted or used up', but Jack Kerouac, its supposed inventor, claimed it was from 'beatitude'.

beatnik *noun* member of the BEAT GENERATION. Also still used informally of any young person with long hair and shabby clothes. The word comes from **beat** in the sense defined at BEAT GENERATION, the **-nik** being borrowed from the Russian *Sputnik* (1957), possibly because *beatniks* rejected many of the values of Western capitalism. The word is said to have been coined by a San Francisco journalist in 1959 to describe the sort of young people coming to the city in search of the *beat* lifestyle.

beautiful people (sometimes with capital letters) *noun* originally (USA, 1960s) FLOWER PEOPLE, HIPPIES and fashionable people more generally; now used of famous, rich and fashionable members of international high society.

behaviour therapy *noun* any of various methods of treating psychological disorders by making a patient systematically learn new modes of behaviour to replace damaging ones. The psychologist HJ Eysenck coined the term in 1959. AVERSION THERAPY is an example.

bell, give (person) a *phrase* contact person by telephone. British slang, early eighties, referring to the bell with its clear ringing sound that once summoned people to the telephone. It is presumably based on the familiar, 'I'll give (person) a ring', and is another phrase given currency by its use on television by the character Arthur Daley in *Minder*.

best-before date *noun* the date by which a food-product must be used in order to ensure that it is still in good condition. In 1980 new UK regulations were introduced for the labelling of foodstuffs, so that it was now obligatory that perishable goods should be marked with the formula *best before* and a date, so that the customer would know when it should be consumed by. It later came to be felt that this phrasing was too vague for certain perishables and USE BY or SELL BY were preferred. The phrase has been adapted to indicate the age constraints on the employability of highish flyers in the City: job seekers have a *best before date* (i.e. age) after which they will seem less attractive to employers. Similarly ageist and/or sexist remarks are sometimes passed about someone (perhaps of the opposite sex) being past their SELL BY DATE.

beta-blocker *noun* a drug able to prevent undue activity of the heart by blocking the 'beta receptors' of the nervous system which are stimulated by adrenalin. Developed in the sixties, now widely prescribed for the treatment of high blood pressure, angina, etc., and also taken advisedly by those needing to manage anxiety in particular situations (e.g. musical performance) but also improperly by some sportsmen when the regulations of their particular sport prohibit it.

beta test see ALPHA TEST.

Bhangra or **bhangra** *noun* a form of popular music combining elements from Western rock and disco with Punjabi folk music. This style of music for dancing originated in the Asian community in the UK in the early eighties; it took its name from a traditional Punjabi folk dance. Bhangra features a strong beat and synthesised effects and has attracted wide audiences.

big bang *noun* the **Big Bang** (or *big bang*) is the deregulation of the London Stock Exchange in October 1986, when numerous changes took place, notably the abolition of the distinction between jobbers and brokers, the admission of international dealers, and the computerisation of operations. The name for this operation comes from the earlier **big bang theory** which, based on the observation that the universe is still expanding, holds that the universe as we know it originated in the explosion of a superdense mass of matter some ten to twenty billion years ago, and that galaxies and stars were formed as the fragments slowed down. This cataclysmic event was given the rather comically inadequate name *big bang* by the astronomer Fred Hoyle, in his *The Nature of the Universe* (1950), to belittle the theory, which he disagreed with. When financial deregulation was under discussion thirty years later, there was a choice between introducing it gradually or all at once. The latter was chosen and named *big bang* because, like the cosmological explosion, it was to be a sudden and comprehensive act of re-creation. The term has proved sufficiently current to be called upon when subsequent one-off changes are in the offing.

big brother *noun* any person or organisation exercising dictatorial control. From the totalitarian leader, Big Brother, in George Orwell's novel *Nineteen Eighty-Four* (1949). Elements of the novel still live in the popular imagination and surface in our vocabulary – for example *Thought Control* and the *Thought Police*, the slogan 'Big Brother is Watching You', and the brutalism of Newspeak. Even Room 101, the place of ultimate horror, has recently surfaced in a jokey form as the title of a TV show where pet hates are consigned to oblivion in Room 101.

bike, on your *phrase* Push off! British slang, usually dated from c.1960, though it may have been in earlier spoken use. In 1981, the then Employment Secretary in the Thatcher government, Norman

Tebbit, described in a speech how his unemployed father had in the thirties 'got on his bike and looked for work.' Tebbit's intention was to advocate sturdy self-help among the unemployed ('Keep pedalling!' rather than 'Push off!'); but his remark is often interpreted as a failure to understand – or even to care – that jobs simply did not exist. In the language of political comment and controversy, therefore, usages of *on your bike* are likely to refer to Tebbit's notorious comment rather than to the usual meaning.

biker *noun* a member of a motorcycle gang. Originally US, but common in Britain since the late sixties. *Biker* is now colloquial rather than slang.

bimbo *noun* a sexually attractive, empty-headed young woman. The word has a long history in American slang, initially as a contemptuous term for a stupid or disreputable fellow (from the Italian *bambino*, meaning 'little boy' or 'baby'), later as a word for a young woman, usually a prostitute. Something of these senses remains in the current usage, which entered British tabloid journalese in the eighties and spread into general circulation as usually derogatory slang. In newspaper parlance, a *bimbo* is an attractive girlfriend of an older affluent man, and is often a fortune-hunter ready to sell her story if the relationship breaks down. There are semi-facetious coinages to cover male bimbos e.g. **himbo** and **bimboy**, but TOY BOY is probably sufficiently close in meaning to see off these potential rivals.

biodegradable *adj.* capable of being decomposed by biological agents, especially bacteria. The popularity of the word, which dates from the early sixties, reflects environmental concerns about pollutants, waste, pesticides, etc., and the need to develop products, including plastics, which can be broken down after use.

bio-diesel *noun* fuel made from rape oil, the oil extracted from rapeseed. In the UK first used by buses in 1992, though used slightly earlier by commercial vehicles in other European countries and welcomed as being environmentally more friendly than normal diesel oil. Rape oil (often called rapeseed oil) had previously been used as a lubricant and in the manufacture of soap and rubber.

bio-diversity *noun* plant and animal species in all their variety – but, post 1992, frequently with the implication that such diversity is endangered and must be protected. Formed by combining *bio*-('having to do with living organisms') and *diversity* ('the state of being different or varied'), the word was restricted to the technical vocabulary of ecological studies and politics in the eighties, but it suddenly leapt to prominence in 1992 when the Earth Summit took place at Rio de Janeiro and the USA, alone among the assembled nations, refused to sign the *bio-diversity convention* that had been prepared for adoption. In consequence **bio-diversity** which had until then denoted the diversity of living organisms came to be used with the implication that it was necessary to prevent any further reduction of the existing diversity.

biofeedback *noun* a technique of therapy in which a patient is taught to control certain automatic physiological activities, such as the rate of heartbeat or breathing, which are monitored by machines and shown, usually in visual form, to the patient. By learning to concentrate on a particular physiological activity, and to note the 'feedback' provided by the machines (including changes in the activity), the patient can be taught to control the activity. Developed during the late sixties, the technique has been particularly applied to problems caused by tension. It is a feature of AUTOGENIC TRAINING.

biogas *noun* gas produced by the action of bacteria on organic waste matter (e.g. sewage or industrial waste) for use as a fuel. An ALTERNATIVE energy source used in some third world countries since the 1970s and likely to become more important as fossil fuels are exhausted.

biological clock *noun* (the internal mechanism supposedly regulating) cyclic or rhythmic activities in a living organism, especially in humans. The mechanism that produces the regular internal rhythm of activity is not known, but does not depend on external time-signals. It governs body temperature in mammals, the migration of birds, the opening and closing of flower-petals, etc. The term originated in the fifties, though since c.1968 BODY CLOCK has been the more usual term when human beings are being referred to.

bionic *adj.* having some human capabilities increased or replaced by electromechanical devices. The scientific study of *bionics* (the design and development of artificial systems that imitate the systems of living things) dates from c.1960 but *bionic* entered the popular vocabulary with the 'bionic man' of an American TV series of 1973–8; he had superhuman strength and powers because parts of his body had been replaced by electronics. *Bionic* is therefore sometimes loosely used to mean 'superlatively strong or skilful' (1970s slang). *Bionics* is a shortening of *bi(ological) (electr)onics*.

biorhythm *noun* a cyclically recurring pattern in the bodily functioning of an organism, such as the sleeping/waking cycle in humans and the rhythm of hibernation or migration among animals. A scientific term (c.1960), also used by some who believe that human behaviour depends on three cycles of physical, emotional and intellectual activity which can be charted in order to explain or predict behaviour or plan one's life to the best advantage.

biotechnology *noun* the use of micro-organisms (e.g. bacteria) in scientific and industrial processes (e.g. the production of vaccines on a large scale). The scientific processes are both chemical and physical, and the applications extend from food manufacture (e.g. cheese, beer) to recycling toxic waste by digesting it. The present sense emerged in the early seventies, accompanying rapid developments in genetic engineering. The word had been used earlier in the sense of *ergonomics* (the study of the relationship between people and their working environment) but the current sense is the dominant one.

bit *noun* one of the two digits 0 and 1 used in binary notation. The basic unit of information in a computer. The word (1948) is formed from **bi**(nary) (digi)**t**. See BYTE.

blackboard jungle   *noun* a school or school system seen as violent or undisciplined. From the title of an American novel by Evan Hunter (1954), later turned into a film. The novel was centred on a New York school and on certain aspects of state education in the USA, but *blackboard jungle* was later applied – and occasionally still is – to an anarchic school in the UK and elsewhere.

black box   *noun* an instrument for recording the operation of instruments and/or crew conversation, etc. during the flight of an aircraft. Originally RAF slang of the Second World War for various items of scientific apparatus, including a navigational instrument and a device by which a bomb-aimer could see in the dark or through cloud. Since c.1964, however, it has been used of the flight data recorder of an aircraft and has become generally known because of the instrument's usefulness in establishing the cause of crashes. The term is also used of any self-contained unit in an electronic system, such that (being a discrete entity) it may be easily isolated and replaced in the event of a malfunction, even by someone who does not understand its internal workings.

black comedy   *noun* a comedy of macabre style and import. Originally (in the sixties) a translation of a French term, and used only in literary contexts, but now more generally applied to any circumstances which are both funny and macabre.

black economy   *noun* that area of a country's economic activity that produces no tax income. This will include, for example, money earned (usually in cash, often by casual work) but not declared for tax purposes, and income not disclosed by people receiving state benefits. The term, in use since the seventies, is probably derived from the earlier *black market*, a term familiar during World War Two and the immediate post-war years for unofficial buying and selling, especially of rationed goods. *Black* has a long history in expressions indicating disgrace or liability to censure or punishment (*black list*, *black books* etc.)

black hole   *noun* a place into which things disappear irretrievably. This is a metaphorical use (c.1980) sometimes jocular, as when confronting a teenager's room, of the earlier astronomical term for a hypothetical object or region in space having a gravitational field so strong that no matter, light, or radiation, can escape from it. Such a black hole is believed to result from the collapse of a massive star at the end of its life, and to be capable of sucking in matter from the space around it. Though first postulated in 1916 the object was not given its present name until the late sixties.

Black Panthers   *noun* a militant Black political organisation. Founded in the USA in 1966 with the aim of ending White domination and extending BLACK POWER. The name comes from its panther symbol, previously adopted by other Black activists.

Black Power   *noun* a grouping of Black radical, often militant, organisations devoted to achieving the social, economic and political advancement of Black people. The specific and ultimate aim of the movement in contrast to the integrationist and pacifist policies of some others, was the establishment of a separate Black state in the USA. Its name is a slogan first used c.1966 by Stokely Carmichail, the US Black leader. Also *noun* the underlying concept and philosophy of this movement.

black propaganda *noun* falsified information, especially that spread among an enemy (often giving the impression that it comes from within their own ranks) designed to lower morale. A COLD WAR term from the early sixties, though practised to good effect by the British and others in the Second World War.

black section *noun* an unofficial group within a constituency Labour party to promote the interests of black constituents. Though much discussed within the Labour Party during the eighties, the idea of black sections was never officially adopted.

blanket, on the *phrase* (of an imprisoned terrorist) wearing only a blanket instead of prison clothing as a protest against being regarded as a criminal instead of as a political prisoner. Irish slang, used mainly of protests by IRA and Orange special category prisoners at the Maze prison, near Belfast, from c.1977. The protests were extended to smearing excrement on cell walls, refusing to use normal prison facilities, etc.

bleep *noun* and *verb*. As both noun and verb, *bleep* dates from the fifties as an echoic word for the short, thin, high-pitched signal made by some pieces of electronic equipment such as computers. Recordings of the plaintive sound made by the first SPUTNIK made the word popular. **Bleeper** belongs to the following decade as the name for the small radio receiver worn by a person on the move, such as a hospital doctor, who needs to be readily contactable. It can be activated to give a bleeping sound and warns the wearer to call in to control. **Bleeper** is also used (c.1990) to designate the remote control unit of a TV set, video or hi-fi; some of them emit a bleep as they are switched from one function to another. See PINGER and ZAPPER.

blip *noun* a temporary irregularity recorded in a process, set of statistics, etc. *Blip* has been the name for a pulse on a radar screen since the 1940s. The present figurative meaning belongs to the seventies, when it grew up in business jargon to denote a temporary problem or disturbance (in exactly the same way that a radar blip denotes a hazard). The word is now no longer confined to economics however.

blow-dry *verb* to dry (and style) hair using hot air from hand-held hair-dryer. Also *blow-dryer* (hair-dryer for doing this). Both 1970s.

blow one's mind *verb* to utterly amaze and (usually) thrill. From 1960s US slang for 'induce hallucinatory experiences by using drugs (especially LSD)'. The phrase remains slang in its present milder meaning. It is presumably based on the older 'blow one's top' (also US) which among its many meanings had 'to be deranged by drugs'.

blue movie *noun* an obscene or indecent film displaying sexual activity. The combination is first recorded from 1965, but *blue* has a long history of denoting smut and dirty talk, at least as far back as the middle of the nineteenth century and continuing into the twentieth to describe blue songs and variety acts.

blue-rinse (brigade) *noun* a group of elderly, probably well-to-do and well-groomed women, usually socially active and occasionally intimidating. The **blue rinse**, a tinting process in women's hair-dressing by which grey hair is given a silver-blue colour, became popular towards the end of the Second World War, but did not acquire its present connotations until the mid sixties. The term is usually found in *the blue-rinse brigade*, the name for any coterie of elderly ladies – who may or may not have blue-rinsed hair – but particularly associated in many people's minds with ladies at the Conservative Party Conference, an association strengthened by the fact that blue is the Conservative Party's identifying colour. The military overtones of *brigade* imply that such a group is a force to be reckoned with.

blush wine *noun* rosé wine. A promotional coinage, originating in California in the mid eighties, to give the sales of rosé wine a boost by giving the product a new name – one that would perhaps lend associations of the first blush of youth and romance. Wine growers elsewhere followed suit.

BMX (abbreviation for) bicycle motocross, a form of cycle-racing and stunt-riding on rough terrain or on a specially constructed obstacle course, using a specially designed and manoeuvrable bicycle. The sport became known in the US in the seventies and was a craze among the young in the UK by the mid eighties.

boardsailing (official name for) WINDSURFING. See also SAILBOARD.

boat people *noun* refugees, chiefly Vietnamese, many of Chinese ethnic origin, who fled from their country in small boats. First given this name in 1977, they became more numerous in 1979, after which their plight, notably their difficulties in finding asylum, began to attract international attention. Later the term was applied to other refugees, economic or political, who escaped in boats, for example from Haiti and Cuba in the early nineties.

body bag *noun* a plastic or rubber zippered container in which accident victims or the battlefield dead are stored and transported. A US term first used in the fifties, but not generally known in the UK until the Vietnam War. TV coverage ensured that the people back home were made increasingly aware of these bags and their contents, and what came to be known as **the body bag factor** (public disquiet in the face of continuing losses) played an important part in pushing the USA towards disengagement from the war. In the Gulf War US strategy and tactics clearly recognised in advance the importance of *the body bag factor* and the need to limit own losses at all costs. The bags themselves were rechristened *human remains pouches* – a more acceptable if less pronounceable name – perhaps more acceptable *because* less pronounceable. The easy to say abbreviation, *HRP*, masks what *body bag* always revealed.

body clock see BIOLOGICAL CLOCK.

body count *noun* a tally of the enemy dead left on the battlefield or after skirmishing. Another US military term from the Vietnam War, and another grim reminder of what war leaves behind (see

BODY BAG). It is said that since the *body count* was taken to indicate the effectiveness and success of individual units and commanders there were inevitable temptations to sacrifice more important strategic considerations to this all-important statistic. First recorded 1968.

body language *noun* those clues of posture, movement and gesture by which a person reveals their feelings, often unconsciously, and so imparts information to an observer (mid sixties).

body-popping *noun* a popular dance with jerky movements, including snakelike movements of head and arms. The dance originated as urban street display among teenagers in Los Angeles in the late seventies and spread rapidly, becoming international by the mid eighties. Related to BREAK-DANCING and HIP-HOP, it has quick, mechanical movements in time to disco music. Its name is probably from the verb *pop*, to make a sudden or brisk movement.

body-scanner *noun* an X-ray machine able to produce cross-sectional pictures of the internal state of the whole body. Developed in 1975. The name was probably based on the earlier *brain-scanner* (1964), and is now also used non-medically for the security device (such as those found at airports) through which passengers have to pass and which can detect objects hidden on the body or by clothing.

bodysuit *noun* a close-fitting one-piece stretch garment covering the whole body. The term was introduced in the late sixties as the name for an all-in-one fashion garment for women, and revived a decade later for a thin body-hugging sports garment.

bomb *verb* to fail disastrously. N. American slang of the 1960s, presumably from the idea of something falling apart as if hit by a bomb.

bomb *verb* to travel at great speed (often in a car) UK slang (1966) used with a variety of adverbs – to *bomb off, bomb along, bomb around, bomb past*, etc.

bonk *verb* to have sexual intercourse with; *noun* an act of sexual intercourse. Not recorded in print before the seventies, though used in slang speech for about twenty years before that. It has been common since 1987, when the tabloid newspapers took it up, especially as their headline writers were not able to resist the pull of its alliteration with the name of German tennis star, Boris Becker, whose disappointing performance at Wimbledon that summer they attributed to his alleged activities off-court. *Bonk* is now a fairly acceptable, slightly humorous colloquialism rather than slang. The word comes from an earlier echoic verb *bonk* (to hit a hard surface with something hard, making a resounding noise) and is in the tradition of using violent words for sexual activity (e.g. *bang, shaft*). Also *noun* **bonker** (person who *bonks*) and *adj.* **bonking. Bonk journalism** is a derogatory term for journalism that focuses on the sexual exploits and peccadilloes of the well-known.

boo-boo *noun* a foolish or embarrassing mistake; blunder. A playful variant of an earlier American slang word *boob*, which has the same meaning and comes from the much older *booby* (a nincompoop). Originally slang (fifties in US; sixties in UK) but now merely informal.

boobs *noun* a woman's breasts. Well-known slang since the 1960s (slightly earlier in the USA), from *boobies* (earlier still). This in turn comes from the now obsolete *bubbies* (Standard English until the late 18th C, after which it became vulgar). Often used semifacetiously this is a comparatively acceptable word in most company, certainly in such a combination as **boob tube**, a sort of sleeveless close fitting garment fashionable in the early eighties.

boob tube see COUCH POTATO and BOOBS.

boomer *noun* (short for) BABY-BOOMER. US slang, late eighties.

boot-boy *noun* a youth, usually member of a violent or would-be violent gang, prone to cause trouble by gratuitous assault, usually involving kicking a victim with his heavy boots. Early seventies variant on the earlier BOVVER BOY. Best remembered for the wall slogans which marked their territory: '(Name of place) boot boys rule. O.K.'

boot in, put the *phrase* to kick an opponent who is down; *also figuratively* take decisive or unkind action, usually to bring a problem, etc., to an end. Slang, c.1964, originally Australian and New Zealand. The phrase gained currency as a result of the activities of the later (1969) SKINHEADS, who wore BOVVER boots and used them aggressively, often to kick someone who had previously been knocked down. The figurative sense, now very common, developed later.

bootstrap (program) *noun* (in computing) a program built into the computer itself that, when the power is switched on, enables the operating system to be loaded and thus ready the computer to begin work. See BOOT UP.

boot (up) *verb* to start up a computer by loading its operating system (e.g. as contained on a 'start of day disc') into its working memory. *Boot* is short for *bootstrap* and refers to the idea of 'lifting yourself up by your own bootstraps'. A computer contains a BOOT-STRAP PROGRAM that when the power is first switched on enables the operating system to be loaded. Thus it allows the computer to get going – to achieve 'lift off' by its own bootstraps. **Bootstraps** dates from the fifties, but it was not until personal computers became common in the seventies and eighties that the shortening to *boot* (for both noun and verb) occurs.

born again *adj.* having experienced spiritual conversion to (evangelical) Christianity i.e. having been born again into a new life in Christ; or (by extension) belonging to any group that claims and values such conversion (e.g. the Southern fundamentalists of the USA); or (figuratively) of converts to quite other causes and movements: having the zeal of the newly converted. Although this is based on the Bible (see John 3:3) it dates only from the vocabulary of fifties American evangelism.

bottle *noun* spirit, guts, courage. Also *phrase* **lose one's bottle**, to lose one's nerve. British slang, first recorded in the late fifties, though thought to have been in spoken use among teenagers for about ten years before that. The origin is obscure. There is a much older expression *no bottle* (from the mid nineteenth century) meaning 'no use, no value, no class', perhaps from Cockney rhyming slang *bottle and glass* (class); this definition of *bottle* as 'value' could have developed the additional sense of 'courage'. **Bottle** became very common in the seventies. **Bottle out** (to lose one's nerve) surfaced at the end of that decade, when television police and crime series, especially *Minder*, popularised the usage.

bottle bank *noun* container in which people may leave used bottles, jars etc. for recycling. Familiar since 1977, reflecting public concern with the conservation of resources. *Bank* was perhaps intended to give a spurious air of dignity or seriousness to a humdrum operation, and has the additional advantage of adding a touch of alliteration. Reports that LOONY LEFT councils, wishing to avoid an identification between recycling and the capitalist system, renamed them 'bottle rehabilitation centres' are a mere invention.

bottom line *noun* the determining factor; final outcome; main point of an argument or problem. A late 1960s development, originally US, of an earlier meaning: the last or bottom line of a financial account shows the total profit or loss, usually the most important single feature of the whole statement. A further metaphorical extension beyond those given above is 'a sticking point, not to be gone beyond.' There is a (so-far) rare verb, **to bottom line**, to forecast what the final cost of something will be.

bottom out *verb* (of prices, trade, etc.) to reach the lowest level. The normal form, since c.1958, of what was previously simply *bottom*.

boutique *noun* a small shop selling fashionable clothes and accessories. The word has a long history in its sense of 'small shop' but developed the more specialised sense given above only in the early fifties in America, and a little later in the decade in Britain. French words, such as this, have long been thought suitably exotic for the merchandising of fashion, perfumes, etc. Large stores often have specialised known-name *boutiques* trading on their floors, and following this pattern large financial institutions that include a number of specialised services operating under the main umbrella have christened these *boutique operations*, where **boutique** *adj.* means 'displaying small-scale specialisation'. Similarly in the late eighties smaller New World wineries began calling themselves **boutiques** to establish a similar claim to specialisation and excellence.

bovine spongiform encephalopathy see BSE.

bovver *noun* trouble, rowdiness, fighting – originally as caused by SKINHEADS. Late sixties slang, a euphemism for 'violence' from the unschooled London pronunciation of *bother*. Also **bovver boy** (skinhead) and **bovver boots**, heavy boots, usually with toe-caps, often ex-Army, worn by skinheads. *Bovver boy* is now occasionally found as humorous slang for a person, such as a politician, with a reputation for abruptness or directness of manner.

box, on the *phrase* on television. *The box* has been British colloquialism for 'the television (set)' since the early fifties when television first started to become generally available in the UK, though the term had previously been used for 'the radio' in the earlier part of the century. There is an occasional verb to **box** (something) (to put it on television).

brain-dead *adj.* having suffered BRAIN DEATH. Also used colloquially of a person to mean 'stupid' (1976).

brain death *noun* irreversible loss of brain function even though respiration and circulation may continue if artificially maintained (1964). This concept is a product of modern medical developments in life-support machinery. It is important as the criterion establishing death before organs can be removed for transplant. Prior to these developments in life support technology there had been no need to refine the definition of 'death' in this way.

brain drain *noun* the large-scale emigration of the ablest – originally of British scientists, doctors, academics, etc., especially to the USA, because of the attraction of better pay or funding and conditions of work. A journalistic coinage of 1963, when anxiety about this drift was strong. It is not at present a high profile issue but the term is still used, and has been extended to less specific contexts, as for example in times of fuller employment when there was said to be a *brain drain* of teachers into other jobs with better pay.

brain-scanner see BODY-SCANNER.

brainstorming *noun* an intensive discussion by a group of people specially brought together to solve a problem or generate ideas. **Brain-storm** is an old US colloquialism for the British **brain-wave**, though in British use **brain-storm** is an informal term for a mental aberration. It is with this US sense that *brainstorming* was invented in America in the early fifties, as a technique for problem-solving in the business world. The word spread into British usage a little later, often in the phrase **a brainstorming session**, though it is no longer confined to business jargon.

brainwash *verb* to systematically attempt to instil beliefs into somebody, or to radically change a person's existing beliefs, often by the use of intensive psychological disorientation including severe physical discomfort and sense deprivation. The term is a US coinage from the Korean War (c.1950) and is thought to be a translation of a Chinese term. American and other UN prisoners of war of the Chinese were subjected to intensive political re-education and indoctrination which in some cases was accompanied by a determined invasion of their personalities. The term is widely used nowadays with the more general sense of 'to expose to repeated propaganda'.

brand image *noun* the impression a commercial product (i.e. brand) makes in the minds of consumers both actual and potential. Originally an advertising phrase (1958) implying that, in marketing, the manipulation of image, appearance, general impression, etc. is more important than fact, truth or intrinsic value.

brat pack *noun* any group of (often) ill-mannered young people, especially those who are successful, precocious, aggressive and well-to-do. Coined in 1985, specifically for a particular group of rising Hollywood stars with an extrovert lifestyle, but now applied to any group of uppish (young) people spoilt by success and indulging in brattish behaviour. **Brat** is an old dismissive word for a child, but was originally chosen with punning reference to an earlier group of Hollywood celebrities who grouped around Frank Sinatra in the fifties and called themselves *the rat pack*. The mid-eighties group were recognised as talented if self-involved, and it was probably their youth as much as their behaviour that attracted the term *brat* (and also perhaps the fact that some of them at least were the children of established stars) but later usages have tended to pick up on the negative connotations of *brat*, so that the term is generally taken to indicate selfish, rowdy and arrogant behaviour. A member of such a group is a **brat-packer**. There have been numerous nonce coinages such as *black pack* and *Brit pack*.

break-dancing *noun* highly energetic and acrobatic, competitive solo dancing. A craze of the eighties, pioneered in the late seventies by Black teenage youngsters in the Bronx in New York as one element in that street culture called HIP HOP. The dancers showed extraordinary agility, often spinning around on their elbows or backs. The **break** was originally an instrumental interlude during a RAP performance.

breathalyser *noun* instrument for measuring the amount of alcohol in the breath, and thus indicating amounts in the blood, in cases when a person may be unfit to drive because of drinking too much. An American invention first demonstrated in Britain in 1960. Slightly later developments include **breathalyse** (*verb*) and **breath-test**. The word is a conflation of *breath* and *analyser*.

breath-test see BREATHALYSER.

brilliant pebbles *noun* (an SDI code-name for) small missiles deployed in orbit to keep watch for and destroy any enemy missiles. Part of the STAR WARS vocabulary (1988) this is one of a series of code-names indicating the different levels of intelligence shown by different sized weapons, ranging from *moronic mountains* through *smart rocks* to *brilliant pebbles*. The *brilliant pebbles* are heat-seeking, computerised and super-smart.

brinkmanship *noun* the taking of a very serious risk (i.e. going to the *brink* of failure or disaster) in order to win a success, advantage, etc. The term was first recorded as being used by the US politician Adlai Stevenson in 1956, though he claimed not to have invented it; perhaps it was previously in spoken use in US diplomatic jargon. In the Cold War atmosphere of the time, dangerous adventurism such as the Cuban missile crisis of 1962 kept *brinkmanship* in use in the language of international affairs. More recently, however, the word has established itself in more general contexts, having to do with negotiations (e.g. in business dealings) or gambles (e.g. in chess).

British disease occasionally used in place of ENGLISH DISEASE.

British Library *noun* the British national library, formed in 1973.

It brings together the British Museum library and other national collections, and is scheduled to be housed in a new building in Euston Road, London, during 1997, later than was originally planned and after considerably exceeding its budget.

broad-brush *adj.* (of policy, strategy, approach, etc.) dealing with the general rather than the particular. From the use of a wide brush, unsuitable for fine detail, in painting, c.1966.

Brownie (or **brownie**) **point** *noun* credit for an achievement. From the idea of scoring fictitious points (good marks) for doing well, but the Brownies (junior Girl Guides) have no such scheme. In fact the origin is vulgar US slang: *brownie* is short for *brown-nosing* (*arse-licking* i.e. currying favour). The shift of meaning from 'sycophantic act' to 'creditable act' (c.1971) was accompanied by the addition of a capital B to *brownie*. This was done in ignorance of the true meaning of that word (or to disguise it facetiously). Thus what was originally a vulgar term has been accidentally transformed into a respectable and commendatory one.

BSE (abbreviation for) bovine spongiform encephalopathy. A fatal viral disease affecting the brains of cattle. It was identified in the UK in 1986 and thought to be caused by the use of cattle-feed containing the brains of sheep infected with scrapie. Fears that it might affect humans led to a fall in the consumption of beef in the late 1980s, and the discovery in 1990 that the disease could be spread to cats, probably through pet-food containing cattle offal, led to international concern about the safety of British beef. These worries returned with a vengeance in 1996 when it was officially recognised that there was a possible connection between CJD (the equivalent disease in humans) and the consumption of infected beef. See MAD COW DISEASE.

B-side *noun* the side of a gramophone record, usually a pop record, that is thought likely to be less popular and commercially successful than the A-SIDE (1962). Sometimes called the FLIP SIDE.

bubblejet *noun* a type of printer used in conjunction with a computer. Various types of printing technology, including the DAISY-WHEEL and the LASER PRINTER, have been used since the seventies; the *bubblejet* (sometimes spelt as two words), developed in the late eighties, has been common since c.1990 and gained favour because of its speed and silence compared with, for example, the DOT-MATRIX PRINTER. With the *bubblejet* system, a minute heating element in a nozzle produces vapour bubbles that rapidly expand and force out a controlled jet of ink. As the bubble cools and contracts, the vacuum created draws in more ink.

bucket shop *noun* a firm that sells cheap airline-tickets. Known in the UK only since the early seventies in this sense, the term has a much longer history in American English where it means an unauthorised stockbroking firm which speculates fraudulently with its clients' funds. The original bucket-shops were low-class liquor-stores selling small quantities of suspect spirits distilled in buckets. The name was later applied to low-grade dealers in small quantities of stocks and shares.

buddy

buddy *noun* a volunteer who acts as friend and support to a person with Aids. A specialised use, since 1982, of the familiar US word. Also *verb*: to undertake buddying, and the *noun* **buddying**.

bullet train *noun* the high speed train developed in Japan in the seventies. So called because it has the shape of a bullet and travels fast and straight.

bum bag *noun* a small zipped pouch attached to a belt and used for holding money, etc. Originally a sports accessory for skiers, racing cyclists and others, who wore it with the pouch at the back (over the *bum*) because they had to crouch. It became suddenly popular in 1989 among children and adults, who wore it with the pouch at the front for convenience or as a protection against pickpockets.

bump *verb* to deny (an airline passenger) a reserved place on a flight because of (deliberate) overbooking. Originally US in late forties, but not in general use in UK till the seventies or eighties.

bungie, bungy or **bunji jumping** *noun* jumping from high places, such as bridges, while attached to an elastic line, so that one has the impression of free fall and the safety of not hitting the ground. A controversial activity known since the 1980s. *Bungie* is a long-established word, of unknown origin, for an india-rubber or eraser. The *g* is soft.

burnout, burn-out *noun* physical or emotional exhaustion, especially as a result of stress at work. (Sometimes used more generally to mean 'depression, disillusionment'.) The condition was first named in print in 1975 by an American psychotherapist, though *burn-out* in the literal sense of 'complete destruction by fire' and *burn oneself out* (exhaust one's strength by over-exertion) were known in the earlier part of the century. There is an intransitive verb **burn out**, to suffer this exhaustion, and an adjective **burned** (or **burnt**) **out**.

business park *noun* an area, usually landscaped, on the outskirts of a town, designated as a site for light industry, business offices, warehouses, etc. (late eighties).

busing, bussing *noun* transporting children by bus to schools outside their neighbourhood to achieve racial integration in schools. A subject of very considerable political controversy in the USA from the late fifties, and especially in the sixties and seventies.

buster *noun* See BABY BOOMER.

butterfly effect *noun* an often quoted illustration of CHAOS THEORY: an extreme case scenario in which the motion of a butterfly on one side of the globe makes minute but crucial disturbances sufficient to tip weather conditions towards cumulatively catastrophic effects on the other side (1980s).

butter mountain see CAP.

buyout, buy-out *noun* the purchase of a controlling share in a company. Coined in the USA in the mid seventies on the pattern of the phrase *to buy (someone) out*. The term is now familiar in the UK and usually means that the purchase has been made by the company's own staff or management. See MANAGEMENT BUYOUT and LEVERAGED BUYOUT.

buzzword   *noun* a fashionable word, often a meaningless piece of jargon. As this word seems to have originated in the vocabulary of American business-management jargon, *buzz* may be an abbreviation of *business* or from the idea of meaningless *buzzing* sounds. In American slang a *buzz* is also a thrill (1942), and an effect of drug-taking (1952) and this too may have given rise to *buzzword*: people who use buzzwords are often thought to do so from the self-indulgent pleasure of making an impression, not in order to communicate sense. But the most likely derivation is from 'meaningless, confused sound' (e.g. a *buzz* of conversation or activity), the sound of the word echoing the noise.

bypass   *noun* an alternative passage for the circulation of blood, created either by an artificial device or by transplanting a vessel from elsewhere in the body. The word has been familiar since the 1920s to denote a road constructed to avoid congestion, but its medical use dates from the first *bypass surgery* in 1958, since when it has become generally known.

byte   *noun* a group of eight BITS processed as a single unit in a computer; the storage space for such a group. Computerese since the mid 1960s.

C2   *noun* a skilled manual worker. *C2* is a socio-economic category taken from a five point scale that runs from A (top management) through B (middle management) and C1 (supervisory and clerical workers) to D (unskilled and semi-skilled workers). It is used by advertisers and marketing people to denote earning power and target audiences more accurately. *C2s* were the subject of particular analysis and discussion by political commentators in the late eighties and early nineties, when their defection from their traditional Labour allegiance to a Conservatism appealing to their wish to get on was thought to be a major factor in successive Labour defeats.

cable television or **cable**   *noun* a television service relayed by cable to subscribers' homes; also the stations and programmes making up this system. Cable TV was first used in the US in the early sixties. It has been available in the UK since the early eighties, though it has been slow to catch on. The name is commonly abbreviated to **cable TV** and then to **cable** once the system is established and familiar. The verb **cable (up)** means 'to connect to a cable television system'.

CAD   (abbreviation for) COMPUTER-AIDED DESIGN.

Callanetics   *noun* (trademark of) a system of exercises to improve fitness and muscle tone through repeated small movements. The inventor, Callan Pinckney, used the name as the title of her book, published in the US in 1984 and the UK in 1989. It is from her first name with the addition of the last part of athl*etics*. It functions as a singular.

camcorder   *noun* a portable video-camera incorporating a sound recorder. From *cam*era + re*corder* (1982).

Camillagate   *noun* the furore surrounding allegations of adultery between Prince Charles and Mrs Camilla Parker Bowles. The affair came to light in 1992 with the publication of the transcript of

camper(-van)

a compromising telephone conversation alleged to have taken place between the Prince of Wales and Mrs Parker Bowles. See -GATE.

camper(-van)   *noun* a van equipped as a caravan. The American terms **camper** (1960) and **camper-van** (1973) have largely displaced the original UK term for such a vehicle – *Dormobile*, a tradename formed from *dorm*itory and *auto*mobile (1952).

can-do   *adj.* confident, positive, go-getting. 'Can do!' is what a typical SELF-STARTER will reply when faced with a request or a problem (to him an opportunity), however daunting they might appear to others. A *can-do attitude* is essential to the ENTERPRISE CULTURE.

can of worms   *noun* an involved problem. An Americanism known in the UK since c.1962. The reference is to the appearance of the contents of a tin can holding worms to be used as fishing bait, and the implication that in 'opening up a whole can of worms' you are looking into something it would be preferable not to.

cap   *verb* to impose an upper limit on something. Also *noun*: the upper limit so imposed. In the eighties and nineties **cap** has been made familiar from its use to describe central government's control of local government spending by placing a top limit on local government taxation. The term probably comes from the *capping* of oil wells when they catch fire or gush out of control, though this is itself a straightforward extension of the long-standing meaning of *cap*: to cover with a cap or capping, as a wall is with a coping stone. Government policy towards local authorities has ensured that the new figurative meaning has been much heard since the mid eighties. Thus in 1990 we find **charge-cap** (to limit the amount of community charge or poll tax) and previously **rate-cap** (to limit the local rate raised on house-holders).

CAP   (acronym for) Common Agricultural Policy. This is the system first implemented in 1962, which requires the member countries of the European Community to organise their agricultural policies jointly. It is probably best known because of the policy of setting 'reasonable' prices for foodstuffs: if market prices fall below this level the EC buys up surplus products, thus creating a vast BUTTER MOUNTAIN (1969) or WINE LAKE (1974) etc. In other words farm products are capable of attracting subsidies whether or not they are actually required by consumers.

capital gains tax   *noun* a UK government tax imposed on the profit made from a person's sale of certain assets. Included under this tax are, for example, the profits made on certain stock-exchange dealings, but any increase in value of one's main home is excluded. The tax was introduced in 1965.

capture   *verb* to convert data into a machine readable form and enter it into a computer. Also *noun*, the action of doing this. Computerese since the early seventies, and short for **data capture**.

car bomb   *noun* a bomb placed in a car for subsequent detonation. This may be a terrorist bomb placed in or under a parked car and intended to kill the driver and passengers, but more often refers to a bomb placed in a car for transportation to the place where it is detonated by a suicide bomber, or (at an opportune moment) by remote control. Such bombs are particularly devastating because of the huge amount of explosives that can be packed into them (as with the Oklahoma bombing of 1995) and because they are so difficult to guard against.

carbon fibre   *noun*   fine, light and strong thread of pure carbon made by heating and stretching textile fibres. Used, normally in bundles, to reinforce resins, metals, etc. and found in aircraft engines, sporting equipment and other items needing to withstand strain (1960).

car-boot sale   *noun*   an event at which people sell their unwanted possessions, which are displayed in the boots of their cars. A form of jumble sale common since the early eighties, facilitated by the popularity of HATCHBACK cars. Such sites now often include trade vendors – e.g. market traders.

card   *noun*   (short for) CHEQUE CARD and CREDIT CARD. See also CASH CARD, PHONECARD, SWITCH, STORECARD.

cardboard city   *noun*   a collection of temporary shelters where homeless people live or sleep; that part of town where these are found. So called because of the use of cardboard boxes or packaging as cover. The term probably originated in the USA in the late seventies or early eighties; during the eighties it became familiar in the UK, particularly with regard to an area under Waterloo Bridge, London, though it is used of other locations also and shows signs of developing more generally in the phrase **in cardboard city**, meaning 'in poverty; on the breadline'. Analogous to French *bidonville* – for a shanty town made of flattened petrol cans (bidons).

cardphone   *noun*   a public telephone operated by a PHONECARD. Because of the newness of the technology (see PHONECARD), its vocabulary has not yet settled down. There are signs that *cardphone* (c.1984) will prevail, though public telephone boxes carry various words advertising the services, and people sometimes refer to 'a phonecard phone' or simply 'a phonecard'.

carer   *noun*   an unpaid person who cares for an elderly, handicapped or sick relative at home. Although the word has been used for three centuries in the general sense of 'a person who cares', this specific and now well established use was not heard until c.1978, when it was felt necessary to find a name for several million people who were increasingly seen to deserve support, better financial allowances, opportunities for part-time employment, etc. because of the strain upon them and the importance of their contribution in the overall pattern of care. Members of the *caring professions* are often called **professional carers**.

caring   *adj.*   (of a person) compassionate; (of a job) offering care to the sick and elderly or otherwise dependent people. *Care* is an ancient word, but *caring* in the above sense is not recorded until the mid sixties, since when it has also been used in such compounds as a **caring society** and even **caring capitalism**, also the **caring professions** (see CARER) and the **caring nineties** – a media forecast that a hallmark of the decade would be a new compassion in contrast to the discredited materialism of the eighties.

car-jacking *noun* the theft of a car after assaulting or menacing its driver. Because the theft of parked cars has been rendered difficult by improved security devices such as better locks and alarm systems, car thieves in the USA have switched since c.1992 to stealing cars when they are actually in use. Such operations include pulling drivers from their vehicles when stationary at traffic lights, making off with cars after stealing the keys from drivers at petrol stations, in car parks, etc., or forcing a driver at the point of a gun to drive a hi-jacker to a place where the driver can be abandoned and the car driven away.

carphone *noun* a radio telephone installed in a car. Also written as two words with or without a hyphen. Known since the sixties but only familiar since the late eighties as a result of better and cheaper technology, at which time they became an essential status symbol for YUPPIES who generally called them CELLPHONES.

cash card *noun* an embossed plastic card resembling a CREDIT CARD and issued by a bank or building society, enabling the card-holder to obtain money from a CASH DISPENSER (late 1960s).

cash dispenser *noun* a computerised machine outside a bank for the use of customers wishing to withdraw cash or obtain information about their account. They are operated by using a CASH CARD and a PIN, and are often referred to as CASHPOINTS. See ATM.

cashpoint *noun* a cash dispenser. Lloyds Bank invented the word, with a capital C, when it introduced its cash dispensers in 1973. Similar facilities soon became popular throughout the UK, and the word quickly passed into everyday use.

cassette *noun*. The original meaning was 'casket' and in this sense the word was used for the small flat box in which early photographers kept photographic plates. With the development of photography the word came to be applied to the small light-proof cylinder holding a spool of film. In the late fifties the word was used for the closed plastic container of a spool of magnetic tape, capable of being inserted into a tape-deck for play-back or recording of sound. Previously, a spool of tape had to be threaded through part of a tape-recorder and attached to a second, empty spool; the new technology provided a more compact all-in-one arrangement. *Cassette-player* and *cassette-recorder* became familiar in the sixties, closely followed by *videocassette* (c.1970) a cassette of tape for the recording and playing back of television programmes.

casual, Casual *noun* a young man, member of a group who wear casual clothes, often support right-wing political views, and who go to football matches to start fights. Although casual, his clothes are expensive; other characteristics include a taste for soul music and materialism. This sub group appeared in the early eighties and were in some senses successors to the mods almost two decades before them.

cat (short for) CATALYTIC CONVERTER (c.1988). Especially *cat car*, one fitted with a catalytic converter.

catalytic converter *noun* device fitted to the exhaust system of a car to reduce pollutants discharged into the atmosphere. Developed in the fifties, introduced in America in the sixties and familiar since the eighties in the UK, though it was not until 1992 that all new cars had to have them.

catch-22 *adj.* consisting of mutually frustrating features; also **Catch 22** *noun* a regulation or other factor that frustrates our endeavours (e.g. funnelling us into a loop which allows no exit). Usually found in **a catch-22 situation**, i.e. circumstances in which it is impossible to succeed, whatever line of action is followed. *Catch 22* is the title of a war novel by Joseph Heller published in 1961. In it *catch* (or 'drawback') number 22 is a regulation to the effect that a pilot who flies dangerous missions is crazy and therefore eligible to be grounded, but if he asks to be grounded he must be sane – because his concern for his safety is rational – and therefore must fly more missions. The homeless unemployed are often said to be in *a catch-22 situation*: without an address they cannot get work; without work they cannot afford permanent accommodation.

CAT scanner *noun* a computer controlled X-ray machine capable of producing three dimensional images; a body-scanner. *CAT* stands for *computerised axial tomography* but is sometimes interpreted as *computer-aided* (or *-assisted*) tomography. See BODY SCANNER.

catsuit *noun* a one-piece tight-fitting trouser suit, usually worn by women. From c.1960, and so called because it reveals the shape of the wearer, like the short fur of most members of the cat family.

CB (abbreviation for) citizen's band radio. A two-way radio system specially popular among drivers, especially US truckers, enabling them to chat with other people to break the monotony of long-distance travel. It became popular in the USA in the late fifties, and in the UK twenty years later (though it was illegal until 1981) after which its use declined.

CD (abbreviation for) compact disc, a small audio disc read by an optical laser system. The technology, invented in the late seventies by Philips, became commercially available in the eighties, and rapidly established itself as the successor to the LP because of its improved sound quality, its near-indestructibility and the compactness of both disc (12 cm diameter; compare SINGLE) and player. Information is recorded digitally (see DIGITAL) on the disc as a spiral of tiny pits, and reproduced by the reading of the reflections of a LASER beam focused on the spiral. The surface of the disc is protected from dust or scratches by a smooth, transparent layer and cannot be worn out because nothing mechanical comes into contact with it during operation. See CDI, CD ROM, CDV for developments of this technology.

CDI (abbreviation for) COMPACT DISC interaction. Form of computer gaming using compact discs. Known in the late 1980s, but its popularity remains to be seen.

CD ROM or **-rom** (in computing) (abbreviation of) COMPACT DISC read-only memory. A form of compact disc developed in the 1980s to store large volumes of data such as encyclopaedias or dictionaries. This can be read by using a computer, and can contain far more information than normal computer discs. It cannot, however, be added to or changed, which is why it is called 'read only'.

CDV (abbreviation for) compact video disc; also of CD-VIDEO. A compact video disc is a compact LASER DISC able to play pictures as well as sound. It was developed in the eighties and is used with CD-VIDEO.

CD-video *noun* a compact-disc player that can be connected to a television set and hi-fi to produce pictures and high-quality sound from a disc resembling a CD. Known since the late 1980s, but its popularity cannot yet be judged.

Ceefax see TELETEXT.

Cellnet see CELLPHONE.

cellphone *noun* (short for) cellular telephone, i.e. mobile radio phone. Also **Cellnet**, trademark for the cellular network enabling the use of such phones. The operating network consists of a huge number of small areas (called *cells*, hence *cellular*), each of which has its own short-range radio transmitter/receiver connected to the main telephone system. Mobile phones have access to this system through radio contact with the transmitter/receiver serving the *cell* where the user happens to be; if the user moves (e.g. by car) to another *cell*, radio contact is automatically switched to that cell's transmitter/receiver. The system, introduced in the late seventies, became familiar in the eighties.

cellular see CELLPHONE.

centrefold *noun* an illustration, usually coloured, spread over the double page (or a triple, folded page) at the centre of a popular magazine; the photograph of a nude woman used as such an illustration; a model who appears in such photographs. Originally US, c.1966, but now more general journalese.

CERN (*acronym* for) Conseil Européen pour le Recherche Nucléaire (European Council for Nuclear Research). A research centre formed by a group of leading European states in 1954 in Geneva (a French-speaking part of Switzerland). Even though the centre has since been renamed the European Laboratory for Particle Physics, it is still known as CERN.

CFCs (short for) chlorofluorocarbons; the shortening uses the initial letters of the three elements that make up that name covering a number of chemical compounds of chlorine, fluorine and carbon. Their commercial use, notably as propellants in aerosols and as fluid refrigerants in refrigerators, came under examination in the seventies when it was discovered that their disposal into the atmosphere contributed to the depletion of the OZONE LAYER. They were much in the news during the following decade as a subject of concern to ecological groups, and several governments have taken action to control their use. One result of this public concern has been the labelling of goods in the shops as **CFC-free**. See HCFC.

chair, chairperson *noun* (a non-sexist term for) a person presiding over a meeting. *Chairman* used to be the normal word for either a man or a woman occupying such a position (and is still widely current), while a *chairwoman* has existed for centuries, though not necessarily in common use. However, in the early seventies **chairperson** and **chair** were invented as non-sexist alternatives by feminists, though *chairperson* (1971) is thought by some people to be ugly. Its slightly later shortening to *chair* prompted further objections because the primary meaning of that word (i.e. a piece of furniture) is sufficiently strong for the new meaning to feel odd, though the long-standing phrase 'to address the chair' provided a clear precedent for its use. Though some still object to these terms both *chair* and *chairperson* are now widely accepted and used by many who once disliked their newness. See -PERSON.

challenged *adj.* suffering from a disadvantage or handicap. Social workers and some other people have often claimed that the use of *handicap, problem, sufferer, victim,* etc. in relation to those they look after can be discriminatory, negative or hurtful. The attempt in the late eighties to introduce *challenged* as a more positive term was greeted with some ridicule (satirists promptly seized on the description of small people as **'vertically challenged'** or gypsies as **'residentially challenged'**, etc.) and it is too early to say whether the term will survive. In fact, as with other politically correct terms (*hair disadvantaged* for 'bald' or *differently sized* for 'fat') it is not always easy to be sure that the coinage is meant seriously – and it may be doubted that *follicularly challenged* or *circumferentially challenged* for these same things ever had serious use or intent. See POLITICAL CORRECTNESS.

champagne socialist *noun* a professed socialist who enjoys an extravagant lifestyle (c.1970). This old sneer (with such variants as *Ramada* or *chateau-bottled socialist*) is based on the curious idea that a person of left-wing political persuasion cannot enjoy the good life without betraying the working classes and socialist principles and must therefore be bogus. It is difficult to say whether the advent of New Labour will remove any surviving sting it may once have had or allow it a new lease of life.

channel surf *verb* (late eighties) see GRAZE and ZAP.

chaos theory *noun* a theory or line of study (in mathematics and various branches of science) focusing on apparently random and unpredictable behaviour in dynamic systems resulting from their sensitivity to small changes, and especially to initial conditions, which may have significant and significantly different outcomes. A 1980s term for a study which actually began twenty years previously. The name comes from the familiar figurative sense of *chaos* ('complete disorder, utter confusion'); originally, *chaos* or *Chaos* was the formless matter or void from which the ordered universe was created. Under this theory the chaos is apparent rather than actual, as the BUTTERFLY EFFECT illustrates.

charge-cap see CAP.

charge card *noun* a form of CREDIT CARD issued by an individual store or business enabling the holder to obtain its goods and services for payment at a later date. The term was originally (US,

1962) – and sometimes still is – interchangeable with *credit card*, but a distinction is beginning to emerge: a **charge card** is now usually limited to a single business concern and its customers, and a *credit card* may be used with any business (or in any country) which has membership of the appropriate agency. Additionally, a *charge card* does not necessarily imply (as *credit card* does) that the holder is entitled to credit facilities.

charismatic movement *noun* a Christian movement consisting of various groups, within existing denominations, that emphasise communal prayer, informality of worship, and charismatic gifts (speaking in tongues, faith-healing, baptism by the Holy Spirit, etc.) in a spirit of spontaneity and enthusiasm. *Charismatic* in this context means 'divinely bestowed', which is the original sense of the word (despite its debased use in modern non-theological contexts). Although it has its roots in much older pentecostalism, the *charismatic movement* was not named until the sixties and is found within the Anglican, Roman Catholic and Orthodox churches as well as within Nonconformist ones.

charts, the *noun* the published lists of gramophone record sales showing the most popular records week by week (early sixties). Later used of other media, e.g. the list of the most popular television programmes during a given period, as measured by audience size.

chase the dragon *phrase* (drug users' slang) to smoke heroin. If a heroin-user heats the drug on a piece of aluminium foil, the molten heroin may move about the surface, and the tube through which the user inhales the fumes has to follow (*chase*) this movement to pick up the smoke. The expression, known since the sixties, though not in the UK until the late seventies, is said to be a translation of a Chinese term, and the movement of the fumes is likened to the movement and appearance of a dragon's tail in the traditional theatre. *Dragon* also suggests the fierceness of the drug.

chat-line, chatline *noun* a telephone service enabling users to join in general conversation with each other. In the UK several such services were introduced after the privatisation of the telephone network in 1984. During the second half of the 1980s, when the word first became well known, there was public outcry over their misuse and particularly over the enormous telephone bills incurred by some users, especially teenagers, and the service was suspended.

chat show *noun* a television or radio programme in which a compère has informal conversation, often light-hearted or trivial, with well-known guests. The term emerged c.1969 as a variant of the slightly earlier *talk show*. As *chat* is more informal than *talk*, there may be an implication that a *chat show* is intended to be more lightweight than a *talk show*, or the two terms may be interchangeable. *Chat show* is certainly the more common term, perhaps because it sounds more friendly.

chattering classes, the *noun* educated, articulate, liberal-minded middle-class people who enjoy talking about social, political or cultural issues, sometimes with no first-hand knowledge or the ability to make any practical difference. This catchphrase is a product of an increasingly media-dominated age, a pragmatic political climate, and British philistinism. Coined in the early eighties, it was originally applied to the mainly metropolitan left-wing intelligentsia who expressed their views over dinner-tables in terms unsullied by practical considerations. The more general modern meaning is derogatory journalese for people, especially pundits, who enjoy talking or earn their living discussing things they may be unable to do anything about. The implication that people who talk are inferior to people who act is, to say the least, arguable. Certain politicians have used *chattering classes* in disparaging reference to the media for daring to disagree with or criticise them.

chauvinism or **chauvinist**   (occasional shortening of) MALE CHAUVINISM/CHAUVINIST.

chequebook journalism   *noun* the practice of paying large sums of money for the exclusive rights to the stories of newsworthy individuals. A derogatory term (mid 1960s) because such individuals are often notorious, or associated with notoriety (e.g. the wives of murderers), and payment to them is seen as a direct or indirect reward for crime or reprehensible behaviour, or else to induce a betrayal of trust. See KISS-AND-TELL.

cheque card   *noun* a numbered card, consisting of a flexible rectangle of plastic, issued by a bank or building society to a customer, guaranteeing payment to a shopkeeper etc. of the card-holder's cheques up to a stated amount. Issued by UK banks since the late sixties. The style of the card has since been copied for CREDIT CARDS, etc.

child abuse   *noun* ill-treatment of a child by a parent or other adult. The term was first used in the seventies (see ABUSE) of physical violence, formerly called *child battering*, or neglect. It is still used in this sense, but since the 1980s it has been mainly used to denote sexual interference, as a result of a succession of notorious cases and growing public awareness of the problem. In this later sense it has largely replaced *child molesting*, perhaps because this term was usually applied to adults other than parents when it is now more generally known that *child abuse* is sometimes committed by parents.

childproof   *adj.* not capable of being operated, misused or damaged by a child. Formed c.1956 from *child* and the combining form *-proof* ('secure against damage by'), though the meaning is no longer restricted to damage.

chill out   *verb* to relax. Originally US slang, from the late eighties. It may have grown up as an elaboration of the earlier *cool down* or, more likely, in drug-users' slang among the young: at crowded ACID HOUSE parties where the taking of ECSTASY is accompanied by energetic dancing, participants need to go out into the open air to literally *chill out*, i.e. recover by a (long) period of cooling off. The term is one of many new US phrasal verbs using *out* to indicate the obliteration of something: see MAX OUT, MELLOW OUT.

China syndrome   *noun* a nuclear disaster caused by failure in a nuclear reactor, followed by MELTDOWN that burns deep into the earth with unpredictable results. Originally (c.1970) a hypothesis taking its name from the facetious idea that the meltdown would pass through the earth's core from the USA and come out at the other side in China. The term was popularised by a film called *The China Syndrome* (1979) about attempts to conceal a nuclear danger, and the catastrophe at Chernobyl (1986) gave it greater relevance, though the idea of penetrating through to the earth's centre remains fanciful, and the term may be applied to any Chernobyl-type disaster. The disaster that overtook the Challenger shuttle in the same year as Chernobyl led to a coinage, **the Ch/Ch syndrome**, (denoting a blow to high technology resulting from undue time pressures in the development of projects) with its punning reference to **the China syndrome**.

Chinese wall   *noun* a restriction on the exchange of information among the parts of a business organisation, especially a financial company that may have conflicts of interest between its different departments. Specially used since BIG BANG on the London Stock Exchange (1986) to denote the separation between brokers (advising people to buy shares) and market-makers (trying to sell shares) within the same institution, and also to discourage insider dealing. The allusion is probably to the strength of the Great Wall of China.

chip   *noun* a tiny wafer of silicon or other thin semiconductor material etched or otherwise processed to form an integrated electronic circuit. Developed in the early sixties and generally known by the seventies as the basis of much modern technology, especially in computing.

chocaholic or **chocoholic**   see WORKAHOLIC.

chopper   *noun* helicopter. US military slang (c.1951) from the Korean War (1950–3), probably from the sound of the rotor blades. The word was later used (1960s) for a motorcycle that has been modified and customised with high handlebars, and for a child's bicycle (c.1971) modelled on this.

Chunnel   *noun* the tunnel under the English Channel linking England and France. Familiar since the late 1950s, though actually invented earlier as a combination of *channel* and *tunnel*. The coinage has never really caught on outside the tabloid press.

ciao   an Italian word of greeting or farewell, pronounced 'chow', affected by some English speakers since the sixties.

cinéma-verité   *noun* a technique of film making which avoids artificiality and depicts events, conversations, etc. that are close to those of real life. The earliest examples, in the early sixties, used hand-held cameras, ordinary people instead of actors, spontaneous dialogue and real-life situations, though the term was later applied to films that used less extreme methods in their search for a feeling of unrehearsed reality. French film-makers were among the pioneers of the style: *cinéma-verité* is literally 'truth cinema'.

CIS   (abbreviation for) Commonwealth of Independent States. Set up in late 1991 by most of the republics which had formerly been part of the USSR.

city technology college *noun* type of secondary school independent of local government control, originally intended to be set up in inner-city areas with the help of funding from industry and normally specialising in technical subjects. One of several government initiatives intended to by-pass local education authorities and attract industrial sponsorship of schools. CTCs were first heard of in 1986, and the first was opened in 1988. Only 15 have so far been created, not all of them in inner cities, and with only lukewarm support from industry.

CJD (abbreviation of) Creutzfeldt-Jakob disease. This is a rare but transmissible and normally fatal progressive disease, usually of the later middle-aged and elderly. The nerve cells in the brain degenerate and dementia and spasticity follow. *CJD* came to general notice in the eighties because it is the human equivalent of BSE and there were fears that eating the meat of infected cattle might put the population in general at risk. More recently (1996) a scatter of cases of *CJD* among much younger sufferers has resurrected these fears, depressed beef prices and soured relationships with our EC partners. Creutzfeldt and Jakob published their researches on the central nervous system (separately) in the early 1920s.

clamp *verb* to immobilise (a vehicle) by using a WHEEL CLAMP.

classist *adj.* showing discrimination because of a person's social class. Also (*noun*) a person who discriminates on grounds of class. From c.1985, on the model of *ageist, sexist*, etc. Some people argue that an unquestioning acceptance (or unconscious assumption) of the superiority of middle class values is one common example of **classism**.

Clause 28 *noun* a clause in the Local Government Bill (1988), now an Act, prohibiting local authorities from 'promoting homosexuality'. As the responsibility of local authorities include the control of public libraries and of most state schools, this legislation was seen as inevitably leading to an infringement of important principles such as freedom of information and speech. The Clause is also thought to reflect the homophobia of much right-wing thinking in the Aids decade. See also NEW MORALITY.

closet, come out of the see COME OUT.

clout *noun* power and/or influence. Originally US slang (1950s) based on the colloquial meaning of *clout* ('heavy blow') but now Standard English.

club class *noun* a class of aircraft travel offering facilities between those of first class and tourist class. Introduced in the late seventies and mainly intended for business travellers. *Club* was no doubt intended to suggest the exclusivity and comfort of a men's club.

COBOL (acronym for) **C**ommon **B**usiness **O**riented **L**anguage. A computer-programming language developed in America in 1959 for commercial programming. It became the most widely used HIGH-LEVEL language.

cock-up theory *noun* the belief that when events turn out badly and plans go awry it is more than likely to be the result of bungling

cocooning

(*cock-ups*) and misunderstandings than of deliberate plotting. *Cock-up* has been a UK slang term for a blunder or confused situation since at least the Second World War and was originally forces slang. The *cock-up* explanation is usually found in tandem with its alternative, the **conspiracy theory**, which explains the disasters of history by the malign and covert influence of secret forces (*conspiracy*). It is common, though of course not invariable, for the two to be evoked, so that cock-up theory can be ultimately preferred.

cocooning   *noun* spending leisure time at home relaxing with one's family; a retreat from hassle on the streets and over-commitment to a career. US YUPPIE slang, late eighties, apparently coined by a New York sociologist in 1986 to describe an apparent retreat from the stresses both of work and social life into the *cocoon* (protective covering) of the family. The reference is to the protective sheath or case of silky threads that silk worms and other insects spin to protect themselves as chrysalises.

coffee-table book   *noun* a large, expensive book usually lavishly illustrated. The implication is that such a book is likely to be put on a low table in a sitting room, either so that it can be glanced through rather than read, or in order to impress a visitor. In fact the name may originally (early sixties) have meant no more than that the book was too big for a normal bookshelf – an outsize book.

cold call   *noun* an unsolicited visit or telephone call to a person by someone trying to sell goods, services, etc. Also *verb* **cold-call** to make an unsolicited call to or on someone for the purpose of selling to them. The expression dates from the early seventies, *cold* indicating a lack of preparation or warm-up, as a car may be difficult to start from cold as distinct from when it has been run for a time. *Cold calling* began by being in person, but is now popularly associated with unsolicited telephone calls.

Cold War   *noun* a state of enmity between nations, involving subversion, propaganda, threats, economic boycotts, etc., but not actual fighting. Usually applied to the hostility between the two superpowers (the USA and USSR) and their allies between 1945 and the collapse of communism in Eastern Europe in the late 1980s or early nineties. The term was coined at the end of the Second World War (its first recorded use being by George Orwell in October 1945) and was commonplace from the 1950s onwards. On 3 December 1989 President Bush declared 'the Cold War is over'.

collateral damage   *noun* unintended civilian casualties (and damage to non-military buildings) during a military conflict. US military jargon since the Vietnam War, and more recently familiar from US comment on the Gulf War of 1991. It is a widely criticised euphemism, as *damage* seems a dishonest understatement for 'death', and though *collateral* is perfectly properly used here as an adjective meaning 'aside from the main line of action or issue; subordinate', it is now an unusual word that most people know only from legal contexts as a noun meaning 'something given as collateral security', and the overall intention of the term seems to be to obscure rather than make clear.

collectable (sometimes **collectible**, chiefly US) *noun* a thing worth collecting. An established adjective but comparatively recently used as a noun (in the fifties in the US, but not until the late seventies in the UK). *Collectables* are not necessarily antique nor of established value but are considered worth collecting for some intrinsic interest, charm or *possible* future value. The term and the trade are now generally familiar, and there has been a great increase in such collecting in the eighties.

colourise or **Colorize** *verb* to add colour to old black and white films by a computerised process. Also *colourisation* (noun). There is a long-established verb meaning 'to colour', but this is a new meaning describing a new process with the trade name *Colorizer*. There has been understandable disagreement about the value (or vandalism) of adding colour to classic black and white films.

come out *verb* to let it be known that one is a homosexual. Probably now Standard English, though it is from a longer expression *come out of the closet* which is slang. *Closet* as a noun meaning 'small cupboard or private room' has a long history in English but has not been much used recently (except perhaps in *water closet*, usually abbreviated to *W.C.*). In the USA, however, it has remained in common use, which is why *come out of the closet* is likely to have originated in an Americanism (despite what some commentators have said), perhaps by reference to *skeleton in the closet*, the US and Canadian version of the British *skeleton in the cupboard*. Both *come out of the closet* and the shorter form *come out* owe their present currency to GAY LIBERATION. For the recent development of this term – the transitive verb **to out** (to expose someone as homosexual, to force a homosexual to come out of the closet) – see OUT.

Common Market *noun* (popular name for) the European Economic Community (see EEC). The term first became familiar in the UK c.1954, at first without capital initials, when certain European countries began to discuss the setting up of a trade association to reduce duties on trade among themselves, and to impose common tariffs on trade with countries outside the association. Capital initials became common with the formalisation of these arrangements in the Treaty of Rome (1957) and their institution in 1958 as the European Economic Community. The term has continued in use long after the later EC broadened the scope of this original collaboration.

community charge *noun* a flat-rate charge payable by every adult to the local council to replace the local property-tax ('rates'). Introduced in Scotland (1989), then in England and Wales (1990), this POLL TAX, as it was popularly called, was widely resented on the grounds that it took no account of the individual's means. It was one of the factors leading to the resignation of Margaret Thatcher (1990) and was promptly replaced by the COUNCIL TAX. See CAP.

commuter belt *noun* a residential area around a city, from which people travel to work in the centre (1960s). For an explanation of *belt*, see RUST BELT and STOCKBROKER BELT.

compact disc *noun*. Although this term is most popularly known as the name for an audio disc (see CD), it is used also of a disc capable of storing other types of information, notably that which can be visually displayed (see LASER DISC, for example).

compassion fatigue   *noun* a reduction in one's ability to feel sympathy for the misfortunes of others as a result of too many demands on one's charity or of too much exposure to others' suffering. The phrase (early eighties) reflected a fear, which was probably exaggerated, that repeated images of starving and suffering people would lead to a deadening of the public's sympathy and generosity towards people in need, especially in third world areas affected by famine. Similar coinages include **condom fatigue** and **fashion fatigue**.

complementary (medicine)   *noun* a therapy or medical treatment that seeks to complement orthodox medical treatments; an alternative therapy. For example, acupuncture, osteopathy, homeopathy, etc. Since it was coined in 1982, *complementary medicine* – also known as *alternative medicine* and, more cautiously as 'fringe medicine' – has become a well-established term that implies a medical treatment working alongside and not in competition with orthodox medicine. Indeed *complementary medicine* has become so familiar that it is now offered in some hospitals. *Complementary* is preferred to *alternative* by many practitioners because it stresses the idea of working in tandem rather than in place of conventional treatments, *fringe* (the other word by which these therapies are sometimes known) has undesirable connotations of being on the outside, or at the margins or of little effect.

computeracy   *noun* the ability to understand and use computers. Also **computerate** (adjective): having this ability. The first of these words has been in colloquial use since the late sixties, and the second since the early eighties, though neither caught on as quickly as NUMERACY and *numerate* (based on *literacy* and *literate*) did in the 1960s. The prevailing terms remain *computer-literacy* or *computer-literate*, familiar since the 1970s when computers began to assume importance in commerce, industry and education. It is too early to say whether the blendings of these into *computeracy* and *computerate* will stand the test of time.

computer-aided design   *noun* the use of computers in the design of products, buildings, etc. (1963). By using computer graphics, the designer can display plans, elevations, etc. and manipulate them on a video screen, perhaps with a view to modifying them or to assessing the effect of changing certain dimensions, tolerances, etc.

computerese   *noun* the technical jargon of computing. This is the popularly accepted sense of the colloquial word (since c.1970) but the original sense ('computer language', c.1960) is still sometimes found in specialist use.

computerise   *verb* to introduce computers into (an office); use a computer to perform or control an operation (c.1960).

computer literacy   see COMPUTERACY.

condo, condominium   *noun* a privately-owned apartment in a building jointly owned by the apartment-owners; also used of the whole apartment building. This system of ownership has been popular in N. America since the early sixties. *Condominium* previously had a much older meaning: '(country under) joint rule'.

cone-headed   *adj.* (of person) intellectual. The British equivalent of the US POINTY-HEADED. It emerged c.1993, and may be short-lived journalese.

conglomerate   *noun* a large industrial or business group resulting from the merging of companies with diverse and sometimes unrelated interests. A 1960s addition to the meanings of a word which was previously mainly restricted to scientific vocabulary.

Connect   see EFTPOS.

consciousness-raising   *noun* the process of increasing one's own or others' awareness of and sensitivity to social, political and other issues. Also a *noun* **consciousness-raiser**: one who raises consciousness *or* the means for raising consciousness. A coinage first recorded in 1968 and quickly a central word and concept in the feminist movement. Among the **consciousness raisers** they embraced were words that denied the MASCULIST assumptions of speech and study – e.g. **manglish** and **herstory** for English and history.

conspiracy theory   see COCK-UP THEORY.

consumerism   *noun.* This word, first coined in the 1940s, has two distinct meanings. The original one, much discussed in the sixties and seventies was 'protection of consumers' interests' and had to do with campaigns establishing the producers' responsibility in selling defective, dangerous or misleadingly advertised goods. The second, which looks like becoming the dominant one, developed in the early sixties: 'the doctrine that continual increase in consumption (i.e. spending) is the basis of a sound economy'.

consumer terrorism   *noun* interference with consumer goods (usually in supermarkets) to make them dangerous to the consumer. The purpose is usually to blackmail the producers or to damage their interests (perhaps in retaliation for some alleged malpractice, e.g. the use of animals in product research). The first important act of *consumer terrorism*, the addition of poison to painkillers, took place in the USA in 1982; by the end of the decade, the term – and the action – had spread to the UK. See TAMPER-EVIDENT.

containerise   *verb* to pack into containers for transport. Also **container-ship** *noun*, a ship suitable for such transport. The first is from the 1950s, the second from c.1966. *Container* itself is much older.

contra, Contra   *noun* a member of the guerrilla forces opposing the Sandinista government in Nicaragua, 1979–90. An abbreviation (c.1981) of a Spanish word for 'counter-revolutionary'. It became widely known from the 'Iran-contra' affair (1986), a controversy involving US officials, and possibly the President, in the secret diversion to the *contras*, contrary to US legislation, of funds raised by selling arms to Iran in exchange for the release of hostages. See -GATE.

contraflow   *noun* temporary two-way traffic on one carriageway of a motorway or other dual-carriageway road. Usually put into operation so that the other carriageway can be repaired, or in the event of blockage by an accident. The word was invented in the 1930s ('flow in the opposite direction') for use in the paper-making industry, and has been applied to traffic since the seventies.

convenience food   *noun* food designed to be convenient, needing little preparation. For example, frozen, cook-chill or pre-cooked foodstuffs. The term, originally American from c.1960, is now general in the UK.

cook-chill   *noun* a method of cooking food, then refrigerating it, for later reheating and consumption. The process became familiar from the early eighties in mass catering, for example by airlines and hospitals, and was later extended to foodstuffs available for retail purchase. Because the food is chilled, not frozen, extra care is necessary with temperature control and storage time, and cook-chill food came under suspicion at the time of the listeria scare of 1989.

cool   *adj.* a key word of the BEAT GENERATION in the fifties, adopted by HIPPIES in the sixties, and still in use, as a colloquial term of general approval meaning 'excellent' or 'very pleasing'. It was borrowed from a slightly earlier use (late 1940s) in American jazz, where it meant 'restrained' or 'relaxed' (as distinct from 'hot' with excitement) and was applied to the music, its performance and its devotees. Its sense of lack of emotional involvement made it specially attractive to young people in subsequent decades who wished to signal their detachment from conventional attitudes and values. The 1950s expressions **cool it** ('take it easy') and **play it cool** ('treat matters calmly'), the 1960s **lose one's cool** ('lose one's composure') and the later, Caribbean **cool out** ('relax') are slang variants of the same general idea.

cop-out   *noun* a desertion of responsibility or commitment. Also **cop out** *verb*: to fail to show responsibility or commitment. The modern sense comes from rather confused American slang of the early sixties when the term meant both 'escape from conventional society' and 'escape from HIPPIE values back into conventional ones'. There are earlier uses of *cop out* in the sense of 'escape'; *cop* is old slang for 'capture' and 'punish' (hence *cop* and *copper* as slang names for policeman) and the addition of *out* implies the opposite: not getting caught or being called to account.

corn circle   (another name for) CROP CIRCLE.

corporate   *adj.* associated with big business. The word has a long history in the sense of 'forming a corporation or belonging to a united group', but since the early seventies a determined hijack has added a new shade of meaning to the word: 'forming a **business corporation** or organisation'. Hence *corporate image/identity* (public presentation of a business firm in a desirable way), *corporate hospitality* (e.g. Wimbledon seats and a private refreshment marquee for people a firm wants to reward or impress), *corporate raider* (person or group acquiring many shares in a business in order to gain control) and even *corporate Britain* (the country seen as a business entity first and foremost).

Cosa Nostra   *noun* the Mafia in the USA. The Italian words mean 'our thing' and the name surfaced in 1963 as a coded way of referring to the Mafia.

cosmonaut   *noun* a member of the crew of the Russian spacecraft. The Russian equivalent of the American *astronaut*, a word coined in the earlier part of the twentieth century when space travel was merely a matter of speculation. *Cosmonaut* is from Greek words meaning 'universe' and 'sailor'; *astro-* = 'star'.

cost-effective   *adj.* (of anything you invest money in or – by extension – time and/or effort) providing an adequate return in relation to its cost (c.1967).

cot death   *noun* the unexplained sudden death of a baby while sleeping. The common name, since c.1970, for what is technically known as 'sudden infant death syndrome'; none of the explanations so far provided seem to hold the key to this worryingly common occurrence.

couch potato   *noun* a lazy person whose favourite occupation is watching television or videos (usually eating JUNK FOOD and drinking) and taking no exercise. In British slang, a BOOB TUBE is a tightly-fitting strapless top worn by women (a tube to cover the BOOBS). In North America, however, it is a television receiver (from its cathode-ray *tube* and the *boobs* (idiots) who watch it); hence a compulsive viewer is, slightingly, a **boob tuber**. The term *couch potato* is from the *couch* on which a viewer slumps and the vegetable he or she is – a *potato* being the best known *tuber*. The expression, coined in 1976 as a private joke, became known with the registration of *The Couch Potatoes* as a trademark for merchandising purposes (e.g. tee-shirts bearing a cartoon of a viewer resembling a potato). This led to a loose cult jocularly dedicated to a lifestyle that rejected physical exercise. The expression became known in Britain in the late eighties.

council tax   *noun* an annual tax payable to the local council for the provision of services. The successor to the COMMUNITY CHARGE, first paid in 1993. The tax replaced flat-rate payment by one based on property values, with a variety of rebate arrangements.

counter-culture   *noun* a radical culture and mode of life, especially among young people, that rejects conventional values and practices. US English of the late sixties and seventies, invented to define the HIPPIE movement and its rejection of consumerism. UK English usually prefers the term the ALTERNATIVE SOCIETY.

counter-insurgency   *noun* government action against guerrillas, rebels, etc. (1962).

cowboy   *noun* an unqualified, often reckless and unscrupulous, provider of goods and services, especially in the building trades. (Also used as an adjective.) A colloquialism dating from the early seventies and deriving from earlier slang for a reckless driver, especially a lorry driver, i.e. a slapdash one interested in doing his job quickly rather than properly, and not conforming with good standards in his trade. This use can be traced back to American slang for a wild young man (1940s), which is rooted in the rough, boisterous and peripatetic lifestyle of the original cowboys, the cattle-herders of the American west.

crack *noun* a highly addictive, processed form of cocaine. *Crack* is made by heating cocaine with other substances, and its name comes from the fact that, as it is hard baked, it has to be cracked into small pieces for use and it also makes a cracking sound when smoked. The name appeared in 1985, though the substance itself was known a few years earlier (as ROCK or FREEBASE). It is now recognised as among the most dangerous of illegal drugs. There is a verb **crack (it) up** to smoke *crack*.

crank (up) *verb* to inject a drug, especially heroin. British drug users' slang since the early seventies.

crash *verb*. **Crash** and **crash out** are slang (originally US, sixties) for 'to sleep', though *crash out* later came to mean 'to pass out' (normally as a result of exhaustion or drink). They originally had the special sense of 'sleep just for one night or in an emergency'; this explains their derivation, which is from *gate-crash*. A related slang word is *crash-pad*, a place to sleep, usually temporarily. All these words recall the informal lifestyle of the HIPPIE period.

creative accounting or **accountancy** *noun* ingenious or misleading but not illegal manipulation of financial accounts to achieve a desired purpose, especially to present them in the most favourable light. A euphemism (early seventies) for a usually suspect activity.

cred *noun* status or standing in the eyes of one's peers, especially as regards adherence to the current fashions and life-style. A slang abbreviation, in young people's language, of *credibility* as used in STREET CRED. The *street* here is the place of youth culture, originally in the US and especially among the urban poor – a vital place but one demanding survival skills (see STREETWISE). To have *cred* is to have contact with and respect from the people on the street, so was particularly important to punk stars and others in the media who might claim to speak to or for them – as well as for all those who wanted acceptance from their peers. *Cred* is a shortening (found from the late eighties onwards) of the earlier eighties *street cred*, itself a shortening of the seventies *street credibility*. As the word has become more familiar it has tended to mean 'in the know about fashion' rather than anything deeper.

credibility gap *noun* a perceived disparity between the claims or statements of a person, government, etc. and the facts about which those claims are made. The expression was first heard during the Vietnam War when the optimistic claims of the US government were often at variance with television and newspaper reports. Gerald Ford, a US Congressman who later became President, has been credited by some with coining the term in 1966 when there was evidence of growing involvement in the war despite the Administration's claims to the contrary, but it was probably coined rather earlier by the US Defence Department, an important source of less than honest English. It was originally a euphemism (*credibility* is a good thing, and a mere *gap* can quickly be repaired) but it quickly became a clear way of saying that someone was being untruthful. The term is now sometimes used more generally to cast doubt on someone's competence and standing.

credit card   *noun* a small rectangular card, usually plastic, issued by banks, finance companies, etc., enabling the holder to obtain goods and services on credit from shops, businesses and others participating in the scheme. Originating in the USA in the fifties, this system was well established in the UK by the early seventies and commonplace in the eighties.

Creutzfeldt-Jakob disease   *noun* See CJD.

criminalise   *verb* to make an activity illegal; to turn someone into a criminal by making their activities illegal, *or* to treat them as though they were criminal. This is a fairly recent formation and its increasing use probably reflects the widespread use of its near-opposite DECRIMINALISE.

critical path analysis   *noun* a technique for planning a complex operation by breaking it down into its component stages, analysing all alternatives, establishing the time required for each, etc., in order to work out the sequence that must be followed to complete the work in the minimum time. The *critical path* is the sequence of the most important (i.e. critical) stages in the operation. The term originated c.1960.

crop circle   *noun* an unexplained flattened area in standing crops (e.g. in a cornfield). Three circular areas of flattened oats were first noticed in Wiltshire in 1980. After that the number of sightings increased, spreading round the globe; there were 1000 in 1990, and in 1991 there were 800 in England alone. England is currently the world leader. The phenomena are still referred to as circles though many other geometric shapes and more complex patterns have been found. Some are the results of hoaxes, but most remain unexplained. Freak whirlwinds and intervention from outer space are among the most popular theories. The whole matter is currently the subject of serious scientific investigation.

crossover   *adj.* successful in more than one style, culture or genre. The word, sometimes as *cross-over*, goes back a long way (e.g. in biological language use) but has been specially used in the vocabulary of popular music since the seventies to describe a performer who has become popular in a type of music other than that in which he or she originally became known. It is also used to describe a type of music which appeals to more than one sort of audience (e.g. Black music which has become popular with White audiences) or which is a blend of two styles. **Crossover** has since been used of other art forms in these senses, and is occasionally used by sociologists to describe an ethnic group who exchange their culture for another, normally one with higher status. The word also exists as a noun for the process of crossing over in all these ways or for those who have done so.

crucial   *adj.* very good, great. Eighties slang among young people, especially children, originating in the vocabulary of Jamaican REGGAE. Like AWESOME and RAD it demonstrates the tendency to weaken or diffuse the earlier meaning of the word ('vital, decisively important').

cruise missile *noun* a continuously powered and guided small pilotless aircraft with warhead, able to fly low so as to be difficult to detect by radar. Developed originally from World War Two German missiles, this was named in the late fifties and a later version became well known in Britain when objections were raised to the basing of such missiles in the UK; they may have a nuclear or conventional warhead. Their name probably comes from naval terminology, in which *cruise* means 'sail in search for enemy vessels'. A *cruise missile* has a very accurate guidance system that can be updated during its flight to a target, as was demonstrated during the Gulf War.

cruelty-free *adj.* (of cosmetics, pharmaceuticals, etc.) developed without being tested on animals. Originally (late eighties) from the vocabulary of animal rights activists who wished to promote commercial products not associated with the experimental use of animals, but now appearing on the labels of branded goods to promote their sale to a concerned public. Sometimes adopted by vegetarians to denote animal-free foodstuffs.

crumblie or **-y** *noun* an elderly person. Older than a **wrinklie**, but also loosely used – especially by the young – of a parent or of any adult thought to be old-fashioned or dull. Originally seventies slang, from the familiar adjective meaning 'crumbling easily' and the assumption by young people that anyone belonging to an older generation is falling apart.

cryo- *prefix.* Recent scientific developments in the creation of very low temperatures have led, since the 1950s, to the creation of new words with the prefix *cryo-* (from the Greek for 'icy cold'), particularly in medicine, surgery and electronics. These include *cryogenics* (the branch of physics concerned with the production and study of low temperatures), *cryobiology* (the study of the effects of low temperatures on organisms) and *cryosurgery* (the use of low temperatures for the destruction of tissue). Perhaps the best known, though scientifically marginal, is *cryonics*, the practice of freezing corpses until, it is hoped, a cure is found for the currently incurable illness or the ageing process that has led to death. This is a lucrative business for *cryonicists* in parts of America, though the means of freezing (and eventual unfreezing) without damage are not thought to be reliable.

CS gas *noun* an irritant gas causing chest pains, coughing, tears, etc., and used in riot-control. Its effects are uncomfortable and immediate but not dangerous or persistent. It was invented in the twenties by two Americans, Corson and Stoughton – the initials of these surnames form the name of the gas. It was not generally known until it came into use during the sixties.

CT scanner *noun* the more normal name for the CAT SCANNER. **CT** stands for *computerised tomography*; tomography is the technique of obtaining X-ray photographs of plane sections of the human body, etc.

Cultural Revolution *noun* the social and political movement to purify and reinvigorate Chinese communism by replacing bureaucrats and intellectuals, reforming the educational system, and re-educating the bourgeoisie by forcible exposure to manual work. This was launched by Mao Tse-Tung in 1966, ostensibly in an attempt to restore the revolutionary vigour and egalitarianism of original Maoist doctrine, thought to have become stagnant. It was more likely an attempt to restore his waning power and crush revisionism. Purges, upheaval, violence and Mao-worship lasted for three years, and continued in diminished form until his death in 1976.

culture shock   *noun* the effect of anything unfamiliar on someone who is unprepared for it or unwilling to accept it. Originally (1940s) a sociological and anthropological term for the feelings of alienation, rejection or isolation when one culture, such as that of a primitive people, is brought into contact with another, e.g. a modern civilisation. Since the 1960s it has been used in a more general sense, including the experiencing of change within our own culture, as for example when an unreconstructed CRUMBLIE encounters the youth culture.

cursor   *noun* a symbol on a computer screen, often a flashing rectangle, to indicate the position of the next character or action. The word has had previous and unfamiliar uses, though it has been well known in formations such as *precursor* and *cursory*. It originates in the Latin for 'runner', which explains its present use: the computer **cursor** can be made to move about a screen by using a keyboard or MOUSE. The name was adopted in the sixties and was in everyday use by the eighties.

cutting edge   *noun* the forefront, especially in technological progress. The literal meaning is 'sharp edge of a blade' etc. A figurative meaning, which emerged in the sixties and is still current, is 'ability to make an incisive difference, effectiveness'; as such it is used of policies, plans and proposals, especially those intended to make changes by 'cutting' into established practices. The present meaning, given above, dates from the eighties and is largely restricted to advertising jargon, and probably emerged as a more incisive variant of LEADING EDGE.

cybernetics   *noun* the scientific study of control and communication systems in machines and living organisms. Practical applications include the construction of inanimate objects (such as robots) able to behave like living systems. The word – coined in the late forties but not generally known until the early sixties – is from a Greek one meaning 'steersman'.

cyberphobia   *noun* (irrational) fear of computers. A rather inaccurate word (1980s) in that it is formed from **cybernetics** which, as its derivation implies, has more to do with control systems than computing. Compare TECHNOPHOBIA under TECHNO.

cyberpunk   *noun* a genre of science fiction featuring a computer-controlled society and violent, nightmarish, mindless behaviour. A mid-eighties word combining **cybernetics** (the science of control systems) and **punk** (the aggressively anti-social youth movement of the 1970s). The future worlds in which **cyberpunk** novels are set normally explore the clash between a scientifically controlled society and unregulated human nature.

cybersex *noun* the pornography available on the INTERNET (eighties users' jargon).

cyborg *noun* a human being whose physical capabilities are extended or replaced by an electro-mechanism. The word is sometimes used more generally of an integrated man-machine, i.e. a *cybernetic organism* (from which two words *cyborg* was blended c.1960).

daisy chain *noun* (literally, a garland made, usually by children, by threading daisies together through small slits made in the stalks.) The term has long been used for any linked arrangement of people or things, and has been most recently (mid eighties) applied to a number of stock-exchange traders who conspire to keep the price of a particular commodity artificially high. *Daisy chain* has also been used as a verb since the mid eighties meaning 'to link (computers) in a series'.

daisy wheel *noun* a component of a computer printer or electronic typewriter consisting of a wheel with spokes, each of which bears a character and (when struck by a hammer) prints onto paper through a typewriter ribbon. The term, introduced in the early seventies, is often loosely applied to the whole printer. The name comes from the fanciful resemblance between the spokes of the wheel and the radiating petals of a daisy.

damage limitation *noun* the (attempted) restriction of damage to one's cause whether brought about by external attack or one's own error. Originally (mid sixties) American military and political COLD WAR jargon for plans to limit damage if deterrence should fail and nuclear war break out, especially if Russia struck first. The phrase was later adopted in political circles, including British ones, as a high-sounding alternative to 'making the best of a bad job' or 'covering up' a mistake, and has since passed into more general use as a term for any attempt to mitigate the effects of a crisis.

DAT (acronym for) digital audio tape. Originally, in the mid eighties, an abbreviation, but now established as an acronym i.e. originally said as three separate letters but now normally pronounced as a single word. This is an audio tape on which sound is recorded by DIGITAL means. Its commercial availability (1992) was a matter of controversy as DAT was expected to provide a cheaper alternative to the COMPACT DISC, offering equivalent sound-quality and additionally permitting the copying of CDs without loss of quality. See DCC.

data bank *noun* a store of large quantities of information, especially in computerised form. From the idea of a bank as a place for deposits or withdrawals (1970).

database *noun* a structured collection of data held in a computer system in a form that enables it to be accessed and processed. Computerese since c.1962. See also DBMS.

data capture *noun* the conversion of data into a form that can be handled by a computer, i.e. from everyday written form to a machine readable one. Computer jargon since the early seventies. See CAPTURE.

date rape *noun* rape during a social encounter, which is usually a 'date' (i.e. a prearranged meeting) but may follow a more casual meeting. Akin to, but not identical with, what is sometimes called *acquaintance rape* in the UK. Both are distinct from rape by a previously unknown assailant, and *date rape* may raise special problems relating to consent. The term is American and has been known in Britain only since c.1991.

dawn raid *noun* an unexpected and rapid purchase of a substantial shareholding in a company, usually as a preliminary to take-over. So called because the operation takes place as soon as the stock market begins trading for the day. The term, originally military, is well known from its use in newspaper reports of early-morning police-raids, but did not appear in financial jargon until c.1980. Since then its use has declined as regulations have been introduced to limit the proportion of shares that can be acquired in this way. A **dawn raider** is one who undertakes such a foray.

Day-Glo (trademark of) brand of fluorescent paint or other colouring material (e.g. in clothing). Registered as a proprietary noun in 1951, presumably on the grounds that the product *glows* in *daylight*. The term, now often spelt without capitals or as one word, is often used loosely to mean 'fluorescent' as in *dayglo socks*.

DBMS (abbreviation for) database management system. A computer programme for retrieving, sorting and generally processing the information stored on a DATABASE. The term dates from about 1970.

DBS (abbreviation for) direct broadcasting by SATELLITE. The term (1984) has an earlier but less common use as an abbreviation of *direct-broadcast satellite* (1981). See SATELLITE.

DCC (abbreviation for) digital compact cassette. An audio cassette tape with a sound quality said to be as good as a CD's; unlike the CD, it can be used to record. Launched commercially towards the end of 1992, it was expected to replace ordinary cassettes in due course. See DIGITAL and DAT.

debt counselling *noun* professional advice for those in debt. Although invented in the sixties, the term was not generally known until the seventies (in the USA) and the eighties (in Britain), coming to notice initially as a result of the increasing popularity of the CREDIT CARD which facilitated the running up of debts. The UK recession, from the late eighties onwards, made the term increasingly common because of unemployment, bankruptcy, mortgage default, etc.

decommunisation *noun* the dismantling of communism in a country. Also *verb transitive* and *intransitive*, **decommunise**: to dismantle communism in a country; to go through the process of decommunisation. Originally an economic term coined in the early eighties when some communist countries allowed limited free-market elements into their communism. As Marxism collapsed in Eastern Europe throughout the decade, and in the USSR in 1991, the term became more general, and was applied to political as well as economic change from communism to various blends of democracy and capitalism.

deck *noun.* Strictly speaking, this is the flat surface of a record-player on which are mounted the turntable, pickup and other apparatus, but the word is most commonly used for this whole assembly or for the turntable itself. It is also used for the entire record-player. It derives (c.1971) from the earlier TAPE DECK (1949) which is sometimes also known simply as a *deck*.

deconstruction *noun* the philosophy and method of critical analysis which breaks down the structure of language to show that meaning results from the differences between words, not from their reference to things, and to explore assumptions and contradictions in the use of language. The word, followed by a number of derivations such as *deconstructionism*, came into English use in the early seventies; it was coined by the French philosopher Jacques Derrida (b.1930) who is chiefly associated with this approach to literature, philosophy and film.

decriminalise *verb* to remove from the legal category of criminal offence. A fairly recent formation (c.1972) from the earlier *decriminalisation* (c.1945). It is usually applied to activities or things, especially drugs, and only occasionally to people, unlike its opposite, CRIMINALISE.

dedicated *adj.* designed to be given over to a particular function. This is a modern (c.1969) extension of the meaning of a familiar word, and is used of facilities or equipment, especially in computing, where it originated.

def *adj.* excellent. Originally US HIP HOP slang of the mid eighties, and a British slang term of approval among the young since c.1987. It appears to come from West Indian English (by way of RAP lyrics) in which *def* is a pronunciation of *death* as an intensifying adjective (compare 'dead funny', 'dead good', etc.). Some dictionaries suggest a less-likely derivation from *definitive*. The word is specially found in **def jam** (very good music) and also occurs in the emphatic form **deffo**. Whatever its derivation **deffo** is certainly used to mean 'definitely' or 'certainly', as in 'I'll be going, deffo'.

defensive medicine *noun* a cautious or even negative approach to the practice of medicine whereby doctors insist on extreme precautions when treating patients, in order to protect themselves against accusations of negligence or in the event of their being sued for malpractice. Such practices include ultra-cautious diagnosis, extensive testing – often costly or unnecessary –, constant referral to consultants and recourse to second opinions. The term originated in America, where suing appears to be a national pastime, but spread to Britain in the eighties along with an increase in the suing of doctors, hospitals, etc. for damages.

degradable *adj.* capable of being decomposed by natural, chemical or biological means. Dating from the early sixties, this term is used of packaging materials, waste products, etc., especially plastic ones, and reflects public concern with preservation of the environment. Compare BIODEGRADABLE.

deliver *verb* to produce the promised, described or expected results; to come good. Originally a colloquial shortening of *deliver the goods*, first found in the fifties and with the same meaning as that much older colloquial expression. Their usage perhaps influences the sense of *deliver* in such contexts as the expectation that teachers will 'deliver the National Curriculum'.

demo *noun* (abbreviation of) demonstration. **Demo**, in the sense of 'public demonstration' (e.g. a protest march) has been in use since the 1930s, but since the 1950s it has also been used attributively in the sense of 'used to demonstrate something to a potential buyer'. Thus, among others, *demo tape* (c.1970) a tape-recording made by a music group to circulate among booking agents and recording managers in the hope of receiving a contract. **Demo** also stands by itself as a shortening of *demo tape*.

demystify *verb* eliminate the mystery from; clarify (1963).

deniability *noun* the ability to deny something. Especially, in US politics, this denotes the capability of the President or some other high official to be dissociated from some scandal because the responsible subordinate is understood to have kept knowledge of it away from him or her. The notion of *providing deniability* for a president or government became generally known in connection with the Watergate scandal of the early seventies and again during the Iran-contra affair (see CONTRA). See also TEFLON.

Denver boot *noun* a wheel clamp. This colloquialism was the normal term for what is now called a WHEEL CLAMP when this solution to illegal parking was first discussed in the UK in the late 1960s, but the expression is no longer general. It comes from the name of Denver, Colorado, where wheel clamping was first used in 1949.

dependency culture *noun* (1980s) see ENTERPRISE CULTURE and NANNY STATE.

deregulation *noun* the removal of regulations or controls. Found from c.1963; also the verb **deregulate** (to remove regulations) from about the same time. Both words were made more common during the eighties by government free-market policies: see for example BIG BANG.

deschooling *noun* the transferring of education from schools to non-institutional systems to allow freer development of the pupil. Also **deschool** *verb*: to abandon the school as the central source of education. The word *deschooling* was coined by Ivan Illich in 1970 and popularised in his book *Deschooling Society* (1971). It is sometimes now used to mean 'full-time education of children at home', as practised by some parents.

deselect *verb* to choose not to (re)select. Also noun **deselection**. Originally (US, 1960s) a euphemism for 'reject' (a trainee during training) and even 'dismiss' (an employee), but most commonly known in the UK since c.1979 in connection with the power of a local constituency party to refuse to renominate a sitting MP and to choose another candidate for a forthcoming election. The word has since spread to other sorts of election or choice.

desertification   *noun* the transformation of fertile land into barren waste or desert, especially as a result of human activity. The process is typically associated with deforestation, the erosion of top soil and the GREENHOUSE EFFECT. The word seems to have been first coined in French in the late sixties; it appeared in English in the early seventies and was familiar by the eighties as a result of public concern with international environmental issues.

desertified   *adj.* subjected to DESERTIFICATION.

designer   *adj.* (of clothes) bearing the name, signature, label or logo of a well-known fashion designer, with the implication that such goods are expensive or prestigious; (of things) contriving to be fashionably trendy, especially in appearance. The first of these meanings emerged in the USA in the mid sixties, and by the eighties had become so popular in the UK, especially among advertisers, (**designer jeans, designer knitwear**, etc.), as to be almost meaningless. The usage also spread to fashion items such as bags. Although not necessarily better than, or even much different from, other goods on the market, *designer* items were more expensive. Their success is a remarkable comment on public taste and a tribute to the ingenuity of the design industry, which caught the mood of an image-conscious age by something as simple as putting labels on the outside rather than the inside of their products. The second meaning is a natural but increasingly ironical or even contemptuous development of the first. In the eighties it has been found in **designer water** (overpriced bottled spring water, promoted as being chic), **designer stubble** (a fashionably unshaven look) and even **designer socialism**, a late 1980s pejorative term for the Labour Party's redefined policies – less left wing, more moderate and voter-friendly. What *designer* implies in all such cases is an emphasis on style or 'image' rather than intrinsic worth. The emerging sense is 'fashionable but meretricious'.

designer drug   *noun* a synthetic hallucinogen or narcotic illegally manufactured from chemicals rather than natural substances. The term (c.1983), is another example of *designer* being used as a vogue word (see DESIGNER). It is sometimes used more specifically to denote a drug which is designed to reproduce the effect of a banned drug but has a chemical structure that is not (yet) illegal, so that both manufacturer and user can hope to avoid prosecution under existing anti-drug regulations. The best known examples are probably ECSTASY and the drugs taken by athletes hoping to avoid detection.

desk top   *noun* (short for) a personal computer that fits on a desk top. Also the representation of a desk-top and its equipment on a computer's VDU, that allows the (new) user to identify and access the files and functions of the computer more readily (see ICON). The term **desk-top computer** is first recorded in the late sixties, in forecasts of what *could* be, though computer systems small enough to stand on an office desk did not become widely available until the eighties. By the mid eighties we find the shortening *desk top*. At that time it became common for those systems that depended on

ICONS and WIMPS to feature a representation of a desk top on screen (with such associated equipment as notepad, files and address book) so that the user could select the desired functions and files with the aid of the MOUSE.

desk top publishing   *noun* the production of printed documents to a publishable standard using a desk top computer system. Desk top publishing packages were introduced in the mid eighties and allowed the user the facilities to design and make up pages utilising graphics and a wide variety of type styles and sizes. A laser printer allowed printing to near professional standard, so that it became possible for an individual or small company to produce high quality printing 'in-house'.

des res   (abbreviation for) desirable residence. Originally *desirable residence* was estate agents' euphemistic jargon for a standard house, and was best known through its abbreviation to *des. res.* in advertisements. Since about the mid eighties it has been generally used as a colloquialism, usually ironic.

developing country   *noun* a lesser developed or underdeveloped country. A sixties refinement of the earlier *lesser developed* and still earlier *underdeveloped* (1949), both of which were felt to be negative. In many cases *developing* is a completely accurate description, but in others is seen as a euphemism that obscures lack of development or even 'backwards progress'.

dickhead   *noun* a stupid or incompetent person. Still coarse slang, first noted in print in 1969, though probably in spoken use before then, but not much heard until the eighties. It is from the old slang word *dick* (penis) + *head* (brain) on the model of *bighead*, *fathead*, ACID HEAD, etc. and is one of many abusive slang words, many of them taboo, others, like PLONKER, less so, relating to genitalia. The derivation of *dick* is obscure: perhaps, like *willie* or *willy*, it originated as a childish term and is related to the familiar form of a name (Richard). **Dick brain** is an alternative. Both are quite likely to be used 'innocently' by people in informal situations who have not registered the words' possible connotations.

diet   *adj.* (of drinks) with reduced sugar content. First used by Pepsi in 1963, this new meaning of an old word is now widely applied to other drinks.

dietary fibre   *noun* roughage. More fully, the fibrous substances, in fruit, vegetables, and cereals, that aid digestion and help prevent overweight and certain diseases. This use of *fibre*, previously confined to scientific vocabulary, became general in the seventies with the discovery that a *high-fibre* (and therefore reduced-calorie) diet was conducive to good health and weight-loss.

digital   *adj.* (of a sound recording) made by converting the musical signal into a digitised code of numerical values which is then stored, to be reconstituted as sound by a player. This method was developed in about 1960 but not introduced commercially until later: see CD and DAT. Compared with the older analogue recording, which it has displaced, the process is not liable to distortion. In

digital audio tape

computing *digital* had meant 'representing data in the form of digits', and this usage is a natural extension of that.

digital audio tape   see DAT.

digital clock   *noun* a clock stating the time in digits (numerals) rather than by hands on a dial. From c.1964. Also *digital watch*.

dinkie, dinky   (acronym) married but childless man or woman where both partners are employed and assumed to be well-to-do because of the lack of family to support. An acronym of '**d**ouble **i**ncome, **no** **k**ids' with *-ie* or *-y* usually added as a suffix on the pattern of YUPPIE (though the *-y* is sometimes said to stand for 'yet'). There was a rash of playful coinages of this sort, most of them short-lived, in North America and then the UK during the eighties, perhaps as a result of market-researchers attempting to identify social groups. This one had some currency as it reflected the fact that better educated and better off women were often delaying their families – in other words this mirrored an observable social change.

dirty dancing   *noun* form of dancing to pop music or DISCO, characterised by gyratory movement and hip-to-hip contact with others. It was a craze in the mid eighties, popularised by a film of the same name (1987). *Dirty* was jocular for 'sexually teasing'.

dirty tricks   *noun* (of politics) underhand activities designed to discredit an opponent. In the singular this is an old and familiar term for an unkind or malicious action. In the plural it was sixties US slang for covert intelligence operations, especially those of the CIA whose plans department was known as 'the department of dirty tricks'. It spread to political vocabulary in the seventies, notably in connection with the presidency and downfall of Richard Nixon, and in particular with the activities of CREEP – the Campaign to Re-Elect the President. This resulted in it being more widely used, in the UK as well as America.

disablist   *noun* a person showing discrimination against disabled people. Formed during the mid eighties on the model of 'racist', 'sexist', etc., but not generally current.

disaster   *noun* (used attributively.) The adjectival use of this word is new. A *disaster area* (1960) is one in which a disaster has occurred. The plot of a *disaster movie/film* (1975) centres on a catastrophe such as an accident, usually one affecting many people.

Discman   (trademark for) portable CD system. Introduced by Sony in 1984, the system gets its name by analogy with the same company's earlier WALKMAN, which it resembles.

disco   *noun* a club (or sometimes a private party) where records are played for dancing, often with a DJ and lighting effects; also the mobile equipment used for such functions; and also the music played for such dancing. Although the word was known in the sixties (for its development see DISCOTHEQUE) it did not pass into general use until the seventies when, under the influence of some popular films, it became associated with heavily rhythmical *disco-music* and vigorous, exhibitionist *disco-dancing*. *Discos* have become a popular venue for young people, where listening to the music, or simply being there, is as important as the dancing. See also DISTCO.

discotheque *noun* (full name of) DISCO. The word was originally coined in France (as *discothèque*) in 1932 to mean 'gramophone-record library' on the model of *bibliothèque*, which means an ordinary library. It was subsequently used for a club where recorded music was played for dancing. In this sense it crossed to the USA and Britain in the sixties, when it became abbreviated. For subsequent meanings, see **disco**.

dish (short for) dish aerial or SATELLITE dish (aerial). Dish-shaped aerials for the reception of broadcasts transmitted via artificial satellites have been familiar in the UK since the late eighties, when satellite television first became commercially available in people's homes.

disinformation *noun* deliberately false information designed to mislead. The word comes originally from the fifties (though it may have originated in Russia, c.1949) when it was used of COLD WAR propaganda disseminated by governments, the military, intelligence agencies, etc., to influence the policies or confuse the opinions of those seen as enemies. It has since spread to the vocabulary of commerce and industry where it is sometimes used of misleading information spread by a company to deceive its competitors.

disinvest *verb* to remove one's investment from a country (or company). Although first recorded in 1961, the word did not become familiar until the eighties when it was used of the withdrawal of investment from South Africa because of objections to that country's apartheid policies.

diss or **dis** *verb* to snub, put down, or show disrespect for a person by insulting language or behaviour. Mid eighties slang originating in US Black culture and spread by HIP-HOP and RAP. The word, formed from the first syllable of *disrespect*, surfaced in the UK c.1989 and has since spread to those parts of the youth culture, White or Black, which attach importance to the maintenance or assertion of self-esteem by the trading of insults.

distco or **disco** *noun* (short for) *dist*ribution *co*mpany (for electricity in England and Wales). Stock Exchange and economic journalists' jargon since the creation of twelve such companies in 1989 and their sale the following year.

DMs (abbreviation of) DOC MARTENS.

DNA test, take the *phrase* submit oneself to GENETIC FINGERPRINTING, usually to determine paternity (c.1990).

dock *verb* (of spacecraft) to join to another vehicle in space. An extension (c.1951) of the familiar meaning of *dock*, 'moor (a vessel) at a dock'. Also action noun **docking**.

Doc(tor) Martens (trademark for) heavy-duty, high-laced workman's boots with air-cushioned soles. Named after their German inventor (1965), they became part of the uniform of the SKINHEAD in the late sixties, and enjoyed a further period of fashion in the eighties and early nineties.

docudrama *noun* a film or television dramatisation based on real events. Although coined as long ago as 1960 from *docu*mentary and *drama*, the word has never quite caught on, and *drama-docu-mentary*, sometimes shortened to *drama-doc* or *dramadoc*, is more commonly used of television programmes. Such programmes have maintained their popularity, though often criticised for blurring the distinction between fact and fiction. *Docudramas* use actors, sets and a script, but often imitate documentary or news pro-gramme techniques, for example by the use of a handheld camera and by their style of editing.

doggy-bag *noun* a bag, usually provided by a restaurant, in which a diner can take home the leftovers, ostensibly for the dog. The custom, and the name, originated in the USA in the late 1950s, though requests for such bags are not welcomed in classy estab-lishments. Sometimes the dog is fictional.

Dolby (tradename of) the noise-reduction system used in tape and video recorders to reduce tape hiss. Named after Ray Dolby (born 1933), the US engineer who invented the system in 1966.

dolly-bird *noun* an attractive and fashionable girl. British slang from the early sixties, though *dolly* is older US slang for an attrac-tive girl and *bird* has long been slightly disparaging British slang for a girl. The term is so firmly linked with the swinging sixties and mini-skirts that it would be unlikely to be used today unless with reference back to that era.

donor card *noun* a card carried by person to indicate that his or her organs, as specified on it, may be used for transplant in the event of the card-carrier's death. In use in the UK since the early seventies, initially for kidney-donors. As a result of advances in transplant surgery the cards now have a wider application.

doom and gloom *phrase* feelings of doom about the future; a pes-simistic forecast. Originally a catchphrase from the musical *Finigan's Rainbow* (1947), it passed into more general use after the show was made into a film in 1968. The alternative form, **gloom and doom**, which also occurs in the musical, is equally common. At the moment they are most current in comment on pessimistic forecasts about ecological issues such as global warming, often by those who take an opposing view and talk dismissively of contribu-tions that are 'all doom and gloom'.

doomwatch *noun* observation of the environment with a view to preventing deterioration by pollution, etc. Also **doomwatcher** *noun* person who maintains such surveillance. *Doomwatch* was the title of a BBC television series (1970) on this subject, the implica-tion being that we need to *watch* in order to avoid *doom* (terrible fate). The word is sometimes used disparagingly by those who feel that environmental degradation is over-emphasised – and that the word is too melodramatic – but it has proved to be a useful coinage for a new activity.

doorstep *verb* (of politicians, etc.) to go from door to door to canvass support (1960s); (of journalists) waylay (person in the news) on his doorstep to obtain story, picture, etc. (1980s). New developments of an earlier verbal use of *doorstep*, 'to go from door to door selling things'. The **doorstepping** of some journalists has been so aggressive and persistent, and sometimes directed at vulnerable people, so that the activity is often denounced as an intrusion on privacy. Also *noun* **doorstepper** someone who *doorsteps*.

DOS   (acronym for) disc operating system. Computerese, 1967.

dot-matrix printer   *noun* (in computer technology) a printer that produces each character by an array of dots. An early (c.1975) form of printer for personal computers. It has already been largely displaced by the **daisy-wheel**, which gives clearer definition, and this in turn may be displaced by the **laser printer** if its price is made affordable to the private buyer.

doublespeak   *noun* jargon, euphemism, gobbledegook or circumlocution designed to mislead, obfuscate, distort or inflate, or to circumvent the truth; pretentious or obscure terminology intended to impress rather than to communicate. The word, a useful and aggressive one, deliberately echoes the dehumanised NEWSPEAK and *doublethink* of Orwellian nightmare. It emerged in the late eighties in the USA, where the language of public discourse, especially as used by the Pentagon, the CIA, the State Department, etc., had a pervasively anaesthetising and sometimes dishonest quality, exemplified by the military lexicon's COLLATERAL DAMAGE (civilian casualties) and 'incontinent ordnance' (shells hitting civilian targets), by describing President Reagan, unconscious during surgery, as being in a 'non-decision-making form', and by calling an unpopular factory closure a 'volume-related production schedule adjustment'. (Quotations from William Lutz, 'The World of Doublespeak', in *The State of the Language* (1990), ed. Ricks and Michaels). The habit is not restricted to politics, however; in an attempt to disguise the vacuity of cheer-leading as a time-tabled activity in some US schools, it has been renamed 'spirit leadership'.

double whammy   see WHAMMY.

doughnutting   *noun* the practice of MPs sitting close to an MP who is speaking in the House of Commons while the proceedings are being televised. This practice is commonly said to be intended to give the viewing public the impression that the speaker is well supported or that the House is well attended; though the clustering MPs may merely wish to be seen themselves. The word *doughnutting* is usually said to have been first used of televised debates in the Canadian parliament; it became familiar in the UK when the proceedings of the House of Commons were first televised in 1989, and has continued in use. It presumably refers to the circular shape of the American or ring doughnut resembling the ring of attendant MPs.

dove   *noun* a person opposed to war. Although the dove has been a symbol of peace since Noah used one to establish that the Flood, the sign of God's anger, was abating, the popular antithesis between doves and HAWKS dates only from the Cuban missile crisis (1962) and seems to have originated with two US political writers, Alsop and Bartlett.

down   *adv.* (of computer system, etc.) (temporarily) out of action (1965).

downbeat, upbeat   *adj*. depressed or depressing; cheerful or cheering. US colloquialism since the fifties, but now familiar in the UK. The terms came originally from music, perhaps by way of jazz vocabulary. A *downbeat* is the strong first beat of a bar of music, indicated by downward movement of the conductor's hand; an *upbeat* is an unstressed beat, indicated by upward movement of the conductor's hand. Figuratively, *downbeat* means 'pessimistic' and *upbeat* 'optimistic' or 'lively'. See also OFFBEAT.

downer   *noun* a depressant drug, especially barbiturate; a depressing experience or a state of depression – something that puts you down. Slang, the first from c.1966, the second from c.1970, from the general association with 'low' spirits.

down-market   *adj*. (of products, services, etc.) cheap, of poor quality, lacking in prestige. From the early seventies. Also used adverbially: to *go downmarket* is to buy – or, in the case of a shop, start to sell – less expensive merchandise. Also used figuratively of an acceptance of lower standards in other, non-market, contexts.

downside   *noun* the disadvantageous aspect (of a situation, etc.). A late seventies metaphorical use of an older but little used word meaning 'the under side' of something.

downsize   *verb* to reduce the size of. Chiefly US (1979) from a slightly earlier use of the word to mean 'design or build a smaller car' in response to government demands for fuel economy (c.1975). By the nineties *downsizing* was in occasional use in the UK as a euphemism for the sacking of employees.

Down's syndrome   *noun* chromosomal abnormality causing mental retardation. Named after JLH Down (1828–96), an English physician who first specialised in this condition, this term was adopted in 1961 at the suggestion of medical writers in *The Lancet*. It replaced *mongolism* – the condition produces some facial characteristics resembling those of Mongolian people – which was thought to have misleading racial connotations and to be hurtful to parents.

drama-doc, dramadoc   see DOCUDRAMA.

dread   *noun* a Rastafarian: a wearer of dreadlocks. Slang (sometimes contemptuous) from the early seventies. The word is also occasionally used of Rastafarian fear of God or sense of alienation from contemporary society. See also DREADLOCKS and RASTAFARIAN.

dreadlocks   *noun* a Rastafarian hairstyle in which the hair is allowed to grow without combing, forming matted locks, or is fashioned in tightly corded strands. The style was inspired by pictures of Ethiopian warriors, and the name (c.1960) reflects the dread which they or their hairstyle inspired or were intended to inspire. Sometimes abbreviated to *dreads*. See RASTAFARIAN.

drive-by   *noun* (of a shooting) committed from a passing car. Initially (mid eighties, USA) used of gang warfare, particularly among young people, but later used of the random shooting of one driver by another who takes exception to the former's driving manners. In the UK the expression has been restricted to journalists' reports of terrorism in Northern Ireland.

drop *verb* to swallow (drug). Mid-sixties slang, found especially in **drop-acid**: see ACID.

drop-out *noun* a person who rejects conventional society; also and earlier (mainly US) a student who drops out of school/college. This term became familiar in the UK in the first sense in the sixties. In the USA, however, where this new sense originated, also in the sixties, the term had a previous (and continuing) use to denote a student who fails to complete a school or college course. In Britain this sense of a scholastic *drop-out* is less often used, and it is the rejection of society's values that the word most often denotes. Also verb: to **drop out**.

druggie, druggy *noun* a drug-taker. Slang, from c.1968.

drug abuse *noun* the non-medical use of drugs, especially narcotics. This term replaced *drug-taking* c.1970: see ABUSE.

dry *adj.* (of Conservative politicians or policy) following a hard line; also *noun* one who supports such policies. This sense arose naturally as the opposite of WET, the term applied by Mrs Thatcher and the Thatcherites to those within the party who had reservations about their policies. *Wet* comes from public school slang for anyone or anything feeble and unimpressive, and as a pre-existing term was more readily accepted than this formation from it – *dry*.

DTP (abbreviation for) DESKTOP PUBLISHING.

dude *noun* a person, fellow. (As form of address) friend. Originally (c.1883) US slang of unknown origin for a dandy or city slicker. Its present, more general and generally favourable sense, comes from US Black English (seventies) and HIP-HOP (eighties) where it is used of young men from within the speaker's own group. It had spread into British English from these sources by the late eighties but gained wider currency, at least among children, in 1990 because of its widespread use by the Teenage Mutant Turtles, a craze imported from the USA at that time.

dump *verb* to transfer stored data to another location e.g. a peripheral device such as a printer for printing or to some other storage. Computerese since the mid fifties.

dump *verb* to defecate (US slang, current in UK since eighties) also *noun* an act of defecation (eighties); **dump on** *verb* to criticise (US slang, current in UK late eighties).

dumping *noun* disposal of waste (especially radioactive) by burial, or into rivers or seas, or by exporting it to other countries. A specialised use of a familiar term rather than a new meaning. The use dates from the late seventies when the dangers of these practices were first made into public issues by environmentalists.

dune buggy *noun* variant (1965) of BEACH BUGGY.

E *noun* (colloquial abbreviation of) ECSTASY. Also *verb* to take Ecstasy.

earner see NICE LITTLE EARNER.

EC (abbreviation for) European Community. The organisation of European States created in 1967 from the merger of the EEC with Euratom (1957) and the European Coal and Steel Community (1952). The abbreviation has been in use since c.1973, though it has been familiar only since the mid eighties. Until then, the European Community was popularly known as the EEC, but this abbreviation was increasingly seen as inappropriate as the Community broadened its operations from the economic to the political, social and monetary. It has been alleged, mainly by those who oppose European integration, that the change from EEC to EC (i.e. dropping the middle E for Economic) was the work of politicians trying subtly and unofficially to alter public perception as they steered European development increasingly towards political integration. The EEC was officially subsumed into the EC on 1 November 1993, after the final ratification of the Maastricht Treaty, and on that date the EC was itself absorbed into the European Union, where it remains in being as one of the three 'pillars' of the Union.

eco- (a combining form made by a shortening of **ecology** or **ecological**) having to do with the conservation of the environment. Earlier this century **ecology** denoted the branch of biology that deals with the relationship of living organisms to their surroundings, and that is the sense that **eco-** carried in scientific combinations from the first half of the century such as *ecoclimate* and *ecosystem*. During the sixties **ecology** began to take on the additional sense (especially in popular, non-technical usage) of 'conservation of the environment', often with the emphasis on such conservation being seen as a political issue or cause. This is the sense, stemming from widespread concern over serious damage to the environment, especially from human activity, that **eco-** carries in combinations from the late sixties onwards. 1969 produced **eco-activist** (a person opposed to pollution), **eco-catastrophe** (major damage to the environment) and **ecocide** (such damage done by human agency). This last coinage gave rise to **ecocidal** (1970); to the same year belong **eco-freak** (a fanatical environmentalist), also called an **eco-nut(ter)** and **eco-politics**. Later inventions include **ecodoom** (collapse of the world's ecology), **ecodoomster** (a person predicting this), **eco-labelling** (the labelling of products as being **eco-friendly** i.e. tending to preserve the environment), and very many others, mainly self-explanatory and coined by journalists and environmentalists, though it is too early to say how much of this **eco-babble** (mid eighties, see PSYCHOBABBLE) will last.

economical with the truth, being *phrase* a famous phrase used in November 1986 by Sir Robert Armstrong, the cabinet secretary, when defining the misleading impression he had intended to convey in a certain letter; he was being cross-examined in an Australian court about the British Government's attempts to prevent the publication of *Spycatcher*, a book about the British secret service. Although the phrase merely described something that is an everyday occurrence in any large bureaucracy, it was seized on as a euphemism for 'lying' and did some damage to the Thatcher government. In fact, as Sir Robert acknowledged at the time, the phrase is not original. Authorship has been ascribed to St Thomas Aquinas, Samuel Pepys and Edmund Burke, among others.

Ecstasy, ecstasy *noun* (street name of) MDMA, an illegal drug acting as a stimulant and capable of producing hallucinations. Also known as E. Although said to have been legally manufactured as early as 1914, *MDMA* was then forgotten and did not become known as a DESIGNER drug until the mid eighties in the USA, when it acquired its current slang name because of the strong sense of well-being it can induce. Although banned in 1986, it became known in the UK with the introduction of ACID HOUSE in 1988 and continued to cause great concern into the nineties because of its widespread popularity among young people, despite evidence of the risk of irreversible brain-damage or even death in the event of over-use. Switzerland is unique in allowing its prescription as an anti-depressant under controlled clinical conditions.

ecu (acronym for) European Currency Unit. The word **ecu** is taken from the initial letters of what it is – the European Currency Unit – but there already existed a French word *écu* for a coin, which no doubt reinforces the possible adoption of this word for the common unit of currency in Europe, though it is possible that a different term may win favour, such as the *euro*. The *ecu*, created in 1972 but little used, did not become generally known in the UK until the late eighties when there was a good deal of political controversy over UK membership of EMS and EMU. It is intended to be the single European currency, replacing national currencies in EC member states, in due course.

EEC (abbreviation for) European Economic Community. Founded as a result of the Treaty of Rome in 1958 (see COMMON MARKET) and merged into the European Community in 1967 (see EC), but the abbreviation **EEC** continued in popular use until the mid eighties when EC became the normal abbreviation, as by this time the European Community had moved beyond its original character as a largely economic arrangement.

EFL (abbreviation of) English as a foreign language. Educational jargon since about 1965.

E-free see E-NUMBER.

EFTPOS (acronym for) electronic funds transfer at point of sale. A method of immediate ('point of sale') payment for goods or services; the customer has a card which is passed through a computer-based system at the cash-desk, and this automatically debits the customer's account. The system came into use in the second half of the eighties, but the ungainly acronym remains restricted to business jargon: most people refer to the system by its commercial names, SWITCH and Connect.

EFTS (abbreviation for) electronic funds transfer system. Any computerised system for the transfer of funds from one account to another. See above.

ego trip *noun* the self-indulgent expression of whatever satisfies or enhances one's sense of self-importance or self-esteem. A colloquialism (c.1969) combining the Freudian *ego* (roughly, 'consciousness of oneself') with *trip* which originally had the sense of 'hallucinogenic experience'.

electronic funds transfer

electronic funds transfer see EFTPOS and EFTS.

electronic mail *noun* the transmission of information (letters, messages, data, etc.) from one computer terminal to another; information thus transmitted. (Now often called **E-mail**.) The term, which dates from the late seventies, combines the familiar sense of *mail* and a newer sense of *electronic* ('computerised', 'machine readable'). Also **electronic mailbox** (1981), a device for receiving and storing electronic mail for retrieval by the recipient.

electronic office *noun* an integrated computer system designed to handle all office work. *Electronic* here means simply 'computerised'. The term is from c.1980.

electronic point of sale see EPOS.

electronic publishing *noun* the publication of text in electronic (i.e. machine-readable) form (e.g. on magnetic tape, discs, CD-ROM etc.) so that it can be accessed by a computer. The term came into use in 1979, though the system had been introduced some years before, but was not widely used until the eighties. It is not to be confused with DESK TOP PUBLISHING, which uses electronic means but still publishes onto paper; whereas this is paperless publishing.

electronic tagging *noun* the attaching of an electronic device to the waist or ankle of a prisoner on parole or an offender serving a non-custodial sentence in order to monitor his or her whereabouts. The device is linked to a central computer through the telephone network; the hope is that this form of electronic surveillance will in selected cases be an alternative to confinement in prison. The system, which came into use in the late eighties, is a development of one used in some US mental hospitals in the sixties, and in many shops including clothes shops in the seventies: *electronic tag* is the name sometimes used of the heavy label which is attached to some goods in shops and which is removed by a shop assistant if the goods are purchased. The label activates an alarm system if the goods are removed by a shop-lifter with the label intact. The words *tag* and *tagging* (which have long meant 'label' and 'labelling') are often used without *electronic*.

E-mail, e mail (abbreviation for) ELECTRONIC MAIL.

EMS (abbreviation of) European Monetary System. The system was set up in the late seventies to stabilise currencies in the EC and to hasten progress towards monetary union (see EMU) and a common currency (see ECU). Its central feature was an exchange-rate mechanism (see ERM); there were also mechanisms relating to balance-of-payments and common credit facilities. The British government's failure to be a full member of the system became a matter of political controversy in the late eighties, and contributed to the downfall of Mrs Thatcher in 1990.

EMU (abbreviation of) economic and monetary union, the achievement of full economic unity in the EC to be achieved by the phased introduction of a common currency (see ECU). Sometimes written as **Emu** and pronounced as an acronym. The idea for such a union within the EC originated c.1970, but the concept did not become familiar in the UK until the setting up of the EMS (1979), the initial

failure of the UK to join its ERM, and the political controversies of
the late eighties, when Mrs Thatcher insisted on standing apart
from the general enthusiasm for progress towards EMU. This was
a factor in her departure from office (1990) but the precise
timetable for EMU, and its final form, remain matters of some
political controversy in the European Union in the 1990s.

encounter group   *noun* a group of people meeting under the guidance of a therapist to improve the emotional adjustments and self-
awareness of its members through the open expression of feelings
and emotions, bodily contact, confrontation, etc. A US term for a
kind of group therapy (1967). Also **encounter therapy**.

end-user   *noun* the person (or organisation, or country) that will
actually use purchased goods, as distinct from the person (etc.) who
makes the purchase. The term, which dates from 1963 although
end-use appeared ten years earlier, is of special importance in international trade. When international embargoes or economic sanc-
tions are in force, for example, attempts may be made to break an
embargo by using an intermediary who is not under embargo and
who is willing to pass goods on to a country which is. Arms dealings
are subject to the signature on an *end-user certificate* giving details
of who will actually use the arms, though in practice this does not
always prevent arms coming into the possession of illegal organisations such as terrorist ones. Advanced technology, such as computer
equipment under copyright, may need similar protection to ensure
that the seller has some guarantee that the buyer is to be trusted.
In these and many other circumstances there is an important distinction between the purchaser and the actual *end-user*.

English disease, the   *phrase* a proneness to strikes and other
industrial action, thought to be typical of industrial relations in
the UK. The term (1969) was mainly used by journalists and for-
eigners, and has been little heard in recent years.

enterprise   (**culture/zone**, etc.) *noun*. This word was heavily politi-
cised by Conservative governments during the eighties, becoming a
key word in an economic theory that stressed free-market capitalism and the application of a monetarist ethic to public services
such as local government, the National Health Service and state
education. The phrase **enterprise culture**, invented by right-
wing theoreticians in the early eighties, indicates their belief that
individual effort and initiative should power and pervade society,
reversing the inertia of the DEPENDENCY CULTURE by such measures
as (alleged) reductions in state spending, the PRIVATISATION programme, BIG BANG deregulation, lower taxation to facilitate CON-
SUMERISM, reduction in state benefits to foster self-reliance, and the
encouragement of small businesses and private home ownership.
Although not entirely in keeping with the principle of non-inter-
vention by central government in business matters, **enterprise
zones** (1978) were created in derelict inner-city areas such as the
London Docklands, the intention being to attract investment and
create jobs and profit by offering tax incentives to entrepreneurs
willing to operate in them.

entryism *noun* the organised infiltration of a political group with the intention of changing its principles and activities. The word originates in advice given by Trotsky to his followers in the 1930s, and is first found in English as *entrism* (1963) in academic writing about Trotsky. It assumed its current form in the seventies when it became familiar as a result of the subversion of socialist groups (e.g. in local government) by the extreme left-wing, especially the MILITANT TENDENCY, who preferred this tactic to the formation of a party of their own. See also LOONY LEFT.

E-number *noun* a code number, preceded by the letter E (for European Community) used to identify a food additive and found on the labels or packaging of food and drink. The term, sometimes abbreviated to E, is now also used to mean 'additive', as in **E-free** ('containing no additives'). It originated with an EC recommendation of 1977 that all food additives should be identified by name or code, and such labelling has been mandatory since the mid eighties. The term has achieved such widespread use in part because of concern that the additives were damaging to health in the long term and might be responsible for such things as disturbed and disruptive behaviour in children.

environment *noun*. The established meaning of environment is that which environs or surrounds us, especially those conditions which influence the way a person or thing lives or develops. Two specialised meanings have grown up in recent years from this starting point. **1.** (in computing) the overall conditions and structure within which an operator or machine functions e.g. the operating system and its protocols, the add-on hardware and software available. This term dates from the sixties but came into more general use with the advent of home and personal computing in the seventies and eighties. **2.** The natural world seen as a unified whole and with a natural balance between its parts which must be preserved. From this comes the extended sense of conservation of this natural world, or ECOLOGY. In this meaning it is often referred to as **the environment** and it became the dominant sense in the eighties and nineties, growing out of our increasing concern with the effects of industrialisation and pollution. *Environment* in this new sense of *conservation of the environment* has led to similar new senses for the adjective **environmental** (concerned with conserving the environment) and the adverb **environmentally**, which is used in combination with adjectives in many vogue terms of the eighties, such as *environmentally friendly* and *environmentally aware*. An **environmentalist** is one who is concerned with preserving the environment. When it was first met in the seventies it could be used as a marginalising term, implying cranky enthusiasm, but now environmental concerns are central and accepted.

EOE (abbreviation for) equal opportunity employer. See EQUAL OPPORTUNITY.

EPOS (acronym for) electronic point of sale. Formed (c.1980) by adding E to the existing POS (1972). It refers to the system, introduced in the UK in the early 1980s, for electronically scanning the BAR CODE of shop goods at the cash-desk as a means of stock control.

equal opportunity *noun.* There is nothing new in the notion of 'equality of opportunity' in the broad sense of 'an equal right or chance to seek success regardless of social factors', but in recent years *equal opportunity* has acquired the particular sense of 'offering employment regardless of sex, colour, creed, race or disability'. In the UK there is an Equal Opportunities Commission, set up under the Sex Discrimination Act (1975) to enforce the provisions of that Act and the Equal Pay Act (1970). Firms often refer to themselves as an *equal-opportunities employer*, often abbreviated to EOE in job advertisements.

ERM (abbreviation for) Exchange Rate Mechanism. The core of the European Monetary System (see EMS). Participating governments must maintain the value of their currencies in relation to the ECU within agreed limits, and take action to correct any disparity. The British government, after some eleven years of abstention, joined the ERM in 1990.

escalate *verb* to increase or be increased, often step by step, in intensity, size or extent. Originally used in this sense (late 1950s) as military jargon, especially in reference to the danger of conventional warfare giving way to nuclear warfare if the Cold War should itself escalate into a shooting war. *Escalate* was new in this sense (it had previously meant 'travel on an escalator'), though *escalation* has a slightly longer history and started life as a military word (1938). Since then it has become a vogue word for 'increase' in a general sense, though some authorities regard this usage as journalistic and imprecise.

Essex man *noun* a self-made lower middle class or working class right-wing Conservative voter, caricatured as ill-educated, bigoted, aggressively anti-intellectual, philistine, and lacking in social grace. Anthropological labelling of this kind is familiar from Neanderthal Man, Piltdown Man, etc.; *Essex* refers to the dormitory towns of that county to which people have moved from east London and several of which have returned THATCHERITE MPs. One of the features of Mrs Thatcher's appeal was that she attracted the votes of working people who might have been expected to be traditional Labour voters. On her political demise (1990), her brand of hard right-wing politics was thought to be somewhat outmoded, and it is likely that *Essex man* (1990) emerged amid the speculation about whether the Conservatives could continue to claim the loyalty of this distinctive type of voter. Although Thatcherism was by no means confined to urban Essex, it did so happen that one of her most prominent and typical supporters, and former cabinet colleague, Norman Tebbit (sometimes known as the 'Chingford skinhead'), was MP for an Essex constituency. *Essex man* as a derogatory term probably emerged from this existing identification between Essex and aggressive Thatcherism, and from attempts to marginalise the latter. The original political sense of the term has now widened to embrace anyone (including women) thought to exemplify loud-mouthed, unthinking self-interest and intolerance, and conspicuous consumption in bad taste. A rush of 'Essex jokes' in the early nineties featured Essex man and Essex girl, momentarily displacing the Irish as a customary butt of (prejudiced) English humour. The people of Essex, however, find the term very offensive, which it is, and it should be used with discretion.

est (acronym for) **Erhard Seminars Training**, from the name of Werner Erhard, American businessman, who devised it, in about 1973. This is a technique to raise self-awareness, develop psychological growth and increase human potential by philosophical, psychological and other means, incorporating some motivational theories from the business world. It includes deprivation of food and water, hectoring by group-leaders, and various sorts of psychological conditioning.

Establishment or **establishment, the**   *noun* a social group exercising institutional authority in society (or in particular spheres of it), especially in government, the civil service and in other state institutions such as the law, the church, the armed forces and the City of London. This influential hierarchy, whose power tends towards the preservation of privilege and the status quo, is thought to exist by virtue of its sense of traditional superiority, common social background and shared assumptions. It represents the pinnacle of the British class system which, though sometimes said to be in decline, continues to exist in the public mind as an important unelected and self-selecting determinant of power and influence within society. Its constituents are said to include senior civil servants, the monarchy, the City of London, judges and academics, with a strong male, public school and Oxbridge bias. This definition of *the Establishment* is usually credited to Henry Fairlie, writing in the *Spectator* in 1955, but the term is now usually found – with a small e – in pejorative references to an inner circle, real or imagined, exercising undue and reactionary authority at the head of an organisation. For example, a late eighties political football, was the *educational establishment* said to determine, irrespective of the wishes of government, parents, etc., how and what is taught in schools; no one has yet identified the membership of this *establishment* or even whether it exists outside the minds of those seeking to scapegoat it.

ethical investment   *noun* financial investment in companies whose business is thought to be ethically acceptable. Investors may have a number of reasons for not wishing to be associated with certain companies. They may object to the arms trade, for example, or to trade with a country governed by a repressive regime (as with South Africa in the days of apartheid); others may feel strongly about environmental or health issues, such as the rainforest or tobacco manufacture. *Ethical investment* aims to take account of such scruples. The term arose in the USA in the early eighties, and had spread to the UK by the end of the decade, though it is largely confined to the vocabulary of people dealing with the financial markets.

ethnic   *adj.* This term used to refer to the racial characteristics (and less frequently to the linguistic and religious traits) that distinguish one human group from another. Since c.1960, it has come to refer to cultural differences as well. Even more recently, it has come to mean 'peasant' in some contexts such as *ethnic food* or *ethnic dress*. In other contexts it means 'of a minority ethnic group' within society, as in *ethnic jewellery* or *ethnic food* and *dress* again.

ethnic cleansing   *noun* the clearing of a people from their land and homes by force and terror. This grim euphemism for a process which may include mass executions among its means of persuasion, is closely associated with the bitter fighting in Bosnia between ethnic groups (Serb, Croat and Muslim) in the early and mid nineties when this term first came to general notice.

Euro, Euro-   (short for) European, usually in the context of the European Community. The development of the European Community during the second half of the twentieth century has given rise to a large number of coinages (with the prefix *Euro-*), many of them journalistic and transient. The more durable of these include *Eurocrat* (a bureaucrat of the EC; 1961), *Euro-sceptic* (a person who questions some aspects of the EC's operations, 1986), *Europhobia* (1990), *Euro-fanatic* (1967) and *Euro-MP* (1975; see MEP). *Eurospeak* (1979), the jargon of EC documents and regulations, has given way to *Eurobabble* (early 1980s, see PSYCHOBABBLE). Economic harmonisation has created the *Eurobond* (1966), a bond issued in a *Eurocurrency* (1963), a country's currency held on deposit in Europe outside its home market (e.g. a *Eurodollar* (1965) held on *Eurodeposit*). More familiar to the general public is the *Eurocheque*, which can be used wherever the EC sign is displayed. Not all **Euro-** words are directly connected with the European Community – *Eurotunnel*, for example, is the name of the Anglo-French consortium that constructed the Channel Tunnel; *Eurocommunism* (1976) was said to differ from the Soviet and Chinese versions by recognising democratic institutions; more recently (1986) the *Euroleft* has emerged as a broader grouping. In British colloquialism, the **Euros** are people who live on the European mainland (and, occasionally, people in Britain who favour the EC), though Americans use the term to mean all Europeans, including the British. *Euros* and *euros* also occur in financial jargon, especially in the USA, as abbreviations for various items traded on European money markets. *Euro* is also the currently favoured term for the ECU.

European Community   see EC.

European Economic Community   see EEC.

European Monetary System   see EMS.

European Monetary Union   see EMU.

Exchange Rate Mechanism   see ERM.

executive   *noun* and *adj.* From meaning, among other things, 'a person holding a responsible position in business', this word has come to be used adjectivally in the informal sense of 'expensive or exclusive', e.g. *executive car, lifestyle, suite* etc. The development has been from the factual (*executive class*, 1962) via house agents' jargon (*executive housing*) to the jocular (*executive toy*, 1971).

exit poll *noun* an unofficial poll in which people leaving a polling station are asked how they have voted. Originally US (late seventies) but now widely known in the UK as an accurate means of predicting the outcome of an election.

Exocet *noun* a high-speed, low-flying, anti-ship guided missile with high-explosive warhead. Developed by the French in the 1960s, officially named in 1970 from a French word meaning 'flying fish', but not generally known by the UK public until the Falklands War (1982) when it did considerable damage to British ships. The word has since been used occasionally as a noun in the colloquial figurative sense of a 'devastating surprise' or 'bombshell', and even as a verb: 'to deliver such a bombshell'.

expert system *noun* a computer system or program that stores, organises and applies the knowledge of experts in a given field so that the user can draw on it. Developed c.1977, such systems are specially useful in performing tasks requiring the logical analysis of large quantities of data, e.g. in medical diagnosis. See also ARTIFICIAL INTELLIGENCE.

eyeball *verb* to stare threateningly or provocatively. Seventies slang, from earlier US slang meaning simply 'stare at' or 'look intently at'. Also *eyeball to eyeball* (1962), in close confrontation with no yielding on either side.

fab *adj.* very good, successful. Teenagers' slang, mainly British, recorded from c.1957, an abbreviation of **fabulous**, and particularly familiar from the catch phrase 'the fab four' for the Beatles.

faction *noun* a literary work, or film or television programme combining depiction of actual events with an element of fiction. The term, invented in the late sixties by blending *fact* and fic*tion*, is not much used outside media circles. Television programmes and films of this kind are more usually known as DOCUDRAMAS.

factoid *noun* a possibly untrue, or partly true or questionable fact, popularly believed to be true, purely because of its publication (and, often, repetition) or because it chimes with the public's perception of how things ought to be. Norman Mailer coined this word in 1973 by adding -*oid* ('in form or appearance') to *fact*, perhaps by analogy with android (a robot in human shape). It has since been used as an adjective meaning 'apparently factual, but not fully so'. It is a useful word in view of the tendency to invention by some journalists, image-makers, etc.

fail-safe *adj.* designed so as to adopt a safe position in the event of failure or malfunction; or *noun* a fail-safe mechanism. Originally a verb in late-1940s aeronautical jargon: a mechanism designed to *fail safe* was able to revert, in the event of breakdown, to a condition involving no danger. During Cold War times *fail safe* referred particularly to precautions and procedures agreed beforehand to ensure that misunderstandings and accidents did not escalate a nuclear war. Nowadays the word has a wider application.

Falklands factor *noun* the supposed boost to the Conservative Party's popularity and electability following the Falklands War, and by extension any fortuitous event that increases the popularity of a political party or candidate. An occasional journalistic phrase (1982) in the wake of the Falklands War. Although this is now widely interpreted as the consequence of political hamfistedness on both sides – acknowledged at the time by the resignation of the British foreign secretary – the outcome produced a surge of popular support for the then prime minister, Mrs Thatcher, and is believed to have played a significant if not determining part in her re-election (1983) at a time of economic difficulty.

fallout *noun* the side-effects or secondary consequences of an action. A colloquial adaptation and extension of the original *fallout* (1950), the radioactive refuse, especially dust, falling to earth after a nuclear explosion.

family jewels *noun* the embarrassing secrets that an organisation, political party etc. wishes to keep hidden. From the euphemistic jargon of the CIA in America in the late seventies; the 'jewels' were details of their DIRTY TRICKS which needed to be kept 'in the family'. The CIA borrowed the term from earlier US slang in which *family jewels* is a term for the male genitals.

fanny pack *noun* same as BUM BAG. A US slang term; *fanny* is the US equivalent of *bum*. The *fanny pack* began life as a sports accessory in the seventies, worn at the back, and became generally popular as a fashion accessory in the late 1980s, retaining its name even though by then it was commonly worn at the front of the body.

far-out *adj.* bizarre; excellent. Originally US jazz slang (1954) for 'daringly progressive', this is now general slang, usually found as an expression of surprise or pleasure.

fastback *noun* a car with a back that forms a continuous slope from the roof to the rear i.e. as distinct from one with a protruding boot. The term originally US c.1965, implies that such styling is conducive to speed.

fast food *noun* food requiring little preparation before serving. Also adjective **fast-food** (of restaurants etc.) serving such food. Also by extension (something) quick and easy. The term has been known in the USA since about 1950 but has been general in the UK only since about 1970 as a result of the opening of American-type fast-food restaurants in Britain. There are signs that the adjectival *fast-food* is spreading to things other than food (e.g. drugs) and even to non-material things (e.g. music) that are easy to fabricate, sell, obtain or consume.

fast lane *noun* a lifestyle that is glamorous and pressured; quickest and therefore most competitive route to success. It is difficult to say which of these two meanings is the most prominent; probably the first, as a result of the hackneyed phrase *(life) in the fast lane*. The term comes from drivers' vocabulary: when the first British motorways were built in the late fifties, the outside lane became popularly known as the 'fast' lane (c.1965) despite official

fast-track

attempts to insist that it was an 'overtaking' lane, for occasional use and not for permanent occupation by fast drivers. Compare FAST-TRACK.

fast-track *adj.* following the quickest and therefore most competitive route to success, promotion, self-advancement, etc. An adjectival and figurative adaptation (c.1966) of the noun *fast track*, an American horse-racing term for a race-track which, being hard and dry, enables horses to run fast. The term became popular in US business circles in the seventies and spread to the UK in the eighties. Compare FAST LANE. Also a transitive verb: to promote (someone) rapidly, to expedite something; and *noun* **fast-tracker** – someone on the *fast track*.

fattism *noun* discrimination against or ridicule of fat people. Also *adj.* **fattist**, discriminating against or ridiculing fat people in this way. The term was coined in 1988 (on the model of *racism, sexism,* etc.) by an American psychologist who wanted to show how we are unduly influenced and prejudiced by the physical appearance of people. The term is often used only half seriously, but there is growing recognition that many people are made to feel badly about themselves, and experience an insidious pressure to change the way they look, so these words also have a serious use, though *sizeist* may perhaps survive longer.

fatwa *noun* an edict issued by a Muslim religious leader. This Arabic word was largely unknown in the English-speaking world until 1989 when Ayatollah Khomeini issued a *fatwa* requiring Muslims to kill the British author Salman Rushdie for alleged blasphemy in his novel *The Satanic Verses*, together with all those involved in its publication.

fax *noun* facsimile transmission, an international system for transmitting a digitised document through the telephone network. Although experiments to develop such a system began in the late nineteenth century, and the word *fax* itself (from 'facsimile') was coined in the 1940s, it was largely unknown until commercial exploitation in the early 1980s, after which it rapidly became standard office equipment. The word now denotes the actual document sent or received, and the machine used, as well as being a verb meaning 'to communicate by fax'.

federalism *noun.* An example of a word used as a political football. Federalism means 'a form of government in which power is divided between one central and several regional governments'. In the political controversy surrounding the relationship between EC member states and the central EC institutions (parliament, commission, etc.), opponents of closer relationship often use *federalism* to mean 'control of a group of states by a central government' (early nineties).

feedback *noun* response to an action, inquiry, etc. with a view to modifying future policies or outcomes. The term originated in the early history of electronics where it denoted the use of part of the output of a signal by sending (*feeding*) it *back* to its input in order to modify performance. The current figurative sense, which emerged in the 1950s, retains the idea of obtaining a response (to a proposal, for example) which may modify a policy or action.

feel-good *adj.* causing pleasant feelings in people. This late eighties adjectival term (often found in political journalism referring to *feel-good policies / factor*, etc.) may be no more than a hyphenation of the familiar expression 'to feel good', but there may be a backward glance to the seventies when Dr Feelgood was a pop group and also, in short-lived slang, an easy-going general practitioner who dispenses drugs.

fibre (short for) DIETARY FIBRE.

fifth generation see GENERATION.

Filofax *noun* a small (normally leather-bound) ring-binder containing loose-leaf and therefore replaceable pages for diary, addresses, notes, etc., with useful printed information and a wallet for pen, credit-cards etc. Although registered as a proprietary name as long ago as 1931 (as a respelling of 'file of facts'), the word was little known until the early eighties when the *Filofax* suddenly became a necessary item for business-people or a fashion accessory – together with a portable phone and brightly coloured braces – for the YUPPY. Sometimes called a PERSONAL ORGANISER or simply ORGANISER, especially as Filofax is a recognised proprietary name so that rival firms had to find an alternative for their versions.

fine print *noun* material in a legal document, especially a contract or written agreement, that is printed in small letters because of its subordinate nature. Often regarded with suspicion because of an assumption that such clauses may have been made deliberately inconspicuous because they contain conditions unfavourable to the person signing. The term emerged in the sixties, though fine has meant 'small' for centuries. Also referred to as *small print*.

firmware *noun* a kind of software containing fixed instructions permanently built into certain sorts of computer and capable of being changed only if the hardware is modified. Part of the language of computer technology since c.1968, based on the familiar HARDWARE/SOFTWARE formation.

first-strike *adj.* (of nuclear weapon) designed to be used in the first attack of a nuclear war in order to destroy the enemy's capacity to strike back. As distinct from *second-strike* weapons, designed to be protected for use in a counter attack if the enemy makes a *first strike*; in this case a nation should have a *second-strike strategy*, allowing it to withstand the enemy's attack and still retain the capacity to retaliate. Both terms are from the sixties, when military strategists were much preoccupied with the relative capabilities of weapons during the Cold War.

First World see THIRD WORLD.

flak or **flak-catcher** *noun* a person skilled in public relations, employed by a company, individual, etc., to deal with bad publicity, or hostile questions and comments. An Americanism from the early seventies, based on the earlier (sixties) use of *flak* to mean 'adverse criticism'. Originally *flak* denoted a Second World War

German anti-aircraft gun and was used by allied pilots to mean anti-aircraft fire. The shift in meaning from 'hostile gunfire' to 'hostile comment' was a natural one.

flaky *adj.* eccentric, unreliable, unpredictable, or crazy; **flake** *noun* someone exhibiting these qualities, a nutter. *Flaky* came first (c.1964 in US), reaching Britain from America in the 1980s; it seems to have originated in US baseball slang. It may come from *flaky* in the sense of 'crumbly', or from *flake out*, earlier slang for 'fall asleep or collapse (from exhaustion, drunkenness, etc.)'; this latter meaning, first recorded in the 1940s and thought to be a variant of *flag* (droop), became popular in the sixties to denote collapse as a result of drug-taking, though it also retains its original sense. The noun *flake* emerged c.1968 and means 'person who has *flaky* characteristics'. It has only recently begun to be used in the UK, in part because of President Reagan's description of Colonel Gadaffi as *flaky* in 1986.

flame *noun* (on the Internet) an angry riposte to or put down of a fellow user who has offended you. Also *verb* to put down in this way. Internet jargon that became more widely known in the early nineties at the time of the expansion of the Internet.

flares *noun* trousers with legs that widen below the knee. Originally US, c.1964, but soon afterwards familiar in Britain when the garment became popular in the late sixties. In the singular, *flare* is a well-established word in tailoring, with the meaning 'a gradual widening or spreading out'.

flavour of the month *noun phrase* a short-lived fad; thing or person enjoying popularity that is likely to be brief. Originally an American advertising phrase, well known (from about 1946) from its use by ice-cream parlours which used it to promote a particular flavour of ice-cream and persuade their customers to try something new, on the questionable grounds that it must be special if it was specially selected. In the UK, where ice-cream parlours are almost unknown, the phrase did not become familiar until its emergence in its current figurative sense in the late seventies. It is used cynically, often derisively.

FLCD (abbreviation for) ferroelectric liquid crystal display. The next generation of LIQUID CRYSTAL DISPLAY, promising to be brighter, cheaper and easier to view than LCD. FLCD was developed from the early eighties, and commercial application began in the early nineties. Pen-based computer systems and large, flat-screen, wall-hung televisions are among the developments expected from advances in LCD technology.

flexitime (occasionally **flextime**) *noun* a system permitting employees to vary their working hours (subject to certain conditions) provided that the number of hours worked adds up to an agreed total. The word (from 'flexible' + 'time') emerged c.1972, and the system is generally agreed to have improved not only working conditions but also productivity.

flip chart *noun* a large display pad mounted on a stand and having the pages bound at the upper edge so that they can be 'flipped' over after use. For use by a teacher, lecturer or other speaker as an alternative to a blackboard, OVERHEAD PROJECTOR, etc. The pages may be written on by the speaker, or contain prepared material which can be displayed in sequence. The device was first used in the USA in the mid fifties and is now a common adjunct at conferences, meetings, etc.

flip-flop   *noun* a light casual sandal secured by thong or strap at the toe end. Because it is not secured at the heel, it flops as the wearer walks, making a sound that has given it its onomatopoeic name (late sixties).

floppy disk   *noun* a magnetic disc capable of storing information, for use in a computer. So called (c.1972) because they were then flexible though they are now commonly rigid: see HARD DISK.

flower   *noun*. The *flower children* or *people* were a young sub group of the HIPPIE culture who were so named (c.1967) because they wore or carried flowers as a symbol of love and peace. This commitment to these virtues (summarised in their slogan 'Make love, not war') and their other beliefs and convictions became known as *flower power*.

fly-by   *noun* the close approach (but not landing) of a spacecraft to a planet (etc.) in order to record or relay information. Originally (1953) an American term for a fly-past, this entered the vocabulary of space travel c.1960.

fly-by-wire   *noun* control of an aircraft by electronic circuitry rather than by mechanical means, so that – theoretically – pilot error is impossible; also such a computerised control system. The increased use of computers in the late eighties' generation of passenger aircraft has been held responsible for a number of accidents, as a result of which this term has begun to assume a pejorative colouring, as if 'wire' implied something makeshift. This was not the case originally.

fly-drive   *adj.* (of a holiday or journey) where the cost includes the flight and the use of a car, to be picked up at the holiday destination (1975).

fly-on-the-wall   *noun* a technique of film-making, especially of documentaries, which seeks to depict events realistically by observing rather than directing them. The term (1970s) is mainly used of television documentary programmes in which events are filmed as they happen and the resultant material is edited and presented with a minimum or absence of linking commentary, on-camera interviews or other arranged elements. More loosely, the term may be used of films (occasionally of plays) in which the material is fictional but the method of presentation apparently lacks artifice. The origin is colloquial expressions such as 'I wish I could have been a fly on the wall', said of an event, conversation, etc. at which one would like to have been present as an unnoticed observer. The technique has been used to film the everyday life of 'ordinary' families, perhaps most memorably the Wilkinsons of Reading in the seventies, when it was hoped that the continued day-by-day presence of the camera crews would mean that they were ultimately

fly-tipping

forgotten by the participants so that the viewer would truly be in the position of a fly on the wall.

fly-tipping   *noun* the deliberate tipping of rubbish in an unauthorised place. Also *verb* fly-tip. Coined in the late sixties, probably on the model of *fly-posting* (in which *fly* refers to the speed with which the posters are put up to avoid detection, or else the speed with which the bill poster departs the scene).

fogey   see YOUNG FOGEY.

folk-rock   *noun* a combination of folk music, especially the style of its lyrics, with rock and roll (1960s).

foodie, foody   *noun* a person interested in cooking, eating, reading about and talking about food; a food 'groupie'. A colloquialism since the early eighties, it implies a more general enthusiasm than the refined taste of the gourmet, and probably reflects the way that the consumer society promotes interest in 'good food' and restaurants through TV series and Sunday magazines. Also **foodism** *noun* a preoccupation with food and things gastronomic.

food processor   *noun* a domestic electrical appliance for rapid chopping, blending, grating etc. of foodstuffs (1974).

Footsie, footsie   *noun* the Financial Times – Stock Exchange one hundred share index, which monitors daily changes in the valuation of shares in the UK's one hundred largest companies. Not to be confused with the idea of *playing footsie* (flirting by rubbing one's foot against someone else's), though the existence of *footsie* in this sense no doubt inspired the formation of *Footsie* from FT (the familiar abbreviation of the *Financial Times*) and SE (abbreviation of 'Stock Exchange') soon after the introduction of the new index in 1984.

forex   *noun* (abbreviation of) foreign exchange. Banking jargon, found occasionally in the financial columns of newspapers, c.1990. It is normally used adjectivally, e.g. *forex dealings*.

FORTRAN, Fortran   *noun* a computer programming language, designed for the solution of complex problems mainly in maths and science. Developed by IBM in the early fifties, this was the first program that made a computer system accessible to the general user.

fourth generation   see GENERATION.

Fourth World   see THIRD WORLD.

fractal   *noun* (in mathematics) a curve of which any small part, if enlarged, has the same statistical character as the original. Coined c.1975 from a Latin word meaning 'to break'.

Franglais   *noun* 1. (for the French) informal French containing many words of English origin, or words and constructions mixing French and English; 2. (for the English) a comic pidgin for the amusement of readers who have some half-forgotten French they can half-remember. The term *Franglais* was coined in France in 1959, as a blend of français (French) and anglais (English) to define and deplore the way that words of English and American usage were being introduced indiscriminately into spoken French. What the English generally understand by *Franglais* is very different and came rather later. Designed for English readers, it is a pidgin containing a larding of French words and phrasing, and is designed to amuse.

freak *noun* a person prone to FREAK OUT. Mid sixties slang for an extreme HIPPIE, not to be confused with *freak* meaning 'enthusiast', which is much older but clearly influences this usage since an *acid freak*, for example, is an enthusiast for the experience of freaking out. *Freak* meaning 'enthusiast' is usually found with a qualifying word (e.g. *health freak*) to indicate the particular activity, and was in use in US English in the early years of this century – the OED cites 'one of your kodak freaks' from 1908 – but it was not in general use in the UK until much later, and *health freak, ecology freak* and *exercise freak* all have a distinctly modern ring.

freak out *verb* to experience (or cause someone else to experience) a heightened emotional state or else a loss of control (e.g. through anger, rage, excitement, terror), especially as a result of taking a hallucinogenic drug. One of the defining terms of the US HIPPIE culture, c.1965, though it has since lost its very close association with drug-abuse and is often heard as a synonym for simply 'lose one's temper', 'behave strangely', 'become drunk', etc. Similarly the noun *freak-out* was originally used of a weird experience, often one caused by drugs: it is still sometimes used in that sense, but it too can more usually be found with the milder meaning of 'loss of control' or 'breakdown'.

freaky *adj.* weird, bizarre. One of a number of mid sixties words associated with FREAK OUT, and also originally with drug-taking.

freebase *noun* cocaine purified by heating with ether. Also *verb*, to refine cocaine for smoking, or to smoke it. US slang, first recorded in print in 1980, though the word was circulating in the private language of drug-takers in the seventies. The derivation appears to be that the *base*, the most important part of cocaine, is set *free* by heating; the fumes are inhaled and what remains is smoked.

free-fall *adj.* dropping rapidly and uncontrollably. Also *noun*. A 1980s development (as in 'a free-fall economy') from earlier uses which had been confined to aeronautic contexts. In parachuting, a free fall is the part of the descent before the parachute opens.

freeze-frame *noun* a still picture forming part of a film or television motion-picture sequence, giving the impression that the action has been 'frozen' for a time; a video-recorder facility allowing play-back to be stopped so that a single picture can be looked at more carefully. Also *verb*, to use this facility. The term has been part of the technical vocabulary of film-making since the sixties, but became generally known in the early eighties when video recorders came on the domestic market and were advertised as having *freeze-frame*. Television recordings do not actually have 'frames': the word has been retained from earlier film use, in which a frame was one of a series of separate pictures that made up a piece of cinematographic film. *Freeze-frame* is developing a figurative use, especially to register those moments of shock and distortion when you have the sensation of time stopping still and reality being frozen.

fresh *adj.* excellent, new, exciting. Young people's slang, chiefly US (late eighties), from HIP-HOP culture.

fridge-freezer *noun* a household appliance combining a refrigerator and freezer, in self-contained compartments, within a single cabinet (1971).

friendly fire *noun* (in a military conflict) firing by one's own side, especially that which kills or injures one's own troops or damages one's own equipment. Although *friendly*, in its familiar sense 'not hostile', has had a comfortable place in military vocabulary ('friendly troops/aircraft', etc.), its use in *friendly fire* in the US jargon of the Vietnam War verged on the euphemistic, if not the foolish, when applied to killing one's own troops. The term reached a wider public in the UK at the time of the Gulf War in which *friendly fire* played an exceptionally murderous role, but most non-military users of the term are sufficiently uncomfortable to put inverted commas round it; BBC newsbroadcasters were speaking of 'so-called friendly fire' as late as 1992 when reporting on an inquest on British soldiers killed by American fire during the Gulf War.

Friends of the Earth *noun* an environmental pressure group established in the UK in 1971.

fringe *adj.* not conventional. This new meaning is a natural development from the older one, 'belonging to the outer edge'. *Fringe theatre* (1971) is experimental drama, usually small-scale and low-cost; the name originated in artistic activity – not exclusively theatrical – said to be on the 'fringe' of the Edinburgh Festival (founded 1947) because it was not part of the official festival programme. *Fringe medicine* (1960) is medical treatment which is not available as a matter of course.

Frisbee *noun* (trademark of) a toy in the form of a plastic disc that can be thrown between players (in a catching game) by being spun by a flick of the wrist. The manufacturers who launched the product in 1957 bought the rights from a Los Angeles building inspector who had been inspired by the airworthiness of the pie tins of the Frisbie bakery, Bridgeport, Connecticut, though it is likely that the aerodynamic qualities of these had first been discovered by Yale students at nearby New Haven. The spelling was changed to avoid legal complications.

fromage frais *noun* low-fat, soft cheese with creamy texture. The French means 'fresh cheese'. Though known previously in France, the product became known in Britain only in the early eighties, and has since become very popular – probably because of its low-fat content – as the basis for a range of dairy desserts.

front-end *adj.* When used of money or costs, this means 'charged at the beginning of a transaction'. If often occurs in *front-end loading* (1962), the arranging of the repayments of a loan so that service charges (commission, fees and other expenses) relating to the whole period of the loan are recovered in the early payments and thus form a large proportion of such payments by an investor (in an insurance policy, etc.). In computing, a *front-end processor*

(1971), often abbreviated to *front-end*, receives data and processes it before routing it to a more powerful central computer able to perform major tasks. This general sense passed into media jargon in about 1979: *front-ending* (noun) is the direct inputting of newspaper material by journalists using their own terminals and bypassing the former printing stage, an innovation that caused a violent and prolonged dispute with newspaper print-workers in the eighties.

front line   *adj.* (of a country) having borders close to a hostile country or a war zone; also *noun*. This modern extension (1975) of the meaning of a familiar military term was specially applied to black African nations bordering South Africa (and, previously, Rhodesia) the Front Line States. In consequence certain streets where the black community came face to face with the police were known as the *front line* during race riots in the UK in 1981.

fudge and mudge   *verb* to demonstrate indecision, evasiveness or prevarication in circumstances where clarity and/or decisiveness are required. Also *noun* indecision and evasiveness at such a time. The expression was first used by David Owen at a speech at the Labour Party conference in 1980: *fudge* ('to fit together in a makeshift or dishonest way') was familiar enough; *mudge* was an invention, perhaps based on *muddle*, probably chosen because of the emphasis that its rhyme provided. Because of its curiosity the phrase has stuck, and is sometimes heard outside political contexts. It has also led to an expanded use of *fudge* as a noun standing by itself.

fundie   *noun* (abbreviation of) fundamentalist. A colloquial nickname for a member of a fundamentalist religious group in the USA and also for a radical environmentalist who does not favour dialogue or collaboration with other interested parties to solve problems concerned with the ENVIRONMENT. Groups of both of these had some political clout, in the USA and Germany respectively, during the 1980s when the word emerged in both countries.

funk   *noun*. Originally a US slang word for a foul smell, (as it was in UK English in past centuries). Perhaps from the association between 'smell' and 'earthiness', the adjective *funky* came to be applied (1954) to jazz and similar music that was down-to-earth, having the roughness of blues, uncomplicated, emotional, like soul but more extrovert. This also became known as *funk* (1959). The word has since been used in many combinations and of a variety of musical styles, but all of them have some relationship with black dance music with strong and usually syncopated rhythms, a heavy bass, and elements of blues and SOUL. There is no connection with the British *funk* (cowardice) which is older.

funky   *adj.* fashionable, deserving approval; unconventional. US slang, c.1969, probably deriving loosely from the *funky* music described under FUNK.

funny farm   *noun* a mental hospital. Facetious slang dating from c.1963. *Farm* implies enclosure, but was probably chosen as much for alliteration as for sense.

funny money   *noun* money associated with crime or dubious practices. A sixties development of an earlier (thirties) US usage denoting counterfeit or otherwise worthless money, probably based on the earlier phrase *funny business*, one of the meanings of which was 'underhand or objectionable dealings'.

fun run   *noun* long-distance run in which the object is for people to enjoy themselves rather than to race competitively. The idea, and the name, originated in the USA in the mid seventies and was immediately taken up in the UK as a way of bringing together and encouraging the new generation of health-conscious but often solitary joggers, and also of raising money for charity by getting friends to 'sponsor' them for every mile (etc.) they completed.

fusion   *noun* popular music that is a blend of two (or more) styles (1975), such as jazz with FUNK or ROCK e.g. *disco-funk* or *techno-funk*.

futon   *noun* a soft Japanese padded quilt or mattress which can be spread on the floor for use as a bed, or folded for use as seating, and easily stored away when not in use. The word, which is Japanese, has been used in this sense in Japan since the nineteenth century, but was almost unknown in the West except for occasional references, mainly in travel literature. Since the eighties, however, futons have become fashionable in Britain and the US but are normally used on a low, slatted, wooden base (also known as a futon) which can also be used for daytime seating.

fuzz, the   *noun* the police; a policeman. Not recorded in the UK before 1959, after which it became common slang. It has a longer history in the US, where it is thought to be related to 'fuss' (an over-particular person).

fuzz box   *noun* an electronic device that breaks up and distorts the sounds as they pass through it. Used mainly by guitarists and named in the sixties (from *fuzzy*, 'imprecisely defined').

fuzzword   *noun* a deliberately vague or puzzling word or term, often jargon, used (sometimes by politicians) as an impressive substitute for good sense. A *fuzzword* is similar to DOUBLESPEAK, though not necessarily as thorough-going in its wish to deceive. This word, based on BUZZWORD and *fuzzy* ('not well defined'), was first used in the *Washington Post Magazine* in 1983 but has not caught on generally in the UK.

f-word, the   *noun* a euphemism for *fuck*. This euphemism has been used since the seventies in discussions about the acceptability of the word's use in the media. Subsequently it was used as a jocular euphemism for *federalism*, a taboo-word for the British government in discussions about closer European union in the early 1990s. It has spawned a number of similar formations, often jocular, for words that dare not say their full names. Thus at the Liberal Democrats' Conference in September 1995 one MP taunted Labour with their inability to confront *the t-word*, by which he meant *tax*, an issue which he considered Labour was unwilling to tackle. Earlier *the T word* had been used as a way of avoiding using Mrs Thatcher's name, by those whose disapproval of her policies meant that they would have us believe they were unwilling to let the dread name pass their lips. Recently (1995) the BBC Radio 4 programme about words and language, *Word of Mouth*, talked of *the m-f word* – a reversion to the original pattern of use as they wanted to refer to a word which they did not want to say aloud – all of which shows that the formula is alive and well.

G7   (abbreviation of) GROUP OF SEVEN.

Gaia hypothesis or **theory**   *noun* the theory that the Earth is not a collection of independent mechanisms but a single living organism in which everything interacts to regulate the survival and stability of the whole. The hypothesis, advanced by the British scientist James Lovelock in 1969, is named after the goddess of the Earth in Greek mythology. Her name is sometimes used of the Earth itself, viewed in a holistic and even reverential way, and adherents to the 'Gaiaist' principle are sometimes called 'Gaians'.

game plan   *noun* a strategy; series of tactics. In its original sense of 'a plan of fixed "plays" pre-arranged by the coach and the team for winning a game of American football', the term goes back to the 1940s, but the more general sense of any carefully prepared strategy (and sometimes no more than a jocular extension of 'plan') is a later development and has been used in Britain only since the late eighties when American football was first broadcast regularly on television.

games console   *noun* a computer purpose-built for the playing of computer games (1987).

gang-bang   *noun* sexual intercourse between one person and several others one after the other, normally against the will of the former. Taboo slang, originally US c.1953. *Bang* is older slang for an act of sexual intercourse. In the US in the fifties a *gang bang* might signify no more than a wild and sexy party (*gang* meaning a group of friends), but the meaning has shifted to that given above, and in the UK (where the term was not generally used before the eighties) it is commonly understood to mean a gang rape. In the late eighties a different meaning has developed in the US for **gang banger** – someone who runs with a street gang and gets a *bang* (thrill) from their activities.

Gang of Four   *noun.* Four leaders of the CULTURAL REVOLUTION, including Mao Tse Tung's widow, were arrested a month after his death in 1976, accused of trying to seize power. They were later tried and found guilty of 'revisionism'. The term is said to have been used by Mao himself when warning his wife and colleagues not to form such a clique. It was later applied, more facetiously, to the four prominent British Labour party members who broke away and founded the short-lived Social Democratic Party in 1981, and occasionally to any group of four people who are taking action together.

garage   *noun.* A low-quality rock group was known in the late sixties as a **garage band**, the implication being that it was so makeshift that it could not afford to rehearse anywhere else. There may be some connection between this and the later **garage**, a mixture of soul and HOUSE music (1980s), but the latter is more likely to have taken its name from the Paradise Garage, a New York venue where it originated. A **garage sale** (1966) is a sale of unwanted possessions, usually held in a domestic garage.

garbology, garbageology *noun* the academic study of a society's refuse seen as a branch of social science or anthropology. Coined (USA, 1976) by W Rathje, a professor of the subject, from *garbage*, the normal American term for domestic rubbish.

gas-guzzler *noun* a large car that has a very high fuel consumption. US slang, first recorded 1973. Such cars appear to drink up the petrol greedily – guzzle the gasoline. The Gulf War was said by some to have been fought to make the world safe for the gas guzzler.

-gate The suffix has been added to a number of words to denote an affair characterised by corruption or embarrassment, often one involving a political cover-up. The most durable example is IRAN-GATE (1986), the scandal involving the US sale of arms to Iran, alleged to have been arranged on the understanding that US hostages would be released, and the diversion of the profits to aid the CONTRA cause despite the vote of the US Congress to ban such aid. The *-gate* in this and many other coinages is from Watergate, the name of the Washington building that housed the offices of the Democratic party, burgled during the 1972 elections on the instructions of supporters of the Republican president, Richard Nixon. The consequences of the 'Watergate Affair' (1972–4) included his resignation, the first of a serving president, when he was threatened with impeachment. Senior White House officials approved the burglary, and Nixon was personally involved in the subsequent cover-up. See IRAQGATE. Though Watergate took place more than twenty years ago the *-gate* suffix has been regularly used and new combinations are still formed. In the UK we had *Westlandgate* (1985) and *Stalkergate* (1986); in the US *Gospelgate* and *Pearlygate* (the scandals surrounding televangelists in the eighties) while *Whitewatergate* is still grumbling away in the US in the mid nineties and threatening to be an embarrassment to the Clintons.

gay *adj.* or *noun* homosexual. Although **gay** in this sense goes back to c.1930 if not earlier, it has only recently become standard English (or at least informal English) rather than slang. Other usages include **gay lib(eration)** (1968), the campaign to combat discrimination against homosexuals, and **gay pride** (1984), a less defensive term for the same concern.

gazump, gazunder *verbs*. The first is old slang, previously spelt in various ways, from a Yiddish word meaning 'swindle' or 'overcharge'. It became suddenly familiar c.1971 in the sense of 'raise the price of a house, or sell a house at a higher price, after a lower one has been agreed with an intending buyer'. House prices were rising extremely quickly at the time, and many house-agents and private sellers found the temptation to break a prior verbal agreement too hard to resist. In the late eighties, when prices stabilised and then began to fall, some buyers got their own back, and *gazunder* was invented to mean 'reduce the price agreed with the seller':

gazundering usually takes place just before the exchange of contracts, when a seller might well be already committed to another purchase. The word is an obvious play on *gazump* (with *-under* reflecting the offering of a price *under* the original one), though there is an earlier slang word *guzunder* for a chamber-pot (which *goes under* the bed). This and the *under–u(m)p* echo may give this word greater currency than the other newly coined near equivalent GAZWELCH.

gazwelch *verb* to withdraw from an agreed purchase of a house at the eleventh hour. An alternative to GAZUNDER, blending *gazump* and *welch* (to default on a debt or other obligation). Also, **gazwelcher** one who withdraws in this way; and *gazwelching* the act or practice of so doing.

GCSE (abbreviation of) General Certificate of Secondary Education. The qualification awarded after public examinations in secondary schools, usually sat at the age of sixteen. The first examinations were held in 1988, replacing the former twin-track system of GCE (General Certificate of Education, intended for abler pupils) and CSE (Certificate of Secondary Education, intended for average and less able pupils). The examination itself is usually referred to as GCSE.

gear *noun* an informal word for fashionable clothing from the sixties, probably influenced by the slang use of *gear* or *the gear* to mean 'excellent' (popularised by the Beatles but actually very much older). *Gear* in the sense of 'illegal drugs' also came to prominence in the sixties, though it originated in the late forties, probably by borrowing a harmless-sounding word (gear = equipment, belongings) to disguise a banned substance.

gel *noun* a jelly-like substance used for various cosmetic purposes. The word has existed in the technical vocabulary of chemistry since the end of the nineteenth century, but only came into more general use in the late fifties as the name for a setting lotion used by ladies' hairdressers. Its use was extended in the late seventies by PUNKS who wore bizarre, upswept styles, sometimes with long sculptured points. In the eighties, by which time *hair gel* had become widely available, it was very popular among young men and boys who wanted a 'wet-look' (often in the shape of short spikes). Firms also marketed *shower gel, shaving gel, shampoo gel*, etc. See also STYLING MOUSSE.

gender-bender *noun* a person with an androgynous appearance, sexually ambiguous clothes, make-up, hair-style, etc. The term was invented c.1980 in the context of a current fashion among certain pop singers and their followers, but has since acquired the more general meanings of 'transvestite' and 'activity in which the traditional roles of male and female are blurred or reversed'.

gender gap *noun* the difference between men and women as regards political, social and cultural attitudes and values. Chiefly US (1977) where the matter has been much studied, particularly in reference to voting patterns.

generation *noun*. In computer jargon, *first generation* computers (forties and early fifties) used electronic valves. The *second generation* (mid fifties to mid sixties) used transistors. The *third generation* (mid sixties to early seventies) used integrated circuits. The *fourth generation* lasted until the early nineties, and had integrated circuit technology with a large main memory and networking facilities. *Fifth generation* computers have multiple parallel processes, are very fast, operate in larger networks, use EXPERT SYSTEMS, and may incorporate voice recognition and speech synthesis.

generation gap   *noun* the difference between successive generations, especially in attitudes, values and cultural behaviour. The term is especially used of the difference in outlook between parents and their teenage children. It was coined c.1967 in the decade of the first identifiable youth culture, which lent customary generational differences a new quality of incomprehension and stress.

gene therapy   *noun* the introduction of normal genes in place of defective or missing ones to correct or prevent the occurrence of hereditary diseases. This medical application of **genetic engineering** has been under investigation since the early seventies but is still at the experimental stage. The possibility of dealing with inherited disorders such as haemophilia is an attractive one, but the replacement or alteration of human genes raises ethical issues needing legal consideration.

genetic code   *noun* the system by which nucleic acid molecules store genetic information. This is the means by which such information (for the building of proteins, the basis of living matter) is stored in DNA. The code, named c.1961, determines the genetic characteristic of each individual.

genetic engineering   *noun* the deliberate alteration of the genetic make-up (i.e. the DNA of a cell) of a living organism. Applications of this technique (late sixties) include the manufacture of animal proteins, the improvement of plants and animals, and the correction of genetic defects in humans. While certain developments, such as the production of plants which are resistant to disease or frost, have been allowed to go ahead under controlled conditions, the modification of human genes raises ethical difficulties which are needing more time to resolve. There is also the risk of producing new, harmful bacteria that, if released, could cause an uncontrollable epidemic.

genetic fingerprinting   *noun* analysis of the pattern of DNA (unique to an individual) as a means of identifying one individual from another. For example, a tiny sample of blood, saliva, semen or human tissue can provide genetic information. The technique, developed in the late seventies and first publicised in the mid eighties, marks a very significant advance in forensic medicine. It can match evidence found at the scene of a crime with samples taken from suspects, or verify blood relationships in paternity suits: see DNA TEST.

gentrification   *noun* the process by which a working-class or run-down urban area (especially in the inner city) is made middle-class. The term is thought to have been coined by Ruth Glass, a

Marxist urban geographer, in an article published in 1964, but did
not become familiar until c.1973 (the verb **gentrify** is only a little
earlier) at a time when the professional middle classes started to
buy homes in traditionally working-class areas of cities. They
restored and renovated the properties to suit their tastes, and this
in turn led to changes in the character of whole neighbourhoods so
that shops went up-market, for example, and traditional pubs
became bistros or wine bars. Because gentrification was sometimes
thought to be pretentious or cosmetic, the word was initially often
rather a mocking one (the *gentry* are, strictly speaking, people of
high birth), but it has since become more neutral. By extension
gentrified and *gentrification* are now applied to a wide range of
objects and institutions.

ghetto blaster   *noun* a large portable radio, usually with a cassette-
player. The informal name (c.1980) came from the very loud noise
(*blast*) it can make and its original association with American
black youths (*ghetto*). Whereas this last word is often used in the
USA to denote a poor area where black people live, it is little used
in this sense in the UK, with the result that *ghetto blaster* lacks
the racist overtones over here that some people thought it originally had in the USA.

GIFT   (acronym for) **g**amete **i**ntra-**f**allopian **t**ransfer. A *gamete* is a
germ cell that unites with another during fertilisation – that is
both eggs and sperm. In *GIFT*, a technique developed during the
mid eighties, egg cells and sperm from a couple who have been
unable to have children are introduced into one of the woman's fallopian tubes for fertilisation. Because this takes place within the
body, if the technique is successful, the method is thought to be
preferable to TEST-TUBE ones on a number of grounds.

GIGO   (acronym for) garbage in, garbage out. Early computer slang
(mid sixties) for the important principle that what you put into a
system affects the quality of what you get out of it.

giro   *noun* (short for) girocheque used in payments of unemployment and other official support benefits. The 'girocheque' is issued
by Girobank plc, originally set up by the Post Office in 1968, as the
National Girobank, and still used by the Department of Health
and Social Security for the payment of benefits by post. From the
colloquialism *giro* (i.e. payment) (c.1976) comes *on the giro* (i.e. in
receipt of benefit; on the dole). This is not to be confused with *giro*
in the sense of 'system for transferring money within financial
institutions', an arrangement which, for example, allows a bill to
be paid by filling in a giro form authorising one's bank to transfer
funds from one's own account to a payee's, thus avoiding the use of
cheques, postage, etc. This system, which takes its name from the
Italian *giro* ('circulation') is very much older and is independent of
Girobank. Giro, as a social security payment, has given us **giro-
drop** – an accommodation address where false claimants say they
live and to which their giros are delivered, and the misleading
girocracy – the UNDERCLASS that must subsist on giros.

glam rock   *noun* a type of popular music of the seventies in which the performers, usually male, wore extravagantly colourful costumes. Some of the performers claimed to be making a statement about decadence; others were suspected of drawing attention away from the words and music.

glasnost   *noun* a policy of frankness, freedom of information, consultation and public accountability. A long-established Russian word, normally translated as 'openness'. Although it was known to specialist students of Russian politics, most people had not heard of it until Mikhail Gorbachev used it in 1985 in his speech accepting appointment as General Secretary of the Communist Party in what was then the USSR. From then on it was a key word in his attempts at reformation which ended in 1991 with the break-up of the USSR and his own consequent loss of power. It may thus have had its day, though there are some signs that it may have taken root in British political vocabulary in the general sense of 'the Government's duty to give information to the public'.

glass ceiling   *noun* an invisible but impenetrable barrier that prevents (women) achieving promotion. The way ahead seems clear, no apparent barriers exist, but it simply is not possible to progress along it. A concern of feminists (and others) in a POST-FEMINIST age (late eighties).

GLC   (abbreviation for) Greater London Council. Part of the two-tier administration (the other tier was the 32 London Borough Councils) for the local government of London. Formed in 1963, it was abolished in 1986 by the then government, who regarded it as superfluous and wasteful (and politically unsympathetic).

glitch   *noun* a snag, hitch; malfunction. Probably slang or at least informal in these senses, but regarded as Standard English in its earlier, slightly more scientific senses. It originates (c.1962) in the electronics jargon of the US space programme when it meant 'surge of current' (which could cause malfunction). Given that German scientists worked on this programme, the word could be from the German *glitschen* (to slip, glide, slide) or the Yiddish *glitsch* which comes from this and means 'slip' (i.e. loss of footing). The word has a subsequent history in computing ('unexpected electronic interference or malfunction'), astronomy ('change in rotation rate of pulsar'), electrical systems generally ('technical error'), and even motor-racing ('skid', recalling the German). By the eighties it had come to mean any hold-up. Also a *verb*: to malfunction.

glitterati   *noun* fashionable celebrities, originally (and sometimes still) those with literary connections. Although coined in 1956 as a pun on *literati* (the educated, literate élite) and *glitter* (sparkling ornamentation; glamour) in a piece of journalism about a literary gathering, the word did not catch on until the late seventies when it was used of show-business celebrities, who are perhaps specially inclined to flaunt themselves. By the late eighties it had settled down to mean famous people in any field, but it is still not much used outside media language.

glitz, glitzy   *noun* and *adj.* The first is a noun (c.1977) formed from the second (c.1966) which is slang (originally US) for 'flashy, gaudy, superficially dazzling, ostentatiously showy, full of tawdry glitter'. *Glitzy* was originally a show-business word, probably via Yiddish from the German *glitzern* (to glitter), but both words are now used in other contexts while still retaining a pejorative sense of hard-edged, calculating artificiality.

global music *noun* another term for WORLD MUSIC.

global village *noun* the world regarded as a unified community because of modern telecommunications. The implication of this term, first coined by Marshall McLuhan in 1960 and later much discussed, is that the mass media reduces national differences and creates an element of economic and social interdependence, as in a small village or tribe where everyone has access to everything that goes on.

global warming *noun* an increase in average temperature throughout the world as a result of the GREENHOUSE EFFECT. The term was first used in the late seventies and had become well known by the eighties as governments began to understand the potentially catastrophic consequences of even a small permanent increase in world temperatures.

gloom and doom (alternative version of) DOOM AND GLOOM.

glue-sniffing *noun* deliberate inhaling of the fumes of plastic cement and similar substances because of their intoxicating effect. This practice, normally seen as the young adolescent's cheap alternative to drug-taking, was first noticed c.1963 and was widely known by the seventies when it had extended to the inhaling of other substances such as cleaning fluids, aerosols, etc. For this reason it was then given the more general and formal name SOLVENT ABUSE.

gluon *noun* (in particle physics) a hypothetical particle thought to be exchanged between QUARKS so that they bind together, forming particles. From *glue* and *on*, 1971.

GMS (abbreviation for) grant-maintained school. The Education Reform Act 1988 allowed state schools, after prescribed voting procedures and subject to the Secretary of State's consent, to leave the jurisdiction of their Local Education Authority and become self-governing, receiving funds in the form of a grant from central government.

goalposts, shift or move the *phrase* to change the rules, conditions, purpose, etc. of an activity after it has already begun. The implication is of unfair dealing, blatant or surreptitious, in breach of agreed arrangements, the equivalent of trying to cheat in a game of football by narrowing the width of the goal or moving the posts just as an opponent is about to score (c.1986).

gobsmacked *adj.* astounded. Although recorded as a word for 'mouth' as long ago as 1550, *gob* has remained obstinately a slang word except in northern England, where it is dialect. *Gobsmacked* – 'as amazed or speechless as if one had been *smacked* in the *gob*' – did not appear in writing until the mid eighties, though it sounds like a word that should previously have existed in spoken slang, probably in the north; Liverpool has been suggested. Its novelty and directness have appealed to some unexpected users, including at least one prominent and well educated politician wishing to grab the headlines, but it will probably settle down into mainstream slang as a colourful addition to the language. There is also an alternative form, **gobstruck**, and a transitive verb by back formation, to **gobsmack**.

God squad or **godsquad**   *noun* any group of evangelical Christians. Originally US college slang c.1969, it spread rapidly to Britain where it is usually derogatory, sometimes implying ostentatious or intrusive piety.

gofer   *noun* someone who runs errands; a general dogsbody. Originally US and Canadian slang (c.1967), perhaps from the broadcasting business, based on the idea of a junior employee whose job is to run errands or 'go for' cups of coffee for other people. The word may also have been a pun on the existing American *gopher* (a burrowing animal). Sometimes applied more generally to anyone who is at another's beck and call, or senior executives who are obliged to run around for their boss.

go for it   *phrase.* As a general exhortation to make an effort in order to achieve something, it is the American equivalent of the British 'Come on!' The origin is probably US university slang of the seventies, when it seems to have been an exhortation to act crazily, but it has had its present sense since c.1980, after which it became a very popular slogan and catch-phrase in the USA and now the UK.

gold   (short for) GOLD DISC.

gold card   *noun* a credit card issued only to people with high income and entitling them to certain benefits not available to holders of ordinary cards. American Express was the first to offer this preferential treatment (in return for a fee) in the USA in the sixties, but the name *gold card* was not coined until the following decade, the implication of wealth being reflected in the colour. It reached the UK in the early eighties, by which time other credit-card companies had adopted the term. Because of the snob value and prestige attached to it, *gold card* has since been borrowed by companies unconnected with the credit-card business who use it adjectivally to denote services or products represented as being exclusive or superior (or, at least, expensive).

gold disc or **gold**   *noun* a gramophone record that has sold 100,000 as an LP or 400,000 as a single. Or in the USA 500,000 of either. This was originally a US term, and it required sales worth $100,000 for a record to qualify, but later the number of copies sold decided the award.

golden handcuffs, handshake, hello, parachute   *nouns* These are all terms to do with the hiring, firing or retention of executives. The earliest of them was *golden handshake* (1960), a payment to an employee on retirement or dismissal; *handshake* represented farewell, and *golden* carried its familiar sense of 'advantageous'. *Golden handcuffs* (1976) are benefits so great as to make it difficult or unthinkable for a valued employee to go elsewhere, and a *golden hello* (1983) is a bonus offered as an inducement to someone to join a company. The less familiar *golden parachute* (1988) is a guarantee of benefits to a senior executive if he leaves, voluntarily or otherwise, following a takeover.

golden oldie   *noun* anything old, long-established and much liked, especially a song or piece of music, and more especially an old hit record. *Oldie* itself is a nineteenth century colloquialism for 'old person' and a 1940s one for 'old song or film'. The rhyming *golden oldie* was a sixties term, much used by DJs, for an old song or tune that had remained loved (*golden* implying value), but it has since widened its application to include anything that is old and popular and, more facetiously, old people.

Golden Triangle   *noun* an area of SE Asia, comprising parts of China, Thailand, Laos and Burma, where most of the world's raw opium (of which heroin is a derivative) is grown. So called (c.1972) because of its approximately triangular shape and the value of its crop.

gonzo   *adj.* wild, eccentric, bizarre. US slang, coined or else promoted by the writer Hunter Thompson in 1971, and applied particularly to his style of journalism. It is apparently from the Italian *gonzo* (fool, foolish) and was popularised in the name of a character in the puppet series *The Muppets*, but it has not caught on widely in Britain.

goth   *noun* (of rock music) a style between PUNK and HEAVY METAL, with a droning sound and mystical lyrics; a follower or performer of such music, favouring black clothes and stark white and black make-up. A late seventies development from punk, and popular by the mid eighties. The name is from 'gothic' very much in its literary sense of 'characterised by sinister gloom and fondness for the ghoulish', and is reflected in their style of clothing and make-up as well as of the music and lyrics.

graphic novel   *noun* a novel in the form of a comic strip. The term was coined in the publishing business in the early eighties when this sort of format began to lose its cult status and be taken up in more mainstream book-production, for adults as well as teenagers. The subjects are usually fantasy and science fiction.

granny-   *noun.* A *granny-flat* (c.1965) is self-contained accommodation within or built onto a house allowing an elderly parent to live independently but close to his or her family. *Granny-bashing* (slang, c.1975) is the assault on or mugging of elderly persons. *Granny-battering* (c.1975) is systematic violence towards an elderly person within the family. These terms are not restricted to grandmothers or even women, but merely reflect the fact that on the whole more women than men live to a vulnerable old age.

graze   *verb* **1.** to eat snacks throughout the day instead of meals at regular times; **2.** to switch continually from one television channel to another. The first of these is from the idea of animals spending much of their time moving about while eating. Originally US, early eighties, it became a British colloquialism a few years later, perhaps as a result of the infiltration of UK business practices and lifestyles generally by American influences. A variant meaning, 'to steal by eating produce while shopping in a supermarket', remains American, however. With the recent proliferation of TV channels, especially cable in the US, the term is acquiring another meaning: 'to switch from channel to channel in search of something worth watching, normally by means of the remote controller' (see ZAP and CHANNEL SURF). This is again a form of snacking when on the move, of browsing rather than sitting down and making a meal of it.

green *adj.* concerned with conservation of the world's natural resources and the improvement of the environment. Also *noun* a person who is concerned about environmental issues; also *verb* to make (people) aware of ecological issues. All these go back to the use of the German *grün* (green) in the names of German ecological groups in the early seventies; they chose the adjective because of its obvious and traditional associations with nature. These groups, originally offshoots of the sixties anti-nuclear movement, became a strong force in Germany and were the first environmentalists to make a political impact. Because of this it was natural that *green* was adopted as a standard description for the organisations and policies which developed in the seventies in other countries and continue to be important: see GREEN PARTY but also GREENPEACE. The result is that *green* has acquired a new and immediately recognisable meaning when used in such contexts as GREEN REVOLUTION and *green labelling* (late eighties), the labelling and advertising of products by manufacturers in a way intended to persuade the buyer that they do no environmental damage. As stated above, the adoption of *green* by German environmentalists was a key factor in its adoption elsewhere, but the association of green with things natural and unspoilt is longstanding – the *green belts*, for example, around UK cities – while *Greenpeace*, founded in Canada in 1971, had independently adopted the colour into its name, just as it can be found in the title of CA Reich's book, *The Greening of America* (1970), though with a rather wider meaning there, perhaps.

Green Cross Code *noun* a code for children giving rules for crossing roads safely. Issued in 1971 and named from the traditional association of *green* with safety (in traffic lights, etc.).

greenfield *adj.* (of building site) in a rural area not previously built on. The term (1962) usually denotes an area which is near an existing town and not protected by being within the green belt or by having qualities of outstanding natural beauty. Developers normally prefer such sites because there are fewer constraints and costs when there are no existing buildings to work around.

greenhouse effect *noun* the retention of the sun's warmth close to the earth's surface as a result of pollution in the atmosphere. The glass of a greenhouse allows the sun's rays to enter but prevents heated air from escaping. Pollution of the atmosphere has, broadly, the same effect, producing GLOBAL WARMING. The *greenhouse effect* was named in the earlier part of the century but the term began to gain currency only in the sixties; by the eighties it had passed into every day use as a result of growing concern. See GREENHOUSE GAS.

greenhouse gas *noun* any of the gases contributing to the GREEN-HOUSE EFFECT. The main one is carbon dioxide, produced by the burning of fossil fuels (coal, oil, natural gas) and of wood during deforestation. Others include methane and the oxides of nitrogen. The generic term came into use in the eighties as more people began to understand the potentially serious consequences of GLOBAL WARMING as a result of the greenhouse effect.

greening *noun* the process of becoming – or making other people – more aware of environmental issues. See GREEN.

green labelling see GREEN.

greenmail *noun* the practice of purchasing a large number of a company's shares on the open market to threaten a takeover, then selling them back to the company at an increased price so that the company retains control of its business. Mainly confined to the US, from c.1983; in the UK, the scope for such a manoeuvre is limited by regulation. The word is based on *blackmail*; the colour is changed because *green* is US slang for money (from *greenback*, the popular name of the US dollar, derived from the original design which had devices in green ink on the back).

Green Party *noun*. In the UK this is the name, since 1985, of what was founded as the Ecology Party in 1973. More generally, it is a leaderless and decentralised international political movement committed to protection of the environment. In several European countries it has political representation in government: in 1987, for example, it had 44 seats in the German parliament, 13 in the Italian, and 9 MEPs. The UK voting system works to its disadvantage, preventing British Greens' representation in the European Parliament despite their 15% share of the vote. For the history of its name, see GREEN.

Greenpeace *noun* (name of) the international organisation which campaigns for the conservation and protection of the environment. Founded in Canada in 1971, it has a policy of non-violent direct action backed by scientific research, and has successfully drawn public attention to such issues as industrial (especially nuclear) activities that cause pollution, and to the killing of whales and young seals. For its name, see GREEN.

green pound *noun* the exchange rate for the conversion of EC agricultural prices to sterling. The prices are set in **Ecus** and then converted into 'green currencies' for each national currency. The arrangement is an aspect of the CAP. *Green pound* dates from 1974; the adjective is a reference to agriculture and has nothing to do with the uses described at GREEN.

green revolution *noun* the new and worldwide concern with environmental issues. Originally (1970) the term was coined to denote the notable increase in cereal production in developing countries as a result of the application of scientific methods to plant breeding and agricultural production. As a result of other and stronger uses of GREEN in the seventies, this new meaning emerged in the eighties.

grey *adj.* **1.** (of a person) faceless, anonymous (c.1965); **2.** of elderly people. Since the late eighties *grey* has been increasingly used to denote the older section of the community, often those of pensionable age, but sometimes those aged over 55 or so. The growth in this newer usage in part reflects the greater longevity of the population, and the consequent fact that older people now own a larger proportion of the disposable wealth than was once the case – also that redundancies and early retirements have taken many people in their fifties out of the anonymous ranks of the employed and made them members of an active but leisured class (see WOOPIE). This means that this group is being consciously wooed by politicians, marketing and media people and that *grey* is now found in such combinations as the *grey vote*, the *grey market* and *grey power*. **Grey** is also an *intransitive verb* (used of a country): to have an ageing population, i.e. an increasingly large proportion of old people.

grey area   *noun* an aspect (of a situation, matter, etc.) lacking clear definition. For example, rules and regulations may have *grey areas* that are not clearly defined and thus give rise to confusion or debate. This use is fairly recent: the original *grey areas* (c.1963) were, in the vocabulary of town planning, areas that could not be defined as slums (black spots) but were depressed enough to need rebuilding.

grey economy   *noun* commercial activity that does not show up in official statistics. In financial jargon (1980s) this is that part of the economy which functions in the area between the illegal BLACK ECONOMY and that part of the economy which appears in official indicators of decline or growth. For example street traders, who may obtain their goods from farms or warehouses, generate a trade which is not officially recorded in the way the sales in supermarkets and department stores are. The name may be influenced by the earlier GREY MARKET.

grey market   *noun* unscrupulous but not illegal selling of scarce goods at high prices; or (late eighties) trading in a company's shares before they have been officially quoted; or (also late eighties) trading in goods manufactured abroad before their official launch in the UK; or (again late eighties) that section of the market represented by older consumers. The first of the meanings given was originally from the US, c.1946, but not known in the UK until the early fifties. The first two meanings from the late eighties are natural developments from that – reflecting such things as the IBM PC. For the last meaning see GREY.

gridlock   *noun* an immoveable jam in which all traffic is halted; also (by extension) a comparable stoppage in any system or organisation. Also *verb* to lock into a (traffic) jam. Originally US; familiar in UK from late eighties.

grockle   *noun* a holiday maker; summer visitor; tourist. A disparaging slang term, mainly used by the permanent residents in places that attract visitors. The word is thought to have originated in Devonshire in the early sixties, either as a use of a local dialect word or as an invented diminutive of Grock, the name of a well-known clown. What is perhaps a nonce word, *grockling* (doing the tourist round of sight-seeing) has also been reported from 1989 (see *The Longman Register of New Words Vol 2*).

gross *adj.* utterly revolting. US slang since the sixties, both as an adjective and a common exclamation of disgust, and subsequently common in the UK among teenagers. *Gross-out* is usually an adjective ('highly objectionable') but is also found as a noun ('disgusting person or thing') or as a verb (usually *gross out*) meaning 'to make (someone) feel strong distaste for'. It is a later variant of *gross*, from the early seventies, but remains largely American.

grotty *adj.* unpleasant, dirty, ugly (1964). A slang abbreviation of 'grotesque', perhaps originating in Liverpool.

grounded *adj.* prevented from going out in the evenings, or associating with friends and enjoying other privileges. Young people's slang, internationally used, for domestic punishment. The term, which literally means 'kept to or put on the ground', was originally used of pilots who lost their licences or of planes prevented from flying. It was then applied, by natural extension, to disqualified or suspended jockeys and truck-drivers in the USA, from which it was adopted by American teenagers (c.1954) to refer to the punishment of being debarred from using the family car. The modern sense is another natural extension, though it has now lost its original literal connection with the ground.

Group of Seven *noun* the group of the seven leading industrial nations (Canada, France, Germany, Italy, Japan, UK and USA) whose heads of state and finance ministers meet to discuss economic policy. The group evolved from the first industrial summit (1976), and its meetings now consider some political issues as well.

groupie *noun* an unusually devoted fan of a celebrity, especially a pop star. The word is also used, jocularly or dismissively, for any supporter, hanger-on or member of a group associated with an activity or cause. The original *groupies* (c.1967) were girls whose devotion to a pop *group* extended to following it round on tour or having sexual relations with its members.

grunge *noun* a youth movement/fashion characterised by the cultivation of ugliness, dirtiness and cheapness, notably in dress, originating in the USA c.1987. A group of young punk musicians in Seattle is said to have begun the trend by affecting a look that made them look ill and ugly. It spread rapidly, reaching the UK by 1992. The style depends on ill-matched old clothes (or new clothes designed to look old), bizarre innovations such as socks worn as hats, unwashed hair, and greasy, unhealthy-looking makeup. Another aspect of the fashion is a type of music combining vacuous lyrics with loud, heavy and chaotic sounds. The word was originally US slang, c.1965, for a person or thing that is dirty or odious. Like the corresponding adjective *grungy*, it seems to be an arbitrary formation based on 'grubby' and 'dingy'. There may be a link with GUNGE and *gungy*, though these are originally British English. Recently *grunge* and *grungy* have been applied more loosely to merely unfashionable and ultra-casual clothing.

GSM (abbreviation for) Global System for Mobile Communications. A digital version of CELLULAR technology, intended for virtually the whole of Europe (there were 17 signatories to the 1987 GSM treaty), and allowing mobile phones to function across the continent.

GUI (abbreviation for) graphic user interface. A method of using a computer by manipulating ICONS (hence *graphic*) on the VDU instead of typing commands. The method was developed in the early eighties and became generally known c.1985 when Apple Macintosh machines made an impact on the UK computer market.

gulag *noun* forced-labour camp in the former USSR. Strictly speaking, the word denotes the department of the KGB (former Soviet secret service and secret police) responsible for such prisons. It is an acronym formed from Russian words meaning 'Main Administration for Corrective Labour Camps', and first came to prominence in the western world with the publication of Solzhenitsyn's *The Gulag Archipelago* (1974–8).

gunge *noun* any sticky, messy, thick or clogging substance. Also **gungy** *adj.*, nasty, messy, slimy. British slang from the sixties. The origin is uncertain, but is perhaps related to 'goo' and 'gunk'. This latter is slang (late forties) for any viscous substance; the word was originally a proprietary name for a brand of detergent solvent.

gut *adj.* (of question, issue, etc.) basic, fundamental; (of reaction, feeling, etc.) instinctive, emotional rather than rational. From the idea of 'guts' (intestines) being a vital part of the workings of the human body and hence of our emotions (1960s). See GUTTED.

gutted *adj.* very disappointed or upset. The word is Standard English when applied to fish ('eviscerated') and to houses which have had the interior but not the exterior destroyed by fire or demolition. It is slang in this new meaning, which implies loss of guts (in the sense of 'motivation, willpower') as a result of something that has happened, though it also suggests the sensation of a blow in the guts. It emerged during the eighties, probably from earlier underworld slang.

H (abbreviation for) heroin or HORSE.

hacker, hack, hacking *nouns*; also *verb* to **hack** or **hack into**. In the computer slang of the 1970s, a *hacker* was no more than a computer fanatic, and *hacking* was the exploration of the computer's potential. The words appear to be from 1950s' US slang in which to *hack* is to cope with, manage, accomplish, etc. (*I can hack it* = I can manage). However, some *hackers* (or *hacks*) extended their enthusiasm to penetrating major computer networks, such as those of government departments and banks; their activities, intended in most cases to be tests of ingenuity, nevertheless were unauthorised, breached confidentiality and were occasionally criminal. In the eighties (by which time these activities had become something of an epidemic and were costing large sums of money to counteract) *hacking* had become synonymous in the public mind with gaining access to other people's computer systems improperly, mischievously or criminally. This is now the predominant sense of *hacking, hacker*, etc., though the words are still used with their original benign meanings among computer enthusiasts.

hackette   *noun* a female journalist. A *hack* is a literary drudge. The suffix *-ette* is used to form the feminine, though it is also used to mean 'small' (*kitchenette*) and 'imitation' (*leatherette*). The result is that *hackette*, coined by the satirical magazine *Private Eye* in the early eighties, is jocularly patronising, though it is not much used outside the slang of journalism, and when used by a fellow journalist is capable of suggesting a half-rueful fellow feeling, as is also the case with *hack* itself.

hack pack   *noun* a group of journalists (1990). Modelled on BRATPACK, the term is mainly confined to use among media people. *Hack* is an old word for a literary drudge, but is used among journalists as quite a friendly term.

hair gel   see GEL.

hairy   *adj.* dangerous, exciting. An abbreviation of 'hair-raising', c.1962.

handbag   *verb* (of women) to deliver a verbal tirade intended to stun an opponent. In the very popular television series *The Muppet Show* (1976–80), in which the puppet-characters were based on animals, the leading lady was Miss Piggy who, though normally coy, genteel and glamorous, was prone to lose her composure and fell with her handbag anyone who offended her. It is possible that this image influenced the emergence (c.1982) of **handbagging** to denote Mrs Thatcher's habitually strident response to those who crossed her. The term remained in use throughout the eighties, but there seems to have been little occasion to employ it since Mrs Thatcher's departure from active politics.

hands-off   *adj.* not involving oneself in close supervision or control. After HANDS-ON became popular in the seventies, *hands-off* followed naturally as its antithesis. It specially appealed to business, as a useful term to describe a style of management, and to governments during the eighties when the free play of market forces was thought to be incompatible with government intervention in the operation of industry, etc.

hands-on   *adj.* having practical experience or involvement. Originally (c.1969) a term in computer vocabulary to describe direct participation in using computers (notably by manipulating the keyboard) as distinct from merely having a theoretical understanding. The term was rapidly adopted for more general application and is no longer restricted to activity requiring actual use of the hands (e.g. 'a hands-on management style').

hang-glider   *noun* a glider consisting of a broad wing and a light framework from which the pilot hangs in a harness controlling the flight with a horizontal bar; *also* somebody who flies such a machine. The term *hang-glider* was occasionally used in specialist literature earlier this century, but was not generally known until the sport of **hang-gliding** (1971) became popular in the early seventies. The verb, to *hang-glide*, has been in use since the mid eighties.

hang in (there)

hang in (there)   *verb* to persist against difficulties; to stay with it. Colloquial, originally US, from c.1969.

hang out, let it all   *phrase* be uninhibited or relaxed, be candidly honest or truthful. Originally Afro-American slang (c.1970).

hang-up   *noun* a problem, inhibition, fixation or preoccupation, usually emotional or psychological. *Hang-up* in the sense of 'delay' or 'frustration' appears among Canadian jazz aficionados from the late fifties. Presumably the sense of 'frustration' led to the current one of psychological difficulty, which was well established by the late sixties and popularised by HIPPIE jargon. It remains colloquial.

happening   *adj.* fashionable, trendy, where it's at. Whereas a *happening* (*noun*) is normally 'something that happens', it became a vogue word during the SWINGING SIXTIES for 'something that is made to happen', usually an improvised or spontaneous performance with unpredictable or outlandish elements, often involving the audience. More recently (late seventies in the USA, mid eighties in Britain) *happening* has emerged as a teenage slang adjective meaning 'fashionable', 'up-to-the-minute', presumably as a shortening of the HIPPIE expression 'It's all happening' (i.e. 'This is exhilarating').

happy-clappy   *adj.* (of religious observance) characterised by overt demonstrations of joy. The modern evangelical movement is sometimes given this epithet because its adherents (also called *happy-clappies*) enjoy informality, audience participation (hand-shaking, hugging, etc.), gospel-music (with swaying and arm-waving) and other ways of sharing their feelings. *Clappy* refers to their custom of clapping in time to the music or to show appreciation. The whole expression is used dismissively by traditionalists who prefer more formal observances.

happy hour   *noun* a period, usually in the early evening, when some pubs or bars sell drinks at reduced prices. A marketing ploy, originally US from c.1960.

hard   *adj.* In US air-force terminology since c.1958, *hard* has been used of military installations to mean 'able to withstand nuclear attack'. It refers to the great strength of the necessary fortification. When applied to drugs (e.g. heroin, morphine, cocaine) *hard* has meant 'highly addictive' since c.1955. Perhaps this use comes from 'hard (i.e. strong) liquor'. *Hard* is also short for HARD-CORE.

hard ball, play   *phrase* to behave in a tough, uncompromising way. US slang, mainly political and business, since c.1973. Playing with a hard ball, as in baseball, is obviously thought to require more resilience than playing softball.

hard copy   *noun* computer output printed on paper. As distinct from output displayed on a screen or machine-readable output held on tape or disc (1964).

hard-core   *adj.* (of pornography) depicting sexual acts or perversions in explicit form, often with violence; (of person) belonging to an irredeemable minority of uncompromising and stubborn adherents to a belief, activity, etc. The primary meaning of *core* is 'central casing of a pulpy fruit, such as an apple or pear, containing the seeds'; it is usually dry and horny, unsuitable for eating. These properties gave rise to such figurative applications as 'the hard core of unemployed people', i.e. those who, despite all efforts, cannot be found work, just as the core of a fruit cannot be put to use. The adjectival *hard-core* emerged from this sort of use in the fifties, and retains the idea of 'impossible to come to terms with'. See below.

hardcore *noun* a style of US rock music that developed out of PUNK in the 1980s and became a popular feature of the RAVE phenomenon. It is aggressively delivered, almost tuneless, and played at high speed. Its name relates to the above senses of HARD-CORE.

hard disk *noun* (in computing) a magnetic storage disk in a sealed unit. Introduced c.1978, this is now common. It is more robust than the FLOPPY DISK, can hold more material, and can retrieve it more quickly. The name comes from the rigid platter which is the storage medium.

hard edge *noun* a type of abstract art with geometrical shapes having sharp outlines. The style, which was distinctive in its lack of personal, emotive content, emerged during the fifties and was named c.1961.

hard landing *noun* a painful solution or ending of a problem. Largely confined to the language of economics, where it indicates a bust following a boom, and is probably borrowed from the earlier (c.1961) language of US aeronautics where it refers euphemistically to an uncontrolled landing by a spacecraft in which the vehicle is damaged or destroyed on impact. See SOFT LANDING.

hard line *noun* an uncompromising policy or course of action. Also *adjective* **hard-line** and *noun* **hard-liner**. *Line* has long meant 'course or method of action or behaviour' but these couplings with *hard* ('unyielding') date only from the early sixties.

hard rock *noun* ROCK music with a simple, pounding rhythm and high volume. Popular in the second half of the sixties. The name represents one of the earliest attempts to distinguish one ROCK style from another. Presumably *hard* related to the harshness of the sound.

hardware *noun* the physical equipment making up a computer system, as distinct from SOFTWARE; *also* heavy military equipment. The first is one of the earliest (c.1947) and most durable examples of computerese; though it has been commonplace in the UK only since c.1960. The second (1950s) now usually refers to tanks and missiles, though *hardware* has been used of smaller weapons since the nineteenth century. Both are slightly jocular extensions of the familiar meaning, 'ironmongery'. In military parlance humans are the *software* manning the *hardware*.

hard-wired *adj.* (of computer) having permanently connected circuits to perform a specific function (rather than using separate software for that purpose) (1969).

Hare Krishna *noun* a sect devoted to a form of Hinduism; a follower of this sect. Officially, the sect was founded in 1966 as the International Society for Krishna Consciousness, dedicated to the

Hindu deity Krishna. *Hare Krishna* (Hindi for 'O Lord Krishna') are actually the opening words of a mantra chanted daily by believers as part of their ritual. The use of these words as the name of the cult and its adherents is therefore informal. The followers practise vegetarianism, avoid gambling, intoxicants, and sex outside marriage, wear yellow robes, study the Hindu scriptures, and are often seen in public soliciting funds. They became known in Britain in the late sixties.

hash *noun* (colloquial abbreviation of) hashish (1959).

hatchback *noun* a car with upward-opening rear door which forms the rear end of the car and gives access to the storage-space. The term, first used in North American automobile language in 1970, was originally coined to refer to the door itself, and is still used in that sense, but rapidly came to be applied to the whole car as the style became popular during the following decades, largely supplementing the protruding lidded boot. The word was formed by adding *back* (the rear of the car) to *hatch* in its familiar sense of 'trapdoor'. *Hatch* was already much used in nautical and aeronautical vocabulary.

have-a-go *adj.* taking a personal risk by intervening to prevent a crime. The Assistant Commissioner at Scotland Yard who, in 1964, advised members of the general public to 'have a go' (step in) if they saw a crime being committed caused something of an outcry at the time. The police no longer give such advice, but the adjectival use of the Assistant Commissioner's phrase still continues, though mainly confined to newspaper reports about *have-a-go heroes*. The phrase previously existed, and still does, as a common colloquialism for 'make an attempt or effort', and was additionally known as the title of a popular radio quiz during the forties and fifties.

hawk *noun* a person in favour of war, warlike policies or aggressive attitudes in the conduct of disputes. Also *adjective* **hawkish**. As a bird of prey, the hawk has a long history in metaphor. 'War hawk' was coined by Thomas Jefferson in 1798, but for the modern antithesis between 'hawks' and 'doves' in the political sense, see DOVE.

HCFCs *noun* (short for) hydrochlorofluorocarbons. Following the discovery of the Antarctic ozone hole in 1985, the chemical industry was alarmed by evidence of its own responsibility as a result of its use of CFCs in coolants in refrigerators, air conditioning equipment, etc. The industry therefore switched to *HCFCs* as being kinder to the OZONE LAYER, though there is evidence that they are powerful agents of GLOBAL WARMING.

headbanger *noun* **1.** a stupid person or (politically) an extremist; **2.** a fan of HEAVY METAL rock music; a devotee of **headbanging** (dancing). It is not known whether these two slang meanings have a common source. The first emerged in the seventies as a term of abuse, mainly among the young, and passed rapidly into the vocabulary of political abuse as a word for an extremist. The origin may be a general idea that people who behave idiotically have damaged their brains by banging their heads against walls, or a more specific observation that mentally disturbed children and adults often rock rhythmically or bang their heads. The second meaning also emerged during the seventies; it may well be related to the first (which was in spoken use before it became more general in the seventies) or it may be an entirely separate coinage based on the fans' violent head-shaking to the beat of the music – a fashion of dancing that raised anxieties in medical circles in the late seventies. This dancing is called *headbanging*, and that term is sometimes extended to apply to 'listening to HEAVY METAL'.

head-case *noun* a crazy person. Eighties slang, perhaps earlier in the USA. Either a variant of NUT-CASE or a reference to the crazy behaviour of a *head* (old slang for 'drug-addict').

headhunt *verb* to recruit an executive, expert or specially able employee from another company. Also *noun* **headhunter**, the agent who does this. The word is now used (without any implication of poaching from a rival company) to denote the recruitment of any skilled person, usually by a direct approach rather than as the result of public advertisement of a vacancy. Neither the word nor the practice was much known in the UK before the eighties; in the USA the word goes back to the sixties and the practice even further. The word itself reflects the distaste which the practice initially aroused: the original headhunters were members of uncivilised tribes who went out in search of heads to cut off as trophies.

head up *verb* to be at the head of, to head. This example of the American practice of creating a phrasal verb (verb + preposition or adverb or both) when the verb is capable of doing its job without embellishment dates from the late fifties and, inevitably, entered British English c.1970 via business jargon.

head-up display *noun* the projection of instrument readings onto the windscreen of an aircraft or car. The term (1960) comes from the idea that the pilot or driver can read the display with his or her *head up*, still able to see through the windscreen and not having to lower the head in order to read the instruments.

heavy *adj.* intense, impressive, serious. All-purpose HIPPIE slang of the late sixties and early seventies: a wide range of meanings is possible for this word, often expressing approbation of youth music or life-styles and deriving from a standard meaning of the word, 'weighty and important'. In other contexts, e.g. describing police or parental reactions, the meaning shades to 'over-serious and oppressive'.

heavy metal *noun* a type of rock music characterised by loudness, harsh sound, and strong repetitive rhythms. The style emerged in the mid seventies as a development of HARD ROCK and by the eighties had established itself as an important element in mainstream rock. The name (c.1973) is not easily explained. *Heavy* may refer to the heavy beat or to the hippie HEAVY (see above); *metal* may be from the music's metallic sound or the metal decorations of the leather gear worn by performers and followers. There is also evidence that *heavy metal* existed as a colloquial term for a

Hell's Angels

motor-cycle in the 1960s slang of the BIKER, and indicates links between biker culture and that of heavy metal music.

Hell's Angels *noun* a (lawless) motorcycle gang originating in California in the 1950s. The name was later adopted by similar gangs in the UK and elsewhere. They wore denims, leather jackets and Nazi-style insignia, their symbol being a winged skull. Often tattooed and sometimes prone to violence, they caused much public anxiety during the sixties and early seventies. Their name seems to have been taken from the title of a film (1930) about air warfare in the First World War.

helpline *noun* a telephone service offering information. The earliest *helplines* were run by charitable organisations for the benefit of people in distress. The term surfaced c.1980, though the actual services often existed before that. The word was later adopted by commercial organisations providing information about their products. It was probably formed on the model of HOTLINE.

heritage industry *noun* the commercial exploitation of historic buildings or sites, natural beauty-spots, industrial archaeology, old customs or working practices, etc. While some argue that this sort of activity preserves and popularises evidence of the country's history, others claim that it cheapens and distorts it, reducing everything to the level of a tourist attraction or a theme park. As a result of this latter opinion *heritage industry* (1980s) is generally taken to be a rather dismissive term, and *heritage* itself is now often understood to mean less 'that which is inherited' than 'that which is inherited and can be packaged and sold' (as in *heritage centre*, formerly 'museum of local history').

herstory *noun* history with an emphasis on the part played by women or an interpretation from the woman's point of view. A feminist pun (US, early seventies) on *history*, as though that meant *his story*, thereby emphasising the point that all too often history has been told from a male point of view. The term is not much used outside feminist writing and, occasionally, more general journalism.

heterosexism *noun* discrimination in favour of heterosexuality. Formed c.1979 on the pattern of SEXISM, this usually implies discrimination against homosexuality, though it is also used by feminists to denote the belief or assumption that the only proper role for women is domesticity within conventional marriage. The noun and adjective **heterosexist** came into use at the same time.

heuristic *adj.* (of a computer) searching through a number of possible solutions and selecting the apparent best before moving on to the next stage of the program. Similar to problem-solving by trial and error. The word is long-established (for example, in education a *heuristic approach* involves discovery methods and pupils learning through the exploration of problems rather than by direct instruction), but it was not applied to computing until about 1960.

hidden agenda *noun* an ulterior motive or secret intention. Although now mainly used in political contexts, this term appears to have originated in the jargon of business management-training in the mid seventies: the agenda of a meeting or negotiations is the official, written statement of issues to be discussed; the *hidden agenda* is the psychology of personal relations, emotions or motives in those taking part, but the term is sometimes used nowadays to indicate a secret intent.

high, on a *phrase* in a state of altered consciousness, usually euphoric or excited. The phrase (c.1953) was initially used of the influence of drugs or drink. As an adjective, *high (on)* (meaning 'under the influence (of)') was used of drugs twenty years earlier: in the senses of 'elated' and 'drunk', *high* is centuries old.

high-fibre *adj.* (of food) containing a high proportion of DIETARY FIBRE (1970s).

high five *noun* a congratulatory or celebratory gesture made by two people slapping the palms of their right hands together high over the head. A member of an American university basketball team claims to have coined the term – the *five* being the thumb and fingers – after the gesture was first used by his team during 1979–80, though a palm-slapping ritual, of one hand then the other, at waist height, seems to have existed earlier among US Blacks as a greeting or expression of satisfaction. The high gesture became popular in British sport in the eighties.

high ground *noun* a position of (usually moral) superiority in a controversy, debate, etc., especially when that position is likely to win the approval of the general public. The term is not new, but this metaphorical application dates only from the eighties and has become specially popular in political language. It derives from military terminology; the occupation of high ground provides conspicuous military advantages.

high-level *adj.* (of computer programming language) largely independent of any particular kind of computer, and easy to understand because it is closer to human language or mathematical symbolism than to machine language. Computerese since the early 1960s. An example is BASIC.

highlighter *noun* a marker pen enabling the user to overlay part of a document with a transparent colour, leaving the words underneath still legible but emphasised. From the standard meaning of the verb *highlight*, 'to bring notice or emphasis to'. *Highlighter* has been, since c.1986, the normal spelling of what was originally 'Hi-liter', a US proprietary name registered in 1964.

high profile *noun* a position of deliberately sought prominence or publicity. Also *adjective*, **high-profile** (1970s). See LOW PROFILE.

high-tech *adj.* (short for) **high technology**: using or including sophisticated and up-to-date equipment, usually electronic, in a factory, office or home, etc. *High-tech* came into use in the early seventies and was a vogue term in the eighties, though it was sometimes used where styling and presentation gave an air of modernity rather than where there was genuine technological innovation. It has generated an antithetical term, LOW-TECH, meaning with little or no technological sophistication. **High-tech** is also a *noun*, denoting technological innovation and its associated gadgetry. It is also used of a style of decor, popular in the seventies, based on a bare and functional appearance suggestive of the technological environment.

hip-hop *noun* a form of popular music consisting of RAP accompanied by a heavy beat, often electronically produced, and jerky dancing like BREAK-DANCING; *also* the youth and street culture surrounding this music and dancing, including the production of graffiti. Popular in the UK since about 1986. In New York, where it originated among young Blacks and Hispanics in the late seventies, it also incorporated particular forms of dress, speech and street culture. Its name combines two old slang words, meaning 'stylish' and 'dance' respectively.

hippie, hippy *noun* a person, usually young, whose behaviour, dress, values and general way of life represents a rejection of conventional society. The word was first coined in the early fifties, when it meant the same as BEATNIK; it is an abbreviation of earlier US slang *hipster*, someone who is *hip*, or, earlier still, *hep* i.e. well-informed, up-to-date, following the latest fashions in music, ideas, dress, etc. In the USA from the mid sixties, and in the UK from c.1967, it was applied to a follower of the youth movement that, originating in San Francisco, spread rapidly throughout America and Europe. The *hippies* favoured an unstructured and sometime peripatetic lifestyle, which in its fullest form often included living communally, advocating free love, taking drugs, wearing colourful and eccentric clothes (characteristically with beads) and preaching a mixture of anarchy, pacifism, oriental mysticism, environmentalism and the rejection of materialism. The term had a new lease of life in the eighties to denote a young DROP-OUT, often unemployed, destitute or homeless, who travelled round the country in old vehicles, sometimes in groups. These came to public notice by wishing to congregate at Stonehenge and at other sites and events in a way that was thought to be a nuisance.

hipsters *noun* trousers worn from the hips rather than the waist (c.1962). Also **hipster**, a skirt worn from the hips.

hi-tech (variant of) HIGH-TECH.

HIV (abbreviation for) human immunodeficiency virus. This virus, isolated by the French in 1983 and officially named three years later, breaks down the body's immune system and can lead to AIDS. The name is often found in the tautological form *HIV-virus* and in *HIV-positive*, which means 'having had a positive result in a test to determine whether one is infected with HIV' or, more loosely, 'liable to develop Aids'. *HIV* is sometimes colloquially known as *the Aids-virus*.

HM (abbreviation for) HEAVY METAL.

hold, on *phrase* delayed, postponed, awaiting action. The hold facility on a telephone enables a caller to be kept connected, but unable to communicate, while the operator (or person called) deals with the caller's request for information, connection to another person, etc. The caller is said to be *on hold*, an expression that dates from the sixties. By the seventies the meaning of *on hold* had been extended to mean 'awaiting action' in numerous non-telephonic contexts.

Holocaust   *noun* the mass murder of European Jews by Nazis during the Second World War. For some centuries the word has been used to mean 'large-scale massacre, especially as a result of destruction by fire'; it originally meant 'sacrifice by fire', from a Greek word meaning 'wholly burnt'. The word was used in its standard sense of 'great destruction of life' in contemporary accounts of the Nazi atrocities in the early forties; it was given a capital H, as a sign of respect, by historians and other writers during the fifties, and has more recently become the generally recognised term for this specific slaughter.

home banking   *noun* a system permitting a bank's clients to use a HOME COMPUTER with a modem to have access to their accounts and carry out routine transactions such as the paying of bills (1980s).

homeboy   *noun* a close friend; person from one's own gang or group. Starting life as US Black slang for 'person from one's own town' in the sixties, if not before, this spread to street culture as 'person from one's gang or peer group' and crossed to the UK in the mid eighties as part of the language of RAP and HIP-HOP culture. It is still slang, chiefly among the young, and has also given rise to *homegirl*, and such shortenings as *home* and *homie*. Home-boy, however, is an earlier term for someone who liked to stay at home and, in Canada, a boy brought up in a 'home' (orphanage).

home computer   *noun* a computer designed for use in the home (1976). Now more usually known as a PERSONAL COMPUTER or PC.

homophile   *(adj. and noun)* homosexual. Originally (c.1960) rare, from the Greek *homos* (same) + *philos* (loving), but increasingly preferred to *homosexual* because it shifts attention away from that word's explicit or even exclusive emphasis on sexuality. Thus it has come to mean 'belonging to a particular social group' rather than 'sexually abnormal'.

homophobia   *noun* hatred or fear of homosexuals or homosexuality. Although it had existed earlier as a little-used word, (meaning 'fear of men') *homophobia* was not used in the now familiar sense until the late sixties when the GAY liberation movement adopted it as defining the prejudice they sought to publicise and oppose. The implication is that the word combines 'homosexual' and 'phobia', though when it was originally coined in the earlier part of the century to mean 'fear or dislike of men' the prefix *homo-* meant 'man', not 'same' as it does in 'homosexual'. Also **homophobe** *noun* one who hates homosexuals and *adj.* **homophobic**.

honcho   *noun* the person in charge; also *verb* to be in charge of. An approximation to a Japanese word, meaning 'leader of a group', which was picked up by US air force personnel based in Japan during the occupation and the Korean War. It has been US slang since the fifties though now more familiar in business rather than military circles, but it has not really caught on in Britain.

honky   *noun* a white man. Derogatory slang used by US Blacks since c.1955, often to imply prejudice and separateness on the part of whites. It is probably a variant of the much older US slang *hunk*, a contemptuous term for an immigrant from east-central Europe. This word may be from the first syllable of 'Hungarian'.

Hooray Henry *noun* a foolish or ineffectual upper-class young man, often idle, affected, loudly hearty or arrogant, who enjoys a social life with others of the same type. (Sometimes shortened to **Hooray** or **hooray**). Although this term became generally known only in the late seventies in connection with SLOANE RANGER vocabulary, it is recorded in print as early as 1959 and may have existed in spoken slang before then. 'Hurrah' occurs in several old slang or colloquial expressions in the sense of 'uproarious' (i.e. prone to shout 'hurrah', perhaps for no good reason); *hurrah boys*, for example, is a 1920s term for college students. The semi-rhyming *Henry* was presumably added as a common upper-class name. *Hooray* is occasionally found as an adjective ('He lacks the Hooray bumptiousness of the Duchess's older male friends').

horse *noun* heroin. Slang, originally US, c.1950 and becoming familiar in the UK in the sixties. The name of heroin, originally a German trademark (1898), is thought to have been based on the Greek *heros* ('hero') because the drug has the effect of making the user feel heroic. *Horse* may be a distortion of *heros* or randomly chosen cant.

hospice *noun* a nursing home given over to the care of the dying and terminally ill. *Hospice* has a long history, coming into English from the French at the beginning of the nineteenth century to designate a lodging for pilgrims and other travellers run by a religious order. By the end of the nineteenth century its use had been extended to cover houses for the destitute, usually run by such orders, including some devoted to the terminally ill. It was not until the beginning of the modern **hospice movement** in the late seventies that *hospice* came to be the accepted word among the general public for a home devoted to the nursing of the dying.

hostile *adj.* (of merger attempt or takeover bid) without the consent of, or resisted by, the company which is the target of the merger or takeover; contested. A US financial term since the mid seventies, and since used in the UK. For the defences against hostile bids see PAC-MAN and POISON PILL.

hot button *noun* a crucial issue, usually political or social, that is likely to influence people's choice (e.g. in voting or buying). This is the button that the politician or marketing man must first identify and then press in each individual if he is to win their vote or loyalty or dollars. The figure of speech probably developed from the idea of pressing a starter button or panic button, though there are other expressions (e.g. 'ring a bell') which have to do with eliciting a response by using a triggering mechanism. *Hot* is used in its familiar sense of 'urgent' (as in HOTLINE), 'current' (as in 'hot from the press') and 'intense' ('hot argument'). The whole expression was originally a US marketing term of the late seventies: it meant a consumer need that required a market response. It became more familiar when it passed into political vocabulary, but it has not yet caught on in the UK to any great extent.

hothousing *noun* the intensive teaching of young children to achieve high levels of intelligence and attainment. There is nothing new in the figurative use of 'hothouse', or sometimes 'hotbed', to mean a place in which the conditions are ideal to make a certain activity flourish as plants do in a greenhouse. What is new about *hothousing* is that it is directed at small children, even babies, individually within their own homes by bombarding them with stimuli (often depriving them of recreation) which they may not understand. The practice became fashionable in the USA during the late seventies and the eighties.

hotline *noun* a direct telephone line for urgent or exclusive use. Originally US military jargon (*hot* having a sense of 'urgent', or 'filled with intense activity') but popularly known from the establishment of a direct communications link between Washington and Moscow in 1963 for use in times of crisis. The agreement for this, made between Kennedy and Kruschev, was seen as an important improvement in relations between the USA and USSR during the COLD WAR. The less specific modern meaning comes from this use, and a natural process of weakening has meant that *hotline* may be used for nothing more urgent that direct ordering of goods by telephone.

hot pants *noun* very short, usually tight, shorts worn by women (1970).

house or **House (music)** *noun* a popular development of DISCO music with a heavy electronic element, fast beat, simplified vocal content and, often, sampling of sound effects or other recordings edited in. A development of FUNK, intended for dancing, and therefore with emphasis on synthesised sound and repetitive rhythm. It originated (1985) at the Warehouse Club, Chicago, from which it takes its name. It came to Britain in the late eighties, becoming widely known from its use at ACID HOUSE parties, and remained popular into the nineties while spawning many sub-forms. See also SAMPLING and WAREHOUSE PARTY.

house church *noun* a religious group, usually Christian, that meets for worship, study, etc. in members' houses rather than within the normal ecclesiastical structures. The term is first recorded in 1964 – like many institutions the Church experienced change and experimentation during the sixties – but the practice of house-meetings goes back to New Testament times.

househusband *noun* a married man (or male partner) who runs a household. Such reversal of traditional roles often takes place if a man is unemployed but his wife is not, or if his wife has a more demanding job which places on him the responsibility for shopping, cooking, child care, etc. The word, derived from 'housewife', was coined in the mid fifties in the USA, though it did not become familiar until the seventies.

HRT (abbreviation for) hormone replacement therapy. This technique, a form of oestrogen treatment used to control unpleasant menopausal symptoms, and particularly the threat of brittle bone disease, became available in the late sixties and is now so well established that it is normally known by its initials.

human resources *noun* people viewed as an asset or as contributors to an organisation, society etc., as distinct from material resources (1961).

human shield *noun* people, usually unarmed, used as a defence to discourage armed attack. The best-known appearances of this expression were in 1990 when the Iraqi government commenced its forcible deployment of Western citizens in military and other installations that were expected to become targets in the imminent Gulf War. The expression had been coined some ten years earlier, but did not become established until this event.

hunk *noun* a sexually attractive, probably beefy, young man, a male pin-up. Earlier Australian slang has *hunk* as 'big man' from the idea of a hunk (large piece) of beef, but the sexual connotations do not seem to have attached themselves until the seventies. The word remains informal. Also the adjective **hunky**.

hydrofoil *noun* a light vessel with hull on ski-like strips of metal to raise it out of the water and permit fast speed. This definition has been familiar since 1959, though the word was coined in the earlier part of the century to denote one of the floats or fins used on seaplanes or submarines. *Hydro-* means 'having to do with water' and a foil is a thin metal strip.

hype *noun* exaggerated publicity or marketing; also *verb*, (sometimes **hype up**) to promote a thing or person in this way. The implication is always that such publicity is organised, and frequently that it is bogus if not dishonest. Indeed, the word meant 'swindle' in US slang long before it came to the UK in the sixties, and one of the earliest and most prominent British uses relates to 'hyping' a pop record by buying up a large number of copies in order to boost its position in the CHARTS. This activity probably accounts for the shift in meaning from 'confidence trick' to 'publicity stunt', though as the word has become increasingly popular the sense of dishonesty has diminished. *Hype* is still regarded with suspicion, however. The origin of the word is unknown: attempts to link it with 'hyperbole' and 'hypodermic' appear to be guesswork because its meaning originally had nothing to do with either.

hypermarket *noun* a very large self-service store, usually on the outskirts of a town. Whereas a supermarket usually deals primarily in food, a *hypermarket* deals additionally in household goods, furniture and clothes. The English word dates from 1970 as a direct translation of the earlier French *hypermarché*.

hypermedia *noun* (in computing) a method of structuring information from more than one machine (e.g. characters, images, sound) so that related items are linked and accessible together (1980s).

hypertext *noun* (in computing) a system of storage whereby documents, graphics and sound are linked, allowing the user to move easily between related items (1980s).

ice *noun* a form of the illegal drug methamphetamine (SPEED). The slang name comes from the drug's translucent, crystalline appearance and became known in the USA in 1989, having spread from

Hawaii. The drug is smoked and is powerful and highly addictive, with unpredictable effects.

icon   *noun* (in computing) a small pictorial symbol that appears on a screen to represent an available function or option. The required facility can then be activated by means of a screen cursor or MOUSE. The system is quicker than tapping instructions on a key board and considered more USER-FRIENDLY. *Icon*, an old word for 'image' or 'representation', has been used in this specialised sense since about 1982.

identikit   *adj.* artificially created by imitating various aspects of an original or like many others of the same type. Applied to people and things, and always implying lack of genuineness. The original *identikit* (*noun*) was a *kit* of transparencies showing drawings of typical facial characteristics; a composite picture of the face of a police suspect could be built up by superimposing some of these on top of each other according to the descriptions of eye-witnesses. The system, first used in the UK in 1961 and borrowed from the USA, where it was introduced in 1959, has now been largely superseded by PHOTOFIT.

immuno-   A combining form of 'immune', 'immunity' and related words in numerous medical terms invented since the late 1950s. Probably the best known is *immunodeficiency* (reduction in the normal immune defences of the body), from the vocabulary of AIDS and HIV.

impro   *noun* a form of entertainment based on improvisation. As a training and rehearsal technique, improvisation – and its abbreviation *impro* – have been known to actors for some time. The new use of the term became known in the late eighties when some stand-up comedians developed a style of performances in which they invited members of their audience to suggest characters, situations, etc. which the performers then used as the basis of an *impro*. Similarly, some experimental or FRINGE theatre groups invited audiences to determine how a story or situation should develop.

in   *adj.* fashionable. A very popular sixties usage, also found in numerous *in-* coinages such as *in-crowd* (fashionable people). Now rather dated, though certain terms persist, e.g. the 'in thing' is 'the fashionable thing (to do, wear, etc.)'.

-in   *Sit-in* goes back to the 1930s as an American term for a form of civil disobedience or sit-down strike in which people simply sit down and refuse to move as a form of protest. The method was much used in the early sixties when there were widespread protests against the racial segregation of Black people in America. Refinements of the method led to developments of the word: Blacks arranged 'swim-ins' and 'drive-ins' at segregated beaches and hotels respectively, and 'kneel-ins' or 'pray-ins' at white churches, to name only four of the numerous coinages. Hippies later adopted the vocabulary for their 'love-ins' and 'kiss-ins'. The craze died down after the early seventies and only TEACH-IN, with a changed meaning, and the original *sit-in* now survive in common usage.

inclusive language *noun* a non-sexist use of words where the phrasing consciously includes women as well as men in contexts where this was not previously so. *Inclusive* here has a new special sense of 'explicitly including women as well as men'. Feminists have long objected to the grammatical convention of using 'he', 'him' and 'his' in cases where the clumsier 'he or she', etc., would be more accurate. Similar objections have been raised to the traditional use of 'man' or words ending in '-man' to signify 'person' (as in 'every man to his trade'). In an attempt to meet these and many other objections inclusive language has been promoted in the US since the late seventies and in the UK since the mid eighties, particularly in relation to the language of Christian scripture and worship and the apparent masculinity of God and mankind.

income support *noun* a social security payment for the unemployed and people on low incomes. Introduced in 1988, replacing supplementary benefit.

incomes policy *noun* a policy for the control of inflation by restricting increases in wages, dividends, etc. Introduced in the UK by the Labour government of 1964–70.

in-depth *adj.* with detailed thoroughness (c.1967).

index-linked *adj.* (of salary, pension, etc.) calculated in relation to rises or falls in the official cost-of-living index (1970).

indie *noun* an independent record company; *also* the sort of music commonly associated with their labels. Also used as an adjective. *Indie* refers to smaller (specialised) companies as opposed to the larger ones that dominate the market. The informal abbreviation, *indie*, was first used as an adjective within the American film industry during the early forties. It was adopted by the pop music industry in the sixties, but did not become generally used until the mid seventies when many small companies were formed to cater for minority interests. By the eighties the word was widely used as an adjective to describe performers, music and even fans: the connotation is that these do not belong to the mainstream of public taste.

industrial action *noun* action taken by employees in industry in order to protest against wage-levels, working conditions, etc. When it was invented in about 1970, the term was probably intended by trade unionists to be a broader term than 'strike' in encompassing work-to-rule, go-slow and other forms of protest. Even so, it has been criticised as a euphemism by those who feel that 'inaction' would be more accurate.

industrial espionage *noun* attempting to obtain the trade secrets of a (usually rival) company by spying, computer-tapping, bribery, infiltration of the workforce, etc. (1962).

INF (abbreviation for) intermediate-range nuclear forces. Officially defined as ground-based nuclear missiles and aircraft with a range of between 500 and 5000 kilometres. The initials were first used in connection with talks between the USA and USSR in the early eighties. The INF Treaty, signed in 1987, required the withdrawal of intermediate-range nuclear weapons from Europe, the destruction of some, and the reduction of nuclear arsenals to an agreed size, subject additionally to inspection. This treaty marked probably the most important arms-limitation in the history of nuclear weapons and brought the end of the Cold War significantly nearer.

infomercial *noun* a short television documentary film produced by a firm to advertise its goods or services. Formed (USA, 1980s) from 'information' and 'commercial' (as in 'television commercial') but an *infomercial* is unlike the latter in being longer and, in the UK, confined to cable and satellite television.

infopreneurial *adj.* having to do with the manufacture or marketing of *information technology*. Originally US, 1980s, by combining 'information' and 'entrepreneurial'. Also **infopreneur**, *noun*, an entrepreneur whose business is the handling of information for profit – its collection, marketing and publication.

informatics *noun* (another term for) information science, the study of the ways that information, especially scientific information, has been or could be gathered, stored, communicated and employed (1967).

information science *noun* the study of the ways that information is generated, stored and handled, especially in the areas of science and technology (c.1960); *also* the development of more effective ways of storing and disseminating information. Also *noun* **information scientist**: one who studies the handling of information; *also* a provider of information services (c.1958).

information technology *noun* the technology dealing with the production, storage and dissemination of information using computers, micro-electronics and telecommunications (1958). Sometimes shortened to **infotech** (from early eighties).

infotainment *noun* a television programme in which a serious subject (e.g. news, documentary material) is presented in a way intended to be primarily entertaining. An eighties coinage, originally US, combining 'information' and 'entertainment'. Although *infotainment* may include worthy attempts to put information across entertainingly, the word became most prominent in the UK during the early nineties when fears were expressed about the trivialising of television as a result of its increased exposure to commercial pressures and competition from satellite channels.

in-joke *noun* a joke enjoyed or understood by a limited number of people, those people in the know. A 1964 coinage probably influenced by the sense of exclusivity in IN.

Inkatha *noun* a black political movement supporting non-racial democracy in South Africa, but also promoting the identity and interest of the Zulu people. The name is a Zulu word for the grass coil worn by Zulu women on their heads when carrying loads: its strength comes from the weaving together of many strands, and it acts as a sacred emblem of unity. *Inkatha* was originally a Zulu cultural organisation (1928) but was revived as a political one in 1975, open to all Black people, though still predominantly Zulu. It has generally been less radical than the much older African National Congress, with which it has had sporadic and often violent conflict, both before and after the dismantling of apartheid, the establishment of the new multiracial state and the holding of the first multiracial elections.

ink-jet (printer) *noun* (a machine, usually used with a computer, for) a printing method employing a fine jet of quick-drying ink which is directed on to the paper, forming characters as it lands. The jet is electrically charged and then shaped by a varying electrical field. The system, developed in the early seventies, is faster and less limited than mechanical devices such as the DAISY WHEEL.

in-line *adj.* (of roller skates) having four, occasionally five, wheels in a straight line instead of side by side in pairs. Invented in the early eighties by two US ice-hockey players who wanted high-speed out-of-season training. By the early nineties *in-line skating* was a multi-million dollar industry in the US. The use of the skates permits very high speed and improved manoeuvrability, though accidents are correspondingly more serious.

inner city *noun* the central parts of a city, especially those having substandard housing, overcrowding, poverty, unemployment and other forms of social deprivation. Also *adjective*: of or belonging to those areas of the city. First used c.1968, originally in the USA, where it tended to be used as a euphemism for 'slums'. In the UK it is now often associated with areas populated by ethnic minorities.

inner space *noun* the part of the human mind that is not normally within one's consciousness (1958). *Inner space* is a comparatively recent term for those usually unexplored regions of the mind that different societies and generations have believed *could* be explored, for example via meditation in past centuries or through drugs in the psychedelic sixties and seventies. The coinage of the term seems to have followed the renewed interest in (and feasibility of exploring) outer space at that time.

Inset or **INSET** (acronym for) **in**-**se**rvice **t**raining. Educational jargon since the mid seventies: the statutorily required training for teachers during term-time in state schools in the UK. Also INSET day (see BAKER DAY) and INSET course.

insider dealing or **trading** *noun* profitable trading in stocks and shares by someone who has confidential information about a company which, if or when generally known, would affect the price and thus the 'insider's' profit. On the stock-exchange, where such a practice is illegal, the term has been used since the sixties, though it did not become generally known until the eighties, as a result of important prosecutions in the USA and UK. In this context *insider* means 'a person with confidential knowledge or inside information'.

instant replay *noun* (the original US term for) ACTION REPLAY (c.1973).

integrated circuit *noun* a miniature electronic circuit with all the components formed on a single CHIP. The first, consisting of a transistor and resistor, was created in 1959, since when the number of components has considerably increased so that a highly complex system can now contain over a million transistors. Integrated circuits are commonly used in computers and most electronic equipment.

intelligent *adj.* (of a machine, and especially of computerised functions) able to modify its actions according to circumstances, events, etc. An extension of the use of *intelligent* as in INTELLIGENT TERMINAL. It is now used of electronic consumer goods and, since the eighties, of buildings, especially offices, in which not only office equipment but also heating, lighting, air-conditioning, security devices, etc. are controlled by a central computer system which is programmed to respond efficiently to changing conditions without constant human intervention. See also (as applied to weaponry) SMART and BRILLIANT PEBBLES.

intelligent terminal *noun* a computer terminal with its own program so that it can process data without further access to the main computer to which it is linked. Such a function is additional to the terminal's capacity to send data to the central processor and receive information from it. This use of INTELLIGENT dates from 1969.

intensive care *noun* the specially careful and continuous treatment of an acutely sick patient. The term, and also *intensive care unit* as the name for the specially designed facility providing this treatment, date from 1963.

interactive *adj.* (of an electronic device) allowing two-way transfer of information between the device and its user (1967). Used of video games, television (e.g. immediate viewer reaction to questions asked by a broadcaster), shopping by television, and especially video hardware (often called *interactive video*) that allows the user to manipulate images via a computer-optical disc system. *Interactive fiction* (1980s) is fiction stored on computer with several sets of story-lines enabling users to choose from those available and, so to speak, 'create' their own plot.

InterCity *adj.* and *noun* British Rail jargon (note the capital C) for what used to be called 'express' (1955). *InterCity 125* is a high-speed service introduced in 1976.

interface *noun* the boundary or place at which independent systems or organisations come together, communicate or interact; also *verb* to connect (usually scientific equipment) so as to permit joint operation. Previously a little known scientific word for the surface forming the boundary between two portions of matter or space, *interface* emerged with this new meaning in the early sixties and rapidly became a cliché with a popular meaning of 'meeting'.

interferon *noun* a naturally occurring protein released by an animal cell (usually as a result of the entry of a virus) and able to inhibit the further development of that virus. Discovered in 1957, *interferons* can enhance the capability of the body's immune system in destroying tumours, cancers and viruses, and may have a role in combating HIV.

intermediate technology *noun* modern technology of a sort suitable for technologically backward regions. A seventies term from the vocabulary of THIRD-WORLD aid and development agencies. The technology has to be simple to assemble, operate and maintain and to be sensitive to the needs, working-practices and natural resources of those for whom it is intended. It is *intermediate* in lying between the HIGH-TECH and the primitive or LOW-TECH.

Internet *noun* a network of computer networks. The *Internet* developed from a US military project in the sixties, when fears that a nuclear strike could wipe out any individual computer prompted the decision to distribute data across many linked sites. If one computer went down others on the network would take over. Protocols (agreed procedures) were developed to allow the networks to talk to each other and thus a functioning network developed during the sixties and seventies. One result of its particular history of development is that the *Internet* has no controlling body – it is rather a loose affiliation of its users. You can access the *Internet* provided you have a telephone and MODEM by opening an account with an Internet Service Provider (ISP) – a commercial organisation providing access to the *Internet*.

intifada *noun* the Palestinian uprising against Israel on the West Bank and Gaza strip, started in 1987. An Arab word meaning 'uprising to throw off oppression'. It is not new, but has been familiar in English only since this particular uprising in the late eighties.

into *prep.* interested or involved in; knowledgeable about. Colloquial since c.1969.

intrapreneur *noun* a person employed in a large business organisation who uses entrepreneurial skills to develop and market a new product or service which the organisation may then launch as a subsidiary business venture. This idea was proposed in the USA in the late seventies as an alternative to the riskier procedure of setting up an independent small business or partnership in possible rivalry to the original organisation. The name, which emerged in the mid eighties is a pun on *entrepreneur*, *intra-* meaning 'within'.

investigative *adj.* (of journalism, broadcasting) enquiring into and seeking to expose malpractice. As distinct, that is, from merely reporting something that has happened. This specialised meaning of the word emerged in the USA in 1951, though it did not become well known until the Watergate scandal (1972–4) was largely unearthed by journalists. In the UK it is especially associated with a particular sort of 'watch-dog' programme on television and radio, detecting cases of fraud and other malpractice.

invisible earnings *noun* that part of a country's economy which is related to services rather than goods. The term emerged c.1969 from the earlier technical terms 'invisible exports/imports'. The earnings in question are not actually invisible, but whereas payments for goods traded between countries appear on the returns and show up in the balance of trade, sometimes called the 'visible balance', payments generated by services such as tourism, international insurance and the like do not.

in vitro fertilisation *noun* a technique enabling some women to bear children after having failed to conceive in the normal way. Eggs taken from the woman's ovary are fertilised with her partner's sperm under laboratory conditions and some of them are inserted in the womb and allowed to implant. The world's first so-called 'test-tube baby' was born in 1978 after previous research in the UK; since then many couples have benefited. *In vitro* (Latin, 'in glass') is an old scientific term used of techniques which require a culture dish, test-tube, etc. (*in vitro fertilisation* actually takes place in a dish, not a test-tube), though the term has the more general meaning of 'in an artificial environment'. See GIFT and ZIFT.

in your face *phrase used adjectivally* assertive, confrontational. Originates in Black American English and basketball, where a defensive player closely marking an attacker is 'in the face of' that player. It has recently (nineties) crossed over into British English, preserving that sense of a confrontational approach.

Iran-contra see CONTRA.

Irangate see -GATE.

Iraqgate *noun* (the alleged scandal of) the sale to Iraq of British machine tools capable of manufacturing armaments, and the UK government's involvement in this, beginning in the late eighties. See -GATE for an explanation of the term. Armaments made on such machines may have been used against British and allied forces in the subsequent Gulf War of 1991, so that this and the UK government's alleged cover-up of such deals, inevitably caused a stir when they came to light in 1992, and again when the report of the Scott inquiry into these matters was published in early 1996.

irradiation *noun* the preserving of food by exposing it to a small dose of radiation using gamma rays. In its general sense of 'exposure to radiation', the word goes back to the beginning of the twentieth century, but this specialised sense dates from the 1950s and became well known only in the eighties when the treatment, in common with several other aspects of modern food technology, gave rise to public concern.

ISBN (abbreviation for) International Standard Book Number. Such a number is now given to all books and printed in the publishing details at the front, as well as (usually) on a BAR CODE on the back of the dust-jacket for the purposes of stock-control. The system was adopted by the International Standards Organisation in 1972.

IT (abbreviation for) INFORMATION TECHNOLOGY.

IUD (abbreviation for) intrauterine device. A contraceptive loop or coil, sometimes called IUCD (C for 'contraceptive'), introduced c.1963.

IVF (abbreviation for) IN VITRO FERTILISATION.

Jack-the-lad *noun* an outward-going young man, confident that he knows what's what. British, colloquial. This form and usage surface in the early eighties, but may ultimately derive from the figure of a roystering sailor, celebrated in Victorian nautical songs with refrains containing the phrase 'Jack's the lad'.

jacuzzi

jacuzzi *noun* a bath or pool equipped with a device for creating underwater jets that keep the water agitated. Strictly speaking, this is a proprietary name, Jacuzzi being the name of the American who developed, patented and marketed the product on the basis of a pump invented by his brother. Known since the mid sixties and subsequently internationally popular, it is now so familiar that it is often spelt without a capital J.

JCB *noun* (trademark for) a large earth-moving vehicle with a hydraulically operated shovel at the front and an excavator arm at the back, separately controlled. Known under this name since c.1960, though developed slightly earlier. The name is formed from the initials of JC Bamford, its manufacturer. The company makes other types of construction machinery, but is specially associated with the distinctive and successful vehicle described.

Jesus freak *noun* an evangelical Christian embracing aspects of the HIPPIE lifestyle. The term emerged in the late sixties when some hippies, mainly young, proclaimed evangelical religion rather than drugs as the way to personal fulfilment and a world of peace and love. They did, however, retain some elements of hippie culture, often living communally, dressing unconventionally and behaving fervently: see FREAK. The term is now occasionally used as a pejorative term for any enthusiastic, BORN-AGAIN Christian. See also HAPPY CLAPPY.

jetfoil *noun* a HYDROFOIL boat powered by jet engines. Pioneered by Boeing and given this as a proprietary name in the USA in 1972.

jet lag *noun* the lassitude and sense of temporal disorientation that results from travelling in a jet plane through more than one time zone. The individual's BODY CLOCK does not adjust to the new time for some days but lags behind it (hence *lag*). The phenomenon was noticed and commented on with the development of long-distance jet passenger planes, and first recorded from 1969.

jet set *noun* fashionable, wealthy people who travel in search of social pleasures. The term appeared first in 1951, a year before the first jet airliner came into commercial operation; but the then meaning seems to have been 'high-flyer', drawing on the jet engine's associations with speed and power. With the subsequent development of jet travel, but while it was still exclusive, the term came to have implications of international pleasure-seeking by a smart 'in-set', though the *noun* **jet-setter** and *adjective* **jet-setting** are now also used of businessmen, entertainers and others who travel frequently by jet aircraft in the course of their work.

jet-ski *noun* a powered vehicle resembling a motorbike mounted on a single broad water ski that allows the rider to surge through or glide over the water at speed (late eighties).

jihad *noun* a holy war conducted by Muslims against unbelievers, as ordained by the Koran. The word, from the Arabic for conflict or struggle, has been used in English in specialist writing since the nineteenth century, but it was unknown to the general public until the rise of Islamic fundamentalism became an issue in the 1980s.

job centre *noun* a local drop-in centre of the government-run

employment agency in the UK. *Job Centres* were established in
1972 to take over the job-advertising functions of the earlier
Employment Exchanges, and the new title was no doubt intended
to underline a new emphasis on *jobsearch* and to shed the rather
grim associations that had gathered around Employment
Exchanges as places responsible for paying unemployment benefits. However, as joblessness worsened in the eighties and early
nineties, the centres were not always able to live up to the implied
promise of their name; and in some parts of the country that name
came to be regarded by many as a euphemism for *jobless centre*.

job-sharing *noun* a scheme whereby two (or more) people share
one full-time job, dividing the hours, duties and pay between them.
The term has been known since c.1972 but the idea was not much
taken up until the early eighties, when it was often seen as a
means of attracting women back into employment, for example,
married women returners to teaching or banking whose family
commitments might make them unable or unwilling to take on
full-time work. The *noun* **job-sharer** denotes someone who takes
up such work, and there is also a *verb*, to **job share**.

job splitting *noun* **1.** the division of a job so that it might be
shared; **2.** a refinement of JOB-SHARING that clearly divides the
responsibilities of a *job-share* so as to make time-consuming consultation unnecessary (mid eighties).

jobsworth *noun* a person in a position of minor authority who
enforces petty rules or withholds cooperation. A colloquialism from
the early seventies. The implication is that the *jobsworth* is either
idle or deliberately unhelpful, often falling back on the stock
expression 'It's more than my job's worth (to do/let you do that,
etc.)', to excuse his refusal of permission or cooperation.

jogging *noun* the physical exercise of running at a steady or moderate pace over some distance. *Jog* is an old word and its meanings
used to include 'walk or ride at a jolting pace; move on with a
laboured pace'. The present meaning seems to have originated in
the technical vocabulary of athletics, and has been in every day
use only since the sixties. *Jogging* is also used adjectivally of running shoes, track-suits and other equipment marketed for *joggers*.

joined-up *adj.* showing the interests and aptitude of an adult
(1990). Just as joined-up writing is an advance on a younger child's
printed letters, so by extension *joined-up* humour or debate has
moved a step beyond the simple and rudimentary forms.

joint *noun* a cannabis cigarette. This slang sense was not widely
known in Britain until the 1960s. It is rather earlier in the USA
and may derive from nineteenth century slang for an opium-den or
joint. This is related to an even older slang use of *joint* to mean
'place of meeting', which reflects the primary meaning of *joint*,
'place where two things join'. An alternative explanation is that
tobacco and cannabis are jointly combined in the cigarette.

jojoba *noun* a shrub from the south-western part of North America,
having edible seeds containing an oil now used in cosmetics. This
Mexican Spanish word was not commonly known in Britain until

the mid seventies, when the campaign to 'Save the Whale' generated a search for substitutes for sperm whale oil. The increasing interest in ecologically-friendly cosmetics, using natural ingredients, led to its being used and quoted as an ingredient in cosmetics from the early eighties.

journo *noun* (abbreviation of) journalist. Media slang in the UK since the eighties, but borrowed from much earlier Australian usage, where the suffix -*o* is commonly added to shortenings (see MUSO). Some claim that the form *journo* is modelled on *wino* (a down-at-heel person habitually drunk on cheap wine) but it is not necessarily derogatory in use, though it may carry implications of hard-bitten insincerity.

joystick *noun* (in computer technology) a small lever for controlling the movement of images on a screen. The attachment containing the lever is best known from its use in playing computer games. The name, familiar since the early 1980s in this special sense, is an obvious borrowing of the colloquial term for the control stick of an aircraft.

juggernaut *noun* a very large heavy goods vehicle. The word has been used in this sense since c.1969, when the increasing size of lorries began to cause concern, though it had occasionally been used of traction engines and large motor cars before then. It is originally, with a capital J, a title of the Hindu deity Krishna, and therefore became the name of the huge car on which his image is annually dragged through the streets.

jukebox *noun* (in computer technology) device for storing information discs in CD-ROM form, and for loading them mechanically into a computer so that the data they hold can be retrieved. The original *jukebox* is a large coin operated automatic gramophone containing a collection of records from which the user makes a selection by pressing the relevant button. Its basic function – picking out and playing a disc on command – is therefore similar to that of the computer device. The name was borrowed into computer jargon as early as the 1960s but became familiar only in the eighties when the development of the OPTICAL DISK brought these storage and retrieval facilities into widespread use.

jumbo jet *noun* a large jet aircraft able to carry several hundred passengers. This informal term, first used c.1965, became specially associated with the Boeing 747, the first wide-bodied jet, able to carry over 400 passengers, and introduced into service in 1970. As a word for a clumsy or unwieldy fellow, *jumbo* goes back to the early nineteenth century, probably deriving ultimately from 'Mumbo Jumbo', an eighteenth century name for a West Indian divinity or bogy. It was used as the name of a famous elephant who was kept at London Zoo from 1865–82, and this is when it became popularly associated with great size.

jump jet *noun* a fixed-wing jet aircraft able to take off and land vertically. A colloquial term, first used in 1964 of the Harrier jump jet.

jump-start *verb* to start a car which has a flat battery by linking its battery to the (charged) battery of another car. The linking-device is known as a *jump-lead* because it enables a charge to 'jump' from the charged to the uncharged battery. However, *jump-start* (1976) is now also interchangeable with **bump-start**, presumably because of confusion between 'jump' and 'bump'.

jump-suit   *noun* a one-piece garment combining trousers and top. Named c.1965 when it was fashionable among women. The term was originally used in the USA in the late forties for the one-piece garment worn by parachutists, whence the name.

junk bond   *noun* (in finance) a high-yielding bond carrying high risk. First heard of in the 1970s on Wall Street when such bonds were usually issued to raise capital to finance a takeover. They were called *junk* ('rubbish') because of doubts that a company issuing them would be able to pay the promised interest, given the likely profitability (or the purpose) of the takeover. The term needs to be understood in the context of a type of financial dealing intended to make money rather than improve businesses: see ASSET-STRIPPING, for example.

junk food   *noun* food of a low nutritional value but high in calories, and, because of its instant appeal, often preferred to a well-balanced meal, especially by the young. Commonly used of FAST FOOD, instant meals and snacks containing ADDITIVES and carbohydrates, especially sugar: hamburgers, crisps, confectionery, soft drinks, etc. The term dates from c.1973; *junk* denotes the nutritional worthlessness of such food and reflects anxiety about young people's diet and health. By extension the term can be applied to ideas, books, music etc. that substitute instant appeal for real worth.

junk fax   *noun* unsolicited advertising or other material sent by fax. A late eighties coinage on the analogy of JUNK MAIL.

junk mail   *noun* unsolicited advertising material sent through the post. So called because most of it is judged worthless (*junk*) and destined to be thrown away as rubbish (i.e. *junked*). Originally a North American term (1954) but since the late sixties widely used in the UK.

junkie   *noun* an enthusiast. A recent development (1990s) of an old slang word for a drug addict. It implies an enthusiasm bordering on addiction.

K   (abbreviation for) one thousand pounds or dollars. From the familiar use of *kilo-*, meaning one thousand, in many words to do with measurement. The language of computing adopted K or k as an abbreviation for 1000 (e.g. in a rate of transmission of data) or 1024 (in numbers to the power of 2) in the mid sixties. As computer language spread, it became common to see – and hear – K used after a number, and this led to the fashion of stating salaries in job advertisements as, for instance, 20K (£20,000). By the early eighties this was becoming common (it was previously limited to job advertisements within computing), and the convention has since spread to other contexts such as house and car prices.

kalashnikov   *noun* an assault rifle. Named after its Russian inventor and manufactured since the late 1940s in the Soviet Union and other communist countries; the name of this automatic rifle has become increasingly familiar to the general public in the West from the early seventies onwards because of its widespread use by guerrilla forces and terrorists in many parts of the world.

Kampuchea *noun* the official name of Cambodia from 1976 to 1989.

karaoke *noun* entertainment in which a person sings in public to the pre-recorded sound track of a popular song. The entertainment originated in Japan and the word is Japanese for 'empty orchestra' i.e. an orchestra that provides accompaniment but lacks the central vocal performance. *Karaoke* was successfully launched in Britain during the eighties, proving popular in clubs, bars etc. The word is used attributively in such common combinations as **karaoke bar** and **karaoke night**.

kerb-crawling *noun* driving slowly in a car close to the kerb in order to solicit a prostitute. Used in this sense since c.1971; the offence became a criminal one in 1990. The term had previously been used (in print since 1955 but before that in spoken slang and police jargon) to mean 'walking (slowly) on a pavement on the lookout for a prostitute'.

key (in) *verb* (of computing) to use a keyboard to operate on data or call up information (1963).

keyboard *noun* and *verb*. As a verb meaning the same as KEY (IN), this dates from 1961. More recently (1980s) it has given rise to *keyboarder*, one who uses a computer keyboard. In musical contexts, *keyboard* has been short for 'electronic keyboard' since the seventies: it now refers to one of a number of devices which use microchip technology, consist of little more than a set of keys, and are widely used in schools, in rock music, and for home entertainment.

keyhole surgery *noun* surgery using fibre optic techniques that require only small incisions. Developed in the seventies and given this colloquial name in the late eighties, from the idea of working through a small aperture like a keyhole instead of through a larger surgical incision.

keypad *noun* a small keyboard with push-buttons, as on a telephone, pocket calculator or remote control device for television, etc. (1975). The word is based on *keyboard*: a *keypad* (as in 'notepad') being smaller. It has since been used, in the language of computer technology, for a small input device capable being attached to a keyboard; this has a number of keys for selecting functions.

Khmer Rouge *noun* the communist movement in Cambodia. It became active in the early seventies, seized power in 1975 after a civil war, and was deposed by the Vietnamese in 1979, when it went into exile, though active in guerrilla warfare. Its period in government saw radical upheaval and the murder of an estimated three million citizens: see KILLING FIELDS. The *Khmer* are the indigenous people of Cambodia: *Rouge* is French for 'red' (i.e. communist), Cambodia having formerly been a French protectorate.

kickboxing *noun* a martial art resembling boxing but permitting use of the bare feet (c.1971). Sometimes called *Thai kickboxing* it combines karate and boxing and is akin to KUNG-FU.

kick-start *verb* to take firm and decisive action to begin a process or development, especially one that has come to a halt. A suddenly fashionable metaphor c.1987, from the verb meaning 'to start an engine, especially of a motorbike, by means of a pedal that is kicked downwards'. In 1991 the term began to verge on cliché amid much talk of the government needing to *kick-start the economy*, then in serious recession. The figure of speech is not very apt: a *kick-start* is given to something in working order. 'Bump-start' might be more appropriate.

kidology *noun* the art or practice of deception. A colloquialism invented in 1964, from the slang verb *kid* (to hoax, deceive) with the jocular addition of *-ology*, the suffix which commonly indicates a science or academic study.

kidult *noun and adj.* The word was coined, from *kid* and *adult*, by an American academic to denote a typical modern US child, passing too rapidly from being a *kid* to being an *adult* (particularly under the influence of television and advertising) and growing up a hybrid – immature, materialistic and uncultured. The word has been used colloquially in US media slang since the late fifties when describing television programmes appealing to children as well as adults but, usually, fully satisfying to neither.

kidvid *noun* a video aimed at children. Originally (1955) US slang for children's television. Now known in the UK with its current meaning (since the eighties) as a result of the creation of the video market.

killer bee *noun* the African honey bee, or one of its hybrids, noted for extremely aggressive behaviour when it is disturbed. Known as a very good producer of honey, it was imported into Brazil in 1956 and interbred with native bees, producing an equally or more vicious strain which has since spread to other parts of South America and northwards into the southern USA.

killing fields *noun* a place of battle or mass execution. Mass graves in the countryside round Phnom Penh containing vast numbers of Cambodians killed by the KHMER ROUGE were discovered in 1979 after the government was overthrown. This countryside was first called *killing fields* in an article in the *New York Times Magazine* early in the following year. A British film based on the article was entitled *The Killing Fields* (1984), and helped to establish the expression, which is now used less specifically.

kinky *adj.* sexually abnormal or deviant. A development (c.1959) from much earlier slang meaning 'eccentric' 'crooked' and, according to one authority, 'homosexual'. The word is often used in a milder, jocular but still informal sense of 'attractive or striking in a bizarre way'. *Kinky boots* were popular in the early sixties. They were knee-length, sometimes thigh-length, leather boots worn by women, often with a MINISKIRT. This name implied a hint of sexual ambiguity rather than abnormality.

kir *noun* a drink consisting of a small amount of crème de cassis topped up with white wine. Named after a Mayor of Dijon (d.1968) who is said to have invented it, though others claim that it originated in the Burgundy countryside as a mixture designed to take the edge off poor white wine, and that it was given Kir's name in his honour. It has been known in Britain since the mid sixties. A *kir royale* has champagne instead of wine.

kissagram, kissogram *noun* an arranged visit by a representative of a greetings service to present a message and a kiss, intended to amuse or embarrass the recipient(s). The representative, usually a girl, is often provocatively dressed. Variants include the *gorrillagram* and the *strippergram* (sometimes delivered by a girl dressed as a policewoman or traffic-warden). The idea became popular c.1981, though 'singing telegrams' had previously been known and a 'Kissogram Post Card' could be bought in the 1900s with a space which the purchaser could kiss, above a sentimental verse, before posting it to a loved one. The *-gram* suffix denotes something written, reminding us that a *kissagram* is a form of novelty telegram. See STRIPPERGRAM.

kiss-and-tell *adj.* (of memoirs, newspaper story, etc.) describing a former sexual relationship, usually with someone well known. An adjectival form, originally US c.1970, of a much older expression with the same sense: 'you must not kiss and tell' is found as early as 1695 in Congreve's *Love for love*. The modern expression is often applied to stories sold for large sums of money to tabloid newspapers.

kiss of life *noun* mouth-to-mouth resuscitation (1961). Now also used of other things that reanimate or reinvigorate. The phrase was presumably modelled on 'kiss of death', an apparently well-intentioned act that has disastrous consequences.

kiwi fruit *noun* a fruit with pale green flesh and brown furry skin, resembling a huge gooseberry and also known as a Chinese gooseberry. The name 'kiwi', an informal word for a New Zealander, was given to the fruit for marketing purposes when the first imports of it from New Zealand, where it is extensively grown, began in the mid sixties.

kludge *noun* something makeshift consisting of a collection of ill-assorted parts. Especially used in computer vocabulary of anything improvised, poorly thought out or imperfect. According to the man who coined the term in 1962, JW Granholm, it was an ironic variant of the German *Klug* ('clever, intelligent'); perhaps it was influenced by 'bodge' or 'fudge'. It's use is largely confined to the slang of computing and electronics.

knee-jerk *adj.* predictable, automatic. Especially found in the 'knee-jerk response' of a person to a problem. The term has been used in physiology, to describe a physical reflex action, since the nineteenth century, but the current figurative use dates only from the 1960s, originally in the language of political knock-about. Recently (1989) **knee-jerk** has also been used as a *verb*: to respond instinctively and predictably.

kneesup *noun* a rowdy celebration. The music-hall song 'Knees up Mother Brown' gave rise to a dance or 'knees up', hence this sense of *kneesup* as a party, first recorded in 1963. There are also occasional extended uses to signify any jamboree or celebratory event.

knock-on *adj.* resulting inevitably but indirectly. Usually found in *knock-on effect*, the indirect result of an action; for example, the bankruptcy of a company will have a direct effect on its own employees and may have a knock-on effect on jobs in companies which did business with it. The term is a fairly recent (late seventies) borrowing from earlier scientific use which had to do with the results of atoms and particles 'knocking on' each other in collision.

kooky *adj.* crazy, eccentric, foolish. Also *noun*, **kook** someone whose ideas or actions are kooky. Slang, mainly North American, probably from 'cuckoo' meaning 'mad' (1959).

Krugerrand *noun* a South African gold coin used only for investments. First coined in 1967, it is named after President Kruger, whose picture it carries. The *rand* is the monetary unit of South Africa.

krytron *noun* (in electronics) a type of switch used as a trigger in nuclear explosions (early 1970s).

kung-fu *noun* Chinese martial art with elements of karate and judo. Known in the UK since 1966.

lager lout *noun* a youth, normally in a group, who drinks large quantities of lager (or other beer) and behaves rowdily or aggressively. Commenting on an outbreak of violence in Britain in 1988, a Home Office minister, John Patten, spoke of a *lager culture*, in reference to an increasingly popular and heavily advertised drink particularly associated with young men. A *Sun* journalist has claimed to have coined the more alliterative *lager lout* a couple of weeks later.

laid-back *adj.* relaxed in manner or character; cool, not easily flustered; unhurried. A colloquialism from c.1973, possibly originating a little earlier in HIPPIE vocabulary, from the idea of lying back comfortably as in a chair, and perhaps under the influence of drugs.

lake *noun* a surplus or stockpile of a liquid commodity, usually within European Community arrangements. The most common example is *wine lake* (1974); see CAP.

lambada *noun* an erotic DISCO dance with pelvic movement and stomach contact between couples. Although danced in Brazil for some time (the word is Portuguese for the cracking of a whip) it became popular in the USA in the late eighties, probably as a result of the DIRTY DANCING craze, and reached Britain in 1989, sweeping Europe as well. The music, a mixture of Latin American and Caribbean, is also called *lambada*. Also a *verb*: to dance the *lambada*.

LAN (acronym for) LOCAL AREA NETWORK.

language laboratory *noun* a classroom equipped for learning foreign languages, with tape or cassette recorders etc., and often with direct communication between the teacher and each pupil through the use of headphones. The teaching method, introduced in the early sixties, is based on oral practice.

landfill (site) *noun* a place where waste material is disposed of by burying it. *Landfill*, originally a US term, has been used since the early 1940s to denote a method of rubbish-disposal. Its use to denote a place (as an abbreviation of 'landfill site') emerged during the seventies. Since the mid eighties there has been growing concern over the burial of toxic wastes in such sites and the long term environmental effects of such malpractice. See LANDFILL GAS.

landfill gas *noun* a potentially hazardous gas, rich in methane, produced by the rotting of vegetable and other organic materials when buried in LANDFILL SITES (1989).

laptop *noun* a battery-powered portable micro computer, small enough to be used on a person's lap. Introduced c.1984, and so called by analogy with DESKTOP. See LUGGABLE, NOTEBOOK and PALMTOP.

laser *noun* a device for producing an intense, narrow beam of light capable of travelling over great distances and of being focused to give very great power densities; a similar device for producing a beam of any electromagnetic radiation (e.g. infrared, ultra violet or microwave radiation). The first *laser* was invented in 1960 by Theodore Maiman. It operated by using light to stimulate the emission of more light by exciting atoms or molecules. Its name is an acronym from 'light amplification by the stimulated emission of radiation'. Applications of the technology include the use of laser-beams to guide bombs (c.1967); see also CD, OPTICAL DISC and the following entries.

laser disc *noun* a disc containing the DIGITAL recording of data which is read by directing a LASER beam onto the surface of the disc and detecting the light which is reflected from the pattern of pits and bumps on that surface (also called an OPTICAL DISC). The technology was developed during the seventies and the name has been in use since c.1980. See CD, CD(-)ROM and CDV for applications of the system.

laser printer *noun* a type of computer printer using LASER technology. A laser beam scans a photoconductive drum and the characters produced are then transferred to paper. The definition of print and graphics is very clear, and the machine – now a familiar part of DESKTOP PUBLISHING – is small and quiet.

laser surgery *noun* the use of LASER technology in surgery. Pioneered in the late sixties; the welding of breaks in the retina of the eye was known by 1970, for example. Lasers are also now used to make delicate incisions, seal blood vessels and destroy diseased tissue.

latchkey children *noun* children who have to let themselves into their homes on returning from school (and, sometimes, who have to leave the house empty in the morning on going to school) because their parents are at work. The phrase originated (early 1940s) in the USA, which accounts for the use of *latchkey*, an uncommon word in British English. The term has been used in the UK since about 1960.

lateral thinking *noun* a way of solving problems by unorthodox or apparently illogical means rather than by the application of logical processes and traditional methods. Coined by Edward de Bono and explained in his *The Use of Lateral Thinking* (1967).

launch(ing) pad *noun* a specially constructed and reinforced area on which a rocket stands for launching. The meaning of *pad* here is related to its familiar one of 'something used as a protection against pressure etc.' and dates from the early fifties. Since then it has been used metaphorically to cover anything which provides a basis for launching an idea, campaign, policy, development, etc.

launch window *noun* the period during which a spacecraft must be launched if its mission is to be successfully completed, taking into account the changing positions of the planets and their satellites. From the idea of a window as an 'opening' (opportunity) that can be closed (1965).

launder *verb* to process illegally obtained money through one or more legitimate commercial enterprise (e.g. a bank), especially abroad, so that the funds can later be used with apparent legitimacy. Originating as a colloquial euphemism in the vocabulary of the Watergate scandal of 1973–4, this has now become Standard English and is sometimes used with a general sense of 'process something (not necessarily money) to make it appear respectable'.

law-and-order *adj.* committed to maintaining order and stability in society by a strict enforcement of its laws. The phrase 'law and order' has been common for two centuries, referring to conditions in which the law not merely exists but is actually implemented, producing order. The adjectival *law-and-order* is more recent (early seventies) and is usually employed in political contexts, as *law-and-order candidate / vote / party* etc.

LBO (abbreviation for) LEVERAGED BUYOUT.

LCD (abbreviation for) LIQUID CRYSTAL DISPLAY (1973).

lead balloon *noun* a failure. Originally US slang (c.1960), usually found in the UK in such set phrases as *that will go down like a lead balloon* (fail to elicit a favourable response) – *lead* being a heavy metal.

lead-free *adj.* (of petrol) not treated with tetraethyl lead, an anti-knock agent. The adjective has been applied to motor fuel since c.1970, though it existed earlier (e.g. 'lead-free paint') in the general sense of 'without added lead'. Later it was used also as a noun, short for 'lead-free petrol'. It became common in the eighties, by which time the risks posed to health and the environment by exhaust fumes were better understood, and price concessions were introduced to encourage motorists to use *lead-free* petrol. As time went by, the more common term became *unleaded petrol*, or simply *unleaded*.

leading edge *noun* the leading position, especially in technological development. Also *adjective* **leading-edge** showing an advanced technology, state-of-the-art. Borrowed in the late seventies, originally in the computing field but later more generally, from the language of aeronautics where it is the name for the forward edge of a wing, propeller blade, etc. – something that leads the way or is in the forefront. A later variant in advertising jargon is CUTTING EDGE, which is probably thought to have a sharper impact.

lean-burn *adj.* (of an internal combustion engine) designed to use a fuel mixture with reduced petrol and correspondingly increased air content, in order to reduce petrol consumption and thus pollution from exhaust emissions. In its sense of 'not rich' *lean* has meant 'using a low proportion of fuel in the fuel mixture of an internal combustion engine' since c.1932, but *lean-burn* is a coinage of the seventies, when fuel economy and air pollution became important issues.

Leboyer *noun* a method of childbirth named after Frédérick Leboyer (b.1918), French obstetrician. He advocated that delivery should take place in peaceful, darkened surroundings, with minimum intervention or excitement, and that the baby should be placed in a warm bath to simulate conditions in the womb. His methods, in which the husband is intended to play a part, became popular in the seventies and are described in his book *Birth Without Violence* (1975).

LED (abbreviation for) LIGHT-EMITTING DIODE.

left field, out in *phrase* see OUT IN THE LEFT FIELD.

legionnaire's disease *noun* a form of pneumonia caused by a bacterium that grows in warm conditions such as those provided by air-conditioning ducts, warm-water systems (e.g. showers) and water tanks. After nearly 200 delegates to an American Legion Convention in Philadelphia in June 1976 were affected by a mysterious illness that caused the deaths of 29 legionnaires, the bacterium responsible was identified and named *Legionella pneumophilia*. The conditions for encouraging the bacterium were also identified, and the risk can now be reduced in the planning and maintenance of buildings. The disease can be successfully treated, though it continues to occur, albeit in a less dramatic form than the event which gave it its name. Unpleasant sickness and respiratory problems are more common than death.

legwarmers *noun* a pair of tubular, usually knitted and brightly coloured garments covering the legs from ankle to knee or thigh (1974). Originally worn by ballet dancers at rehearsal to keep important ankle and knee muscles warm, these became popular in the mid seventies as a fashion accessory for women.

leisure centre *noun* a (usually public) facility where a variety of sporting and leisure activities can be practised. A largely 1980s refinement of the SPORTS CENTRE. Such centres, usually operated by a local authority, offer mainly indoor facilities, including some for activities not normally classed as 'sport', such as snooker or keep fit, and are equipped with refreshment and other social areas, such as rooms for meetings.

leisure suit or **wear** *noun*. Although *leisure wear* originally (1969) meant informal clothing that in style, colour and materials approximated more to sportswear than to everyday clothing, it is now more specifically interchangeable with *leisure suit* (1985), a form of tracksuit worn as everyday clothing.

LEM, Lem   (acronym for) lunar excursion module. A craft designed to convey an astronaut from an orbiting command spacecraft to the moon's surface and back (1962).

lens   *noun* (short for) contact lens. This shortening has been colloquial since the seventies, but is now generally accepted as Standard English. Contact lenses were named in 1888, though not widely worn until the sixties.

level playing field   *phrase* equally fair conditions for all participants. This curious expression, heard since the eighties, seems to have originated in the vocabulary of EC politics in discussions about economic and other arrangements which appeared to have a built-in bias in favour of one country or another. In sport, of course, it does not normally matter whether a playing field is level or sloping; the conditions are the same for both sides.

leverage   *verb* to speculate with borrowed money, calculating that the profit will more than cover the interest payable. An American usage; the first two syllables are pronounced to rhyme with 'never'. The word has been in use since the thirties, but for most of that time it was restricted to specialised financial contexts, and it was not until US business practices and jargon became more familiar to the public at large in the eighties that this word entered general usage. As an adjective **leveraged** denotes those companies that are based on borrowed money (see LEVERAGED BUYOUT). There is also a verb **deleverage**: to refinance a company that is leveraged.

leveraged buyout   *noun* a takeover or takeover bid financed by loans for which the collateral is the assets of the target company (and, in some cases, the assets of a smaller company attempting or making the takeover). Mainly a US term, c.1976, often for a MANAGEMENT BUYOUT using outside capital. See LEVERAGE.

libber   *noun* a person, usually a woman, in favour of WOMEN'S LIBERATION. The word is a shortening of *women's libber*, but neither the short nor the longer version was much liked by those to whom it was applied. *Libber* had a brief vogue in the seventies but is now little heard.

liberate(d)   *adj.* and *verb* free(d) from social prejudice and injustice. This special sense of a familiar word emerged c.1970 in the wake of the slightly earlier **women's liberation**, and originally had to do with the liberation of women from male-dominated conventions and roles. As time has gone on it has become used more generally (e.g. of loss of sexual inhibition) and sometimes means no more than 'unconventional'.

liberation theology   *noun* the belief that the Christian Church should work for the liberation of people from social, political and economic oppression by active struggle within those societies where such oppression is thought to exist. The phrase is a translation from the Spanish *teologia de la Liberacion* (1968); the movement originated among Latin American theologians of the Roman Catholic Church who have found themselves in conflict with the Vatican for openly siding with Marxist or radical theory and revolutionary or reformist practice.

Librium

Librium *noun* (trademark of) a popular tranquilliser (1960).

lifestyle *noun* **1.** a set of habits, attitudes, possessions, etc. characteristic of a person or group; **2.** (in marketing terms) this set of attitudes and preferences as it effects a particular customer's or group's choice of goods, bought to conform to their idea of themselves and their way of life; *also* a marketing approach which appeals to the customers' idea of themselves and their style of living. The word was coined in 1929 by the Austrian psychologist Alfred Adler with a technical sense which is now obsolete. The modern sense of 'way or style of life' began to emerge only in the late forties and was established by the sixties. It became one of the buzzwords of the image-conscious eighties, usually in the context of affluent or successful living, when advertisers developed the concept of *lifestyle merchandising* i.e. directing specific products at people by appealing to their sense of *lifestyle* (as distinct from their needs, health, convenience, etc.) with a mixture of snobbery, glamour and conspicuous consumption. Also as an *adjective*: using this marketing approach, or (of a product) conforming to customers' ideas of themselves and their lifestyles.

life-support (system) *noun* (equipment) designed to sustain the normal functioning of the body in a dangerous, hostile or unnatural environment. Originally (1959) part of the vocabulary of aeronautics, used of the sustenance of astronauts when in space, but now more familiar in the vocabulary of the branch of medical science devoted to the care of severely disabled or seriously ill patients, especially those kept alive by machinery. The term is also used figuratively.

lift-off *noun* the moment or act of a rocket achieving vertical take-off; (hence figuratively) the successful initiation of any activity or operation. As in the phrase, 'We have lift-off'.

ligger *noun* sponger, hanger-on, freeloader; person who gatecrashes parties. Slang, mainly in the entertainment industry, especially the rock business, since c.1977. It is from the earlier *lig* (1960), a northern dialect variant of 'lie', which meant 'laze around' until it was adopted by showbusiness and media people in the seventies and developed its present narrower meaning. Also *verb* **lig**: to freeload.

light *adj.* (of food and drink) low in calories, especially in fat. *Light* has been used of food for a long time, and its sense of 'not too filling' (*light pastry*, *light lunch*) has implied 'not too fattening' rather as a *light wine* or *light ale* has meant 'low in alcohol content'. In the eighties the adjective has been widely used by advertisers to make this healthful implication explicit, so that the word has now acquired a new specialised sense. See LITE.

light-emitting diode *noun* a small semiconductor device that emits light like a bulb. Familiar as the indicator light on a television set, video, hi-fi etc. and particularly useful in that it requires only a very low current and works at low voltages. The term is also found abbreviated in *LED display*, a flat-screen display using light-emitting diodes. Such displays were common on pocket calculators, digital watches, read-outs on laboratory instruments, etc. during the seventies, but have been largely replaced by LCDs.

light pen   *noun* (in computer technology) a hand-held device resembling a pen, the photosensitive tip of which can be placed on the screen of a cathode-ray tube to draw diagrams or select from a menu by feeding information to a data-processing system. A similar device is also used to read bar-codes at a cash-desk, etc. The name (1958) comes from its shape and light-sensitivity.

light show   *noun* a display of moving coloured lights, especially used to shine on the performers or backdrop at a rock performance (1966).

Likud   *noun* right-wing nationalist alliance, formed in Israel in 1973 to oppose Labour monopoly government.

limousine liberal   *noun* a wealthy person who professes sympathy for the less fortunate members of society. An ironic term (1969) in the USA, where a *limousine* is an expensive car; a *liberal* has social and political views favouring the deprived, and the juxtaposition of the two is intended to imply lack of genuineness. A British equivalent is CHAMPAGNE SOCIALIST.

line   *noun* a quantity of a powdered drug, usually cocaine, laid out in a thin line on a mirror or other hard surface and snorted or sniffed up through a narrow tube. Drug users' slang from c.1970.

linkage   *noun* (in international diplomacy) the linking of different and distinct issues in the process of bargaining, compromising, negotiating, etc. A specialised meaning of an old word. It originated (1960s) and remained prominent in the political vocabulary of the Cold War; for example, the USA sought to establish *linkage* between an offer of arms reduction and the quite different issue of improving human rights within the USSR. A more recent example occurred at the time of the Gulf War when Iraq attempted to raise the question of an independent Palestinian state on being called on to withdraw from Kuwait.

liposuction   *noun* a surgical method of removing excess fat (e.g. from hips and stomach) by sucking out fat cells through a device inserted into the body. The technique was developed in the early eighties. *Lipo-* is a combining form used in many pathological terms, from a Greek word meaning 'fat'.

liquid crystal display   *noun* a visual display, usually of numbers and letters, using liquid crystals. Liquid crystals were discovered in 1888, though their potential was not realised until 1963 when it was discovered that, though they are transparent, they can be made opaque if an electric field is applied. *Liquid crystal display* (1968) was originally used in watches and calculators, but later spread to remote controllers, lap-top computers, personal organisers, CD players, colour camcorder viewfinders, etc. See also FLDC.

lite   *adj.* (in brand names) light. An arbitrary respelling (probably on the model of the American *nite* for 'night' in entertainment vocabulary) first used by a US beer company in the sixties and since copied by others, for LIGHT (see above) e.g. for low-fat margarines, low-tar cigarettes or low-alcohol beer.

live-in *adj.* (of employee) residing at one's place of employment rather than in a house of one's own. When the term was first coined c.1955, it was applied to people such as hospital or hotel staff who live on the premises. It has now, especially in the combination *live-in lover*, also come to mean 'living in a sexual relationship and sharing accommodation with a partner to whom one is not married', a sense which emerged c.1970.

liveware *noun* people working on a computer system (1966). Based on the model of **hardware** and **software**, this is among the more durable of numerous jocular and sometimes transient *-ware* coinages in the language of the computer industry. See also WET-WARE.

living will *noun* a document drawn up by a person giving instructions that he or she is not to be kept alive by artificial means in the event of becoming severely disabled or terminally ill. The name comes from the idea of a *will* that defines acceptable *living* conditions for the testator. The notion was first discussed in the USA as long ago as the late sixties: the first *living will* was drawn up by a Chicago lawyer in 1969. Such documents were subsequently recognised as legally binding in most US States by 1990, but they have yet to be fully tested in the UK courts. However, their use has been endorsed by the British Medical Association, and their name became familiar to the general public in Britain in 1992 as a result of two controversial cases to do with allowing very sick people to die.

LMS (abbreviation for) local management of schools. The Education Reform Act 1988 required local education authorities to delegate to the governors and heads of individual schools a large share of the responsibility for financial and administrative management. 'Local management of schools' and its now common abbreviation were, however, coined beforehand in a report by a firm of consultants in January 1988. In its operation, *LMS* is largely a matter of finance, and one effect has been to turn headteachers and senior staff into bureaucrats and accountants.

loadsamoney *noun* (respelling and colloquial pronunciation of) loads of money. The British comedian Harry Enfield used this term first as a taunting catch-phrase, then as the name of a grotesque ESSEX MAN plasterer who mockingly waved fistfuls of banknotes in people's faces (1988). He intended to satirise the greed and vulgarity that was a by-product of THATCHERISM; not everyone understood his point, but his coinage encapsulated a mood.

local area network *noun* a computer NETWORK which links a number of stations within an area (e.g. an office building or university campus) and enables users to share resources. Developed in the late seventies and in widespread use within ten years. Now commonly shortened to LAN. See WIDE AREA NETWORK (WAN).

log in/out or **on/off** *verb* to enter or leave a large computer system from a terminal (1963).

logic *noun* (in computer technology and electronics). The principles underlying the representation of logical operations by electrical signals on a computer system (1950).

logic bomb   *noun* a set of instructions inserted into a computer program so that when a certain set of conditions occurs the instructions will cause the system to break down. An eighties term for the sort of computer sabotage which began to occur as a result of the widespread introduction of computer systems during the seventies. A breakdown may be induced by a disgruntled employee, who may well have left the organisation by the time the fault is triggered off; but other cases have involved attempted blackmail or the suppression of evidence of fraud. The term is based on 'time bomb', and that is also the name for a similar device in computing, but whereas a *time bomb* causes havoc after a predetermined passage of time, a *logic bomb* does so when certain conditions occur within the program's LOGIC. See TROJAN HORSE, VIRUS and WORM.

longhair   *noun* a hippie, beatnik (1969). The term is still occasionally found in its older meaning (from the twenties) of 'intellectual person, especially an artist or musician'. Both meanings imply deliberate non-conformity with normal (male) convention. Also *adjective* **long-haired**.

longlife   *adj.* (of milk) treated to last longer than fresh milk (1966). Also as *noun*: long-life milk.

loon   *verb* to spend time in an enjoyable way such as dancing to popular music, lounging or wandering about, etc. A term from the mid sixties, used mainly by young people. It is better known in *loons* or *loon pants / trousers* (1971), tightly fitting trousers flared below the knee, presumably worn by 'looners'. The origin of the word is unknown.

loony left   *noun* the extreme left-wing of the British Labour Party (and perhaps beyond). The domination of some local councils by extremists, often as a result of ENTRYISM by the MILITANT TENDENCY, was an important political issue during the second half of the seventies (when it may have contributed to the election of Margaret Thatcher's first government in 1979) and throughout most of the eighties, as the Labour Party sought to marginalise and finally neutralise them, which they had done by c.1991. The *loony left*, a term coined by the tabloids c.1977 ('loony' is slang for 'lunatic') also included some prominent trade unionists and a few MPs, but their influence had largely gone by the general election of 1992, the Labour Party having recognised that it would remain unelectable as long as it remained associated with them.

lose one's cool   see COOL.

love-bombing   *noun* a style of recruitment practised by some religious cults whose members saturate potential converts with affection, care and idealistic feelings. A US term (mid seventies) which is intended to express the intensity of the process by comparing it to a bombardment intended to bring about surrender. The technique is sometimes called *flirty fishing*.

love-in   see -IN.

low-level   *adj.* (of a computer programming language) closer to machine language than to human language (1961). Generally faster and in that sense more efficient than a HIGH-LEVEL language.

low profile

low profile *noun* a position of deliberately sought lack of prominence or publicity. Also *adjective*, **low-profile**. Usually in *keep a low profile* (keep in the background). The term *low profile* first appeared in a specialist sense in 1967 (applied to car tyres that were wide in proportion to their height). Its new meaning dates from c.1970. Since then it has given rise to an opposite, **high profile**.

low-rise *adj.* (of building) having only a few storeys (1957). As the high-rise flats of the fifties and sixties began to show the drawbacks of such development, *low-rise* came to be used more generally to designate a rival solution to the problems of urban renewal.

low-tech *adj.* using simple or traditional technology. A jocular derivative (1980s) from HI-TECH, usually implying no technology at all. See also INTERMEDIATE TECHNOLOGY.

LSD (abbreviation for) lysergic acid diethylamide (1950). Best known from its widespread use during the sixties as an illegal hallucinogenic drug – though it is also used in experimental medicine – informally called ACID.

luggable *noun* a computer that is larger than a portable but able to be carried about with some difficulty. Also an *adjective* (of a computer) capable of being carried with difficulty. It weighs perhaps twenty to thirty pounds and is the size of a (small) suitcase. The term dates from the eighties and is from the verb *lug* ('to carry with difficulty') and will perhaps be only a short-lived addition to the vocabulary of computing: it belongs to a period when portable computers of various sizes and weights were coming onto the market.

lumpectomy *noun* the surgical removal of a tumour in a woman's breast, leaving the rest of the breast intact. Used in cases of known or suspected breast cancer, and often accompanied by radiotherapy to destroy any remaining cancer cells. The technique, known since c.1972, is obviously an improvement of the much older mastectomy, which entails the amputation of the entire breast.

lurk *verb* to hang back from full participation in discussion on the INTERNET; to observe a newsgroup rather than joining in. Internet users' jargon, describing a natural response of most *newbies* (beginners) on first accessing a newsgroup. The image is perhaps of someone lurking in the shadows rather than coming into the firelight to be recognised. The word became more generally known at the time the Internet was expanding (early to mid nineties).

luvvies *noun* (a semi-satirical term for) actors, actresses and other people employed in the theatrical profession. Media slang c.1990, based on the assumption that people connected with the stage habitually address each other gushingly as 'love', 'lovie', etc. in keeping with their generally flamboyant manner – a rather dated view of theatrical behaviour, though perhaps true of some senior members of the profession. *Luvvy* first appeared in print in the satirical magazine *Private Eye*, and may have been coined by the editor.

Lycra *noun* (trademark of) a shiny, synthetic elastic fibre and fabric used in tight fitting garments, especially sportswear (1958).

Lyme disease *noun* an infectious, occasionally fatal, disease affecting the joints, heart and brain, and transmitted by ticks. So called because it was first identified among children in the town of Old Lyme, Connecticut, USA, in 1975. It was identified in UK patients about ten years later.

Mace *noun* (tradename for) a type of tear gas causing a burning sensation in the eyes, nose and throat, used in riot control. Known since 1966 (sometimes in its full form as *Chemical Mace*) and specially associated with the suppression of US demonstrations against the Vietnam War. It is also available in aerosol form as a weapon of personal protection (e.g. to spray in the face of an assailant) though this use is illegal in the UK. The word is also found without a capital letter, and sometimes as a verb meaning 'to attack with Mace'.

M(a)c Guffin *noun* an event, object, etc. serving as the impetus for the plot of a book, film, TV series, etc. Sir Alfred Hitchcock, the film director, started to use this word c.1935 to describe something (e.g. the theft of secret documents) which starts off the action of one of his film plots and occupies the attention both of the characters and of the audience, but which is merely a plot device to get the action under way and is not of central interest to the filmmaker. Hitchcock claims to have borrowed the word from a Scottish joke (hence the *M(a)c*); there is probably some connection with *guff*, slang for empty or ridiculous talk. The word passed from Hitchcock's private vocabulary into more general use, with a more general meaning, after the sixties, as a result of interviews he gave about his technique, but it remains largely confined to the language of film criticism.

machine code or **language** *noun* (in computer technology) the code representing the operations built into the hardware of a computer (1954). Usually the binary code sequence that can be understood and executed by a particular computer. Instructions in **machine code** can be executed much more quickly than if they were translated into a HIGH-LEVEL language such as BASIC.

machismo *noun* masculine pride and virility, especially when exaggerated. A Mexican–Spanish term, used by English speakers since c.1948, but it has become much more familiar in recent years as the roles and expectations of the sexes have been debated.

macho *adj.* notably virile, showing qualities thought to be typically masculine, especially physical strength, aggressiveness or sexual appetite. (Also *noun*: a man displaying such characteristics.) This Spanish word for 'male' or 'vigorously masculine' has been occasionally used in American English since c.1928, but has been found in Britain only since the 1960s. It is now often used mockingly or pejoratively. The corresponding noun is MACHISMO.

macro *noun* (in computing) a macro-instruction (1959). A computer instruction, often the pressing of a single key, that initiates a more complex set of instructions. The term uses the familiar combining form *macro-* (large, long).

macrobiotics *noun* a dietary system based on natural foods such

mad

as whole grains (e.g. untreated brown rice) and vegetables grown without chemical additives. The word has been used in this sense since the mid sixties, though it has a much longer history as a word meaning 'the science of prolonging life', being derived from two Greek words meaning 'long' and 'life'. The dietary system it now denotes is based on the principle of Ying and Yang and is related to Zen Buddhist ideas for prolonging life.

MAD   see BALANCE OF TERROR.

mad cow disease   *noun* (informal name for) **BSE**. A late eighties journalistic coinage, based on the fact that BSE affects the nervous system of cattle, making them stagger or fall as if deranged.

Madison Avenue   *noun* and *adj.* (typical of the attributes or methods of) the US advertising and public relations business. The name of the street in New York where the business used to be centred has been used allusively, sometimes pejoratively, in this sense since the fifties.

magalog(ue)   *noun* an advertising or marketing publication combining the characteristics of the magazine and the mail-order catalogue. Coined by US advertisers in the late seventies, and known in the UK since the eighties, as a blend of 'magazine' and 'catalogue'. It is normally issued free, its main purpose being to advertise, though that purpose is disguised by a style of presentation which makes it look like a general-interest magazine.

magic mushroom   *noun* any one of various types of mildly hallucinogenic fungi. An informal name coined in the late sixties. *Magic* is something of an overstatement.

magic realism   *noun* a style of fiction writing in which the realistic and everyday are mingled with the unexpected or inexplicable (e.g. dream, fairy-story, mythology) in a kaleidoscopic manner. The term was adopted in this sense by a number of young British writers in the seventies; they included Emma Tennant, Angela Carter and Salman Rushdie. It is a translation of a German term originally coined in 1925 to describe the work of a school of contemporary painters who portrayed the mythical or fantastic in a representational, realistic or rational way. The term has also been used to describe the work of other painters and writers at various times since 1925.

magnetic resonance imaging   *noun* a diagnostic scanning system providing sectional images of the internal structure of a patient's body. Developed in the mid seventies as a means of avoiding exploratory surgery, and in use since c.1983. It works by radiating a part of the body in the presence of a magnetic field, then using a scanning machine to produce a computer aided image of the soft tissue. Commonly abbreviated to *MRI*.

mail merging   *noun* computer software for producing a large number of personalised letters ('mail') by combining ('merging') a file containing a standard letter with one containing names and addresses (c.1985).

mail shot   *noun* (the dispatch of) a circular, leaflet, advertising material, etc., sent to a large number of people by post. (Also

mailing shot.) Originally (c.1963) used of an advertising campaign, which probably explains *shot* with its implication of firing something at a selected target, but the word is now used of other material, including simple information, sent to a mailing list.

mainframe   *noun* the largest type of computer installation, having great store capacity and capable of supporting numerous input and output devices. Used by large organisations such as banks. The word was coined c.1964, but was originally applied – before the development of the MINICOMPUTER and MICROCOMPUTER – to the main framework of a central processing unit on which the arithmetic unit and associated logic circuits were mounted, and subsequently to the central processing unit itself, before acquiring its present meaning in the mid seventies.

makeover   *noun* a complete remodelling. The noun, formed from the old verb *make over* ('to refashion'), originated in the late sixties in the jargon of professional hairstylists and beauticians, and gradually infiltrated the vocabulary of women's magazines, changing its sense from 'refashioning' to 'total restyling', i.e. changing not merely aspects of one's appearance, such as one's hairstyle or make-up, but its totality. Since the eighties the word has been applied to other kinds of remodelling (e.g. interior decoration) and is now often used of the restructuring of a business company or the adjustment of its corporate image.

male chauvinism   *noun* prejudice by certain men against women, based on a belief that men are inherently superior to women, whose role in society should be restricted to a traditionally subservient, domestic and sexual one. This odd but memorable variant of *chauvinism* ('aggressive or fanatical patriotism') arose in the vocabulary of the WOMAN'S LIBERATION movement c.1970 and rapidly became established in general use.

male chauvinist (pig)   *noun* a man who exhibits MALE CHAUVINISM. The addition of *pig* (a traditional term of abuse) transforms a critical description into a derogatory one. Sometimes abbreviated to *MCP*, this term derives from the women's movement and the early seventies.

male menopause   *noun* a period in middle age when a man's sense of purpose and of his own identity falter, perhaps accompanied by, or even caused by, a diminishment of his sexual drive. The term is often slightly jocular as the menopause proper can be experienced only by women. However, the female menopause is usually associated with other effects besides purely physical ones, and it is these – and the age at which they occur – that are alluded to in *male menopause*. Depression, for example, and a sense of having been side-lined may be experienced by both sexes. First recorded 1949, but not in general use until the sixties.

mall   *noun* a covered shopping complex, now often out of town. The normal US term for what the British still often refer to as a SHOPPING MALL, though the shorter form is now sometimes found in the UK also. *Mall* has been used for several centuries in the UK to mean 'a sheltered walk serving as a promenade', and was given a new lease of life in the early sixties when it began to be applied to the pedestrianised central alley that was a common feature of the open-air as well as covered shopping precincts in the UK; but the concept of large covered areas dedicated to shopping and with individual shops opening onto walkways became most familiar and fashionable in the eighties.

management buyout   *noun* the purchase of a company by its own managers (1977). Such purchases are usually with the financial assistance of a bank or other institution and almost always when there are financial difficulties in the company.

Mao suit (collar, jacket, cap, etc.)   *noun* of the type worn by Mao Tse-Tung, China's communist leader (1893–1976). He usually appeared in a simple cotton suit of loose trousers and a straight jacket with a close-fitting standing collar (plus a plain cotton, peaked cap outdoors) indistinguishable from the clothing commonly worn in China at the time. His name was given to the style of collar in 1967 in Paris, and in subsequent years applied to other items. Hong Kong influenza was briefly called 'Mao 'flu' during the same period.

margarita   *noun* a drink of tequila and lemon juice, drunk from a glass with the rim dipped in salt. First heard of in the mid sixties (apparently called after the woman's name) and popular in the seventies, though the word had previously existed as the name of a Spanish wine and, with a capital letter, a Caribbean island.

marginalise   *verb* to make to seem unimportant; to treat (people) as belonging to the fringes rather than to the centre of one's own or society's interest or concern. In its original meaning ('to make notes in the margin') the word was rare. It was taken over by sociologists in the seventies and given this entirely new meaning, since when it has rapidly became established, especially in the vocabulary of pressure groups refusing to be pushed to the 'margins' of public interest and those describing the way that sections of our society have been disempowered and their interests ignored.

market maker   *noun* a dealer in securities on the London Stock Exchange, permitted to make a profit rather than earn a commission. The deregulation of the London Stock Exchange in 1986 – see BIG BANG – established the distinction between brokers and jobbers and created *market makers* who guarantee to deal in the stocks for which they are registered and then to *make* a *market* in them. The term existed previously on the Stock Exchange, but with a different meaning.

MARV (acronym for) manoeuvrable re-entry vehicle. It is a missile with one or more warheads which can be controlled electronically to avoid enemy defences, or to take account of atmospheric conditions, etc. (1983).

mascarpone   *noun* a soft, mild, Italian cream cheese, often eaten as a dessert. Suddenly popular in the eighties in the UK, though long known in Italy.

masculist   *noun* a person who upholds the rights of man; or (sometimes) one who opposes feminism. Coined in the early eighties on the model of 'feminist' and as a response to what were felt to be the excesses of feminism or WOMEN'S LIBERATION. The word is sometimes used to mean 'a person opposing feminism', in which case it is a milder alternative to MALE CHAUVINIST, but the more usual meaning implies being in favour of something rather than opposing something. Also *adj.* **masculist**, typical of male attitudes *or* upholding men's rights.

MASH (acronym for) mobile army surgical hospital. An American term (1950) made famous as the title of a popular television series (1972–83).

massage *verb* to manipulate (information, data, statistics or the way they are presented) to give a more acceptable result or support a particular interpretation. Initially (c.1966) this figurative use of the familiar word was applied to written documents which were 'improved' as a person is by literal *massage* (perhaps the model for this was the figurative use of *doctor*). Since the mid seventies, however, the word has mainly been used of figures, and the rapid spread of computers has made *data massage* much easier in business circles. It implies gentler dishonesty than actual 'doctoring'.

master class *noun* a class for trained musicians given by a virtuoso player. This sense dates from c.1963 (the term earlier meant 'the governing class in society'). It is now sometimes used of a teaching session given by an expert other than a musician.

max (out) *verb* to achieve the maximum. Also **to the max**, *phrase* completely, to the maximum. Eighties US youth slang, mainly West Coast, showing some signs of taking root in the UK, especially in the adjectival *maxed out* ('at the brink of one's capacity', etc.). All the forms are new applications of the abbreviation of *maximum*.

maxi(-skirt) *noun* an ankle-length skirt. As a new abbreviation of 'maximum', *maxi* (1966) was probably inspired by the huge current popularity of MINI. It was also used in *maxi-coat, maxi-length*, etc., and is still heard in the vocabulary of fashion.

McKenzie friend *noun* a person who attends a court of law to help a party to a case by making notes, giving advice, etc. Called after the case of McKenzie v McKenzie (1970) in which it was first established that such a helper had a right to attend a trial to assist someone who did not wish to use a lawyer.

MCP (abbreviation for) MALE CHAUVINIST PIG (1971).

MDMA (abbreviation for) methylene-dioxymethamphetamine, better known as ECSTASY. See also ADAM.

ME (abbreviation for) myalgic encephalomyelitis, an often long-lasting, post-viral condition causing general fatigue, muscular pain, depression, headache, loss of coordination, etc. Because of its lack of observable physical symptoms, this condition was rather dismissively known as 'malingerers' disease' and sometimes thought to be no more than psychosomatic when it first came to prominence in the late seventies (though cases had been noted since the fifties). During the eighties, when the current abbreviation came into common use, it was taken more seriously, and some progress was made towards finding a cause. High achievers seem to be especially prone to it (hence another of its nicknames, YUPPIE FLU) but it remains a mystery, often affecting sufferers for many months with flu-like pains and malaise.

meathead   *noun* an idiot. US slang since the forties, and in UK usage since the mid eighties. Probably on the model of AIR-HEAD, but implying a grosser stupidity because of the assertion that the person so described has meat in the place of brains. See also DICKHEAD.

mechatronics   *noun* a technology in which electronics engineering, including CAD, combines with mechanical engineering to develop and control automation in a manufacturing process. Since its first appearance in the early eighties the word has been mainly used of the development of robots in the car industry, particularly as pioneered by the Japanese, but it is beginning to spread to other aspects of manufacturing industry, again with the Japanese as the leaders, for the technology started with them.

medallion man   *noun* (derogatory term for) a type of man who wears a neck chain and (large, gold) medallion, often with his shirt open several buttons to display it (and, preferably, his hairy chest) as a sign of style, wealth and virility. A seventies term characterising the MACHO, but fading into history after the mid eighties.

Me decade or **me generation**   *noun* The American writer Tom Wolfe (b. 1931) called the seventies 'the Me Decade' in a magazine article of 1973 because of what he saw as the narcissism of the younger generation in the USA: he interpreted their self-absorption (manifested in therapy, health clubs, etc.) and obsession with self-improvement as a sort of new theology. The later term, *me generation*, was a broadening intended to include in its embrace the THATCHERITE eighties, widely perceived as a period of selfishness, material greed and unconcern for the dispossessed and MARGIN-ALISED.

medevac   *noun* a US military helicopter used to transport the wounded to hospital (1966). Also *verb*, to transport by this means. In UK military jargon the word (from 'medical' and 'evacuation') is usually used to cover the evacuation of casualties from forward areas to the nearest treatment centre.

media, the   *noun* (collective name for) newspapers, television, radio and magazines as the most common means of communication with large numbers of people in a short time. *Media* is, strictly speaking, no more than the plural of 'medium', but the current definition has been common since c.1958 when the word began to establish itself as a shortened form of the more specific 'mass media (of communication)'.

media event   *noun* an event specially staged for the MEDIA, having no intrinsic importance or genuineness but designed to generate maximum publicity, notably on television or in the press. Originally (US, 1972) and still predominantly a political device during electioneering, but also a favourite contrivance of the public-relations industry for a variety of purposes, especially advertising.

mega *adj.* extremely good, great, successful, satisfying, important, etc. Slang term of general appreciation ('It's mega'), from the mid eighties, probably as an independent use of the combining form MEGA-. See below.

mega- This prefix, with or without the hyphen, has long had two uses: **1.** denoting a million; **2.** indicating largeness or greatness more generally. Modern examples of **1** include *megabuck* (a million dollars (1946), though the term is now used colloquially and in the plural to denote any very large sum of money) and *megadeath* (the death of a million people in a nuclear war), a word used by military bureaucrats to calculate the effects of such a war (1953). The second use is now much more common, and during the eighties was freely used in combination with numerous nouns and adjectives, e.g. *mega-successful*, *megahype* (see HYPE), sometimes as a free standing word (e.g. *mega deal*, a business transaction involving large sums of money) related to or indistinguishable from the use of MEGA described in the previous entry. See also the following entries.

megabyte *noun* (in computer technology) 2^{20} or 1,048,576 **bytes**. The memory capacity of computers and the storage capacity of discs are measured in *megabytes* (1973). Strictly speaking, the word means a million bytes (see MEGA-, sense 1), but the approximation is allowable.

megaflop *noun* (in computer technology) a measure of processing speed consisting of a million floating-point operations a second; (colloquially) comprehensive failure (of an event, attempt, etc.). The first (mid seventies) is from MEGA- (sense 1) with an acronym from *flo*ating-*p*oint. The second is an example of MEGA- (sense 2).

megastar *noun* an internationally famous and highly paid performer, usually in the entertainment business. Since the mid seventies this term has replaced 'superstar' (1925) in media hyperbole; see MEGA- (sense 2).

megastore *noun* a very large store. See MEGA- (sense 2). The term is from the mid eighties.

mellow out *verb* to relax; become LAID-BACK. US slang, mid seventies, known but not (yet) much used in the UK. It appears to be related to the earlier (1940s) US slang word of *mellow* as an adjective meaning 'relaxed and happy after drug-taking', but the current verbal use does not necessarily imply the release of tensions or inhibitions by drugs.

meltdown *noun* the melting of fuel rods in a nuclear reactor as a result of failure in the cooling system, with the possible release of radiation into the environment; (figuratively) very sudden or uncontrollable disastrous failure with the potential to cause far-reaching harm. The first meaning (1965) gave rise to the second in the mid eighties, probably because the word had become recently well known as a result of the accidents at Three Mile Island (1979) and Chernobyl (1986).

menu *noun* (in computing) a list of options (commands, facilities, etc.) displayed on a screen, enabling the operator to select one by moving a cursor or depressing a key. One of the earliest and most familiar computing terms (1967) borrowed from the restaurant *menu*, a list of dishes from which the customer makes a selection. Computer software which is *menu-driven* (1979) is that which functions in response to the operator's selection from a *menu*.

MEP (UK abbreviation for) Member of the European Parliament (1976).

metal (occasional abbreviation for) HEAVY METAL.

methaqualane *noun* a hypnotic and sedative drug (1961). Used widely in sleeping tablets and as a relaxant since the sixties, especially in the US where it is sold as Quaalude. Its use is controlled because of abuse by some users.

metrication *noun* conversion from nonmetric to metric units. Attempts to change British measurements to the metric system have progressed slowly outside science and engineering. The Metrication Board, set up in 1969 to complete the process throughout commerce and industry by 1975, disbanded in 1980 without having succeeded. At least the name for the process was agreed on: *metrication*, and the *verb metricate*, were officially adopted in 1965 after consultation with the editor of the *Concise Oxford Dictionary*.

Mexican wave *noun* a wave-like effect created by a large crowd of spectators in a sports stadium when successive sections of the crowd stand while raising their arms and then sit, so that the motion passes round the stadium. The practice originated with spectators at American football matches in the early eighties but did not become generally known until it was seen on international television during the World Cup football competition in Mexico in 1986.

mezzanine funding *noun* intermediate funding during a financial process. Typically this is the funding of a take over by using unsecured loans (at a high rate of interest) as an 'intermediate' between a conventionally financed (i.e. secured) loan on the one hand and offering a share of equity on the other. It offers a high risk but also a high return. See JUNK BOND. The use of *mezzanine* in this sense (c.1980) is based on the architectural sense of the word, which is 'an intermediate storey in a building (usually a low one between the ground floor and first floor)'.

micro (short for) MICROCOMPUTER, MICROPROCESSOR, MICROWAVE.

microchip *noun* a small piece of semiconductor material carrying many integrated circuits. From *micro-* ('very small') and CHIP (1975).

microcomputer *noun* a cheap, small computer with a central processing unit contained in one or more CHIPS (1971). Now more usually called a PERSONAL COMPUTER. When such machines began to appear in the early seventies as a result of developments in MICROCHIP technology, they were largely used for video games, but they are now in widespread use for wordprocessing, DESKTOP PUBLISHING, etc.

microdot *noun* a tiny tablet containing LSD (1971). In the sense of 'photograph (of document, etc.) reduced to about the size of a dot', as used in espionage, the word originated c.1946.

microelectronics *noun* the branch of electronics dealing with tiny INTEGRATED CIRCUITS (1960).

microlight *noun* a small one- or two-seater aircraft weighing not more than 150 kg when empty, and having a wing area not less than 10 square metres. Introduced c.1981, used for pleasure flying, and sometimes spelt *-lite* or *-lyte*.

microprocessor *noun* (in computer technology) a simple INTEGRATED CIRCUIT on a small CHIP acting as the central processing unit of a small computer (1970). In addition to its use in MICROCOMPUTERS, its applications include cookers, washing machines, aircraft, cars, video machines, telephone boxes, cash dispensers and machine tool control.

microwave (oven) *noun* an oven in which food is cooked rapidly by passing microwaves through it. As a scientific word, *microwave* belongs to the earlier part of the century, but its now everyday use as an abbreviation for *microwave oven* (and also as a verb and adjective) dates only from the mid sixties in the US and from the seventies in the UK.

MIDI (acronym for) musical instrument digital interface. Such an interface allows electronic musical instruments, synthesisers, computers, etc. to be connected and controlled simultaneously. Since its introduction c.1983 it has been widely used in popular music for mixing sounds from different sorts of sources.

midi system *noun* a compact medium-sized, home stereo system designed as a single stacked unit and usually comprising CD, record and tape decks, amplifier with radio, and speakers. Introduced in the mid eighties, it was welcomed as a cheaper, neater and smaller set of equipment than previous systems, but the appearance in 1990 of an even smaller and, it is claimed, equally sophisticated *mini system* (approximately half-size) may make it short-lived. The name is modelled on MAXI and MINI: see MIDI(-SKIRT) below.

midi(-skirt) *noun* a skirt reaching to midcalf (1967). The name derives from 'mid-' or 'middle' and is modelled on the slightly earlier MAXI and MINI. It is sometimes used adjectively (*midi-length*) and occasionally applied to other garments, especially coats.

midlife crisis *noun* an emotional crisis occurring in middle age, especially among men, and associated with the realisation that one is no longer young and that life may be passing one by. The psychologist who coined the phrase, in 1965, referred to the typical age of crisis as being 35 – which may be biblically *midlife* but not what most people think of as middle age. As the phrase has passed into general use, however, it has become more associated with middle age than with one's mid-thirties.

Militant Tendency *noun* a Trotskyite group within the British Labour Party. It became active in the seventies and took control in local government in a number of areas, pursuing radical policies which others considered extravagant and unbalanced. After causing disruption and division, it was banned by the Labour Party during the late eighties at a time when the Party was striving to make itself electable in preparation for the General Election of 1992, which it lost.

milk round   *noun* the personnel managers' (usually annual) round of visits to universities to recruit potential graduates into industry, etc. In RAF slang of the Second World War, the term was used of any regular flight, especially a routine night-bombing raid that returned at dawn (when milkmen begin their rounds). The current usage (c.1970) may derive from this, or simply from the idea that the recruiters aim to 'milk' (extract) the best talent from the universities.

mind-bending, -blowing, -boggling   *adj.* so astounding as to be difficult to comprehend. All seem to be originally associated with sixties vocabulary for the effects of hallucinogenic drugs. *Mind-bending* is c.1965; *mind-blowing* is from BLOW ONE'S MIND; *mind-boggling* (c.1964) is British rather than American English, from a previously little-known verb *boggle* ('to surprise or alarm').

minder   *noun* an aide or experienced adviser who looks after someone in the public eye, especially a politician or political candidate, and handles public relations, prevents gaffs or unwelcome publicity, etc.; the bodyguard of a celebrity. This second meaning is a natural development from much earlier criminal slang which euphemistically (compare 'child-minder' or 'machine-minder') used *minder* to mean 'a con-man's assistant', 'a bodyguard e.g. for a prostitute', 'a club bouncer', etc. The first meaning emerged in the mid eighties, no doubt under the influence of a very popular television series called *Minder* (1979 onwards) about a secondhand-car salesman and dubious 'entrepreneur' or petty crook and his 'minder'. The word has become so general that, though initially jocular and colloquial, it is probably now to be regarded as Standard English. It was used, for example, during the Gulf War of any military officer attached to a journalist, ostensibly to assist but actually to censor.

mind-expanding   *adj.* same as PSYCHEDELIC (1963).

mindset   *noun* a state of mind; attitude; opinion. In the earlier part of the century, the term had a precise and useful meaning in psychology and sociology: 'habits of mind formed by previous events or earlier environments'. The current usage, which seems set to displace this, reached Britain from the USA in the early eighties, and is both weaker and more general, suggesting a characteristic attitude or set of assumptions.

mini   (abbreviation of) **miniskirt** and **minicar** (see MINI-). For *Mini* as the name of the popular small car, see MINI-.

mini-   Beginning in the 1960s, this has been an extremely popular prefix, attached to numerous nouns to add the sense 'small of its kind' (*mini-budget, mini-holiday, mini-crisis,* and many others too numerous to list). The derivation is from 'miniature' (or 'minimum'), though the vogue for 'mini-' words may have been influenced by the launch, in 1959, of the revolutionary and very popular (Austin) Mini car. However, it is to be noted that the three-wheeled Bond Minicar had been invented in 1949, *minicameras* were known in the thirties, and the *minibus* was named in the nineteenth century, though not of course in its present form. The most durable coinages include *miniskirt* (reaching mid-thigh or higher, 1965), *minicab* (an ordinary saloon car, and therefore having less capacity than a taxi, but available for hire only by telephone or personal call, not by hailing in the street, 1960), *minicomputer* (intermediate in power between a mainframe and microcomputer, 1973) and *minipill* (a low-dose oral contraceptive, 1970).

Mini Disc   *noun* small CD capable of being used in a portable as well as a stationary system. Commercially introduced in the UK in late 1992.

minimal art   *noun* a style of abstract art, especially sculpture, with an emphasis on simple geometric shapes, primary colours, and a minimum of expression of meaning, emotion or illusion (1965). From c.1974 *minimal* was also applied to music that used a form of composition characterised by short phrases and repetitive rhythms or harmonies rather than by complexity of style.

minimalism   *noun* (another name for) MINIMAL ART (1969). Also *minimalist*, a practitioner of minimal art (1969).

minimum lending rate   *noun* the minimum rate at which the Bank of England would lend to discount houses from 1971–81. It thus controlled the rate of interest operated by banks, building societies, etc., throughout the economy. After 1981, when government wished to indicate a relaxation of its controls, it was replaced by the less formal *base rate*. Before 1971 it was known as the *bank rate*.

mini-series   *noun* a television programme in several parts, shown over a short period. For example, for three consecutive nights or weeks, whereas most television series run for much longer. The concept of the mini-series came from the US but they were staple fare in the UK by the mid eighties, and are a favourite way of adapting best selling novels and biographies for television.

mini system   see MIDI SYSTEM. The first word is a stand-alone form of MINI-.

MIPS   (acronym for) million instructions per second. A measure of computing speed and power (1974).

Miranda   *noun* the name given to a set of rules specified by the US Supreme Court and requiring the police to tell suspects, before interrogation, of their rights to counsel and their privilege against self-incrimination. The name, used in the US in a variety of contexts but known in the UK only from US television programmes, comes from the court case of Ernesto Miranda v State of Arizona (1966) which led to the Supreme Court's notable ruling and to changes in police procedure.

MIRAS   (acronym for) mortgage interest relief at source. Such relief was introduced in 1983 when the UK government wished to encourage home ownership. Previously, home owners with mortgages made their repayments in full and then claimed tax relief on that part of the repayment which was interest. Under the new scheme, this relief was paid directly by the government to the mortgage company.

MIRV

MIRV (acronym for) multiple independently targeted reentry vehicle. A nuclear missile with several warheads, each one of which can be programmed to hit a different target (1967).

missionary position *noun* a position for sexual intercourse in which the man lies on top of the woman, face-to-face (1969). The name is popularly said to derive from missionaries' advocacy of this position to their flocks as the only acceptable one.

mission impossible *phrase* any impossible task. A popular catchphrase which is the title of a popular American television spy thriller originally broadcast from 1966 to 1972 and also shown in the UK.

mission statement *noun* a published statement of the policy and objectives of a business firm, government department, etc. *Mission* means 'task' or 'duty' and carries associations of 'vocation' (one's mission in life) or even of a religious calling. A *mission statement* is therefore rather highflown business jargon, originally US and first heard in Britain c.1991, for something that may be rather ordinary and essentially commercial. Schools, Health Authorities and similar organisations are now also required to develop a mission statement.

mix *noun* the final version of a recorded song. So called because the final version blends several tape tracks, each of them recording a different voice or instrument, not necessarily at the same session, which is why some rock groups are unable to reproduce in live performances the songs of their own recordings. This current use of *mix* (c.1980) is a specialised application of a usage which goes back to the earliest vocabulary of broadcasting and films, in which it means 'the action or result of mixing two pictures or sounds'.

mixed media *noun* a work of art combining two or more media. The earliest applications of the term (1962) were to painting which combined media that had customarily been used separately (e.g. water colour, oil paint, crayon, ink etc.). Later it was applied to other art forms or entertainments, for example combining light and film projection with varieties of recorded sound. Compare MULTIMEDIA.

mod *noun* an adherent of a fashion-conscious sub-culture among British teenagers who cultivated smart Italian-style clothes (especially suits), careful grooming, Italian scooters and cool jazz. The group emerged in the late fifties and the name was established by 1960, but most people were unaware of either until Bank Holiday clashes with ROCKERS at several seaside resorts in 1964. The cult was short-lived, but was briefly revived in the late seventies. Their name came from 'modern' or 'modernist', the implication being that they were modern in being fashionable and sophisticated, especially in comparison with rockers.

modem *noun* (in computer technology) an electronic device for connecting computers by a telephone line for the transmission of messages. It modulates computer signals (i.e. digital) into electrical signals (i.e. audio) that can be transmitted, and demodulates the latter into the former when receiving. The word (1958) combines *mo(dulator)* and *dem(odulator)*.

mole *noun* a spy who has infiltrated an organisation and gained its trust. John Buchan used the word in something approaching this sense in a 1920s novel, in reference to the mole's burrowing and its inoffensive and inconspicuous appearance. It did not become part of our language, however, until the publication (1974) and subsequent televising of John Le Carré's *Tinker, Tailor, Soldier, Spy*; he himself claimed it was KGB jargon. The word is now sometimes more loosely used of any informant or discloser of confidential information even if he acts of his own volition and has not been deliberately placed within an organisation for that purpose.

moment in time, at this *phrase* now. First recorded in 1972, subsequently becoming an epidemic, apparently incurable.

Monday Club *noun* a club of right-wing Conservatives founded in 1961. They originally met for lunch on Mondays, and they continue to see themselves as the guardians of 'true' conservatism.

mondo *adv.* extremely. Formerly US slang meaning 'very weird in a decadent, seedy or anarchic way', though it existed earlier in the sense of 'the bizarre world of . . .'. The origin was a curious but popular Italian film, *Mondo Cane* (1961), in which *mondo* is the Italian word for 'world'. The term reached Britain only with the TEENAGE MUTANT HERO TURTLES, by which time it had changed to an adverb with a simpler meaning. It is now used mainly by young people in expressions of approval.

monetarism *noun* an economic theory that control of the money supply is the only way to control inflation, and that an expansion of the money supply will increase unemployment; an economic policy based on free market forces, balanced budgets, and the belief that high wages cause unemployment. This theory is usually contrasted with that of John Maynard Keynes ('Keynesianism') which holds that it is for governments to create jobs and wealth through public-spending programmes. The word was first heard c.1969 in connection with the economic theories of Milton Friedman, and became commonplace in the eighties because of its association with THATCHERISM.

monokini *noun* a one-piece bathing costume worn by women and consisting of the bottom half of a bikini (1964). Here *mono-* ('one') is something of a pun, because the *bi-* of *bikini* does not mean 'two', as it often does (e.g. bicycle). The bikini or two-piece bathing costume was named in 1948 after Bikini Atoll in the Pacific, the site of an early atom bomb test in 1946.

Moog or **moog** *noun* (short for) Moog synthesiser, an electronic musical keyboard capable of making instrumental and other musical sounds. Actually a tradename from the name of its inventor, RA Moog (b.1934), an American engineer. The name did not become known in the UK until after 1969, though Moog had developed his first synthesisers during the 1950s.

moon *verb* to display one's bare buttocks to passers-by. American women students appear to have originated this practice in the mid fifties, in order to amuse, impress or affront. Its name, based on the supposed resemblance between the buttocks and the moon,

Moonie

presumably originated at about the same time but is not recorded in print until the late sixties. The practice **mooning**, became known in the UK c.1974, though it is usually performed by men, especially those travelling on football coaches.

Moonie *noun* (informal name of) a member of the Unification Church. The church itself is usually called *the Moonies* after Sun Myung Moon (b.1920) who founded it in South Korea in 1954. He claims to be the Second Messiah, but his organisation – which spread to the USA in the sixties and then, less strongly, to the UK – is thought to be political and sinister. Moon himself has built up a large business organisation in the USA but has been imprisoned for tax avoidance.

moonlight *verb* to have a secondary job, especially at night, sometimes illegitimately, in addition to one's regular employment. Although this meaning dates only from c.1957, originating in the US, the word has long been used to denote a variety of illegal activities at night, as in **moonlight flit** the unannounced departure from rented rooms to avoid paying the rent.

moonwalk *noun* and *verb*. Coined, initially with a hyphen, in the late sixties in connection with man's first walk on the moon (1969). It was revived in the mid eighties as the name of a form of BREAK-DANCING in which the dancer gives the impression of sliding on the spot, suggesting the slow-motion effects of actual moonwalking.

MOR (abbreviation for) middle-of-the-road. Used since the seventies in the jargon of the music industry, radio stations, etc. to denote simple pop music for average, undemanding listeners – a large and therefore commercially important group – who do not want anything experimental or unusual.

moral majority *noun* a (presumed) majority of people believed to be in favour of traditional (or stricter) moral values in society. The original Moral Majority movement – the name was based on SILENT MAJORITY – was founded in the USA in the late seventies to promote a conservative Christian viewpoint (which some would describe as a right-wing reactionary opposition to liberal values and reforms on such matters as abortion and homosexuality). It became prominent in US politics during the Reagan administration, but changed its name in 1986. The current phrase (without capital letters) is less specific in its connotation, though some who use it in the UK still do so in a proselytising way, assuming that most people agree with them.

MOT *noun* the compulsory annual test for all road vehicles over a certain age. Also used for the **MOT certificate**, issued when a vehicle has passed this test: without it a vehicle may not be licensed or operated. *MOT* are the initials of the Ministry of Transport, which was responsible for the testing scheme when it was instituted by the Road Traffic Act of 1960. Although the Ministry has subsequently been renamed the Department of Transport, the original initials remain in popular use, and even official use, as the present certificate publicises 'The MOT Hotline' to advise the public on stolen or forged certificates.

motormouth *noun* a person who talks a lot, often loudly and to little purpose. Originally US black slang, c.1971, based on the idea that a motor usually cannot switch itself off. It reached UK slang in the late eighties. It is sometimes used to express speed and energy of delivery, but more often in a derogatory sense, suggesting running on without purpose or control.

motorway *noun* a main road for fast-moving traffic with limited access, separate carriageways and (usually) six lanes of traffic. The word did not come into general use until after the opening of the London–Birmingham M1 in 1959, though a short stretch of what was to become the M6 had been opened earlier near Preston, Lancashire. Credit for coining the word, however, seems to belong to a visionary writing in 1903. The first recognisably modern motorway linked Milan and Varese, Italy, in 1924.

Motown *noun* music of a type made popular by black musicians and singers from Detroit, USA, particularly that blending rhythm and blues and pop or combining gospel music with a modern ballad style. Detroit is the centre of the US car industry, and *Motown* is from its nickname, *Mo(tor) Town*. Strictly speaking, the name is a trademark of Tamla-Motown Records (founded 1960) who did much to promote this type of music, which was very popular in the late sixties and the seventies.

mountain *noun* a great surplus or stockpile of a commodity, usually foodstuffs within European Community arrangements. The best known examples are *butter mountain* (1969) and *beef mountain* (1974); see CAP. This metaphorical use of the word has spread from the language of journalism and politics.

mountain bike (or **bicycle**) *noun* a sturdy bicycle with light frame, thick tyres, straight handlebars and many gears (usually at least 16). Originally developed (N. America, early eighties) for use on rough cross-country or mountain tracks, it was adopted by the fashion-conscious for general town use during the late eighties, reaching the UK c.1987 and becoming something of a status symbol, particularly among the young, by c.1990.

mouse *noun* (in computing) a device in the shape of a small plastic box which when moved over a table top or a foam rubber pad moves a cursor on the VDU screen and enables the user to enter commands by 'clicking' a button or buttons. First invented in the US in the mid sixties it was not generally known and used until the eighties, when the user-friendly WIMP system popularised it as a means of instructing the personal computer. Its compact size and shape and its trailing lead are sufficiently like a stylised mouse's body and tail to explain the name. See ICON.

mousse *noun* a mixture of sea-water and oil resulting from spillage of oil into the sea. Originally *chocolate mousse*, a journalistic term used in reporting the *Torrey Canyon* disaster of 1967 to describe the colour and frothy texture of the resultant oil slick, and which compared it to the culinary chocolate mousse, a dessert of whipped cream and eggs. Shortened to *mousse*, it is now found in scientific or technical vocabulary as well as in press reports.

mousse

mousse   see STYLING MOUSSE.

movers and shakers   *noun* powerful and influential people with the means and energy to make things happen. The phrase occurs in *'Ode'* (1874) by the British minor poet Arthur O'Shaughnessy: 'Yet we [poets] are the movers and shakers/Of the world forever it seems.' The poem, though occasionally anthologised, can hardly be said to be well known, so it is odd that one of its phrases should have cropped up as a US colloquialism c.1972 and subsequently have passed into British usage, though not with quite the sense that the poet intended.

Mr Clean   *noun* an honourable and incorruptible person, often a politician or other public figure. Elliott Richardson, the US Attorney-General, appears to have been the first person to be given this appellation (originally the name of an American household cleaner) after his resignation in 1973 because he refused to accept President Nixon's restrictions on investigations into Watergate (see -GATE). Perhaps the name of the household cleaner was based on earlier coinages such as Mr Right (a man who will be an ideal husband) and Mr Big (head of a criminal organisation).

MRI   (abbreviation for) MAGNETIC RESONANCE IMAGING.

Ms   *noun* a title used before a woman's name in place of Mrs or Miss to avoid making a distinction based on marital status. The US National Office Management Association proposed this usage in 1952 so that typists could avoid the problem of deciding how to address women they had to send letters to. The usage was unknown in the UK until the seventies when it was advocated by the supporters of WOMEN'S LIBERATION, initially in the USA. Since then it has become increasingly common, though it is not universally accepted and some women object to it as being a feminist label.

MTV   (abbreviation for) music television, a 24-hour US rock channel now available on various satellite and cable channels (1984).

muesli belt   *noun* a middle-class area where people are likely to eat muesli and other health foods. The jocular implication is that such people, as well as being health-food faddists, are probably left-wing, intellectual, GREEN, feminist and generally trendy. The term (late seventies) is based on established uses of *belt* in the sense of 'area', e.g. green belt, stockbroker belt. *Muesli-belt malnutrition* is the undernourishment of children brought up on an over emphasised health food diet: research by the University of Surrey (1986) suggested that children reared on FAST FOOD are better nourished than children where food takes so long to chew that they do not eat enough.

multilevel marketing   *noun* (another name for or development of) PYRAMID SELLING. American jargon (early seventies) which was probably intended to give a more favourable impression as pyramid selling had been much criticised. *Multilevel* was coined c.1952 to mean 'having or operating on several levels'.

multimedia   *adj.* (of artistic, educational, commercial or other presentations) combining various media such as television, sound, graphics, animation, slides, etc. (1962). The word has subsequently been used in other contexts, such as computing, and in *multimedia CDs* which combine text, sound and images on a single disc.

multinational   *noun* a large business company operating in several countries. As a noun, this emerged only in the late sixties. The adjective meaning 'of several countries' as in *a multinational peace-keeping force*, is much older.

multitasking   *noun* (in computer technology) the simultaneous execution of various different tasks by the same machine (1966).

Murphy's law   *noun* if something can go wrong, it will. For example, if a piece of toast is dropped on the carpet, it will land with the buttered side downward. Although this term may have originated in Second World War military slang, it does not seem to have appeared in print until 1958 and it was certainly not in widespread use before then. The *Murphy* is simply the archetypical Irishman, the butt of many jokes about the alleged illogicality of the Irish. See SOD'S LAW.

musicassette   *noun* a tape cassette of prerecorded music (1966).

music centre   *noun* an integrated domestic hi-fi system consisting of record turntable, cassette tape deck and tuner-amplifier in a single unit, usually with separate speakers. Introduced c.1974 when the miniaturisation of components had been made possible by the MICROCHIP, but later supplemented by the MIDI SYSTEM.

muso   *noun* a musician. Originally (late sixties) Australian slang for any professional musician. In the UK, where it appeared about ten years later, its use is mainly limited to the rock scene. Its meaning is not easy to pin down: it is sometimes derogatory (compare **journo**), is sometimes applied to a player more preoccupied with technique than content or expression, and sometimes implies fanaticism. It has been said to be a bad musician's word for a good one, and has even been applied to a keen follower of music.

Muzak   *noun* (tradename for a system of) recorded light music played in public places such as shops. The word was patented in this sense in 1952 though it has been coined and patented earlier in a different but related sense. It was modelled on Kodak, this being a well-known tradename thought to be successfully memorable. Because piped music is disliked by some people as intrusive, the word became a term of abuse and is now sometimes used (with a small m-) to denote any unmemorable, poor quality or 'wallpaper' music.

MX   *noun* (abbreviation for) missile-experimental, a sophisticated US ICBM with up to ten nuclear warheads capable of being very accurately targeted. The weapon was developed during the seventies and designed to be operated from mobile launchers so that it could survive a FIRST-STRIKE attack by an enemy. It was the subject of some controversy because some people suspected it to be a disguised first-strike weapon itself, and in 1983 the US Congress refused to vote more funds for research into mobile launching systems, which had proved difficult to develop successfully.

nacho   *noun* a tortilla chip, usually grilled with a topping of cheese, peppers, spices, etc. and served as a side dish. Although known in regional cookery since the forties in N. Mexico and Texas, this did not become generally known until its adoption by FAST-FOOD outlets in the eighties. The name is thought to be from the first name of the Mexican chef who invented it: *Nacho* in the diminutive of the Spanish *Ignacio*.

naff *adj.* lacking style; socially inept; inferior or shoddy; unfashionable, in poor taste. British slang from c.1969 that enjoyed a sudden vogue c.1982. Its origin is unknown: it may be related to a northern dialect word meaning 'simpleton'. There appears to be no connection with NAFF OFF.

naffing *adj.* a euphemistic substitute for 'fucking'; 'effing'. Its origin is doubtful; naffing was widely used as an expletive and intensifier in the RAF in the Second World War, which suggests a possible connection with the NAAFI (Navy, Army and Air Force Institute) the organisation which provides cheap canteen and shop facilities for the armed forces. There seems to be no connection with the adjective NAFF (shoddy) above. As with NAFF OFF the word did not pass into widespread use until its popularisation in *Porridge* (mid seventies onwards).

naff off *verb* go away; 'eff off'; a euphemistic substitute for 'fuck off'. Not recorded in print until 1959, 'naff off' was given exposure by the popular prison life television comedy series, *Porridge*, from the mid seventies onwards.

naked ape, the *noun* the human species. Popularised by *The Naked Ape* (1967), a study of human behaviour by the British zoologist Desmond Morris (b.1928).

name of the game, the *phrase* the object or essence of an action. A N. American colloquialism from the early sixties, perhaps originally in the vocabulary of sports coaching. It was popularised by being the title of a US television series (1968–71) and has been common in the UK since the early seventies.

nanny state *noun* the state seen as dominating or being over-protective of its citizens, preventing them from achieving sturdy independence and self-reliance. The phrase is thought to have been coined in the early sixties (perhaps by the Conservative politician Ian Macleod) to describe the post-war welfare state, but it first came into prominence in the eighties when it suited the tone of many THATCHERITE attacks on institutions such as nationalised industries, social services and general bureaucracy which were thought to inhibit the flourishing of individualism and private enterprise. The British nanny (children's nurse) has been much discussed as a formidable and stunting influence on the psychology of the male governing class, and metaphorical uses of *nanny* as both noun and verb have been common in the language of political controversy since the Second World War.

nano- *prefix Nano-* is prefixed to the name of units to denote units a thousand-millionth times smaller (1947). See NANOSECOND.

nanosecond *noun* one thousand-millionth of a second (1959).

nanotechnology *noun* technology based on the smallest possible units of measurement (1990). This as yet unproven technology is believed by some to offer the possibility of reshaping matter and rebuilding materials from scratch. It works on the level of molecules and is theoretically capable of rearranging atoms. It is projected to have the added advantage of being pollution-free. If this promised technology comes about it would allow us to detoxify polluted environments and to perfect non-invasive health care, leading to what some have labelled **nanotopia**.

narcoterrorism *noun* terrorism against anti-drug agencies, including government and the police, instigated by those profiting from drug-trafficking, notably in South and Central America. Because of the newness of this term (mid eighties, mainly US), its meaning has not yet settled down. It has also been used to mean 'any violent crime associated with drug traffic' and even 'the manufacture or sale of illegal drugs' (i.e. 'terrorism' against the people who buy them or against society generally). *Narco-* is a combining form which can be used to mean 'related to illicit drugs'.

Nashville *noun* name of the capital of Tennessee, USA, used to describe a type of country and western music originating there. The name has been used in this context since c.1963, though the music began to evolve there as long ago as the twenties and was spread by a number of popular broadcasts. The installation of music publishing and recording industries there in the forties was an important step towards establishing the city as the home of country and western music.

nasty *noun* (short for) VIDEO NASTY.

national curriculum *noun* the curriculum of subjects designated as those that must be taught in state schools in England and Wales. Introduced by the Education Reform Act (1988). Responsibility for the school curriculum had previously rested with Local Education Authorities and in effect had usually been delegated to the individual Head Teacher.

National Front *noun* (in Britain) a small, right-wing political party with racist and other extremist policies, formed in 1967.

native American *noun* (North) American Indian. For a time *(North) American Indian* was the preferred term for those once called Red Indians, partly because of the unfortunate associations and past prejudices that the earlier term brought with it, partly because of the manifest inaccuracy of 'red', as not all American Indians have coppery-coloured skin. The use of *Indian* has itself been objected to, as enshrining Columbus's mistaken assumption that he had reached the Indies, thus imposing a European error on the native people. Even the present preferred term, *native American* (common since the early seventies, though it has existed at least since the fifties) has its detractors as it incorporates the name of one of the Europeans who 'discovered' and dispossessed them, Amerigo Vespucci.

natural *adj.* (another word for) AFRO (1969) i.e. not straightened or bleached.

necklace *noun* a tyre soaked in petrol, put round the neck of a victim and set alight, as a means of unofficial execution. Also *verb*, to kill by this method. Used by South African black activists on other blacks who were thought to be traitors. The grim euphemism, used by the activists themselves, emerged (1985) in newspaper reports of township violence.

needle time   *noun* the proportion of broadcasting time allocated by a radio channel to the transmission of recorded music (1962). The time has to be agreed for a number of purposes, including the payment of royalty fees.

neighbourhood watch   *noun* a system by which residents, usually with police advice, agree to keep an eye on each other's property and generally to be vigilant in their neighbourhood in order to discourage and combat crimes such as burglary and theft. The scheme originated and was named in the US in the early seventies and spread to the UK in the mid eighties.

neocolonialism   *noun* the acquisition or retention of political control of a sovereign country by another country, especially by economic means (1961). That is to say, not actual *colonialism* (which implies physical occupation, direct government, etc. of a country by a foreign power) but a new version of it, as a result of which a country remains theoretically independent but its economy and thus its political processes are controlled from outside.

neo-conservative   *noun* (also abbreviated to **neo-con**) a supporter of a US political movement allowing a degree of welfare-state interventionism within democratic capitalism while rejecting liberal utopianism. The word, though coined in the sixties, was not widely used until the emergence of the US 'soft right' during the seventies, at the end of which the abbreviation *neo-con* had become familiar as a noun and adjective.

nerd   *noun* a stupid, boring, feeble, insignificant or contemptible person; (in young people's slang) a conventional, puny or studious person. Slang, probably US in origin, though it appeared almost simultaneously in the UK in the later fifties. It may be a polite evasion of *turd*, but its first recorded appearance is as a nonsense-name in a children's book of 1950, and it may simply have spread from there, or that use may be an unrelated coincidence. The term became very popular in the seventies and eighties and spawned such variant forms as **nerdy** and **nerdish**. A *nerd* typically takes himself and his doings too seriously, is interested in gadgetry and is deadly dull and without style. See DWEEB and ANORAK.

nerk   *noun* a foolish or objectionable person (1966). Also *adj.* **nerk-ish**. Slang, probably from **nerd**, perhaps under the influence of the much older slang *jerk*.

net   (in computer technology) abbreviation of NETWORK (seventies).

Netiquette   *noun* the (unwritten) rules of behaviour for Internet users. A punning eighties coinage.

network   **1.** (in computer technology) *noun* a system of interconnected computers; also *verb* to link computers together into a network. **2.** (in business use) *verb* to form business contacts through informal social meetings; also *noun* **networking**. The first usage (no doubt based on earlier terms such as 'broadcasting network') goes back to the sixties and most typically denotes a number of terminals operating from a large central computer which can provide a degree of power not available on a stand-alone machine. The second usage surfaced in the THATCHERITE eighties when even social engagements had to be justified in terms of value for money: social lunches with business acquaintances therefore became *networking lunches*, and drinks parties could be regarded as opportunities for *networking*. This usage appears not to have been named after computer networking but to have originated in North America from the older (1947) sense of *network* as 'an interconnected group of people' (as in *old boy network*). Also in the eighties (though it may have began a little earlier) networking was used of professional people coming together in groups to help each other in their work and the furtherance of their careers by providing information and advice. This has been specially prominent among women who have been excluded from traditional male groupings (e.g. clubs or *the old boy network*) which provide such support. Senior women executives have begun to organise themselves into groups of one sort or another to make social and business contacts that will be helpful to them. There are signs that *networking* is spreading to fields outside business (e.g. politics) in the sense of 'the cultivation of useful contacts who may be helpful, influential, etc.'

neural network or **net**   *noun* a computer system designed to mimic the operation of the human brain (eighties). The meanings of *neural* include 'related to the central nervous system'. In medicine, a *neural network* is an interconnected series of neurons (cells conducting nervous impulses) in the brain or other parts of the nervous system. In computing, it is an analogous system of electronic components, connected in patterns similar to that of human neurons. It dispenses with a central processor and employs a number of elements working in parallel, and is designed to 'learn', make allowances for errors in initial data and solve problems by trial and error. This whole field is currently one of the most important areas of research into ARTIFICIAL INTELLIGENCE.

neurocomputer   *noun* a type of computer designed to simulate the action of the human brain, using electronic NEURAL NETWORKS. Also called *neural computer* (eighties).

neutron bomb   *noun* a type of nuclear weapon designed to destroy life by high radiation but cause little blast (and therefore little damage to buildings) and little long-term radiation. First discussed in the late fifties, named c.1960, developed by the USA in the early seventies but not so far used.

New Age   *noun* a philosophy or approach to life characterised by the rejection of Western materialistic values and culture and the promotion of spirituality, ALTERNATIVE medicine (esp. homeopathy), astrology, Eastern religions and mysticism, meditation, parapsychology, and conservation of the environment by such methods as organic farming, etc. Many of these were not 'new' (e.g. astrology) and some go back to HIPPIE preoccupations of the sixties. **New Age**

New Age (music)

emerged from this COUNTER-CULTURE, originally on the West Coast of the US, and spread to Europe in the seventies though it did not become generally known under its present title until the eighties. Unlike the HIPPIE movement, which was largely confined to the young and strongly associated with drug-taking, **New Age** is more diffuse, is seen to be more positive and health-conscious, and has attracted the interest of the middle-aged and the middle-class as well as the young and nonconformist. It is variously defined, but generally it seems to stand for universal brotherhood, the merging of religion and science, and ecological concerns. The name of the movement appears to be associated with the *Age of Aquarius*, an astrological age characterised by world peace, brotherhood and spiritual awareness, which is variously said to have begun during the sixties or to be due in the late 20th or early 21st century. *New Age* has long been an alternative name for this in astrology.

New Age (music) *noun* a style of music combining elements of jazz, folk and classical music, and played mainly on a variety of electronic instruments, sometimes with piano and harp, without strong rhythm or insistent vocals. Popular from the mid eighties, originally US, and characterised by restful sounds and a dream-like atmosphere, as if to promote meditation. The music is clearly associated with the spirit of the NEW AGE culture, especially its search for inner peace and a sense of the oneness of life.

New Age traveller or **New Ager** *noun* a person who rejects conventional society, lives in a caravan or other conveyance, and moves from place to place. People who would previously have been known as itinerant HIPPIES or DROP-OUTS now prefer this name (c.1992) and newspapers have adopted it, usually when reporting irregular or illegal gatherings or festivals, especially when associated with the summer solstice or such places as Stonehenge. These have caused public nuisance and attracted bad publicity, with the result that the use of *New Age Traveller* in such contexts is resented by more conventional exponents of the **New Age** philosophy as well as by gypsies who feel that **traveller** belongs to them; both insist that neither term should be associated with anti-social behaviour, drug abuse or exploitation of the welfare system. 'Genuine' *New Age Travellers* claim to practise none of these, insist that the well advertised problems are caused by casual visitors or hangers-on, such as RAVERS, and stress that their own interest is in the freedom of the road, a variety of mystical beliefs, a distaste for urban life and a rejection of conventionally organised society. Many of their recruits now include well educated and/or middle-class people.

New Commonwealth *noun* those countries which have achieved self-government within the British Commonwealth since 1945 (as opposed to Canada, Australia and New Zealand – the old Dominions). The use of the term (1970) in the context of UK immigration has been criticised because in effect it permits the official identification of coloured immigrants.

New Frontier *noun* part aspirational concept, part slogan and in part a programme of social improvement advocated by John F Kennedy (1917–63) during his 1960 presidential campaign. Although the term was not new, Kennedy made it famous. In the event it came to very little: foreign issues dominated his term of office, the narrowness of his victory deprived him of a popular mandate, and assassination ended his presidency in 1963.

New Left *noun* Left-wing radicalism. The term was coined in 1960 by the US sociologist Wright Mills as the name of a group of predominantly young US radicals who rejected the values and approaches of 'old' Liberalism and advocated a more energetic attack on social injustice. They came to prominence in protests against the Vietnam War, but have been little heard of since. The name, however, has been used of other groupings of left-wing radicals, especially student ones, in many other countries since 1960.

new look *noun* a new or more up-to-date appearance or style or change of policy, procedure, etc. An extension and adaptation of the original 'New Look', a style of women's clothing characterised by long, full skirts and introduced in Paris by Christian Dior in 1947; after the restrictions of wartime, it created a sensation.

New Man, the *noun* type of caring and considerate modern man who plays a full part in running a household and bringing up children, and who shows none of the MACHO, MALE CHAUVINIST attitudes condemned by the WOMEN'S LIBERATION movement. Still largely a journalistic term (c.1975).

New Maths *noun* a type of maths teaching in schools in which discovery methods and principles of set theory are introduced at an early stage (early sixties).

new morality *noun* the term came to prominence in the sixties to characterise a changed set of moral standards, mainly in sexual behaviour, that was establishing itself. Influenced by a general challenging of convention, especially by the young, and facilitated by the availability of the PILL, the *new morality* implied sex before or outside marriage, the depiction of such behaviour in films, on television and in fiction, and the loosening of traditional family values, though the expression was often extended to embrace GAY and WOMEN'S LIBERATION and such issues as the legalisation of abortion and certain drugs. Although it is still too early to be certain, a new and more prudent *new morality* appeared to be in course of definition during the eighties partly as a result of the emergence of AIDS: promiscuity was actively discouraged and the Thatcher governments of that decade occasionally proclaimed 'Victorian values' and, most notably, passed a Local Government Bill (1988) which included in clause 28 a measure preventing Local Authorities from presenting homosexuality in a favourable light. Whether this and the Major government's proclamation of Family Values add up to a 'morality', and whether the Aids pandemic will result in more protection rather than less promiscuity, remains to be seen.

New Right *noun* a political movement that arose in opposition to the **New Left**. It rejected socialism, emphasised the traditional conservative values on law, morality and social issues, and (in the US) reaffirmed free-market capitalism (1966).

newspeak *noun* any corrupt, misleading and ambiguous form of English as used by politicians, propagandists and bureaucrats. The original **Newspeak** was the official language of the totalitarian state which is the setting for George Orwell's *Nineteen Eighty Four* (1949). It reduced vocabulary, introduced ugly neologisms, eliminated subtlety and emotive quality, and was designed to make any mode of thought impossible except that which was approved of by the state.

new wave or **New Wave** *noun* a movement in the French cinema in the late fifties and the sixties; rock music of c.1976, originally associated with PUNK ROCK but later with a toned-down, more melodic and more sophisticated version of rock; any movement that consciously breaks with traditional ideas. The first (1960) is a direct translation of French *nouvelle vague*: the cinematic style valued spontaneity and is the work of directors who embraced AUTEUR THEORY. The second is a borrowing from the first, and denoted the main form of rock, HEAVY METAL apart, during the late seventies and early eighties. The third is a general application from the first.

nibble *noun* (in computer technology) half a **byte**; four **bits**. Originally jocular slang (1970s), but now more established in computer jargon. It is a punning reference to **byte**, a 'nibble' being (in the world outside computing) smaller than a 'bite'.

nicad, ni-cad or **Nicad** *noun* a rechargeable battery of nickel and cadmium. Though invented in the fifties and in use in the US space programme, these batteries were not generally known until the eighties and their use in portable computers needing high power for short periods (e.g. a few hours). Their name is an acronym from *ni*ckel and *cad*mium.

NICAM *noun* (acronym of) near instantaneously companded audio multiplex (late eighties). NICAM is a system used in UK television for coding audio signals into digital form and thus improving the quality of stereophonic sound. The verb *compand* comes by back formation from the device that is used, a *compander*, so called because it *comp*resses and then ex*pands* the signal.

nice little earner *noun* a means of making money easily, though possibly illicitly. A colloquialism made popular from its frequent use in the TV series *Minder* (1978 onwards) by the central character, a shady dealer in second-hand cars and other merchandise, though it previously existed in criminal and police jargon. *Earner* itself is Standard English for 'person who (or thing which) earns'.

niche *noun* (in retailing, advertising, etc.) a gap in a profitable, new or specialised area of the market. Although first used in this sense in the early sixties, the use did not become popular until the eighties in such terms as *niche market(ing)/analysis/business*, etc. Literally, a *niche* is a recess; the word has long been in figurative use to mean 'a position or role particularly suitable for the person who occupies it'.

nightmare scenario *noun* the worst circumstances that could possibly occur. An intensification (c.1990) of 'WORST CASE scenario' which appears to have originated in the jargon of US military bureaucrats. See SCENARIO.

-nik   see SPUTNIK,

Nikkei index   *noun* the index which monitors daily changes in the valuation of representative shares of the Tokyo Stock Exchange. The Japanese equivalent of FOOTSIE. Its name similarly comes from the initial syllables of words in the name of Japan's main financial newspaper, which has calculated and published the index since 1974. The internationalisation of stock exchanges during the eighties made the word familiar.

nimby   *noun* a person who objects to the location of some new development (e.g. a school, prison, housing) near his or her home. The implication is that such a person is happy to see such developments as long as someone else is affected by them. The term (originally US c.1980) is an acronym for 'not in my back yard'. In US English a *yard* is the area around a house, even if it is grassed, whereas a yard in Britain is hard-surfaced, and the British 'back garden' would be called a *back yard* by an American. The original coinage has been attributed to a member of the American Nuclear Society when adversely describing the anti-nuclear movement, though the truth of the matter was that the movement did not want nuclear developments at all, whether in their own back yard or anywhere else. In the UK the term was called into use against Nicholas Ridley, the then Environment Secretary, in 1988, when it was reported that he had objected to developments near his own home, even though they were of a type that his official policy recognised needed to go ahead (somewhere).

nine to five   *noun* normal office hours (1959). Also **nine-to-fiver**, person working such hours; person whose job makes only routine demands; person whose commitment to a job is strictly limited.

ninja   *noun* a Japanese warrior trained in ninjutsu, originally the art of stealth (including assassination by stealth), later a martial art. The word was virtually unknown in the West until the seventies when it started to circulate as a result of Western interest in martial arts; it also featured in some comics and computer games. It achieved popularity as a result of its appearance in the name of the Teenage Mutant Ninja Turtles, though the *Ninja* was changed to *Hero* when they were introduced in the UK, perhaps because of its unfamiliarity. See TEENAGE MUTANT HERO TURTLES.

NIREX   (acronym for) Nuclear Industry Radioactive Waste Executive, set up in 1982 to deal with the disposal of nuclear waste in the UK.

nod (out)   *verb* to lapse into stupor, especially as a result of taking heroin. Slang, originally US (c.1968).

no-go area   *noun* an area which is impossible or dangerous to enter, or which is barred to certain individuals or groups. First used in police jargon c.1971 of parts of Northern Ireland dominated by the IRA, but now used in more general and non-military contexts, so that a particularly sensitive topic of conversation might be described in this way. It is based on an earlier but now rare noun, *no-go* (an impracticable situation) or on the colloquial *it's no go* (the attempt is hopeless).

nonaligned *adj.* (of country, government, etc.) not part of an alliance, especially not with one of the (then) two major powers or power blocs (1960).

non-event *noun* a disappointing or insignificant occurrence, especially one which had been promoted as being important (1962).

non-ism *noun* the avoidance of self-damage by abjuring all foods, drinks, drugs, ADDITIVES and those activities in an ever-increasing list of things said by experts to be bad for one; a form of self-definition by self-denial. An apt non-word (1990) it has a prefix and suffix but no middle. Non-ism is a reaction against the hedonism and self-indulgence seen around us, but also a reflection of early nineties concern with health and fitness.

non-judgmental *adj.* (of an attitude, comment, etc.) unbiased; refraining from moral judgment (1965).

noov *noun* (abbreviation of) nouveau. A slang noun, c.1980. *Nouveau* is itself a shortening of French *nouveau riche*: a newly rich person. Both *nouveau* and *noov* have been used since the eighties for those who have come into money and so moved up in the world, usually with a (snobbish) implication that they have yet to adjust to their position or wealth.

Noraid (blend from) Irish **Nor**thern **Aid** Committee. An American organisation providing support for Republicans in Northern Ireland; it has been alleged to be an IRA front organisation and to have contributed funds and possibly arms. Its short name was first heard in 1974, though the Committee existed before then.

North, the *noun* the economically and technically advanced countries of the world. So called since the mid seventies because most of them are north of the Equator, but the usage is not general, perhaps because *the North* already has strongly established and different meanings in the UK and other English-speaking countries. Compare SOUTH.

North Sea gas or **oil** *noun* natural gas or oil obtained from reserves discovered beneath the North Sea. These terms became general after the discovery of gas in 1965 and oil four years later. *North Sea oil* was particularly prominent in political and economic vocabulary during the seventies and eighties because of its contribution to national wealth in the UK and fears that this would be short-lived and not put to best use.

nose job *noun* a surgical operation to remodel the nose to improve its appearance. Originally US slang from c.1963.

nosh *noun* food; *verb* to eat. Also **nosh-up** *noun* a (large and satisfying) meal. Early sixties slang, though the word occurs much earlier in the US, where it was normally associated with snacks because it originates in a Yiddish word meaning 'to eat on the sly'.

notebook *noun* a small portable, battery-operated personal computer. The name (1990) comes from its size, which is about that of an A4 notebook if not smaller, though it also has *user-friendly* implications of helpfulness and everyday ease of use.

nouveau *adj.* used before a noun or adjective to mean 'having recently become (what follows)' on the model of the familiar *nouveau riche*. The usage is facetious or derogatory, and may have begun with *nouveau pauvre* (the newly poor, 1965) though the second word does not have to be French. *Nouveau(x)* is also an occasional colloquial shortening of *nouveau(x) riche(s)* (late seventies; see NOOV).

nouveau roman *noun* the ANTI-NOVEL. The normal academic term for the *anti-novel* – meaning the 'new novel' it was first used in France in the mid fifties and in Britain c.1961.

nouvelle cuisine *noun* a style of French cooking employing the use of fresh and healthy ingredients, light sauces in place of traditionally rich ones, quick cooking to retain the colour and texture of ingredients, and artistic presentation. This last feature probably did most to bring the style into disfavour: miniscule portions of oddly assorted items, invariably including red, green and yellow ones, were carefully arranged on the plate, separated from each other so that each one and the surrounding area of plate could be admired. *Nouvelle cuisine* ('new cookery'; 1975) was developed in the seventies by a group of French chefs, and later became fashionable outside France, in the more expensive type of restaurant. Its influence persists, especially as regards health-consciousness, experimentation and aesthetic presentation, but public protest (in France and elsewhere) has brought about modification of the original severity: portions are now more sustaining, and some traditional elements of French cooking have reinfiltrated. In the UK the term is sometimes abbreviated to *nouvelle* to describe a restaurant or any method of cooking using some of the features of *nouvelle cuisine*.

no way (as exclamation or sentence substitute) it cannot be done; It is impossible. Colloquial; originally US slang of the late sixties.

now (*as informal adjective*) modern, fashionable, up-to-date (1963). Not much used outside MEDIA circles, except ironically.

no-win *adj.* (of contests or positions) in which one cannot succeed, whatever one does. A cliché when in *no-win situation*, otherwise slightly informal (1962).

nuclear club *noun* the nations that possess nuclear weapons. Probably so called (1957) because of the wish of these nations to restrict ownership of such weapons to the smallest possible number of countries, in the way that a club often seeks to remain selective or exclusive.

nuclear-free zone *noun* an area in which the storage and deployment of nuclear weapons is forbidden. Originally (1958) applied to Germany and part of central Europe during the Cold War, but the phrase became familiar when it was taken up by some left-wing local government authorities in Britain; they announced on roadsigns, official notepaper and envelopes, etc. that they were nuclear-free zones, not in the above sense (they were hardly in a position to prevent over-flying by missiles, etc.) but to declare their support for nuclear-disarmament.

nuclear waste *noun* radioactive waste material, especially from the reprocessing of spent nuclear fuel. The term (1974) is much heard in connection with public concern about the (long-term) safety of the storage and disposal of such waste.

nuclear winter *noun* the blocking of the sun's rays, and subsequent darkness and coldness, caused by debris in the atmosphere as a result of nuclear war. The theory of a post-nuclear-war winter was formulated and named in 1983 by a group of American scientists who held that any survivors of such a war would face starvation as crops would be unable to grow. Because of its scientific rather than political or military nature, the theory attracted much attention and may have contributed to the mood favouring disarmament later in the decade. The term **nuclear autumn** (late eighties) covers later less pessimistic versions of the theory and also the prediction that the explosion of only a very small number of warheads would trigger off a lesser but still disastrous chill.

nuke *noun* a nuclear weapon (1959); *verb* to attack or destroy with nuclear weapon (1967); to cook or heat in a MICROWAVE (1980s). All are chiefly US slang, the first two being originally US military terms. The third is a jocular allusion to electromagnetic radiation.

number crunching *noun* (in computer technology) the large-scale processing of numerical data (1971). Also **number cruncher** *noun* a computer designed to handle this (1966). 'Crunch' normally means 'to crush, or to bite or chew with a crushing sound'. Its use in *number cruncher* probably owes more to euphony than strict sense, though it could be argued that the computer 'crushes' lengthy and complex calculations into a short space of time, or 'crunches' numerical data into a different form.

numeracy *noun* the ability to understand and practise basic mathematics. Also **numerate** *adj.* having this ability. Despite their familiarity, these are comparatively new words, coined in 1959 in a Ministry of Education report, though *numerate* (not *numeracy*) existed as an obsolete word with a different meaning. In that report they denoted familiarity with the basic principles of maths *and* science, though they are now normally used only of mathematical facility, presumably because of a perceived link with such words as *number* or *enumerate*. The report in question makes it clear that they were coined on the model of *literacy* and *literate*: the argument was that science and maths specialists in school sixth-forms should be able to communicate with those having a literary education, and that the latter (historians, linguists etc.) should be able to follow what scientists and mathematicians are talking about.

nurd less common spelling of NERD.

nuts and bolts *noun* essential or practical details; the basic elements or mechanics (of a situation or thing). An obvious metaphorical use (1960) of items that are fundamental to the assembly and holding together of components in a larger construction.

oater   *noun* a Western film or television series (sometimes called a 'horse opera'). Mainly US, originally from 1951, and then largely confined to show business usage, though now more generally familiar from the brief reviews of films on television. The reference is to the amount of money that has to be spent on oats for food for the horses taking part.

ocker   *noun* an uncultured or boorish Australian (1971). The name of a character in a series of Australian television sketches by Ron Frazer. It was in previous colloquial use as a nickname for people called Oscar or O'Connor.

OCR   (abbreviation for) optical character recognition (or reading). The process by which characters (e.g. printed letters or numbers) can be scanned by a computer device, encoded, then stored in its memory (1966).

OD   (abbreviation for) overdose (of a drug). Informal, originally US, used as a *noun* since c.1960 and as a *verb* since c.1970 (*he OD'd*, he took/died from an overdose).

off-air   *adj.* (of a recording) made from a broadcast transmission (1973). The reference is to *air* as the medium for the transmission of radio waves as in *on the air* ('being broadcast').

off beat   *adj.* unconventional. In music off beats are unstressed beats, especially the second and fourth beats in a four-beat bar. They may be accented in some sorts of music, either as a matter of course or as an occasional device (syncopation), and it is this sense of the unexpected or unusual that has given *offbeat* its current meaning as an adjective. The word has been found in Britain since the fifties and has now lost most if not all of its original (American) informality. Compare DOWNBEAT, UPBEAT.

off-Broadway   *adj.* (of New York theatre productions) experimental, low-budget or non-commercial. That is to say, not in the style of mainstream productions found in theatres on or in the area of Broadway, the theatrical centre of New York (1953). Also **off-off-Broadway**, highly experimental, often radical or impromptu, sometimes presented in cafés or small rooms (1967).

off-roading   *noun* driving (or racing) a vehicle over rough country or along unmade roads as a leisure activity. Also **off-roader** *noun*, a vehicle, often having four-wheel drive, used in such pursuits; a person following such pursuits. Also *adj.* **off-road**. Originally US from the late sixties, but *off-roading* has been known in the UK since the late seventies as an organised activity.

offshore   *adj.* (of financial operations, funds, etc.) based abroad in places where tax arrangements are more advantageous than they are in one's own country. This use (1972) is derived from a slightly earlier use of *offshore* to designate goods bought with US dollars by or from countries other than the US, mainly in the context of Marshall Aid. Dollars used in this way were also called *offshore*.

off-the-wall   *adj.* unusual, unorthodox, eccentric, crazy. Slang, originally US (1968), probably from the use of the phrase in handball and squash to describe a shot that is unexpected or a ball that bounces off the wall at an unusual angle.

Ofgas

Ofgas *noun* the regulatory body set up in 1986 to control British Gas prices, to protect the interests of the consumer and to facilitate competition. Its title combines **Office** and **gas**.

OFSTED (acronym for) **OF**fice for **ST**andards in **ED**ucation. Established in 1992, a non-ministerial government department that keeps the Secretary of State informed about standards and management practices in English schools and monitors the inspection system.

Oftel *noun* the non-ministerial government department that supervises telecommunications activities in the UK, promoting effective competition and looking after the interests of users (1984). Its full title is the **Office** of **Tele**communications, which is combined to make the shortening *Oftel*.

Ofwat *noun* (shortening of) **Office** of **Wat**er Services, set up in 1989 to support the Director General of Water Services in his regulation of the economic framework of the water industry in England and Wales, and in the protection of the interests of consumers.

old boy network *noun*. Strictly speaking, this is the interconnection of former pupils (old boys) from a small group of British public schools in a system of favours, especially employment in or promotion to positions of power. The phrase – which dates only from c.1959, though the system goes back much further than that – is now also used more generally to denote any closed system of privileges conferred on the basis of shared background or interests.

ombudsman *noun* an official who investigates complaints by individuals against maladministration by public bodies. The word is Swedish for 'commissioner', and is used because Sweden was the first country to appoint such an official (to oversee the legal system) in 1809. It became familiar in 1966 – though it had been used previously in specialist circles – when the UK appointed the first Parliamentary Commissioner for Administration, commonly called *the Ombudsman*. As other officials were appointed, notably for local administrations, the word lost its capital letter.

one-nation *adj.* (of political philosophy or policy) designed to reduce social inequalities. The conservative politician Benjamin Disraeli (1804–81) had an interest in social reform and in his popular political novel *Sybil* (1845) dramatically characterised the rich and the poor as 'two nations' having nothing in common, not even the same laws. Allusions to **one-nation Conservatism** became common in the seventies and eighties usually linked to assertions that this was the pure mainstream of Tory thinking, and sometimes to allegations that THATCHERISM by contrast was extremist, divisive and aberrant. The phrase goes back to the One Nation group of liberal Conservatives formed in 1950 to press the case for greater Conservative commitment to the social services. Their name was consciously chosen to echo Disraeli's earlier concern.

one-night stand *noun* a sexual encounter lasting one night; person acting as a partner in such an encounter; casual sex. A slang and punning use (1963) of an older term for a theatrical or musical performance given only once at any one place, the *stand* being a halt on a tour.

one-off   *adj.* single and not to be repeated. In commercial jargon since the thirties *off* has been used with a preceding number to indicate the number of items required or produced, as in 'Re our order for 50 off flange couplings . . .'. During the sixties *one-off* started to move into more everyday use and to be applied to things other than manufactured products, as in 'a one-off occurrence'. This usage, now common, was initially disliked by some people because of its associations with what they thought ugly commercialese.

one-on-one   *adj.* in direct confrontation with one other person. A US slang variant (1967) of the standard British expression 'one-to-one'.

one-parent family   *noun* a family consisting of a child or children and either the mother or father, the other parent being dead or permanently absent (1969).

onsell   *verb* to sell on (usually something recently bought or acquired) in a premeditated way. Mainly financial jargon of the late seventies. The prefix *on-* implies the existence of a chain of buying and selling for the sake of making a profit rather than of possessing or using something.

op art   *noun* a style of abstract art in which the central or sole object is to give an illusion of movement by exploiting optical effects such as those created by precisely executed spirals, fine grids and other geometric forms (1964). The *op* is an abbreviation of *optical*; the movement of the observer's eye, or its inability to focus, produces 'dazzle', or else an illusion of movement in the picture.

OPEC   (acronym for) Organisation of Petroleum Exporting Countries. Formed in 1960; the acronym came into immediate use. The purpose of the cartel, dominated by Middle Eastern countries, though including some South American, African and SE Asian ones, was to counter the power of Western oil companies, encourage nationalisation, and bring about a transfer of wealth to those nations having oil deposits.

openers, for   *phrase* to begin with; for a start. This colloquial phrase is first recorded in the USA in 1967, which suggests that it comes from baseball, where an *opener* is the first game in a match.

open-heart surgery   *noun* surgery performed on the heart while it is exposed (1960). Such operations require the heart to be motionless and bloodless and this was made possible by the introduction of the heart-lung machine (1953) which maintains blood circulation mechanically during the heart-surgery.

open marriage   *noun* a marriage in which the partners have agreed to be free to have other sexual relationships (1968).

Open University   *noun* a university for adults studying by correspondence courses and by following television or radio broadcasts, with the help of local counselling and summer schools. Founded during the Labour administration in 1969, this provides education to degree level for mature students who for various reasons, including their own full-time employment, are unable to enrol at a conventional university.

optical disc or **disk**   *noun* an inflexible disc with a large storage capacity on which information is stored in DIGITAL form by LASER technology and read by a laser scanner. (Also called **laser disc**). The technology was developed in the seventies and the name has been established since c.1981.

opt out (of something)   *verb* to choose not to participate (in something). Much heard since the later eighties, when government policy allowed state schools and hospitals to choose to become self-governing instead of remaining within existing administrative structures. The verb was actually coined about forty years earlier as a useful elaboration of the slightly older (late 19th C.) *opt* (choose). Also *noun* and *adjective* **opt-out**.

Oracle   see TELETEXT.

oral history   *noun* tape-recordings of the memories of people who have experienced certain events or social conditions. These are preserved as historical evidence and sometimes transcribed for use in written history (1971).

orbital (party or **rave)**   *noun* an ACID HOUSE party taking place near the M25 motorway. British youth slang, 1989, based on the M25's official name, the London orbital motorway. This motorway gives access to a number of industrial estates where warehouses were sometimes used for such parties, and was a means whereby the necessary large numbers of attenders could conveniently travel.

organic   *adj.* (of food) organically grown i.e. grown without using chemical fertilisers, pesticides etc. In its sense of 'using natural substances' the adjective *organic* was first applied to fertiliser in the nineteenth century and to farming methods in the forties. The present sense (c.1972), describing the food grown by these methods, is a development from these uses and became common during the eighties as a result of the growth of GREEN consciousness and of public concern about the effects of agricultural chemicals on farm produce and therefore on people's health.

organiser   *noun* something which helps one to organise one's belongings, appointments, etc. Until recently an *organiser* was always 'a person who organises'. From the late sixties the word began to be used of things, often adjectivally. Examples include the *organiser bag* (a ladies' handbag with several compartments, pockets, etc. for different items) introduced in the late seventies, and the PERSONAL ORGANISER, often shortened to *organiser*. In the eighties pieces of furniture or equipment with shelves, compartments etc. were often described as *organisers*, e.g. 'a hanging organiser' to keep clothes smart.

OTE   (abbreviation for) on-target earnings. That is to say, the basic pay plus the amount of commission that an employee (usually a salesperson) can expect to earn if performance 'targets' are reached. Since the second half of the eighties this abbreviation has started to appear in job advertisements either alongside or in place of the basic salary being offered.

OTT   (slang abbreviation of) OVER THE TOP (c.1980). Said to have originated among television crews, the abbreviation became popular as a result of its use as the title of a 1982 television comedy show which set out to be outrageous.

out   *verb* to expose (a public figure) as being a fellow homosexual. First used in the US c.1990 and derived from the expression 'COME OUT of the closet'. The highly controversial practice of **outing** was particularly associated with a New York gay magazine and was used by gay activists to draw attention to the lack of concern for people with AIDS. It was felt that they – and gay rights generally – deserved the support of prominent figures who preferred to keep their homosexuality private. The word and the practice soon spread to the UK.

out in the left field   *phrase* out of touch, crazy, bizarre. Also a variant: **out of left field**. The first of these is a long-established baseball metaphor in the US, though it has only recently begun to be heard in the UK. The *left field* is an area of play outside the centre of activity, any player marooned there is out of touch with events, so that it is an easy step to 'unconventional' or 'crazy'. The second phrase is sometimes heard with the apparent meaning that something is coming at you from an unexpected quarter.

out of one's tiny mind   *phrase* utterly crazy. An emphatic form (1970) of 'out of one's mind'.

out of order   *adj.* (of behaviour) unacceptable, wrong. British slang, late eighties, based on the earlier and rather formal use of the phrase to mean 'not following the rules' in debates, public meetings, parliament, etc.

out of sight   *adj.* amazing. Hippie slang, c.1967; probably an intensification of FAR-OUT.

outplacement   *noun* (a service offering) assistance in finding a job after redundancy. The assistance may be provided or paid for by the employer who has made an employee redundant. The word means *placement* which is *out*side one's own staff. It has been used in the UK since the mid eighties, though it originated in US business jargon at the beginning of the seventies. It smacks of euphemism, especially if it is used, as it sometimes is, to mean 'dismissal'.

outreach   *noun* (of social welfare work) the policy and practice of going out to discover and meet needs, instead of merely responding to approaches from those who have them. Also *adjective*: (of social work and workers) seeking out people who appear to need a service and persuading them to accept it. A specialised use of the word, dating from the seventies, though it had previously been used of similarly active reaching out by churches.

outsourcing   *noun* using outside experts to run part of one's business. Industrial jargon, c.1990, from the idea of using a *source* of help that is *out*side one's own organisation. It is specially used of telecommunications experts, though it has been seized on by apologists for PRIVATISATION who use it as a euphemism for putting work out to contract and reducing the directly employed workforce.

out-take *noun* a length of film or tape that is rejected during editing and not included in the finished work. A technician's term (1960) made familiar by popular television programmes which have shown selections of *out-takes* containing humorous accidents (actors forgetting their lines, scenery falling over, etc.) during filming or recording.

out to lunch *adj.* stupid; not aware of what is happening or needed. Slang, c.1955. The comparison is between a person whose mind is not working and a person who has gone out to lunch i.e. taking a break.

Oval office, the *noun* the United States presidency. Although the oval-shaped private office of the US president was added to the White House in the thirties, its name has been used in this metonymical way to stand for the presidency itself only since the sixties.

oven-ready *adj.* (of food) bought already prepared for cooking in an oven (1960).

oven-to-table *adj.* (of ovenware) designed also to be used at the table for serving (1977).

overdub *verb* to add extra sound track(s) to a recording (1962). Also *noun*, the addition of such sound.

overkill *noun* an action that is greater than the circumstances warrant. This meaning (1965) developed from an earlier US military term for the capacity to deploy weapons, especially nuclear ones, able to effect destruction in excess of strategic requirements e.g. to destroy a target many times over (1958).

over-react *verb* to react excessively (1961). Also *noun* **over-reaction** (1967).

over the top *phrase* (of a person's behaviour or opinions) lacking restraint, propriety or a sense of proportion; excessive, outrageous, extreme, exaggerated. The expression originated in *go over the top*, a First World War term widely used among front-line infantry: it referred to the action of climbing out of one's trench by clambering over the top of the protective parapet, and advancing on the enemy – thus embarking on something unusual and extreme. Because of its widespread use among soldiers, it became generally known after the war and soon passed into metaphorical use meaning 'to do something dangerous or notable'; some commentators say that it also entered theatrical slang in the related sense of 'to overact'. In its current sense (c.1968) **over the top** is more commonly found with **be** rather than **go**, and is sometimes used adjectivally before a noun. See also OTT.

own brand *noun* an item marketed under the retailer's name, not the manufacturer's. Also *adjective* **own-brand**. This form of corporate packaging and marketing was adopted by some retailers, usually large supermarket chains, c.1970.

own goal, (score an) *noun* or *phrase* (cause) damage to oneself or one's own cause. A footballer who inadvertently puts the ball into his own goal, thus scoring for the opposing side, has long been said to 'score an own goal'. The first metaphorical application of the term has been attributed to military forces in Northern Ireland during the eighties when describing the action of terrorists who blew themselves up with their own bombs, but it is now widely used for acts which rebound upon the doer.

Oxfam *noun* name of a charitable organisation providing famine relief and other forms of aid internationally. Founded in 1942 as the Oxford Committee for Famine Relief to provide food for starving people in Greece during the German occupation, though it later broadened its scope. The abbreviated name was originally a convenient nickname but was officially adopted by the organisation in 1965.

ozone layer *noun* the concentration of ozone molecules in a layer of the stratosphere, absorbing harmful ultraviolet radiation from the sun and thus protecting organisms on earth (1951). Sometimes called the **ozone shield**. As a result of the concern first expressed by environmentalists during the seventies, and shared more generally by the public in the eighties, a number of new coinages relating to ozone became familiar from the mid eighties. The best known include **ozone depletion** (the reduction of the ozone layer by pollution, especially by the action of CFCs) and **ozone hole** (an area of serious ozone depletion; the first was discovered over the Antarctic in 1985). **Ozone-friendly** and similar expressions (e.g. *ozone-benign* or *ozone-safe*) are now used of products which do not contain chemicals damaging to the ozone layer, serious depletion of which would have catastrophic effects on human and animal life, agriculture and the weather. For example, depletion would vastly increase the incidence of skin cancers and cataracts and have disastrous effects on single sense organisms, such as plankton, at the bottom of the food chain.

p (abbreviation of) penny, pence. In use since the decimalisation of the British currency in 1971, and usually used as a spoken word, pronounced *pee*, except by those who dislike this as an unnecessary and ugly shortening. Strictly speaking, *penny* is singular and *pence* is plural. The use of *pence* as a singular in 'one-pence piece', etc. is therefore either incorrect or colloquial.

PACE (acronym for) **P**olice **a**nd **C**riminal **E**vidence Act. Introduced in England and Wales in 1984 to reform the procedures by which the police may investigate crime.

pacemaker *noun* an electronic device providing stimulation of the heart and implanted to correct abnormal heart beat in certain cases of heart disease. Initially called an 'artificial pacemaker' (1951), this has been commonly known by its shorter name since it became familiar during the sixties. The word continues to be used in its original sense of 'person, horse, vehicle, etc. that sets the pace, i.e. determines the rate at which a group proceeds, in a race or other activity'.

Pacific Rim *noun* those countries bordering the Pacific Ocean and viewed collectively as an important area of present and future commercial development (1980).

package *noun* and *verb*. An old-established word, but some of its figurative applications are new and very much in vogue. As long ago as the fifties the growth of the travel industry gave rise to the **package holiday/tour**, etc., for which the traveller makes a single payment to an agent who offers a *package* not only of travel arrangement but also accommodation, meals, excursions, guides etc. *Package* is now widely used in place of *salary* in the business world to mean the financial rewards available to an employee, i.e. not just salary but also bonus payments, allowances, travelling and other expenses, perks, etc. During the eighties *package* became common in computer jargon for a set of programs designed for a specific type of problem or task (e.g. in statistics or production) and sold as a unit, making it unnecessary to write a separate program for each particular problem. As a *verb*, **package** has moved from its plain sense of 'wrap up' to one implying attractive or seductive display likely to appeal to a consumer; thus people in the public eye, such as politicians, sportsmen or entertainers, may be *packaged* for popular or commercial success, often with a greater emphasis on external appearance and style than on substance.

packager *noun* firm specialising in design and production, but then selling the finished product to another firm for distribution. Also **packaging**, the business of doing this. Originally (c.1959) used of independent television programme-makers who sell their work to broadcasting companies. Later (c.1970) applied to people in the book trade who deal with all aspects of producing a book but then sell the distribution rights.

packet-switching *noun* (in computer technology) a mode of transmitting data in units which are sent independently by the optimum route (1972).

Pac-Man *noun* (tradename of) a computer game launched in 1980 featuring a small electronic blip (also called Pac-Man) which had to be guided through a maze, avoiding other blips, and which appeared to eat electronic dots. Its popularity led to other uses of the name, with various spellings. From 1982 a company which responded to a take-over bid by threatening to take over the bidding company was said to be using the *Pac-Man strategy* or *defence*. Similarly in 1989 a computer VIRUS was called Pac-Man.

pager *noun* (short for) RADIO PAGER; another term for BLEEPER (1968). From the *verb* **page**, 'to communicate with someone by means of a page' (as in page-boy).

page three girl *noun* a scantily dressed, usually TOPLESS young woman appearing in a photograph, usually in a tabloid newspaper. The *Sun* newspaper was the first to publish such photographs on page three, shortly after its launch in 1964, and the term has now became so well known that *Page Three* has been registered as a proprietary name by the paper's publisher.

page-turner *noun* an exciting book, usually a novel: i.e. it makes the reader want to turn over quickly to the next page (1974).

paintball(ing) or **paintball game** *noun* a war-game in which teams of players in protective clothing try to eliminate opponents by firing paint pellets that explode on impact and mark the players that have been 'shot'. Points are gained according to the number of hits, and the object of the game is usually to capture the opponents' flag. The sport grew up in the US in the early eighties and spread to the UK in the second half of the decade. It originated as a training exercise in the Canadian Mounted Police, though paint pellets fired from pistols had previously been used in North America as a means of marking cattle.

Paki *noun* (abbreviation for) a Pakistani; (loosely) a person originating from any part of the Indian sub-continent. Derogatory British slang, 1964. Also **Paki-bashing**, brutal physical assault of Pakistani immigrants or their descendants, or other Asians, residing in Britain (1970).

palimony *noun* money paid by one partner to the other after the collapse of a long-term but unmarried relationship. Mainly US, a blend of *pal* and *alimony* (1979).

palmtop *noun* a portable personal computer slightly smaller than a NOTEBOOK. The name (1990) is intended to imply that the computer can be operated in the palm of one's hand. Its name is formed on the pattern of LAPTOP and DESKTOP.

panda *noun*. The **panda car** (1966) is a British police car. The name comes from the broad white stripe painted on it, resembling the marking of the giant panda, and may have been suggested by **panda crossing** (1962), a now-discontinued type of pedestrian crossing marked with black and white chevrons, also reminiscent of the panda's appearance.

panic button, hit or **press** *phrase* to become excited or panicky; to call for or take emergency action, often over-hastily, in an apparently threatening situation. A *panic button* is now a button to be pressed in the event of an emergency, e.g. in a hospital ward. It originated in US aeronautical language of the early fifties, especially that of test-flying, when it denoted the trigger mechanism of any safety device to be used in a dangerous situation.

pantihose, pantyhose *noun* women's tights. The preferred American term since c.1963, though sometimes found in Britain. From *panties* (legless knickers) and *hose* (stockings).

pant-suit or **pants-suit** *noun* a woman's suit consisting of matching jacket and trousers. Mainly a US and Canadian term (1964) for what has been known in the UK as a 'trouser suit' since the late thirties.

paparazzo *noun* a freelance photographer who specialises in photographs of celebrities, usually by invading their privacy. Plural **paparazzi**, and abbreviated (e.g. in tabloid headlines) to *pap* and *paps*. An Italian word meaning 'buzzing insect'. It was used as the surname of a prying photographer in Fellini's film *La Dolce Vita* in 1959, though it may have been in earlier use in Italian slang to denote this type of photographer, who appears to have originated there. Another theory is that the word comes from the 'pop' that photographic flash bulbs used to make. The word, which became known in the UK c.1968, has remained in use even though the intrusive photographing of famous people is now far from being confined to Italy.

paragliding   *noun* the sport of cross-country gliding using a parachute shaped like wings. The parachutist launches himself from an aeroplane and glides to a predetermined landing spot. The sport dates from the late sixties, though *paraglider* is an earlier term for a device, either unmanned or piloted, incorporating the principles of both parachuting and gliding.

Paralympic Games   *noun* a sporting event for disabled competitors, modelled on the Olympic Games. Also called **the Paralympics**. Formed from *para-* ('resembling') and *Olympic* (1965).

paramedic   *noun* a person who supplements the work of the medical profession (e.g. a skilled ambulance worker). Short for the earlier *paramedical* in which the prefix *para-* means 'subsidiary to, alongside or in support of' (1970). Not to be confused with the earlier US *paramedic* (1950), a person trained to be dropped by *para*chute to give medical aid.

paramilitary   *adj.* (of an armed force) having a military structure but not a professional personnel, and probably conducting operations that are outside the law. Also *noun*: a member of such a force. This has been the dominant sense in the UK since the early seventies when the word became familiar because of the Northern Ireland conflict: both the IRA and armed Protestant groups are *paramilitary*. In other contexts, however, the word is still sometimes used in its original thirties sense to denote civil forces acting legitimately in support of professional military ones, *para* signifying 'subsidiary to' or 'alongside'. See PARAMEDIC.

parasailing   *noun* a sport in which a water skier wearing a parachute is towed by a speedboat, becomes airborne, and is then towed while suspended from the parachute. Introduced in the US in 1969, though not much known until the late seventies. The word is from *para*chute and the idea of *sailing* through the air. Compare PARASCENDING.

parascending   *noun* a sport in which a person using an open parachute is towed by a vehicle or speedboat, becomes airborne, casts off the tow-line and then descends by parachute. Introduced in the sixties, slightly earlier than **parasailing**. The word is from *para*chute and *ascending*.

parasuicide   *noun* an attempt at suicide which may not be intended to be successful; a person who makes such an attempt. The prefix *para-* means 'near' or 'resembling' (1990).

parenting   *noun* the care and upbringing of a child by a parent or parents; caring for someone as a parent does. A relatively new (1959) use of the noun from the older verb *to parent* ('be or act as a parent'). More recently (late eighties) *parenting* has been used of the parent-like relationship in which, for example, a son or daughter cares for their elderly parent(s).

park-and-ride *noun* a system enabling motorists to travel by private car to designated parking areas outside a congested zone (e.g. a town centre) and then to complete their journey by public transport (1966).

parking meter *noun* a coin-operated meter which shows how long a car may be parked, usually in a street. The first such devices in the UK were installed in Mayfair, London, in 1958, though they had been known in the USA since the thirties.

Parkinson's Law or **law** *noun* a facetious law of economies to the effect that work expands to fill the time available for its completion. Professor C Northcote Parkinson, the British historian and journalist, first promulgated this notion in an article in *The Economist* in 1955, though it was his book *Parkinson's Law* (1959) that made it famous.

partner *noun* either member of a couple in a RELATIONSHIP. As the practice of living together without marriage became familiar during the second half of the twentieth century, there was a search for a substitute for 'husband/wife/spouse' that was more explicit than 'friend', more adult than 'boyfriend' or 'girlfriend', and less tabloid than 'lover'. Since the mid eighties *partner* has been adopted as a suitably neutral term that avoids any reference to marriage or even sexual orientation.

part-work or **partwork** *noun* a series of magazines, usually educational or reference works, published at intervals but designed to be kept together to form a complete book, course of study, etc. The concept is not new though the name is comparatively so (1969).

party *verb* to have a good time; celebrate. Well established US usage, but not much known in the UK until the eighties.

PASCAL or **Pascal** *noun* (in computer technology) high level, general-purpose programming language which also, because of its well-structured coding, became a standard teaching language in universities. Devised by Niklaus Wirth, known since 1971, and named after the French scholar, philosopher, mathematician and scientist Blaise Pascal (1623–62), who built a calculating machine.

passive smoking *noun* the involuntary inhalation of other people's tobacco smoke. Named by medical researchers c.1971. Its recognition as a hazard to non-smokers has increased pressure for the banning of smoking in public places.

patrial *noun* a person who has the right of abode in the UK. This specialised new use of an old and rare word was introduced by the Immigration Bill of 1971 and became a subject of some controversy, being seen as a thin disguise for 'a white person'. The word is not much encountered outside the vocabulary of immigration control, deportation, etc.

Patriot *noun* a surface-to-air computerised missile system with multiple launch capability, used for the radar detection and destruction of incoming aircraft or missiles in mid air; also the missile employed in that system. Developed by the US in the late 1970s and put into service in 1985, but not generally known until they were first used operationally during the Gulf War (1991) against Iraqi missiles.

PC abbreviation of POLITICAL CORRECTNESS and PERSONAL COMPUTER. During much of the 1980s, *PC* was also specifically used as a shortened form of IBM PC, a personal computer marketed by the IBM Corporation, though this model was withdrawn at the end of the decade. *PC* is now the standard term for any computer capable of being used by an individual, as distinct from a MAINFRAME. See also PERSONAL COMPUTER.

PCB (abbreviation for) polychlorinated biphenyl, any of a group of chemical compounds in which chlorine atoms are added to biphenyl. Widely used in the fifties and sixties (though developed earlier) in electrical insulators and the manufacture of oils, paints and plastics, *PCBs* did not begin to enter the general vocabulary until c.1966 when they began to be recognised as extremely toxic pollutants; they accumulate in soil and water, entering the food chain and causing liver damage in humans. Several countries restricted their use during the seventies, but the problems of disposing of existing ones remained an issue into the eighties and beyond.

PCN (abbreviation for) Personal Communications Network. More advanced form of the CELLPHONE using digital technology. PCN mobile phones are for operation in town centres and built-up areas by means of high-frequency links to traditional telephone exchanges via a system of relay stations. PCNs started to become known to the public in 1992.

PCP 1. abbreviation and tradename of the drug phencyclidine, used initially (c.1959) as an anaesthetic but subsequently restricted to veterinary use. In the sixties it was used illegally as a hallucinogen, and returned to prominence with ACID HOUSE in the eighties. Also known as ANGEL DUST. 2. abbreviation of pneumocystis carinii pneumonia. Though named in the fifties (the abbreviation grew up in the seventies), this fatal form of pneumonia did not become generally known until the eighties, mainly in the US, because of its spread among people with Aids.

peace camp *noun* a camp set up by campaigners for peace, usually outside a military base, as a form of protest (1981). Such protests were particularly associated with anti-nuclear demonstration. The best known was the women's peace camp established in 1981 outside the US air base at Greenham Common, Berkshire, where cruise missiles were installed in 1983. The camp survived the arrest and imprisonment of many of its members and, though reduced in size, remained in place after the removal of the missiles (1988–9) and even after the announcement of the closure of the base in 1990.

Peace Corps *noun* a US government agency that sends American volunteers to work on educational and other projects in developing countries for (usually) two years and on low wages. The organisation was set up by President John F Kennedy in 1961 to provide skilled manpower and to promote mutual understanding: the volunteers work in agricultural and rural development projects, and as teachers and health workers, and are expected to share the living conditions of the communities where they are working.

peace dividend *noun* the benefit to a country as a result of reduced military spending at the end of a war, particularly the Cold War. Although the term was used in the US with the approach of the end of the Vietnam War, it was not familiar in the UK until 1989 when the end of the COLD WAR first became a strong possibility, bringing hopes of a reduction in the size of the armed forces and in spending on weapons and research.

peacenik *noun* a member of the pacifist movement, especially (in the sixties and seventies) someone in the US opposed to the Vietnam War. Coined c.1965. The -*nik* suffix (see SPUTNIK) was perjoratively intended to imply both Russian and BEATNIK associations, though these have weakened with the passage of time.

peace sign *noun* a gesture made by raising the index and middle fingers in the shape of a V, with the palm of the hand turned outward, as a sign of peace or desire for peace. Dating from 1969 or slightly earlier, this is said to be based on the symbol (1958) of the Campaign for Nuclear Disarmament, which is an inverted V bisected by a vertical line within a circle, the lines representing the semaphore signals for N.D. (for nuclear disarmament). It is more likely, however, to be a copy – signifying 'we shall overcome' – of Winston Churchill's famous 'V for Victory' sign during the Second World War, or else a slight variation of the centuries-old sign of benediction in Christian churches; the priest raises his right hand, palm outwards, with the forefinger and middle finger extended and the thumb holding the other two fingers across the palm. Some ancient art depicts this gesture as being made with the thumb and forefinger extended in a sort of V shape.

pedal steel guitar *noun* an electric guitar mounted on a stand (rather than hand-held) and having foot pedals that alter the pitch of the strings and can produce glissando effects (1969).

pedestrianise *verb* to convert (a street) into an area for pedestrians only, by banning vehicles from it. The word has been in occasional use since the early nineteenth century with two fairly rare meanings ('to go on foot' and 'to produce something commonplace') but the current meaning, introduced c.1963, has now displaced these.

pelican crossing *noun* a pedestrian crossing controlled by traffic lights with a push-button system operated by pedestrians. A loose acronym for *pe(destrian) li(ght) con(trolled)* (crossing), 1966.

people mover *noun* an automated means of transporting people over short distances. For example, driverless vehicles or moving pavements (1971).

people power *noun* political or other pressure exercised by ordinary people, usually through public demonstrations of popular opinion. The term was originally (1976) used of physical effort exercised by people, as opposed to machines, but the definition given has been the usual one since c.1983.

PEP (acronym for) personal equity plan. Under arrangements introduced by the UK government in 1986 to extend share ownership and encourage personal savings, people were able to invest limited sums in a PEP and enjoy freedom from tax on capital gains or dividends provided that certain conditions were met.

P/E ratio (abbreviation of) PRICE–EARNINGS RATIO.

perestroika *noun* the reconstruction of the Soviet economy and political system as promoted by Mikhail Gorbachev from 1985 onwards; any radical reorganisation, especially of a socialist system. This Russian word (literally 'restructuring') leapt to sudden prominence in the West after Mikhail Gorbachev came to power in 1985 and made it one of the keywords (see also GLASNOST) of his policy. During the tumultuous events that followed – the open criticism of the Soviet system at the Party Congress in 1986, the granting of freedom to Eastern European Communist countries, the end of the Cold War, the break-up of the Soviet Union and the political demise of Gorbachev himself because his own post ceased to exist – the word passed into everyday use in the news media. It is now less frequently heard, though its place in history is assured. So is its association with Gorbachev, even though it was in political use in its now familiar sense some years before he made it famous.

performance art *noun* a form of theatrical art often combining drama with music, dance, painting, film etc. Since its introduction c.1971, the term has been loosely used to denote a variety of avant-garde activities, often including the participation or commentary of the artist himself as a central feature. *Performance art* appears to have developed from the 1960s HAPPENING.

performance car *noun* a car that performs very well in terms of speed and the high quality of its engineering. A shortening, since c.1976, of 'a car capable of high performance'.

peripheral *noun* any device used in conjunction with a computer without being an integral part of it. Peripherals are linked to the Central Processing Unit (CPU) and can be input devices (such as a keyboard) output devices (such as the monitor or VDU or a printer) or storage devices (such as discs). The word is most often found in the plural and has been used as a noun with this sense since c.1966; it was previously an adjective, and its use as a noun originates in the abbreviation of the slightly earlier *peripheral equipment* or *device*, etc. (mid fifties).

permissive society, the *noun.* The term was originally coined c.1968 to describe the sort of society that was emerging from the social upheavals of the SWINGING SIXTIES. It referred primarily to greater sexual freedom (including greater tolerance or latitude in such matters as divorce, contraception, abortion and homosexuality) but also embraced a whole gamut of issues: increased informality in behaviour, customs and dress; the alleged decline of Christian values and family life; the growth of affluence, hedonism and irresponsibility; lack of respect for conventional values, perhaps associated with the development of the welfare state and an apparent reduction in the sense of individual dignity and responsibility; and changing attitudes to matters as varied as censorship, drug-taking, war, racial equality, the rights of women and gay people, etc. For some, *the permissive society* was a term that summoned up a new liberalism and tolerance; for most it was a pejorative term implying the breakdown of important social and moral values. It is now not much used and is of largely historical interest, as many of the changes it stood for have been either absorbed or forgotten.

-person   Since the early seventies this has been often used in preference to *-man* at the end of numerous words relating to jobs, activities etc. that can be done by people of either sex: thus *salesperson* instead of *salesman*, which previously was used to do duty for either sex. See also CHAIRPERSON and SPOKESPERSON. The use of words ending in *-man* to describe either sex (e.g. chairman, statesman, craftsman) was an early target of the WOMEN'S LIBERATION movement. Subsequently, legislation about equal opportunities and sex discrimination has led to job advertisements, for instance, having to be carefully worded so that they cannot be taken to imply a preference for either sex: a plethora of *-person* words has resulted, though few of them are actually in daily use. A number of allied coinages (e.g. *personkind*, early seventies) have been deliberately intended to mock both their own clumsiness and what is thought to be the excessive zeal of some feminists in objecting to words which others may not think of as sexist.

personal computer   *noun* a small computer suitable for operation by a single user in the home or office. When the term was first used, c.1977, it applied to elementary machines – many of them used in conjunction with cassette tape recorders and domestic television sets – which were used for little more than computer games or simple programming at home. Later, and often abbreviated to **PC**, it was applied to more sophisticated machines able to perform a wide range of tasks such as word-processing, DESKTOP PUBLISHING and the storage of material. Such machines are still used domestically, but also in many offices and businesses. PC is now the standard term for any computer which is designed to be operated by an individual user, as distinct from a MAINFRAME.

personal organiser   (another name for) FILOFAX or a similar product from a rival firm; an electronic device having a similar function. Because *Filofax* is a registered tradename, manufacturers who wanted to take advantage of its sudden popularity in the early eighties (see FILOFAX) by producing similar products had to think up an alternative name. Because of the popularity of the term ORGANISER, the *personal organiser* came into being, though its name is usually shortened to *organiser*. Both forms of the name, however, are now also familiar as applied to the electronic device, resembling a large pocket calculator with letters as well as numbers, which stores telephone numbers and details of appointments, acts as a calculator, and gives the time in Phnom Penh, etc.

PERT   (acronym for) programme evaluation and review technique. A method of planning, controlling and monitoring the progress of

Peter principle, the

complex and usually long-term operations (e.g. the manufacture of an aircraft) by analysing each successive step, checking how long it takes to finish each important part, etc. (1959).

Peter principle, the   *noun* 'in a hierarchy, every employee tends to rise to his level of incompetence'. The quotation is from *The Peter Principle* (1968) by Dr Lawrence J Peter (with Raymond Hull). Peter based his self-styled *Peter principle* on his observation that within an organisation people are promoted until they reach a job which they are incapable of doing, at which point they stop being promoted. Peter's principle is often referred to facetiously, but he claims to have based it on a study of hundreds of cases of occupational incompetence.

petrodollar(s)   *noun* dollar(s) earned by oil-exporting countries. The term (1974) is often used of surplus dollar earnings from the sale of oil, i.e. the earnings over and above what an oil-exporting country can spend on imports.

PG   (abbreviation for) parental guidance. A symbol indicating that a film contains scenes that may be unsuitable for children and advising that parental guidance should be sought before children attend. Originally a US certification, c.1970, but later adopted by the UK.

phallocrat   *noun* a person who advocates or assumes the existence of a male-dominated society; a man who argues that he is superior to women merely by being male. Also **phallocracy**, **phallocratic**. Probably borrowed from similar words in French (1977), and used as terms of abuse by feminists against those unsympathetic to their cause. Based on the pattern of *aristocrat* and *aristocracy*, *phallus* was a late Latin word for the penis and derives from the Greek word for the same.

phonecard   *noun* a plastic card, resembling a CREDIT CARD, available from various retail outlets and then used to operate certain public telephones. When the card is used, a display in the call-box shows how many units of time the caller is entitled to, and then the rate at which they are used up during a call. The system, announced in the UK in 1980 and widespread after 1984, has some confusing terminology: *phonecard* is used to mean the card but sometimes also the phone which accepts it. However, there are signs that *phonecard* will come to be the name of the card only, and that **cardphone** will become the standard name for a phone that does not accept coins.

phone-in   *noun* a radio (and occasionally television) programme in which members of the public participate by telephone. The term is first recorded in this sense in 1968, though it had existed a little earlier in the sense 'a protest in the form of mass telephone calls of complaint'. This earlier usage, obviously related to the terminology described under -IN, appears to have been transitory. Whether the now current usage grew out of it or occurred independently is uncertain.

phone phreak or **freak**   *noun* a person who makes long-distance telephone calls by using an electronic device (the blue box) to avoid payment. Possibly a short-lived term (1972) formed by re-spelling *freak* (in the sense of 'enthusiast') to match the initial letters of *phone*. The phone-freak, like the hacker into computer systems, is likely to take pleasure in demonstrating his mastery of the system, and often claims that as his motivation.

photofit　*noun* a method of combining photographs of facial features into a composite picture of a face. Used by the police, who ask eye-witnesses to supply details of the facial characteristics of a suspect so that a photograph can be issued in an attempt to trace a wanted person. The method is a refinement of IDENTIKIT, which used drawings rather than photographs. Strictly speaking, the word is a trademark for a process developed for Scotland Yard in 1970, though it is invariably spelt without an initial capital.

photo novel　*noun* a fictional work consisting of a series of photographs with speech represented by superimposed 'bubbles'. Developed in Europe, especially in Italy, during the fifties for the teenage or young adult market, the idea was taken up in the US in the late seventies and spread to the UK by the mid eighties.

photo opportunity　*noun* a staged opportunity for the press to take photographs of a celebrity. The expression was first used in the US as a piece of media jargon in the mid seventies, but did not become well known until the eighties when it was used of the organisation of newsworthy pictures of President Reagan and Mrs Thatcher by public relations advisers who realised the advantages of giving press photographers what they wanted rather than leaving things to chance. Although photo opportunities continue to be a feature of political life, they are increasingly criticised as substitutes for real news – evidence of the manipulation of journalism by interested parties and the trivialisation of politics by treating it almost as a branch of show business.

pig　*noun* a policeman. Derogatory slang, c.1967. The word had been used of the police in the nineteenth century, but mainly of plain-clothes officers: the idea seems to have been that they used their 'noses' to sniff out criminals in the way that pigs use their noses to forage. This slang use was therefore fairly mild. The 1960s use was not: it was intended by radicals to insult and taunt what were seen as the repressive and unsympathetic forces of conventional society.

pig out　*verb* to gorge oneself. US and Canadian slang, first recorded in print in the late seventies but in spoken use before then. It is a variation of two existing slang expressions, to 'pig it' (devour food greedily) and 'make a pig of oneself' (overindulge oneself). For the addition of *out* see MELLOW OUT.

pill, the　*noun* (an informal shortening of) the oral contraceptive pill. Such informal expressions as *taking the pill* or *being on the pill* have been common since the oral contraceptive was made commercially available in 1960, though *the pill* (sometimes with a capital P) occurs slightly earlier (1957) during the time it was being developed.

PIN　(acronym for) personal identification number. A confidential number issued to the holder of a cash card or credit card. When

pina colada

such a card is used in an automatic cash dispenser or similar self-service machine, the *PIN* (usually known tautologically as the *PIN number*) must be keyed in, otherwise the machine will not work. The *PIN* is a security device to prevent the card's use in the event of theft or loss. The card-holder is expected to memorise the PIN and keep it secret. The PIN was introduced in the early eighties and is now used internationally.

pina colada *noun* a long drink consisting of pineapple juice, coconut and rum. From the Spanish, meaning literally 'strained pineapple'. The drink became popular in the UK during the late sixties.

pin down *noun* solitary confinement of children and young people in residential children's homes (particularly in Staffordshire), sometimes for as long as three months. Alleged to be 'behaviour modification therapy', but widely interpreted as an unacceptably severe way of dealing with difficult children, this treatment was used in Staffordshire during the eighties, was stopped by High Court order in 1989, and came to light in a report published in 1991, achieving immediate notoriety. The word, social workers' jargon based on the familiar verb *pin down* ('hold (person) still'), was widely used in newspaper reports at the time of the affair.

Pinyin *noun* a system of spelling used to represent Chinese characters in the Roman alphabet. From the Chinese *pin-yin*, literally 'spell sound'. The system was officially adopted by China in 1958 and was introduced gradually. It attempts to reproduce Chinese sounds and has been responsible for the respelling of some familiar words, e.g. Beijing for Peking.

pipelining *noun* (in computer technology) a technique for speeding up the operation of powerful computers whereby when one step of the program is completed the results are passed on to separate hardware so that the original hardware is free to begin processing new data. Rather as on a car assembly line, each step is being performed simultaneously but on different pieces of data, which are then pushed along the 'pipeline' – which greatly reduces the time taken.

pirate radio *noun* illegal radio broadcasting. The term did not become familiar in the UK until the mid sixties when the first unlicensed broadcasting of radio programmes took place; it was in use in the US, however, in the 1940s, and the use of 'pirate' to mean 'an unlicensed individual radio-operator' belongs to the early part of the century.

piss *noun* recent additions to the use of this word, which is not in polite use, include *piss artist* (a boastful or incompetent person, 1975), *pisshead* (a drunkard, 1961) and *piss-up* (bout of heavy drinking, 1952). *Piss-taker* (one who engages in mockery) appeared in print in 1976, though *take the piss (out of)* (make fun (of)) goes back to the 1940s.

pixel *noun* any of the tiny elements that make up an image on a VDU or television screen. Formed from *pix*, a respelling of 'picts' as an abbreviation of 'pictures', and *el* as an abbreviation of 'elements' (1969). The full term *picture element* goes back to the 1920s.

plank *noun* an important element in a policy, argument, project, programme, etc. The idea of 'a plank in a political platform' goes back to the middle of the nineteenth century: 'platform' meant 'policy as proclaimed by a politician from a wooden platform, e.g. during an election campaign'. Since the mid sixties, however, *plank* has been used on its own, without reference to 'platform', 'campaign', etc. and is no longer restricted to politics.

PLA, PLWA (abbreviations for) person living with AIDS. The first is mainly British, the second mainly American. The terms, which are intended to stress survival rather than death, are later variants of PWA but are not much used outside the specialised vocabulary of pressure groups and those professionally concerned with AIDS.

planning blight *noun* the damage to property prices, to economic or community activity or the general quality of life in an area affected by a development plan or by rumours of one. A figurative application (1962) of the primary meaning of *blight*, 'a diseased condition in plants, preventing their growth and blossoming'.

plastic *adj.* and *noun* **1.** an informal shortening (early eighties) of *plastic money* (credit cards made of plastic); the latter, originally US, dates from the early seventies. **2.** subsequently *plastic crime* (credit card fraud). **3.** *plastic bullets* are PVC cylinders, about 4" long and 1½" in diameter, fired from a gun and used in riot-control. Plastic ammunition was used for gunnery training in the Second World War, but plastic bullets did not become known until their use (c.1972) in Northern Ireland after the troubles resumed. See BATON ROUND and RUBBER BULLET. **4.** *plastic* is sometimes used to mean 'superficially attractive but artificial or synthetic' (*plastic food*). Applied to people, it means 'artificial, superficial, insincere' (c.1963).

plate tectonics *noun* (in geology) the study of the earth's surface based on the theory that it consists of large blocks (plates) able to move and interact (1969). *Tectonics* is a much older (late 19th C) geological term for the study of rock structures, especially large-scale ones.

platinum disc *noun* a gramophone record certified to have sold 300,000 copies as an LP or 600,000 as a SINGLE. Or a million of either in the USA. Compare GOLD DISC.

player *noun* a participant, especially a major one, in a particular field of activity. An informal extension (c.1980) of existing senses of *player*. It is usually applied to an individual or group taking part in a business transaction such as a merger, takeover or negotiation.

playing field see LEVEL PLAYING FIELD.

play it cool see COOL.

plea bargaining *noun* (in court proceedings) the reaching of an agreement, usually initiated by the defence, as a result of which the accused pleads guilty to a lesser charge in return for the dropping of a more serious charge. Originally US, 1969. Also a *verb*: **plea bargain** to negotiate for such an agreement.

PLO (abbreviation for) Palestine Liberation Organisation. Founded in 1964 to bring about an independent state of Palestine. It has a number of groupings, the main one being al-Fatah, and was for many years associated with terrorist activity, though it is now recognised as the legitimate representative of Palestinians. In 1988 it renounced terrorism and endorsed a UN resolution recognising Israel's right to exist, and is currently embarked on the Peace Process with Israel.

plonker *noun* a stupid person. The word has had a number of vulgar meanings in British slang, notably 'penis' (i.e., that which is *plonked*: see below). The present meaning (c.1966) probably comes from this, but the word became so current as a result of its widespread use in the popular television comedy series *Only Fools and Horses* of the 1980s that it cannot now be described as vulgar, though it is still colloquial. The origin is the colloquial onomatopoeic verb *plonk (down)*, to put (down) firmly, abruptly or unceremoniously. The adjectival form *plonking* (often used of remarks, statements, etc.) means 'blunt, often tactlessly or foolishly thoughtless', and these qualities are often implied in *plonker*.

plonking see PLONKER.

ploughman's lunch *noun* a meal, usually a bar snack, consisting of cheese, bread and pickle, often with some salad trimming. Far from being part of British agricultural or gastronomic heritage, the name was coined by the chairman of the English Country Cheese Council in 1970 and enthusiastically taken up by virtually every pub in the country.

PMT (abbreviation for) premenstrual tension (1960s).

pogo *verb* to dance by jumping up and down on the spot. (Also *noun*, the name of such a dance.) An aspect of PUNK culture, c.1977. The name comes from the earlier *pogo-stick*, the use of which produced a similar motion.

point of sale *noun* the place at which a retail transaction takes place (1953). Now often abbreviated to **POS** (see EPOS) and part of the terminology of cashless shopping.

pointy-head *noun* an intellectual person; a (supposed) expert. Also *adj.* pointy-headed. Derogatory US colloquialism, c.1972, though *pointy* and *pointy-eared* are much older. Perhaps the assumption behind the insult is that clever people have high, domed (pointed) heads to accommodate large brains.

poison pill *noun* a tactic used by a company facing an unwanted takeover in order to make itself less attractive. One common tactic is a share issue, which, in the event of a successful takeover, would be unfavourable to the new owners because of an option written in to it, though other spoiling tactics have been used. The term, said to have been first used in this sense by a US lawyer in 1982, is a metaphorical application of the older and actual *poison pill* carried by spies so that they can kill themselves in the event of capture.

poke or **POKE** *noun* (in computing) a statement or function in BASIC for altering the contents of a memory location; an addition to a program, perhaps by a HACKER, that alters the contents of that program. Also a *verb*: to store a new value in a memory location, thus altering the program (1978).

pole position *noun* an advantageous starting position; any position of advantage, especially the leading position. These senses are recent (c.1971) borrowings and developments of the motor-racing term (c.1953) for the most advantageous starting position on the grid, namely, at the front and on the inside (as regards the first bend). This in turn was taken from a horse-racing term going back to the middle of the nineteenth century: the *pole* was the inside fence of a racecourse and also the starting position closest to it. A horse was said to 'have (drawn) the pole' if the jockey had drawn the starting position nearest the inside fence of the track. The fence was made of wood, whence 'the pole'.

political correctness *noun* a movement aimed at eliminating racism, sexism, HOMOPHOBIA and other alleged prejudices in language and thought, though it has itself often been accused of intolerance. The movement originated in American universities and began to be heard of in Britain in 1991. In its most extreme form it has led to the boycotting of certain teachers, the removal from a US college of a Goya nude thought to represent sexual harassment, and the renaming of flowers such as pansies because of possible offence to gay men. So poor has been its press that the term is now sometimes loosely applied to any trend thought to display intolerance, self-righteousness, fanaticism or even fascism, though it originated as a definition of a sensible and intentionally enlightened movement.

poll tax *noun* (an informal name for) the COMMUNITY CHARGE. As it was a tax per head of the population, the highly controversial and short-lived 'community charge' was properly dubbed 'the poll tax' as soon as it was announced in 1985: *poll* is an old word for 'head', and *poll tax* was used as early as the seventeenth century to mean 'capitation tax'. However, the term has strong historical associations with civil oppression and consequent unrest. For this reason – though few people knew it – government spokesmen studiously avoided it in favour of the more emollient 'community charge', perhaps hoping to disguise a tax as a 'charge'. Everyone else called it 'the poll tax'. Perhaps opponents of the tax also hoped that the name would remind people that failure to register might imply their disqualification from voting (in a *poll*). Se also ROOF TAX.

poly (colloquial abbreviation for) polythene. Thus *poly-wrapped* (wrapped in polythene, 1965) and *polybag* (shopping bag made of polythene, 1971).

pooper scooper, poop scoop *noun* a device used to scoop up a dog's excrement (1976). *Poop* is old slang for 'to break wind' and (of children) 'to defecate'.

pop *noun, adj.* and *verb*. As an abbreviation of *popular* applied to modern music of general appeal but appealing particularly to young people, **pop** originated in the 1950s, as did *top of the pops*, *pop concert, pop singer* etc., though the word was sometimes put in inverted commas as if to apologise for it or to draw attention to the fact that it was being used in a new sense. It had been used since the nineteenth century as an abbreviation in *pop(ular) concert* and in the early part of the twentieth century in such expressions as *pop song* – these are the origins of the current term – but since the fifties *pop* came increasingly to signify the sort of rock and roll music that established itself in that decade and the next. *Pop* and ROCK were interchangeable terms until the end of the sixties, when a distinction began to appear: ROCK became the preferred term for popular music thought to be more meaningful and innovative, and *pop* was used for the more lightweight, conventional or commercial. As time has gone on, *pop* has become a more dated and even dismissive term which has virtually dropped out of the vocabulary of many of the young. As a *verb*, *pop* has meant 'to take a narcotic drug' since the mid fifties. This use is based on the *noun pop* ('an injection of narcotic drug'), a 1930s term probably based on the idea of 'popping' (bursting) a vein. Later it was drugs in the form of pills that were popped – and the sense has recently (mid eighties) been extended to cover the greedy consumption not of drugs but of food, drink or medicines as though one were addicted to them. See also POP ART and POP CULTURE.

pop art *noun* an art movement using the themes and techniques of mass-produced urban popular culture such as comic strips, advertising, science fiction and magazines. The term was coined by the English critic Lawrence Alloway for a movement which originated in meetings of a group of artists during the winter of 1954–5. It became prominent, mainly in the USA and Britain, during the late fifties and throughout the sixties; its best known products include Andy Warhol's silk-screen of soup tins and Marilyn Monroes, and Roy Lichtenstein's paintings of comic strips. In this context *pop* does not refer to pop music: the reference is to POP CULTURE, as the movement reacted against the traditional elitism of fine art and the traditional distinction between good and bad taste by adopting the styles, artefacts and preoccupations of popular taste, however commercialised, as a fitting subject for artistic exploration.

pop culture *noun* culture based on popular taste and disseminated widely, usually on a commercialised basis. Although the dominant modern sense of *pop* has to do with music (see POP), the word has often been used to denote 'popular taste' as it is in *pop culture*, **pop art** and a number of less durable expressions. The word began to be used in this sense in the late 1950s: *pop culture* may have been coined by Colin MacInnes in *Absolute Beginners* (1959).

popmobility *noun* a form of keep-fit exercise in which movements are performed to the accompaniment of POP music (late seventies).

popper *noun* a capsule of amyl nitrate. A slang term, c.1968, from the vocabulary of drug abuse. The capsule is broken ('popped') open so that the contents can be inhaled.

popular capitalism *noun* the extension of capitalism among the general public by widening the ownership of shares, houses, small businesses, etc. Measures to encourage such ownership were a feature of Mrs Thatcher's governments during the 1980s, though the term is first recorded in 1979. *Popular* in this context means 'pertaining to the people as a whole'.

porn or **porno** *noun* (abbreviation for) pornography. The usage dates from c.1962, though *porno* as an abbreviation for *pornographic* had occurred about ten years previously. *Porno* as a noun came a little later, probably under the influence of numerous new *porno-* combinations such as *porno-film* and *porno-movie* (both 1969).

porridge *noun* a term of imprisonment. (Usually **do porridge**.) British slang, first found in print in 1953 (though thought to have been in spoken use for twenty years or so before then) and later popularised as the title of a successful television comedy series. A much earlier slang term for 'prison' was *stir*, said to be from a Romany word and *porridge* is probably a pun on this: porridge is something one has to stir.

port *noun* (in computer technology) the place, such as a socket, where signals may enter or leave a data-transmission system. Also *verb*, to transfer data by way of a port. Used since 1970 – a port is where a peripheral is connected to the micro-processor for the input and output of data. *Port* has a long history in engineering in the sense of 'aperture for the passage of something' and is the word used for openings in the side of a ship, or port-holes.

Portakabin *noun* (tradename of) a portable building for use as a temporary office, classroom, etc. (1963).

POS see EPOS.

posey *adj.* affectedly trendy, pretentious. Also *noun*, a person, usually a man, who seeks to impress, a trendoid. Both colloquialisms are from the early eighties and are based on *poser* (or *poseur*). An old but once uncommon word, **poser** enjoyed a revival in the late seventies in the derogatory sense of 'a person who hopes to impress by wearing trendy, clothes and being seen in the right places'.

position paper *noun* a written statement of views, attitudes or intentions. Originally US, 1965, and used of a statement which sets down a person's or, usually, a group's version of a particular state of affairs. It is used for information or as the basis for discussion in a negotiation, etc.

positive discrimination *noun* the provision of special opportunities or resources for a disadvantaged group such as a racial minority, handicapped children, etc. *Discrimination* is normally thought of as unfair treatment based on prejudice, though it does have other less negative meanings. *Positive discrimination* (1967) entails making a distinction in favour rather than against.

posse *noun* (in the US) a Black, especially Jamaican, street gang; (in the US and UK) one's own gang, crowd or group of friends. Youth slang, originally US Black teenage slang of the early eighties. The second, milder sense spread to White youths and to the UK at the end of the eighties mainly by way of RAP lyrics. Since the mid eighties, the word has also been used in the USA to refer specifically to a gang engaged in organised crime, often drug-related, though this meaning is not the original one nor the UK one. The word was borrowed from Western films, where it is widely used: a *posse* (short for the Latin legal term *posse comitatus*, literally 'force of the county') consists of the able-bodied men of a district on whom the sheriff can call for help in maintaining law and order.

postcode   *noun* code of letters and numbers used at the end of a postal address to aid the sorting of mail (1967).

post-feminist   *adj.* and *noun*. Because of its newness (mid eighties) the term has not yet acquired a clear definition; for example, one dictionary describes it as an adjective meaning 'resulting from or including or differing from or showing moderation of the beliefs and ideas of feminism'. It is also used as a noun for a person who believes in these ideas, though the implication of *post-* is that such a person belongs to a younger generation than those who fought to establish these ideas in the 1970s. From this comes another meaning, sometimes derogatory: a woman who accepts and benefits from the beliefs of feminism but has no ideological interest in them. In all cases the underlying assumption is that a time of great change and commitment has given way to one of consolidation or reassessment.

post-it   *noun* a slip of gummed paper on which notes may be written, and which may then be stuck in a prominent position as a message or memo. Usually sold in a pad, in yellow or other bright colours, and sometimes decorated with humorous slogans or drawings, they have been familiar since the mid eighties. Their modified adhesiveness allows them to be stuck to most surfaces and prevents them being blown away, but allows them to be peeled off and reattached at will.

post-modernism   *noun* (in the arts) any movement, tendency, style or school of thought that rejects, breaks with or reacts against modernism. As modernism stands for different things in different fields of art, there is no single definition of post-modernism that can characterise it much more helpfully than this, except perhaps in architecture: – the term is used so liberally and idiosyncratically that it sometimes seems to mean no more than what an individual writer wants it to mean. Although *post-modernism* appeared in print as long ago as 1949, it was not until the sixties that a number of critics began to claim that a break with the past was occurring, and that the aesthetic of the Modern Movement, familiar during the first half of the twentieth century, was beginning to ebb in the post-Second World War years. *Post-modernism* made its appearance in the seventies. It is most commonly used of architecture: the Lloyds building, London, designed by Richard Rogers, is often cited as an example of post-modern architecture. Whereas the predominant style of modern architecture used to be stark, geometrical, functional and unornamented, post-modernist architecture borrows from many styles (especially the Classical) with playful, colourful and sometimes ironic or vulgar use of decoration. Words such as discontinuity, fragmentation and ephemerality, and ideas having to do with the blurring of traditional distinctions between 'serious' and 'popular' culture, sometimes crop up in discussions of the meaning of post-modernism.

post-natal depression *noun* depression experienced by some women after giving birth. Not given this name until c.1973, though the condition itself is far from new.

post-traumatic stress (disorder) *noun* the psychological disorder suffered by someone who has experienced a traumatic event such as a major disaster. The symptoms may include anxiety, depression, withdrawal, nightmares, mood swings or proneness to physical illness. The term was invented by US psychologists dealing with casualties of the Vietnam War in the early 1970s; it was more accurate than the earlier term 'shell shock', coined at the time of the First World War. It has since passed into more general use.

pot *noun* cannabis. Slang, probably an abbreviation of a Mexican Spanish word *potiguaya* ('marijuana leaves'). The word was known – though not widely – in the US in the late 1930s, and entered spoken British English in the late 1940s, though it did not become widely known in the UK until the sixties.

poverty trap *noun* a situation in which poverty is almost inescapable because one is dependent on state benefits which are reduced if one succeeds in gaining any extra income (1972).

power *noun*. This word has featured in a number of recent coinages, including some now familiar ones such as *power saw* (1960) and *power drill* (1961). *Power base* (a source of authority or support) appeared in 1959; *power-mad* is from 1962. *Power-sharing* (1972) was a short-lived attempt to solve the Northern Ireland problem by guaranteeing the Roman Catholic minority a share of seats in an executive assembly, though the term has continued in use, sometimes in other contexts. *Power play*, a sporting term from c.1961 which originally described the concentration of players at a particular point in order to provide overwhelming force (in rugby, American football, ice hockey, etc.), has since been adapted to mean any display of power in a sport, e.g. *power golf*, *power tennis*, *power running*, where *power* means no more than 'powerful'. See also the following entries.

power broker *noun* a person who intrigues to exercise influence or to affect the distribution of political power. Originally and chiefly US, thought to have been coined by TH White in *The Making of the President*, 1960.

power dressing *noun* a style of women's dress intended to project an image of efficiency and the exercise of power. Popular in the early eighties, especially among businesswomen, it favoured severely tailored suits, shoulder pads and the limited use of such ornamentation as jewellery.

power lunch *noun* a business meeting attended by powerful people and held over lunch (late eighties).

prat *noun* a stupid, incompetent or ineffectual person. Slang, often a term of abuse, from c.1968. It is probably from *prat(t)*, a slang word for 'buttocks' since the sixteenth century and still in use in this sense. A number of slang words, including some taboo ones, refer to the human bottom and its bodily functions, but *prat* is relatively innocuous.

pre-emptive

pre-emptive *adj.* (of military action) designed to damage or eliminate enemy strength before it can be used. Usually found in *pre-emptive strike* (1959).

preppy or **preppie** *adj.* (of clothing style, especially among young adults) neat, classic, expensive. Also *noun,* a person dressed in such a well-groomed style. The word is also used to denote other aspects of personal appearance (clean cut, short hair, smart bearing) as well as manners, vocabulary and background, all of them indicative of wealth, conservatism and a sense of privileged superiority. Originally (c.1970) and still chiefly US, it is from the US 'preparatory school' or 'prep', the equivalent of the British public school.

prequel *noun* a film, television programme or book about an earlier stage of a story or characters that have already been the subject of a work. Modelled, c.1970, on the more familiar *sequel,* which of course deals with events subsequent to those described in an existing (and usually popular) book or film.

Prestel *noun* (trademark of) a computerised visual information system operated by British Telecom. Data selected from various databases may be made to appear on a suitably adapted television screen by dialling the appropriate telephone number (1978).

pre-teen(ager) *noun* a child (usually just) below the age of thirteen (1960).

price-earnings ratio *noun* the ratio of the price of a share on a stock exchange to the earnings per share. Used as a measure of a company's profitability in the future (1961). Normally abbreviated to P/E RATIO.

primal (scream) therapy *noun* a type of psychotherapy in which patients (often in groups) are encouraged to scream and behave violently to relive birth and the sufferings of infancy and to express aggressive emotions about their parents. Developed by the US psychologist A Janov and named by him in his book *The Primal Scream,* 1970.

prime time *noun* (in broadcasting) the time of day when an audience is expected to be at its largest. Adjectivally, *prime-time.* Mainly used of television, and denoting the period from (approximately) 7.00–10.30 p.m. (1964).

print journalism *noun* writing for magazines or newspapers. Coined c.1975 to make a distinction between it and television or radio journalism, though *print media* had been used a little earlier (1968) to mean 'newspapers and magazines'.

prioritise *verb* to arrange (items) in order of their importance; *or* to establish (something) as a priority. Originally US, 1973, and potentially ambiguous: a promise to prioritise something may mean either that it will be given first place in one's attention or that it will be given the place it deserves relative to other matters that have to be dealt with. The word is also disliked by some who think that the habit of adding *-ise* and *-isation* to existing nouns merely to save a syllable or two (*prioritise* = give priority to) has gone far enough.

186

prisoner of conscience *noun* a person in prison or detention because of their political or religious beliefs (1961). A term made familiar by Amnesty International's adoption of it.

privatise *verb* to transfer a nationalised industry to private owner-ship (early seventies), also *noun* **privatisation** the transferral of nationalised industries and public utilities to the private sector. Also **privatiser** *noun* (early eighties) one who advocates and/or enacts the transfer of national service industries to private enter-prise.

priviligentsia *noun* Communist Party intellectuals and officials who enjoyed economic and other privileges in some Communist countries; by extension, any privileged group. A blending of *privi-lege* and *intelligentsia*. Though coined in the fifties, the word was not generally known until the eighties, the decade of Soviet unrest and Gorbachev's reforms (resisted by the *priviligentsia*), when it began to be used in the press. It also broadened its meaning to include those who advocated or enjoyed privilege in the UK or else-where.

proactive *adj.* taking the initiative or anticipating events (1971), i.e. as opposed to *re*acting or responding. As a prefix, *pro* can mean 'before in time or position'. The word has since been taken up, especially in management or business contexts, as a vogue substi-tute for 'innovative' or 'making things happen' – highly prized qualities in the ENTERPRISE CULTURE.

pro-choice *adj.* (of person or group) supporting the right of a woman to choose whether or not to have an abortion. Originally US, mid seventies; compare PRO-LIFE. Both terms have importance in US political and electoral controversies about abortion, which is not as prominent an issue in UK politics. Also **pro-choicer** *noun*: a supporter of this movement (late seventies). See ANTI-CHOICE.

pro-death *adj.* (US, derogatory) supporting a woman's right to choice in abortion; also *noun* **pro-deather** a supporter of a woman's right to choose abortion. These are derogatory coinages of the pro-life, anti-abortion lobby in the USA in the eighties, using their own preferred title (PRO-LIFE) as the model rather than PRO-CHOICE. See ANTI-CHOICE.

product placement *noun* arranging for recognisable branded goods (e.g. foodstuffs, drinks, clothes) to be prominently used in a film, television play, etc. as a means of indirect advertisement and to imply endorsement by a well-known actor or actress. Well estab-lished in the USA, where payments by advertisers have improved sales of their 'placed' products, but not known in the UK until c.1991, notably on commercial television.

professional foul *noun* (in sport) a deliberate foul committed, usu-ally as a last resort, to prevent an opponent from scoring. This notorious euphemism, which stretched the already elastic meaning of *professional* to breaking-point, was greeted with widespread con-tempt and hilarity when it first came to light in the 1970s (it may have been in earlier use within the private vocabulary of foot-ballers). It remains in occasional use, however, though most frequently as a colloquial or ironic expression to denote a spoiling tactic in, for example, business or politics.

profile   *noun* a characteristic personal manner or stance (1961); the public position or policy adopted by a government or other group (1970). These are developments from an earlier meaning, 'a character study or biographical sketch', which comes from a primary meaning of the word, 'drawing or representation of the outline of anything, especially the human face'.

program   *noun* a series of coded instructions that enable a computer to carry out specified operations. In computing terminology, this has been the standard spelling since c.1950. It is also the standard US spelling, and was presumably adopted because of its widespread use in US scientific writing during the early days of computer development. Actually, the US spelling is no less 'English' than the standard British English *programme*, which only displaced the original spelling *program(e)* comparatively recently in the development of the language.

program trading   *noun* trading on international stock exchanges using a computer PROGRAM to benefit from the differences in value between stock-index futures and actual share prices. Originally US, early eighties, a product of the computerisation of financial markets.

pro-life   *adj.* (of person or group) supporting the right to life of the unborn. That is to say, opposed to abortion. The term originated in the US in the late seventies, presumably because it was thought to be more positive (*pro-* means 'in favour of') than the more familiar *anti-abortion*. It spread to the UK by the end of the eighties. See also PRO-CHOICE and ANTI-CHOICE.

promo   *noun* (abbreviation for) promotion (1963), or (as an *adjective*) promotional. Usually denotes something used to promote a product and increase sales e.g. advertising and marketing ploys and promotional events or freebies.

Provo   *noun* (abbreviation for) a Provisional, a member of the Provisional Irish Republican Army. A northern group of the (Official) IRA broke away in 1970 to become the Provisional IRA, with a special commitment to the expulsion of the British from Northern Ireland. The abbreviation came into use almost immediately.

PSBR   (abbreviation for) public sector borrowing requirement, i.e. the amount which the government of the UK borrows each year from the banks or the public in order to make up the deficit between its spending and its receipts from taxes: *borrowing requirement* is a euphemism for 'debt'. The initials date from 1976.

pseud   *noun* a pretentious or insincere person (1962). Also *adjective*. *Pseud* is usually found as a noun, sometimes meaning 'a pseudo-intellectual person', but often applied more generally as in the definition above. It is a shortening of the rather earlier *pseudo* (1945), though that is used more as an adjective than a noun, and is a colloquial adaptation of the familiar combining form *pseudo-*, meaning 'false, sham, spurious'.

psychedelic *adj.* (of drugs) capable of producing altered states of consciousness, changed mental and sensory awareness, hallucinogenic experiences, etc.; (of such effects) produced by or relating to the use of psychedelic drugs; (loosely and informally) having the strong colours, complex patterns or bizarre effects resembling those produced by psychedelic drugs. Also **psychedelia** *noun* (1967), psychedelic objects or the subculture associated with psychedelic drugs. The word was coined in 1956 by Humphrey Osmond in a letter to Alduous Huxley, who had also experimented with hallucinogenic drugs. He took it from Greek words meaning 'mind' (*psyche*) and 'made manifest', and it was intended to signify the heightened or profounded state of awareness that he believed hallucinogenic drugs could produce, though it is now generally recognised that awareness is not 'heightened' but merely changed or distorted. The word entered the UK from the USA in the mid sixties, when it was associated with HIPPIE culture and the taking of LSD. In the late sixties it was used to describe the vivid colours and kaleidoscopic, swirling patterns used in paintings, posters, fabric designs and other artefacts, all of which were attempts to replicate the effect of LSD. The Beatles' *Sergeant Pepper* album was similarly called *psychedelic music*, but in its most extended form the word came to mean little more than 'excitingly new' or 'avant-garde'.

psych *verb* to influence (person) psychologically. Originally a US colloquialism, c.1957, probably as an abbreviation of *psychoanalyse*; the verb has little to do with psychoanalysis, however, but merely denotes an influence based on a supposed understanding of someone else's personal 'psychology', whatever that may mean. A more familiar form is *psych out* (1963), which originally meant 'lose one's nerve'; it is now most frequently used to mean 'gain a psychological advantage over (a person); intimidate, frighten or demoralise', though the original sense is sometimes found in the form of 'to break down; lose one's control psychologically'. Other meanings include 'guess (person's) intentions correctly', 'outguess' and 'analyse or solve (a problem) using psychological means'. Inevitably so many possible meanings for one verb are likely to lead to confusion. *Psych up* (c.1968) in simpler and probably the most common form. It means 'make oneself (or some other person) psychologically ready for an event, especially for a performance', and usually implies a state of controlled excitement.

psychobabble *noun* language, usually jargon, that is influenced by concepts in psychology, psychoanalysis and psychotherapy. Coined in the US in 1976 and subsequently popularised as the title of a book by RD Rosen (1977). *Babble* is incoherent, meaningless or foolish speech or prattle, usually continuous; **psychobabble** is the impenetrable and often self-centred *babble* used by the numerous American exponents and followers of ever-multiplying new therapies and forms of analysis, especially those talking endlessly of their own personalities and relationships in jargon they only imperfectly understand. Although the word originated in an American (and particularly Californian) obsession with therapy and pseudo-therapy in the seventies, it has come to acquire the more general sense of 'jargon associated with psychology, especially psychoanalysis', and as such has given rise to other coinages such as TECHNOBABBLE, *eurobabble*, *ecobabble* (the jargon of the environmental movement; mid eighties) and other more transient -*babble* words that denote the jargon of a particular field of activity.

Public Lending Right *noun* authors' entitlement to payment when their books are borrowed from public libraries. The term was used from c.1960 during the campaign to establish such a scheme, though it was 1981 before the UK government established one.

pull-down *adj.* (of a computer MENU) capable of being accessed during the running of a program (mid eighties). The menu, a list of commands or options, is typically selected using a cursor controlled by a MOUSE, and is revealed on the screen rapidly and line by line, as if, the information were being 'pulled down' for use, rather as a roller blind is.

pulsar *noun* an extremely dense star emitting regular pulses of radiation, especially radio waves, with great regularity. Discovered in 1967 and named the following year from 'puls(ating) (st)ar'.

pump iron *verb* to exercise with weights in fitness-training or for body-building. US slang, c.1972. *Pump* implies the regular up and down movement of the plunger in a pump or of a person's arm or leg when using a pump; *iron* refers to the material from which weights are made.

punk *noun* (short for) PUNK ROCK or PUNK ROCKER (mid seventies).

punk rock *noun* a basic and deliberately loud and simplistic rock music, characterised by raucous and simple anti-establishment lyrics and a rejection of conventional values. *Punk* flourished from the mid to late seventies, a deliberately working class British youth culture, aggressively independent and typified by the music of Sid Vicious, Johnny Rotten and the Sex Pistols.

punk-rocker *noun* a follower of the fashions and music of punk rock (early seventies), i.e. distinctively dressed in cut or torn clothing, with various forms of self-mutilation, such as safety pins through the ears, and seeking to express a rejection of middle-class values and manners.

purple heart *noun* a stimulant pill consisting mainly of amphetamine. The colloquial name for Drinamyl, 1961, because of the shape and colour of the pill.

put-down *noun* a (cruelly) humiliating remark or snub. From c.1962, though the verb to *put down*, the senses of which include 'humiliate', is much older. A **put down** can sometimes be casual and merely deflating rather than deeply humiliating.

PWA (abbreviation for) person with AIDS. At an Aids forum held in the USA in 1983, a group of people declared that they did not wish to be labelled as 'victims' of Aids, which implied defeat, or as 'patients', which implied passivity. They wished to be known as 'people with Aids'. The term and its abbreviations have since become quite common, especially in the USA. See also PLA, PLWA.

pyramid selling *noun* the sale of goods to distributors who recruit other distributors and sell them the goods at a profit, after which this second batch of distributors do the same, and so on. The inevitable consequence is that the final distributors, such as door to door salesmen, are likely to find themselves with stock that is too expensive to sell, which is why the system is illegal in the UK. The term *pyramid selling* dates from 1975, though *pyramid* was used in the same sense in such expressions as 'pyramid profits' in the mid sixties; the reference is to the shape of a structure which has a single franchise holder at the apex and progressively widening layers of regional, district and local distributors underneath.

Quaalude (proprietary name for) METHAQUALONE (1966).

quadraphonic *adj.* (of a sound system) employing four loudspeakers, each broadcasting suitably differentiated versions, so that the listener who is at their centre receives the impression of being fully wrapped around by their sound (late sixties).

quaffable *adj.* (of wine) suitable for being drunk copiously. This new formation (c.1982) from the old verb *quaff* (drink copiously) probably originated in wine-writers' vocabulary as an amiable substitute for 'pleasant, not expensive, palate-friendly' etc., or 'drinkable'.

quagma *noun* (in physics) hypothetical plasma-like body of matter consisting of QUARKS and GLUONS. The theory was postulated in the mid eighties, the name being a combination of *qua(rk)*, *g(luon)* and *(plas)ma*.

qualities, the *noun* the QUALITY broadsheet newspapers.

quality (as an *adjective*) of good quality (1962).

quality circle *noun* a group of employees who meet to discuss ways of improving production, resolving problems, etc. within their organisation, especially in factories. An idea originally developed in Japan, and known in the UK since c.1980, partly as a result of Japanese ownership of some businesses and the consequent introduction of certain Japanese management methods. Bosses and employees meet together in small groups for the purpose of troubleshooting and the exchange of ideas.

quango (acronym for) **qu**asi-autonomous **n**on-**g**overnmental **o**rganisation (1973). A body of people, usually including some civil servants, appointed by a government minister to carry out a public duty at public expense. It is not fully independent in that it is answerable to the appropriate minister (hence *quasi-*) but it is not a department of government as the civil service is (hence *non-*). However, a few quangos have been governmental, in which case the n and g of the word have been said to stand for 'national government', though only rarely.

quangocrat *noun* one of the great and good who by virtue of a place on a QUANGO joins a self-appointing elite class thought by some to have an undue (because unelected) role in governing the country (early nineties).

quantum leap

quantum leap *noun* a sudden huge and spectacular advance; a breakthrough. In physics, a *quantum* is the smallest quantity of some physical property, and it is odd that the word should figure in an expression associated with hugeness. *Quantum leap* dates from c.1970 as a variant of the much older (1920s) *quantum jump*, which means 'the sudden transition of an electron, atom, etc., from one energy state to another'. This is significant, though certainly not 'huge' in terms of size or amount. *Quantum jump* was used figuratively for any highly significant change or development from c.1955, after which it was displaced in popular use by *quantum leap*, perhaps because a leap sounds more dramatic – it is certainly bigger – than a jump. *Quantum leap* is now common, verging on cliché. In short, something which originally meant 'a significant change in state' is now used to mean 'a huge step forward', probably because most people wrongly assume that *quantum* must have something to do with hugeness of *quantity*.

quark *noun* (in physics) a hypothetical sub-atomic particle carrying a fractional electric change and thought to be a constituent of known elementary particles. The idea was first put forward by the US physicist Murray Gell-Mann in 1964. He borrowed the word, an invented one, from James Joyce's *Finnegans Wake* (1939). It is usually pronounced to rhyme with *fork*, though some authorities prefer a rhyme with *park*.

quasar *noun* a star-like object outside our galaxy that is a powerful source of radiation such as radio waves. Quasars are the most distant and probably the most powerful observed objects in the universe. They were first detected in 1963 and named the following year from *quasi(i-stell)ar (radio source)*.

queer-bashing *noun* an unprovoked physical assault on homosexual(s), usually by a gang of thugs. Also **queer-basher**, one who does this, and *verb* **queer-bash**, to do this. Slang from c.1970, though *queer* as a slang word for a (male) homosexual goes back to the first half of the century.

quick and dirty *phrase* makeshift; hastily put together; producing the desired result but without final polish. Originally US slang, 1960s, for a cheap café, though this sense appears to have been displaced by the current one, which has been colloquial since the seventies.

quilling *noun* decorative craftwork in which paper (and occasionally other material) is formed into small bands, curls or rolls and used in pictures and designs. A modern extension (1970s) of the sense of the old verb *quill* ('to form into small cylindrical plaits or rolls'), this is now the standard term for a craft previously known as 'paper filigree' in the UK.

Quorn *noun* (tradename for) a vegetable protein derived from a type of edible fungus and used as a vegetarian meat substitute in cooking. The product, which came on the market in 1987, is named after the Leicestershire company that first made it. The company itself is named after the Leicestershire village of Quorn (now called Quorndon), well known for the fox-hunt in its area.

Rachmanism   *noun* exploitation of tenants of dilapidated or slum property by an unscrupulous landlord (1963). Probably coined by Harold Wilson, from the name of Peter Rachman (d.1962) whose use of intimidation and racial fears to drive out sitting tenants from his properties in Paddington had been brought to light a little earlier. The tenants paid low fixed-rate rents and could be removed only (or most cheaply) by thuggish action. *Rachmanism* no longer implies such tactics, and is now mainly used of the charging of extortionate rents for badly maintained accommodation.

rack up   *verb* to achieve (a score); accumulate (points). Originally and still chiefly N. American, from c.1961. The derivation is uncertain. In pool-playing, to *rack up* means to place the balls in the triangular wooden frame (called a *rack*) in order to set them in position at the start of a game. The balls as set up in this position when the *rack* is removed are also known as the *rack*. Players are then in a position to start play and thus accumulate points.

rad   *adj.* very good, excellent, up to the minute. US young people's slang, c.1982, abbreviated from RADICAL. It spread to the UK by the late eighties and was popularised by the TEENAGE MUTANT HERO TURTLES.

radical   *adj.* very good, excellent, 'cool'. Originally Californian surfers' slang of the late sixties, meaning 'at the limit' (of control, excitement, etc.). It came to be no more than a general term of approval, and by the early eighties had spread into general use among the young, soon being abbreviated to RAD.

radical chic   *noun* a fashionable affectation of left-wing views, dress, style of life, etc. Coined by the US writer Tom Wolfe in 1970 to denote high society's adoption of radicals and radical issues (such as environmentalism) as fashion accessories. The term is now used more generally of anything left-wing (or even working-class) that seems to have been embraced because it is fashionable (or new) rather than because of personal conviction.

radicchio   *noun* an Italian variety of chicory, eaten in salad, having purple leaves with white veins. Known in the UK since the mid eighties. The -*cc*- is pronounced *k*.

radio pager   *noun* a small radio receiver fitted with a buzzer. Usually worn by someone whose job entails being on the move (e.g. around a hospital). The buzzer can be made to sound in order to warn the wearer to go to a telephone to obtain a message. The term first appeared c.1968, though the device had been invented a few years earlier; see PAGER, the normal abbreviation.

rage   *noun* a dance or party; a good time. Nothing to do with anger; it is from the verb *rage*, 'to move violently or boisterously'. Originally an Australian colloquialism, it has been known in the UK since c.1987 as a result of the popularity of Australian soap operas. Also *verb* **rage**, to party, and *noun* **rager**, a party-goer.

rag-rolling   *noun* an interior decorating technique in which paint is applied with a bunched-up rag to produce a mottled effect. An old technique, but not given the name until the mid eighties when the style became popular again.

rah-rah skirt

rah-rah skirt *noun* a very short flounced skirt. Fashionable among teenage girls in 1982, it was similar in style to the skirt worn by American cheer-leaders, known in US slang as *rah-rah girls* since c.1970 because of their cries of 'rah-rah' (from 'hur*rah*').

rai *noun* a type of Algerian popular music based on traditional Arabic and Algerian folk music and influences of Western POP or ROCK (c.1986).

rainbow coalition *noun* a (political) coalition of minorities. When the term was invented in the Southern US in 1982, it referred to a possible coalition of racial minorities and disadvantaged whites (i.e. literally of different colours, as a rainbow is) together with such minorities as women's groups and the peace movement. The term was additionally useful because of the rainbow's traditional association with hope. In British use, however, since the mid eighties, it has referred to a coalition of political 'colours', notably of Labour and the Social Democrats.

rain check, take a *phrase* to postpone acceptance of an offer, invitation, etc. until a more convenient time. This colloquialism has long been known in America but has only recently (1970s) been used in Britain, not always very accurately because of an assumption that 'check' means 'inspection' or 'verification'. A *rain check* is actually a ticket given to spectators at an outdoor event enabling them to obtain a refund or a ticket for a subsequent event if there is interruption by rain. This practice, common in North America for over a century, though not in Britain, has given rise to the present metaphorical use of the term.

rallycross *noun* a form of motor sport in which cars race over a circuit combining rough territory and hard-surfaced sections (1967). From AUTOCROSS and *rally*, a form of racing on public roads, usually over long distances.

RAM (abbreviation for) RANDOM ACCESS MEMORY (1955).

Rambo *noun* a film character noted for mindless violence. Also *adjective* **Ramboesque** in the style or tradition of Rambo, and *noun* **Ramboism**: behaviour or attitudes characteristic of Rambo. The central character of David Morrell's novel *First Blood* (1972), made famous by the film of the same name (1982), is a Vietnam veteran and loner who is driven by hatred and a desire for violent retribution because he believes that society has treated him wrongly. In subsequent films Rambo is more of a national hero, fighting the Soviets in Afghanistan (1985) and rescuing US prisoners of war in Vietnam (1988). Although (or because) he was praised by President Reagan, Rambo has been ridiculed for macho posturing and reviled because of his blood-lust and brainlessness. His name has been used in many contexts, both serious and derisive, and is no longer specifically US, though Rambo has been thought to typify a number of American attitudes and foreign-policy adventures in the second half of the twentieth century.

ram-raiding *noun* a smash-and-grab burglary using a car (usually stolen) to ram the door or plate-glass window of premises to gain access (1991). Variants of this method have included the use of a

JCB or fork-lift truck to break down part of the outside of a building to remove a wall-mounted cash-dispenser, safe, etc.

ranch-style *adj.* (of house) built in the style of an American ranch-house (1961). That is to say, spacious, surrounded by land, and on a single storey or built in a way that gives the impression of being on a single storey.

random access memory *noun* (in computer technology) a set of storage locations which can be accessed directly without having to work through from the first one. *Random access*, called 'direct access', has been computerese since c.1953. Its abbreviation is RAM.

rap (music) *noun* a style of popular music in which a monologue is spoken quickly and rhythmically with instrumental accompaniment or over a pre-recorded instrumental track. Like BREAK-DANCING, this was pioneered by Black teenagers on the streets of New York in the seventies and spread rapidly, reaching Britain – among White as well as Black youngsters – in the mid eighties. *Rap* (talk) is old US slang, but it had been adopted by Black Americans in the sixties as the name for a distinctive style of verbal display and repartee in competitive street culture. It is this, when allied to music, that has given rise to the present sense. By the end of the sixties, the sense of *rap* as 'talk' had been adopted by the HIPPIE movement and some other groups as a slang term for impromptu talk or conversation: hence *rap group*, a group that meets to discuss problems (1970) and *rap session*, a group discussion (1969).

Rastafarian *noun* a member of an originally Jamaican religious and political sect which believes that Blacks are the chosen people, that the late emperor Haile Selassie of Ethiopia is their Saviour, and that their homeland is Ethiopia. Sometimes abbreviated to **Rasta**. The name, which has been generally known since the fifties though the sect originated earlier, is from Ras Tafari, the name by which Haile Selassie was known before 1930, when he became Emperor; *Ras* means 'duke' and Tafari was a family name. The sect spread to the UK in the sixties and is associated with a number of moral, religious, political and personal attitudes: see DREAD-LOCKS, for example.

rate-cap see CAP.

rat-fink or **rat fink** *noun* a contemptible or undesirable person. Chiefly US and Canadian slang, c.1964. It is an intensification of the much earlier US slang *fink*, a pejorative term of unknown origin, which means 'unpleasant person' and in particular 'informer, double dealer'.

rat pack see BRAT PACK.

rat run *noun* a suburban or minor road or route used regularly by fast or heavy traffic as a short cut or to avoid congestion on a major road. A *rat-run* is literally a maze of small passages which rats use when moving (running) about their territory. The term has often been used metaphorically (e.g. of the London underground system), as it is in its present meaning (1970s), and implies something disagreeable, as rats usually do – here the selfishness of the drivers. Also *verb*: to follow a rat run through minor roads.

raunchy *adj.* sexy, smutty; sexually uninhibited, provocative or exciting; aggressively licentious. Also *noun* **raunch**, crudeness, vulgarity, licentiousness. These meanings are from the sixties. *Raunchy*, though not *raunch*, existed earlier, largely confined to US slang in the sense of 'sloppy, cheap, slovenly' (perhaps from the Italian *rancio*, rotten). It also exists in the slang of rock and jazz as a term of approval meaning 'raw unsophisticated'. **Raunchy** came into particular prominence in the tabloids in the early nineties as a largely approving description of flaunted sexuality.

rave(-up) *noun* a lively party. Late fifties slang, though *rave* goes back to the sixteenth century in the sense of 'frenzy, great excitement'. The word took on a new meaning c.1989, when it was used to denote a large-scale ACID HOUSE party and the culture (the *rave scene*) and music associated with weekend gatherings of many thousands of mainly young people. The parties, often arranged secretly in derelict buildings, warehouses, fields or other unorthodox locations, were for the purpose of dancing, drinking soft drinks and enjoying an atmosphere of goodwill, but also (for many) for the consumption of ECSTASY. See RAVER.

raver *noun* person, usually young, who attends ACID HOUSE parties (see RAVE). Colloquial, c.1989.

razor-cut *noun* hair-cutting and styling using an open razor, mainly on wet hair. Also *verb*, to cut in this way. Introduced in the 1950s and named in the sixties.

ready-mix *adj.* having ingredients already blended. Originally US, c.1950, as an adjective for foods that were ready to cook or eat after the addition of milk or water. Since the 1970s the term has been used as a noun for concrete mixed before or during delivery to the place where it is to be used.

Reaganomics *noun* the economic policies of Ronald Reagan, US President 1981–9. He advocated reductions in income tax, welfare provision and all public spending except defence, arguing that such reductions would be bound to stimulate economic growth. In the event, the policy produced a huge federal deficit and a doubling of the national debt. The word *Reaganomics* was a variation on *Reaganism* (c.1966), coined during an earlier phase of the future president's career to denote his politics in general. *Reaganomics* (1980s) was originally a derisory term, intended to indicate that *Reagan('s econ)omics* were not worthy to be called 'economics', but the word was later used as a factual and unemotive term. It has continued in use during the first half of the nineties because of the relevance of the economic policies of Reagan – and his ally, Mrs Thatcher – to the severe economic depression that followed.

real ale *noun* beer which is allowed to ferment in the cask and which is served from pumps that do not use carbon dioxide. From about the middle of the century, the brewing industry in the UK introduced mass-production methods which included the chilling, pasteurisation and carbonation of beer; it was stored in metal kegs and finally served, fizzy and bland, under gas pressure. Of the voices raised in protest, the most effective were those of the

Campaign for Real Ale (CAMRA), founded in 1972; the name implied that too much beer was 'unreal', artificial and unpalatable. The success of the Campaign has been notable: traditionally brewed beers, previously threatened by 'convenience' beers as well as by industrial mergers, were saved, as was the service of beer by hand-pumping rather than by pumping under gas pressure, and public opinion was educated in favour of 'real' ale, so much so that many public houses now advertise it prominently.

real-time *adj.* (of computer data-processing system) able to accept data, update its records and feed back results immediately. The term (originally 1953) has a number of uses and slightly different meanings, but is most usually found in the context of the data-processing of constantly changing information, e.g. an airline-ticket booking system. The *real time* is the actual time when an activity or process takes place, or a situation is analysed. A computer able to work in *real time* is analysing a current situation, things as they are and not as they were.

reception class *noun* the first class in an infant school. So called because it specialises in the reception of children attending school compulsorily for the first time (1972).

recombinant DNA *noun* DNA containing DNA fragments from a different species or organism. The basis of GENETIC ENGINEERING (1975). *Recombinant* means 'formed by recombination'.

record-book *noun* a book containing details of the best performances ever attained, usually in some field of sport (1961). *To go into the record-book* may also be used figuratively (and colloquially), often when no *record-book* actually exists for the activity in question: 'He goes into the record-book as one of the few former prime ministers to refuse a peerage'. Thus the expression may mean no more than 'do something unusual'.

record of achievement *noun* a statement setting out not only the educational record but also the general personal development of a school pupil. First heard of in educational circles in the mid 1980s as one of a number of innovations which the UK government wished to see introduced by state schools. The *record of achievement* was to be an open document, not a confidential reference, prepared during the pupils' schooling (perhaps in consultation with them) for presentation to them on leaving school.

recreational drug *noun* a drug taken not for medical reasons but for pleasure. The implication is usually that the drug-use is optional, i.e. not as the result of an addiction (c.1970).

recycle *verb* to convert (waste) into reusable materials. This meaning (c.1960), closely related to the earlier one of 'to reuse (a material) in an industrial process by returning it to an earlier stage in that process' (thus beginning a new 'cycle'), became more prominent as a result of the GREEN revolution, especially during the eighties when manufacturers began to advertise *recycled* goods or packagings. *Recyclability* (1973) became a more familiar word, and *recyclable* (1971) developed into a noun.

red card *noun.* Since 1976 a player who commits an offence in soccer is shown a yellow card by the referee as a warning or a red card if he is to be sent off for a more serious infringement. This practice has given rise to a number of colloquial and figurative expressions: to *get* or *be shown a red/yellow card* is to be dismissed/warned.

red-eye or **red eye** *noun* an overnight aeroplane flight, especially one crossing time zones. This has been a US colloquialism since c.1968, alluding to passengers' eyes being red from lack of sleep, and was originally used attributively, as in 'red-eye flight'. The term spread to the UK in the eighties.

Red Guard *noun* a member of the Chinese youth movement that attempted to implement the CULTURAL REVOLUTION. The Red Guards, often students or school children, were first mobilised in 1966 and dispatched around China to destroy anything thought to represent impure communism. They wore red armbands and carried Mao's 'little red book', and their name was probably a conscious copying of that of the Red Guard of the Russian Revolution.

redline *verb* (of a bank, finance house, or building society) to refuse a loan (mortgage, etc.) to a person who lives in a certain area, usually an INNER CITY. A specialised application, c.1973, of the old but rare verb *redline*, 'to underline (person's name) in red ink in one's records to signify a presumed risk'. The modern sense (mainly US) implies that a 'red line' has been drawn round a whole area.

red triangle *noun* a reflective warning sign in the shape of a hollow triangle (late sixties). In some European countries all drivers must carry one of these devices, which fold up into a small size, in their vehicles and erect it on the road-side, several yards behind their car or lorry, in the event of a break-down so that following drivers are warned of the obstruction.

reel-to-reel *adj.* (of magnetic tape) wound from one end to another during use; (of tape-recorder) using two reels between which a tape is passed during use (1961). Now largely displaced by CASSETTE arrangements.

reflag *verb* to change a ship's flag to that of another (friendly) country in order to gain protection during a war. This practice, the propriety of which is controversial, became an issue at the time of the Iran–Iraq War (1980–8) when exports by means of oil-tankers were threatened in the Persian Gulf. In particular, reports in the media drew attention to the *reflagging* of Kuwaiti tankers under the US flag so that they could then enjoy the protection of US warships in the area.

reflexology *noun* a technique for relief of tension by foot-massage. The word is not new, though this development of its meaning is (c.1976), as is the popularity of the technique as an ALTERNATIVE therapy, especially during the eighties. *Reflexology* means, originally, the study (*-ology*) of the body's reflexes: its underlying principle has to do with pressure points in the feet which are linked to parts of the body, so that action on a pressure point has a reflex ('reflected') action on some other organs.

refuge *noun* a place offering shelter to a woman who has been abused by her husband or PARTNER. The word has always meant 'place of shelter or safety' but this special use dates only from c.1976.

refusenik *noun* a Jew in the Soviet Union who has been refused permission to emigrate; (colloquially) a person who refuses to follow instructions. The first meaning (c.1975) is now largely of historical interest, as permission to emigrate became much more freely available as a result of Gorbachev's policy of GLASNOST. The word is a translation of a Russian one which comprises part of the verb 'refuse' and the Russian suffix *-nik* ('person associated with'): compare SPUTNIK. The second meaning is mainly journalistic, c.1986. It is accurate in that it implies dissent from a higher authority (most of the original Soviet *refuseniks* had been dissidents) but inaccurate in that they were so named because they had 'been refused', not because they were doing the refusing.

reggae *noun* a type of West Indian popular music with strongly accented upbeat in a four-beat bar, frequently associated with the RASTAFARIANS. Other characteristics include sophisticated rhythms in the sung melodies and the use of a short repeated tune in the bass. *Reggae* emerged in Kingston, Jamaica, c.1969 as a combination of indigenous music and US rhythm and blues, and spread to London in the early seventies. Its name is thought to be from West Indian English *rege-rege*, a quarrel or argument.

relationship *noun* a sexual affair. A common euphemism since the early seventies.

relaunch *noun* (of a commercial product) a renewed launch. Also a *verb*. The implication, usually, is that the original launch was not successful.

remaster *verb* to make a new master audio-recording (from an earlier recording). The implication is that the remastering is done digitally and that the result will be CDs (or records) of improved sound quality even though the original recording was made with older technology (1967).

remit *noun* a set of instructions or a brief; an area of responsibility or authority given to a person or group. The dominant sense of the noun since c.1963. The previous (and rare) meaning of the word was 'the conveyance of a (usually legal) matter to some other authority for settlement'.

rent-a- (as a prefix) *Rent-a-(car/Ford)* goes back to the 1920s as the name or part of the name of some car-hire firms, and has been registered as a propriety name in the US. For many years the expression was used both as a noun and adjective in a number of contexts having to do with car hire. In 1961, a right-wing British newspaper coined *rent-a-crowd* as a facetious and derogatory name for any group of people who could be relied on to take part in a public demonstration: the implication was that their voices were as worthless as if they had been paid to take part. The term, later intensified to *rent-a-mob* c.1970, was satirically apposite at a time when left-wing DEMOS were common and could be made fun of by the suggestion that the same people turned up whatever the subject – nuclear disarmament, gay lib, strikes – as though they had been hired from some agency. Later coinages such as *rent-a-gob* and *rent-a-quote* (an MP always and instantly available to the media to give an opinion on any subject) are probably transient, but *rent-a-crowd/mob* is likely to persist as long as the PHOTO OPPORTUNITY remains a prominent part of political life.

rent boy   *noun* a young male prostitute for men. The term has been generally known only since c.1969 when it first appeared in print. However, the less explicit *rent* has had the same meaning (though without drawing attention to youthfulness) in private homosexual slang since at least 1930, if not much earlier.

repetitive strain (or **stress**) **injury**   *noun* a painful condition of arm, shoulder, neck or wrist caused by prolonged and repetitious mechanical activity. First named in the 1980s, and subsequently recognised as an industrial injury justifying compensation, because of the sharp increase in sufferers as a result of the introduction of computer keyboards and VDUs into the workplace. The condition had existed previously, among musicians, for example, and writers suffering from 'writers' cramp', though on a smaller scale. Often shortened to RSI.

reprography   *noun* a branch of technology concerned with the reproduction of documentary or graphic material. A direct translation, c.1961, of a slightly earlier French coinage: the word is a blend of *reproduction* and *photography*, though it is used of any form of facsimile reproduction, not necessarily a photographic one. The adjectival form *reprographic* is also from c.1961, and a noun **reprographics** (c.1967) has virtually displaced *reprography*, probably because of the latter's ugliness.

rerun   *noun* a repeated occurrence or attempt (1976). As in 'the 1992 election was a rerun of the one in 1987'. This sense comes from an earlier one 'a *repeat* showing of a film' (1955), later applied to broadcasts, etc. The verb *rerun* ('to put on or broadcast again') is from the same time. The common origin of both the verb and the noun (which was in earlier US use) is the much older verb *re-run*, 'to run (over) again'.

resale   (as adjective) second-hand. A popular euphemism since c.1960 especially in the housing market as in 'resale value', though very much older in its sense of 'the selling again of something already bought'.

residency   *noun* a regular series of performances by a band, musician etc. at one venue (1966).

reskill   *verb* to retrain (the workforce) in the new skills required for today's businesses (1985). Also *noun* **reskilling** (1983).

Restart   *noun* a UK government programme for retraining and re-employment particularly for the long-term unemployed (1988).

retread   *noun* a person or thing pressed into use again. Because the original meaning is 'a tyre having a new tread bonded on to a worn casing' (now more usually called a *remould*) the figurative uses of the word can sometimes imply 'a lesser substitute for the real thing'. A *retread* is often 'a retrained person', which was its meaning in US slang of the fifties, when it was perhaps borrowed from Australian military slang for a retired soldier recalled for service in the Second World War. The word has been in general use in the UK since the mid eighties and is used not only of retrained people but of film sequels and re-makes of old films, updated versions of old government policies, and anything else thought to be refurbished so it can go round again.

retro *adj.* revived from or associated with the past; nostalgic for the past. In 1973, when the year's Paris fashions echoed the 1930s styles, the French abbreviated their word *rétrograde* to *rétro* to describe them; in French as in English the prefix *retro-* signifies 'backwards'. English borrowed the new adjective, which has since been applied to styles and fashions in other fields such as literature and popular music. The abbreviation also exists as a noun meaning 'style, etc., that looks back to an earlier period; nostalgia for the past.'

retro-chic *noun* the fashionability of past fashions (late eighties).

retrovirus *noun* any of a group of RNA viruses that are able to reverse the normal flow of genetic information (i.e. from DNA to RNA) by 'transcribing' RNA itself into DNA (i.e. by forming DNA during the replication of their RNA). They do this by using a unique enzyme called *Reverse Transcriptase*, and their name is formed from the initial two letters of each of these words + *o* + *virus* (c.1977). The word became familiar because HIV is a *retrovirus*.

returner *noun* someone returning to their paid work after a break – most usually a married woman returner coming back after childbearing and rearing (late eighties).

returnik see SPUTNIK.

reverse discrimination *noun* discrimination against the majority group in a society as a result of giving preferential treatment to a minority group. The term came into use after the passing of the Civil Rights Act in the USA in 1964; this required businesses to include among their employees a certain proportion of people from ethnic minorities, and led to allegations that such POSITIVE DISCRIMINATION had a negative ('reverse') effect on those who were in a majority. The term had reached British English by 1969, e.g. in connection with the allocation of reserved places for Roman Catholics within the Northern Ireland police.

rhythmic gymnastics a form of gymnastics involving rhythmic movement and the use of hand apparatus such as ribbons, hoops and balls. Not a new term, but an official one only since the style was recognised in the 1970s, since when it has become well known through television.

right-on *adj.* modern, trendy; politically sound, socially aware or relevant, ideologically correct. Colloquial since c.1972, though the second group of meanings are sometimes used ironically, implying self-righteousness. The origin is the popular slang exclamation *Right on* (c.1966), a US expression of general agreement, approval and encouragement borrowed from much earlier Black slang.

right to die *noun phrase* the (alleged) right of an incurably ill person to have life-support systems withdrawn. The phrase, from the early seventies, reflects a comparatively new moral dilemma brought about by the sophistication of modern life-support mechanisms. It is usually found in the adjectival form *right-to-die* (movement, legislation, etc.). See also RIGHT-TO-LIFE for a distinctive US sense of that term.

right-to-life *adj. phrase* anti-abortion (mid seventies). Also the *noun* **right-to-lifer**, an opponent of abortion. In the US, and increasingly in the UK also, the **right-to-life** *movement* dislikes the negativeness of 'anti-abortion' and prefers the positive affirmation of the rights of the unborn child. Members of the movement have also supported the rights of the incurably ill not to have their lives artificially prolonged: their right to *quality* of life. See RIGHT TO DIE.

ring-pull *adj.* (of a can) having a seal which is opened by pulling a ring attached to it (c.1970). Also *noun*: the ring itself; the can itself.

riot shield, helmet, gear *nouns.* The *riot shield* was first heard of c.1967; it is usually a long or full-length transparent shield used by the police during disturbances when missiles may be thrown at them. At the same time came *riot gas* (see CS GAS) *riot helmet* (1969), a hard hat worn as protection by the police, and, a little later, *riot gear* overall protection (1978).

rip-off *noun* something grossly overpriced; a fraud, swindle, theft. Also *verb* **rip off**, to cheat, steal from. All these are slang, originally US, late sixties, from the familiar sense of *rip* 'to tear violently or roughly'.

RISC (acronym for) reduced instruction set computer. Introduced in 1983, this is a computer designed for a limited set of operations. As a result of the simplification of its circuitry, it is able to perform at high speed.

ritual or **satanic abuse** *noun* improper, mainly sexual, use of children (see CHILD ABUSE) by adults in organised events having some features of satanic ritual. These terms were much used c.1990 in connection with some notorious apparent examples, but it is not certain that such practices are common enough to ensure that the terms will survive. See ABUSE.

roach *noun* the butt of a cannabis cigarette. Originally US slang, c.1953. It had previously meant a cigarette end, thought to resemble a cock*roach*.

roadie *noun* (abbreviation for) road-manager. In practice extended to anyone, not just a manager, who travels (or goes on the road) with a band or group to set up their equipment.

road movie *noun* a genre of film in which the main character takes to the road or travels, either as an escape from something or in a search (e.g. for self-discovery). The name (early seventies) was probably borrowed from the earlier and very different *Road movies*, an occasional description of a group of popular film comedies which began with *Road to Singapore* (1940s) and continued with other 'Road to . . .' titles.

road rage *noun* an uncontrollable anger that overtakes and takes over some drivers (including normally reasonable people) as a result of the frustrations of late twentieth century traffic conditions. The sense of powerfulness, of being in control, that driving sometimes lends to people – or more particularly the withdrawal of that illusion under some driving conditions – no doubt also contributes to the loss of self-control that has led to incidents of assault and battery. The phenomenon came to general notice and was named in the early nineties.

rock *noun* (slang for) a crystallised form of cocaine. Another but now less common name for CRACK. The word has been known since the middle of the eighties, though it may have existed earlier in the private vocabulary of drug users. It refers to the hard, rock-like consistency of the substance. See ROCK (MUSIC).

rockabilly *noun* a style of White ROCK music originating in the US South during the mid fifties. The name, and the music, blend ROCK AND ROLL and hillbilly.

rock and roll, rock 'n' roll *noun* a type of popular music of the 1950s which developed into POP and ROCK. The basic ingredients combine US country music and Black rhythm and blues with an insistent beat and energetic delivery; the best known practitioners were probably Elvis Presley and Bill Haley and his Comets, who came to prominence in the mid fifties, though the style had been known as *rock and roll* since c.1951. The origins of the name are unknown. There was a song entitled 'Rock and Roll' in a film of 1934, but it was about the movement of a ship and does not seem to have been particularly well known. It has also been suggested that *rock and roll* was playful Black slang for sexual intercourse; if this is so, it could have found its way into music, as a number of Black terms have, especially given the sexual demonstration in rock-and-roll – witness the number of tight-jeaned performers such as Elvis ('the pelvis') Presley. The simplest explanation is that the vigorous dancing which grew up with rock-and-roll involved bending the body backwards and forwards and from side to side and that this was described as rocking and rolling.

rock (music) *noun* (originally, abbreviation of) ROCK AND ROLL; (now) any of various styles of electronically amplified popular music derived from rock and roll. In the early stages of its development during the fifties and sixties, ROCK was generally indistinguishable from ROCK AND ROLL and POP. Since the early seventies, however, *rock* has become the standard term covering all types of heavily rhythmical, usually loud and often frenetic popular music: see HEAVY METAL, ROCK and HARD ROCK as examples. Meanwhile *pop* has become an almost historical term for the style of lighter, more tuneful and commercial music associated with the sixties and *rock and roll* tends to be reserved for the music of the fifties.

rocker *noun* a member of a youth cult which was interested in motor-cycles, wore leather jackets and long hair, and enjoyed ROCK AND ROLL. The word originated in the 1950s, when it merely meant 'a devotee of rock-and-roll', but it rapidly became associated with

rock opera

more complex interests and became well known as a result of clashes between rockers and mods: see MOD for further detail.

rock opera   *noun* a drama set to ROCK music. A rather pretentious (or ironic) term, 1969, given opera's position as a high art form, but it is one of the earliest indications that rock wished to break away from the more frivolous association of POP and the commercialism of ROCK AND ROLL. The first successful examples of the genre were *Hair* (1969) and *Jesus Christ Superstar* (1970), though subsequent examples have usually been called 'musicals' rather than 'operas'.

rock steady; rocksteady   *noun* a slowed-down version of SKA, with more elaborate vocal lines. It succeeded ska c.1965, and developed into REGGAE c.1969. Its name comes from ROCK AND ROLL and 'steady' (because of its slowness in comparison with the original rock and roll).

role-playing game   *noun* a form of game in which players play the part of imaginary characters in an imaginary setting. Role-playing as a technique in psychiatry goes back to the 1940s, but the present term dates from the late seventies when a number of new games, notably *Dungeons and Dragons*, were devised which involve the participants as characters in a particular setting, often a fantasy one. By the mid eighties, computer games in similar style were available for home use and also called *role-playing games*.

rollerball   *noun* a type of pen with a writing tip consisting of a tiny ball in metal, plastic, etc. at the end of an ink cartridge (late 1970s).

roller disco   *noun* DISCO-dancing on roller skates (c.1978).

roll-on roll-off   *adj.* (of a ship, usually a ferry) designed so that vehicles can be driven on and off (1955). Sometimes abbreviated to RO-RO.

ROM   (acronym for) read only memory. In computer technology, a storage device (*memory*) that holds data or instructions permanently (e.g. the operating system) and cannot be changed or added to by the computer or the user because it is fixed at the time of manufacture. It is 'read only' because it cannot be 'written to' i.e. altered, erased, etc.

roof tax   *noun* a property-based local tax. During the political controversy surrounding the introduction of the COMMUNITY CHARGE, which the Labour Party insisted on calling a POLL TAX, Conservative politicians invented the term *roof tax* (c.1990) to describe Labour's counter-proposals for a tax on property. Conservatives were stung by the implications of 'poll tax' and hoped that their riposte, 'roof tax', would be similarly offensive, implying that not even the roofs over people's heads would be safe if Labour had its way. In the event, when the poll tax was finally abolished by the Conservatives and replaced by the COUNCIL TAX, it turned out to be mainly a *roof-tax*.

roots   *noun* ethnic origins perceived as a special cause for Black consciousness or pride. There is nothing new in the definition of *roots* as 'a person's origins or background, socially and culturally'. What is new (late seventies) is the specific association with Black heritage, probably as a result of the popularity of *Roots* (1976), an exploration of his own African origins by the Black US writer Alex Haley. Hence *roots music* (expressing the cultural uniqueness of a particular ethnic, especially Black, minority), *roots reggae* (strongly Jamaican in character: see REGGAE) and *rootsy*, which originally meant 'having a strong feeling of Black cultural heritage' though it has since (1980s) broadened into 'earthy, unsophisticated, having a sense of ethnicity' without specific reference to Black culture.

rootsy   *adj*. see ROOTS.

ro-ro   (acronym for) ROLL-ON ROLL-OFF (1969).

round-tripping   (in financial dealings) a form of trading in which money borrowed from one source is lent to someone else in order to make a profit from a short-term rise in interest rates, after which the original sum is repaid. A metaphorical use, c.1977, of the familiar *round trip*, a journey to a place or places and back again.

routier   *noun* (in France) a restaurant (occasionally hotel) catering for lorry-drivers though open to the general public. Specifically, an establishment displaying a sign signifying that it is listed in the *Guide des Relais Routiers* and therefore subject to regular inspection and approval by the official organisation of *routiers* (French for 'lorry-drivers'). The word has been known since the 1960s by British tourists wanting quickly-served, reasonably-priced, simple but substantial meals of good quality. Since the 1980s, British hotels and restaurants have been able to register as *routiers*, though many of them are far more expensive and up-market than the French ones.

RSI   (abbreviation for) REPETITIVE STRAIN (OR STRESS) INJURY.

rubber bullet   *noun* a projectile made from hard rubber and fired from a special gun. Intended for riot-control and best known from its use in Northern Ireland since c.1971. It is intended to be bounced off the ground, and, like the PLASTIC bullet, it is not designed to kill but is solid enough to do so if it strikes a vulnerable part of the body, so it has in fact been responsible for a number of deaths. See BATON ROUND.

rubbish   *verb* to disparage, criticise. An (informal) verb in the UK only since the 1970s, taken over from an Australian colloquialism, though as a noun it is very old.

Rubik('s) cube   *noun* (trade name of) a popular toy puzzle invented by Professor Erno Rubik, Hungarian inventor, in 1975, launched in the UK in 1979 and given this name in 1980. It consists of a cube composed of 26 smaller cubes which have differently coloured faces. Each layer of cubes is rotatable. The object of the game is to rotate the layer so that each face of the large cube has a single colour. There are many billions of possible permutations.

rude boy or **rudie**   *noun* an unemployed Black youth, stereotypically seen as indolent and apt to commit petty crime by his critics but as daring by his friends. Originally Jamaican c.1967, and later a distinctive youth cult.

rumble   *noun* a gang-fight, mainly pre-arranged, usually among youths. UK slang since the sixties, though known in the US and

rumble strip

elsewhere in the forties. As a verb, *rumble* is old slang for 'handle roughly or unceremoniously'.

rumble strip *noun* one of a series of small ridges set across a roadway approaching a junction or other hazard to alert drivers to slow down. As the tyres pass over them, these ridges cause a drumming sound (or, depending on their thickness, a certain discomfort) which is gradually intensified because they are placed closer together as the hazard is reached. The name is American, known in the UK since c.1962, and is based on the rumbling sound the strips are intended to cause.

rumpy-pumpy *noun* sexual intercourse. 1980s slang, presumably based on the familiar meanings of *rump* and *pump*.

run time *noun* (in computer technology) the time taken to execute a computer's program (1965).

rust belt *noun. Belt* has long been used in the US to denote a region which has a particular characteristic or principal product, indicated in an immediately preceding noun: thus *Bible belt* (area where Protestant fundamentalism is prominent), *corn belt*, *cotton belt*, etc. The expression *rust belt* seems to have originated as *rust bowl*, presumably a pun on *dust bowl*, the familiar US term for an agricultural region which has been made destitute because drought has turned the soil to dust. During the presidential election of 1984, the Democratic candidate Walter Mondale, claimed that President Reagan's economic policies (see REAGANOMICS) had caused the industrial areas of the USA to decline into a *rust bowl*; the implication was that steel works, for example, were rusting away. This gave rise to the phrase *rust belt*, which has since been used of manufacturing areas in the UK (e.g. the west Midlands) and of industrial areas in former communist countries in eastern Europe.

S and M (abbreviation for) sadism and masochism or sado-masochism. Sometimes S-M. In general use since the mid sixties; previously restricted to US homosexual vocabulary.

sab *noun* a person who disrupts a fox-hunt as a form of protest against blood sports; a person who commits sabotage as a form of protest against the abuse of animal rights. Also *verb*, to commit sabotage of this kind. A slang abbreviation of *saboteur*, originally confined to the private vocabulary of hunt saboteurs, but since the late seventies increasingly found in newspaper and television reports.

SAD (acronym for) seasonal affective disorder. A state of depression experienced by some people in winter, thought to be associated with lack of sunlight. The condition, now officially recognised though without an agreed physiological explanation, first became widely known in early 1987.

Saddamgate *noun* (the alleged scandal of) loans made by the US to Iraq, of which the leader was Saddam Hussein, during the years before he came to be the villain of the Gulf War, 1991, and the enemy of the -US. The word, one of many based on -GATE, emerged shortly after the Gulf War, though the affair appears to have originated in 1989 when President Bush issued a secret directive which ordered the pursuit of good relations with President Saddam Hussein.

safari jacket or **suit**   *noun* The former (c.1972) is a casual jacket or shirt of denim or cotton with a belt and four pockets, two above and two below the belt. It was previously known as a *bush jacket*. A *safari suit* consists of a safari jacket with matching trousers, shorts or skirt. Modelled on the outfits worn on safari or by game wardens, it became fashionable in the late 1960s.

safari park   *noun* a large enclosed park where imported wild animals roam comparatively free and can be viewed by the public who either drive through in cars or coaches or remain in safe viewing areas. A leisure development of the late sixties: the Windsor Safari Park, for example, was opened in 1969, and others have been opened in the grounds of stately homes. The name is obviously intended to evoke the exotic excitements of a safari, which is a longer and rather more adventurous expedition, often in Africa, to hunt or view wild life in its natural habitat. A car trip in parkland is hardly comparable.

safe   *adj.* excellent. Also **well safe**. A slang term of general approval among the young (late eighties). Its origin, in US Black street culture, is perhaps from the idea that certain fashions, clothes, music, behaviour etc. are 'safe' (and therefore desirable) in that they do not excite ridicule from the peer group.

safe house   *noun* a place of refuge or meeting-place, usually a house or flat of which the ownership and use are unknown to the authorities and which is used, especially by intelligence or terrorist organisations, to house hostages, defectors, agents, etc. or to plan operations, conduct interrogations, etc. The term has been known since the early sixties, since when it has been a commonplace of spy stories, though it may have existed earlier in the private vocabulary of intelligence services.

safe sex   *noun* sexual intercourse using physical protection, such as a condom, or non-penetrative practices to prevent the spread of Aids and other sexually transmitted diseases. The term has been common in the vocabulary of health education, government campaigns etc. since c.1985 as a result of attempts to control the transmission of Aids among the homosexual community and, later, in society as a whole. *Safe sex* sometimes also implies a limitation in the number of one's sexual partners – often to one. The expression *safer sex* (i.e. safer than unprotected sex) is sometimes preferred as not appearing to guarantee an unguaranteeable absolute safety.

sailboard   *noun* a moulded board like a surfboard but with a mast and sail, used in WINDSURFING. The word, originally US, has been used in this sense since the 1970s when the sport developed; in fact the sport itself was originally known as *sailboarding*, though its official name is now BOARDSAILING and its common one is WINDSURFING. During the 1960s, *sailboard* had been the name of a surfboard with mast and sail but also with centre board and rudder – a sort of elementary dinghy – but this usage seems to have been short-lived.

salsa *noun* a type of Latin American dance music; the dance that is performed to this music. Popularised by Puerto Ricans in New York c.1975, this is fast big-band music combining Latin American with jazz and rock. The name comes from a Spanish word for 'sauce'.

SALT (acronym for) Strategic Arms Limitation Talks. A series of US–Soviet negotiations (1969–79) during the Cold War. SALT 1 lasted from 1969–72, and the accord that was signed in 1972 was regarded as an important slowing down of the arms race. SALT 2 started in 1974 and a document was signed in 1979, but the US Congress refused to ratify the treaty. The rapid developments of the 1980s, culminating in the break up of the Soviet Union, made SALT issues suddenly less relevant.

Salyut *noun*. The name (Russian for 'salute') of a series of seven Soviet space stations, the first launched in 1971 and the last in 1982, to which cosmonauts were ferried for long periods (e.g. 237 days in 1984). The Salyut programme was superseded by the Mir space station.

SAM (acronym for) surface-to-air missile (1958).

samizdat *noun* the clandestine printing and publication of banned or subversive literature in the former USSR and other totalitarian countries. The word, an abbreviation of the Russian for 'self-publishing house', has been used in English since 1967. It may soon have no more than historical significance, though it has shown some signs of taking root as a word for any underground press, minority or dissident opinion, or voice of protest.

samosa *noun* small triangular pastry containing spiced vegetables or meat and served fried. A staple of Indian cookery and known in the UK since c.1955. The word is from Hindi.

sampling *noun* (in popular music recording) taking a piece of digitally encoded sound, such as extract(s) from existing records, and mixing it into a new recording. This technique has been popular in the production of recorded popular music since the mid eighties as a result of developments in computerised recording technology. It may involve quotation from a hit record (e.g. the rhythm track); at a more sophisticated level, the entire style, tone or phrasing of an existing work may be applied electronically to new material by the use of a synthesiser. Much HOUSE music and TECHNO has been fabricated from different and variously modified and blended sound sources. There is a *verb* to **sample**, and *noun* **sampler**, the musical computer which samples sounds.

Sandinista *noun* a member of the Sandinist National Liberation Front. The original Sandinistas were followers or supporters of Augusto Sandino, a Nicaraguan nationalist leader who founded a revolutionary guerrilla organisation; he was murdered in 1934. However, the name is best known from more modern Nicaraguan history. In 1963 the Sandinist National Liberation Front, also named after Sandino, was set up; in 1979 these Sandinistas took power and formed a socialist coalition government, but were opposed by the USA, who supported the CONTRA rebels by methods which created the scandal known as IRANGATE. A ceasefire in 1988 led to free elections in 1990 and the fall of the Sandinista government.

sarnie, sarney   *noun* a sandwich. Slang, not recorded in print until 1961, but known well before that in Northern colloquialism, especially in Liverpool where it may have originated. It is based on the first syllable of *sandwich*.

SAT   (acronym for) standard assessment task. The Education Reform Act of 1988 introduced a NATIONAL CURRICULUM for state schools in England and Wales and provided for the testing of all pupils at specified stages. This testing is based on *SATs*; the jargon rapidly entered the vocabulary of teachers, pupils and parents.

satanic abuse   See RITUAL ABUSE.

satellite   *noun* (short for) satellite broadcasting or satellite television: the broadcasting of TV programmes by means of communications satellites which receive signals from ground stations and retransmit them to special aerials (see DISH) in subscribers' homes; a television service using this technology. This system was pioneered in the late 1960s. The present shortening of what was originally called 'direct broadcasting by satellite' and then 'satellite broadcasting' dates from the late eighties when a dedicated service was first introduced into the UK.

scag   *noun* heroin. US slang of unknown origin from the mid sixties. The word had first cropped up about half a century earlier, meaning 'cigarette (stub)'.

scam   *noun* a swindle, especially a dubious business deal or fraudulent bankruptcy; a racket, especially one involving drug-trafficking. Also *verb*: to perpetrate such a fraud or swindle. Originally and chiefly US slang, c.1963. The origin is obscure, but may be related to an obsolete sense of *scamp* 'highway robbery'.

scattershot   *adj.* random, haphazard, indiscriminate. A figurative use, chiefly N. American (1961), of a word which literally denotes a type of shot designed to be scattered over a wide field of fire. The British equivalent of the American *scattergun* is a shotgun. *Scattergun* is also used attributively (e.g. 'scattergun approach') in a similar sense.

scenario   *noun* a predicted sequence of events; a description of an imagined situation; outline of plans or intended course of action; (loosely) any circumstance, situation, scene, etc. The word enjoyed a long and blameless existence in the sense of 'outline of the plot of a play' and later 'full film script' until 1964 when it was taken up by US military bureaucrats and strategists, who turned it into an overworked BUZZWORD with the above sense. See also NIGHTMARE SCENARIO and WORST-CASE.

scene   *noun* an activity, pursuit, interest; a way of life, chosen occupation; the place where a particular activity (especially connected with BEATNIK interests) is taking place. Originally US jazz and beatniks' slang c.1951, now often found in *not one's scene* (not what one enjoys doing). This usage is a development of 1930s colloquialisms in which *scene* meant 'an area of human activity or the environment in which it takes place' e.g. *the social scene*.

schtum (occasional spelling of) SHTOOM.

score *verb* to be successful in seducing a person. A fairly recent slang development (1960, originally US) from the much older meaning, 'achieve success'. A slightly earlier meaning is to succeed in buying drugs, and (by extension) to take them (1953), again originally US.

scratching *noun* rotating a gramophone record manually on a turntable, or moving it backwards or forwards, to produce a scratching or percussive effect, often as a rhythmic accompaniment to another record being played. A technique used from the early eighties, notably by disc jockeys when playing records of popular music, especially RAP. See SCRATCH VIDEO.

scratch pad *noun* (in computer technology) a limited but very fast and reusable memory for temporary storage of data during execution of a program. Sometimes called **scratch file**. Named (c.1965) from the older US *scratch pad*, a notebook for jottings. One of the meanings of *scratch* is 'a hasty scrawl'.

scratch video *noun* a video consisting of a collage of images, often from existing films or television programmes, with a synchronised sound track, frequently one using RAP music. So called, c.1985, because it appears to have developed from the example of the popular music, called *scratch-mix*, created by intercutting several records to create a collage of sound using the SCRATCHING technique.

scream therapy (another name for) PRIMAL THERAPY.

Scud (missile) *noun* a Soviet-made surface-to-surface missile capable of carrying different kinds of warheads, including nuclear ones, and of being launched from a mobile launcher. Though developed as early as the late 1950s, this missile was not generally known outside military circles until its use by Iraq during the Gulf War of 1991. It was too inaccurate and easily intercepted to be a significant military threat, but its deployment against urban areas in Israel, a non-combatant, threatened to bring Israel into the war and thus destabilise the anti-Iraq alliance. Its name is simply a Nato code-word, one of several beginning with *S* and denoting surface-to-surface missiles deployed by the Warsaw Pact countries.

scumbag *noun* an offensive, unpleasant or despicable person. Slang, c.1971, originally US or Australian. It may be an elaboration of the familiar *scum* (worthless person or people) or an adaptation of the slightly earlier (1967) coarse US slang *scumbag*, (condom) from US slang *scum* (semen).

scungy *adj.* mean, miserable, unpleasant, sordid, disreputable, disgusting, dirty. Colloquial, c.1966, mainly Australian and New Zealand, probably from the Scots verb *scunge* which means, among other things, 'scrounge'.

scuzzy *adj.* dirty, disreputable, unkempt, shabby, unpleasant, squalid. Also **scuzz** *noun*. Chiefly US teenagers' slang from the mid sixties, probably from *disgusting*. The corresponding noun *scuzz* (disgusting person or thing) occurred at the same time. In the eighties it was elaborated into *scuzzbag*, *-ball* and *-bucket*, which are mainly used of people who are disapproved of. There are signs that all these are now taking hold outside the US.

SDI (abbreviation for) Strategic Defence Initiative. A US defence system against foreign nuclear missile attack. It was planned to use artificial satellites equipped with laser-beam weapons, operating in space and capable of destroying all incoming missiles. Proposed by President Reagan in 1983, it had cost 16.5 billion dollars by the end of the decade. Despite criticisms of the astronomical costs, doubts about the feasibility of the whole plan, and the collapse of the only country (the USSR) capable of posing any major threat to the USA, the strength of the military and armaments lobbies in the USA is likely to secure at least some form of continuation. See STAR WARS.

search-and-destroy *adj.* (of a military operation) involving an intense and detailed search for enemy guerrillas in a designated and limited area, with a view to destroying them and their equipment. Originally a US term from the Vietnam War, c.1966. In practice, such uncompromising operations often led to general destruction.

second-strike see FIRST-STRIKE.

Second World see THIRD WORLD.

Securitate *noun* the secret police of Romania during the communist era. Although founded in the late 1940s, this organisation was not generally known in the West until the revolution of 1989, when it fought viciously on behalf of the dictator Ceauşescu. The collapse of his regime led to the disbanding of the hated secret police, whose name was colloquial Romanian for 'security'.

security blanket *noun* secrecy, usually temporary, imposed officially (e.g. by police) to protect a person or place from danger or risk; soft blanket to which a baby or young child becomes attached, using it as a comforter. Both date from the mid fifties, the second meaning being specially associated with the US comic strip *Peanuts*, in which one of the characters is inseparable from his *security blanket*. It is likely, however, that the first meaning came first and that the author of *Peanuts*, Charles M Schulz, borrowed it. In the sense of 'something all-embracing', *blanket* (e.g. *blanket insurance*) goes back to the nineteenth century, and *security blanket* is a figurative use clearly related to this.

self-starter *noun* a well-motived person capable of exercising initiative, especially at work. Mainly confined to the jargon of business management, and apparently originating in the vocabulary of job advertisements, c.1960, the term seems to be a rather unlikely borrowing from motor mechanics: *self-starter* is the somewhat dated name of the electric motor which starts an engine by the use of a car's own power systems. Previously, the engine had to be cranked by hand.

sellathon *noun* an extended sale or protracted marketing campaign. Almost entirely US, from the late seventies, formed by combining *sell* and the *-athon* of *marathon*.

sell-by date *noun* the date by which perishable goods should be sold by a retailer or withdrawn from sale. So called because the date is stamped on the packaging preceded by the words *Sell by* (early seventies). The phrase has become so well known that it has passed into informal figurative use: a person or thing that is *past (its) sell-by date* is past its prime. See also USE-BY DATE and BEST BEFORE DATE.

September people   *noun* those approaching the Autumn of their days – say fifty-five and older. A euphemistic term, probably originating in the advertising agencies, avoiding the use of the word 'old' and perhaps reflecting the advertising industry's recognition of the potential of this growing and often affluent sector of the market (late eighties).

Semtex   *noun* (trademark for) a pliable, odourless plastic explosive. First manufactured in Czechoslovakia (where it was invented) in the early 1970s but not generally known until the mid 1980s when it was widely used by terrorist organisations: its pliability allowed it to be easily hidden, and its odourlessness made it difficult to detect. Its name seems to come from that of the village of Semtín, near which it is made.

Senderista; Sendero Luminoso   see SHINING PATH.

senior citizen   *noun* an elderly person, usually one in receipt of the state retirement pension. Although this term was coined in the USA in the 1930s, it did not reach Britain until the late sixties; but by the late seventies it was quite common. Some people find it a rather contrived expression (*citizen*, for example, is a somewhat formal word in British English) while others find it an unnecessary and ultimately patronising revision of *(old-age) pensioner*. See SEPTEMBER PEOPLE.

sequencer   *noun* (in computer technology) an electronic device that puts data into the right sequence for processing, or determines the sequence in which a number of operations occur; a device that stores and reproduces sequences of musical notes. The first meaning goes back to the fifties; the second arose in the seventies but did not become widely known until the eighties, when a number of styles of electronic music, such as HOUSE, came to depend on this technology.

serial killer   *noun* a person who commits a series of murders. The term emerged in the late sixties after a number of multiple murders had attracted public attention. *Serial*, an adjective and noun having to do with occurrence in a series, had not previously been used in such a context.

serious   *adj.* worthy of note or regard because of its substantial quantity or quality. Especially found in *(talk) serious money*, short for '(refer to) a serious (i.e. weighty, not trifling) sum of money'. This American colloquialism entered British English in the late eighties, a decade during which a large amount of US business jargon became familiar in the UK. There is nothing new in the use of *serious* to mean 'important'; what is new is its application to things rather than abstractions.

SERPS, Serps   (acronym for) state earnings-related pension scheme. Introduced by the UK government in 1978 to provide all employed people with an earnings-related pension in addition to the flat-rate state pension payable at sixty-five for men and sixty for women. Employees may contract out of SERPS as long as they have a personal or occupational pension instead.

service industry *noun* an industry that provides services rather than goods. For example, tourism, banking and entertainment. These – and many others – have been known as 'services' since the 1930s, but *service industry* has been familiar only since the mid sixties.

set-aside *noun* (in the European Community) a scheme for taking farmland out of production in order to reduce surpluses, increase demand, etc. Also verb **set aside**, to leave uncultivated. *Set-aside* in the general sense of 'something set aside' has been used in the US since the 1940s, especially in relation to agricultural produce reserved by government order for some special purpose such as feeding the armed forces. The present meaning, which is obviously based on this, is restricted to the vocabulary of EC policy and of comment on it and has been generally known since the early nineties.

sexism *noun* discrimination based on a person's sex, usually in the form of prejudice against or oppression of women by men. Also *noun* and *adjective* **sexist**. *Sexist* was coined in 1965 on the model of *racist*. *Sexism* followed two or three years later. Both coinages are from the years when the WOMEN'S LIBERATION movement came into being.

sex shop *noun* a shop selling erotica, pornography and aids that are thought to increase sexual pleasure (1970).

sex therapy *noun* treatment (usually by counselling, behaviour modification, etc.) of sexual problems, such as psychological impediments to sexual intercourse (1961). Also **sex therapist** *noun* someone who offers such treatment.

sexual politics *noun* the principles and practice determining relationships between the sexes and the role of gender in society, especially as regards feminism, gay rights, the women's movement, sexual discrimination, etc. The term originates as the title of a book (1970) by the feminist Kate Millet.

sexual revolution *noun* the liberalisation of attitudes to sexual behaviour and morality during the sixties. Although changes in behaviour and standards were clearly evident during the sixties, it was not possible to designate them as a 'revolution', as distinct from a temporary aberration, until later. The term *sexual revolution* emerged during the late seventies, and is now usually preferred to NEW MORALITY, as that morality is no longer new.

sexy *adj.* interesting, exciting, trendy. This definition (which has nothing directly to do with sex) originates as a media colloquialism of the sixties, and is now an established extension of the standard meaning of *sexy*, 'provoking or feeling sexual interest'.

shades *noun* sunglasses. Originally US colloquialism, c.1958, probably from the much older *eye-shade* worn to protect the eyes from strong light. It has been British slang only since the eighties.

shareowner *noun* a person who owns shares. Also **shareowner-ship**. Both of these words cropped up in the sixties, and have to do with investment in general, whereas the much older *shareholder* usually denotes someone who holds shares in a specific business. *Shareownership* often has political overtones when used of the extension of capitalism, e.g. by the privatisation of utilities in which the general public have been actively encouraged to buy shares at favourable rates.

shareware   *noun* (in computer technology) software distributed free to users, though a fee may be chargeable for updates, a manual of instruction, etc. One of many variations on the **-ware** of *(soft)ware* that entered computer vocabulary during the eighties. See WETWARE. The distribution of shareware may represent a form of trialling and product development, or it may be a form of promotion and marketing.

Sharon   *noun* (derogatory nickname for) any (usually working-class) girl represented as lacking intelligence, taste and social graces. British slang from the late seventies. The name was extremely popular among many families during the sixties. As the first wave of Sharons reached young adulthood during the following decade, humorists seized on the name as a handy label for a stereotype. Such humorists continue the joke by nominating Tracey as her girlfriend and Kevin and Jason as their boyfriends. In her day Jane Austen considered Richard and Rebecca similarly amusing names: *plus ca change* . . .

shell company   *noun* a company that has stopped trading but, having retained its registration, is available for sale to anyone wishing to buy a company name either without the cost of registering a new company or in order to use the defunct company as a vehicle, e.g. for tax avoidance (1964).

shell suit   *noun* tracksuit with soft lining and an outer showerproof nylon *shell*. A fashion garment of the late eighties and early nineties at a time when sportswear was specially popular as general leisure wear. Because of its garish colours, the shell suit was often regarded as NAFF, suitable only for ESSEX MAN.

sheltered accommodation or **housing**   *noun* accommodation for the elderly or infirm consisting of a group of self-contained flats or houses with the services of a resident warden and, sometimes, shared recreational or laundry facilities, etc. *Sheltered* originally (early sixties) meant 'suitable for the handicapped' as in *sheltered workshops*. The present terms have been familiar since the late seventies and are mainly used in connection with the elderly.

shiatsu   *noun* a type of therapy in which pressure is applied by hand to particular parts of the body. A Japanese word of some antiquity, but known outside Japan only since the late sixties. The more usual term is now ACUPRESSURE.

Shining Path   *noun*. The English translation of *Sendero Luminoso*, the name of a revolutionary guerrilla organisation in Peru, founded in 1970. Adherents are called *Senderistas*. The origin is a quotation from an earlier Peruvian Marxist about 'the shining path of revolution'.

Shoah   *noun* (same as) the HOLOCAUST. In secular Judaism this is a

Hebrew word (literally 'destruction') brought to general notice as the title of a film by Claude Lanzmann (1985).

shock-horror   *adj.* sensationalistic. A facetious phrase that parodies tabloid newspaper headlines. It is thought to have originated in the satirical magazine *Private Eye* during the 1970s and has remained in use, sometimes as a jocular exclamation, sometimes as an adjectival expression meaning 'shocked and horrified'.

shoe-box   *noun* a building resembling a shoe-box (i.e. the sort of box that shoes are sold in) in having a rectangular shape and plain, utilitarian appearance. Mainly used of tall buildings of the sixties and seventies.

shoot-out   *noun* a gunfight, usually one that continues until one side is eliminated; (in football) a tie-breaker. The first is originally US, 1953, based on the earlier expression *to shoot it out* (to settle something by shooting). The second emerged from this c.1978. Attempts to popularise association football in the USA were thought to be inhibited by the American need for a winner – which ruled out drawn games – and so the *shoot-out* was invented for use in the event of a tie at the end of full time. Five players from each team were given a free shot at goal; starting from a 25 yard line, they were given five seconds to dribble the ball before shooting. If the result was still a tie, a 'sudden-death' shoot-out was played between pairs of opponents until a winner emerged. A version of this, the *penalty shoot-out*, was later adopted in some cup matches in UK and continental football, with penalty kicks taking the place of the dribble and shoot method.

shopaholic   *noun* a compulsive shopper. Originally a US colloquialism of the mid eighties, sometimes used facetiously but sometimes denoting a psychological abnormality associated with an inability to control one's use of credit cards. Like WORKAHOLIC this coinage is modelled on *alcoholic*.

shopping mall   *noun* a large, enclosed shopping centre containing several different types of stores and shops. In British usage a 'shopping precinct' is a pedestrianised area containing shops and other facilities (e.g. restaurants, car parking) forming an architectural unit, sometimes with a central open-air avenue called a MALL. A *shopping mall* (which Americans call simply a *mall*) is, however, a single building, though it may incorporate features of a shopping precinct including car parking and a central (enclosed) avenue. Increasingly, shopping malls have been built on the outskirts of town in the UK in the American way. The term has been familiar only since the eighties, though it has existed, chiefly in North America, since the sixties.

show house   *noun* a new house, furnished, decorated but unoccupied, on a new estate of similar properties (normally still under construction), available for inspection by prospective buyers. Also **show flat** (1962).

shrink   (slang abbreviation for) headshrinker, itself slang for a psychiatrist or psychoanalyst (1966).

shrinkage   *noun* (in the retail trade) the reduction in takings and profitability as a result of shoplifting, damage to goods, fraud by employees, etc. A euphemism from c.1961.

shrink-wrapping *noun* the packaging of an article in a wrapping of thin plastic film designed to contract ('shrink') around it so as to cling to its surface and seal it (1959). Also *noun* and *verb* **shrink-wrap**.

shtoom, shtum *adj.* silent, dumb. Found especially in *keep shtoom*, keep one's mouth closed. Of Yiddish origin, from the German *stumm* (silent), it is first recorded in print in the late 1950s, but was almost certainly in widespread spoken use before this, e.g. in the East End of London.

shuttle *noun* (short for) the space shuttle, a reusable spacecraft for transporting people and materials to and fro between Earth and a destination in space. The familiar meaning of *shuttle* as a means of transport plying between two points and offering a frequent service goes back to the end of the nineteenth century. This was a figurative application of the original *shuttle*, an implement used in weaving to carry the thread from one side of the cloth to the other and back again. The *space shuttle*, first heard of in the sixties, was launched in 1981: with wings like an aircraft, it was fired vertically, attached to rockets and a fuel tank which were discarded in space, and it was able to re-enter the earth's atmosphere and glide to a landing on a runway. Its uses included the carrying out of experiments in the SPACELAB.

shuttle diplomacy *noun* negotiations conducted by a diplomat or other intermediary who travels back and forth between two or more hostile countries or parties in an attempt to find a solution to a dispute, usually when the opposing sides refuse to talk to one another. First used in 1974 of the efforts of the US Secretary of State, Henry Kissinger, to find a solution to the Middle East problem. The term makes reference to an airline's shuttle service, as for example between New York and Washington, especially one that is so frequent that seat reservations are not required.

sick building syndrome *noun* a group of symptoms, usually including headaches, eye irritations, lethargy, dizziness and nausea, suffered by people working in some air-conditioned or centrally ventilated (office) buildings. Presumably such a building is 'sick' in as much as it is not functioning properly. *Sick building* was coined c.1980; *syndrome* was added a few years later. The problem is caused by poor air quality, many modern buildings being airtight in the interests of energy conservation and keeping heating costs down. The result is the recirculation of air (i.e. the lack of fresh air) and its heavy contamination.

sicko *noun* a person who is sick in the head (mentally ill) or perverted, e.g. a psychopath or sexual deviant. North American slang c.1977, a variant of the slightly earlier *sickie*. It has been known in the UK since the mid eighties.

SIDS (abbreviation for) sudden infant death syndrome (1970). See COT DEATH.

silent majority *noun* the people in society who may be overlooked because of their moderation but who actually form the great majority of citizens and ought to make themselves heard. This is now the dominant meaning of the expression, which achieved this political emphasis in 1969–70 when Richard Nixon used the term a number of times in speeches appealing for support from 'Middle America'. The expression, however, is not new; it was used in the nineteenth century to mean 'the dead' and later came to mean 'the mass of people whose views remain unexpressed', from which the current and specifically political meaning developed.

silicon chip   see CHIP (1965).

single   *noun* an unmarried person (1960s). Also *singles bar*, *club*, etc. for social gatherings of *singles* (1970s).

single market   *noun* the European Community free trade association, implemented in 1992 and allowing for the unrestricted movement of goods, capital and workers. Although a long-standing aim of the European Community, this plan was not given a completion date until the Madrid summit of 1985 and did not become widely known until publicity campaigns at the end of the eighties.

single-parent family   (same as) ONE-PARENT FAMILY.

sink   *adj.* (socially) deprived. From its meaning of 'a pool, basin or drain for the disposal of waste materials', *sink* has long been used to denote any place associated with other sorts of unpleasantness such as vice or corruption. The new adjectival meaning (c.1972) is often used of rundown housing estates or schools that have more problems than they can cope with.

sinsemilla   *noun* a type of marijuana with a very high narcotic content. From American Spanish, literally 'without seed', and known since c.1975.

sister   *noun* a woman who supports WOMEN'S LIBERATION. Also **sisterhood**, the bond between such supporters. Both terms (late sixties) were used by the more militant feminists and applied to their fellow enthusiasts. They have become rather dated as the WOMEN'S MOVEMENT has become more established. *Sister*, also used as a term of address, was probably borrowed from earlier use by Black women when addressing or speaking of one another.

sitcom   (abbreviation for) situation comedy (1964).

sit-in   see -IN.

Six Day War   *noun* the war in which Israel defeated Egypt, Jordan and Syria in June 1967. Israel occupied the Gaza Strip, the Old City of Jerusalem, the West Bank and the Golan Heights, thus securing a number of significant advantages which have remained contentious ever since.

six-pack   *noun* a package, usually of cardboard or plastic, containing six items (e.g. bottles) wrapped together so as to be easy to carry. Originally US, c.1961, now usually applied to packages containing six cans of beer.

sixth form college   *noun* a British educational establishment for students aged 16–18 following courses of study similar to those available in the sixth forms of secondary schools (1965). Usually found in an area where it has been decided to centralise sixth form provision either in the interests of economy or because local secondary schools are not big enough to generate viable sixth forms of their own.

sixty-four thousand dollar question *noun* the big question, the one that everything depends on (1957). Taken from the name of a US TV quiz show of the 1950s. Contestants had to answer a series of questions for cash until they reached the ultimate question that would bring them $64,000. After running successfully for many years the show was discontinued amidst scandals about rigging. An alternative phrase 'the $64 question' is sometimes used. This is not a shortening but a reversion to an earlier phrase stemming from an earlier radio quiz show of the forties, 'Take it or leave it', which had a $64 prize for each contestant's culminating question.

ska *noun* a type of popular dance music of Jamaican origin, with a fast tempo, emphasis on the off-beats, a mixture of rhythm and blues with native forms, and an element of social comment in the lyrics. Popular during the early sixties, and a forerunner of REGGAE. It enjoyed a revival in London in the late seventies, and was a potent influence on British popular music more generally. Its name is of unknown origin. Compare ROCKSTEADY.

skag (same as) SCAG.

skateboard *noun* a short board mounted on four roller-skate wheels, ridden by a child or young person, usually standing up, often with the performance of stunts. Also **skateboarding** and **skateboarder**. First used in California in 1963 and intermittently popular ever since, though without ever regaining the status of international craze it enjoyed in the mid seventies. Both **skateboard** (the term) and its use seem to have been modelled on the earlier *surfboard*.

ski-bob *noun* a vehicle consisting of two connected short skis, one placed behind the other, the front one having a steering device and the rear one having a seat (c.1966). Used for unpowered travel down snow slopes.

skin (informal shortening of) SKINHEAD.

skin flick *noun* a pornographic film. Slang, c.1968. *Skin* refers to the amount of bare flesh on view; *flick*, dated slang for 'film', is an abbreviation of the obsolete *flickers* or *flicks* (the movies), a reference to the flickering quality of the images in early films.

skinhead *noun* a youth, usually male, white and one of a gang, with shaven head, tight jeans with braces, heavy boots and aggressive (often violent) tendencies. *Skinheads* were originally a British phenomenon, emerging in 1969 in succession to the earlier MODS, some of whom had taken to cropping their hair in imitation of the short styles of the West Indian RUDE BOYS. Their taste for violence was often directed against ethnic minorities, and at the end of the seventies the National Front had some success in recruiting from the skinhead movement. Skinheads, often tattooed, are nowadays found in several other countries as a nonconformist youth cult, often associated with racism, football hooliganism and other anti-social behaviour. The word *skinhead* was first recorded some time before all this, in the USA in 1953, when it denoted a bald-headed person or one with closely cropped hair, especially a recruit in the US Marine Corps.

skinny-dip   *verb* to swim naked. Originally US slang c.1966, from *skinny* (with the skin showing) and *dip* (to plunge into liquid).

skyjack   *verb* to commandeer an aircraft (usually in flight). The purpose is usually to make the pilot fly to an unscheduled destination or to hold the passengers hostage in the pursuit of political ends. The word is a journalistic pun (1961) on *hijack*, and is little used outside newspapers.

Skylab   *noun* a US unmanned space station, launched into orbit in 1973, and used by a number of crews before it re-entered the Earth's atmosphere and burnt up in 1979. Used for scientific investigations (e.g. experiments in weightlessness), observations (e.g. of the Sun) and photography of the Earth's surface.

slag off   *verb* to abuse, insult, criticise, make disparaging comments about (a person). Although *slag* as a slang noun is best known in its sense of 'coarse or promiscuous woman', it also means 'unpleasant, worthless, rough, contemptible person (usually men)', especially a criminal'. It is these associations that lie behind the verb *slag off*, British slang since c.1971, perhaps originally dockers' slang.

slam dance   *verb* to fling oneself about so as to 'slam' into other people or against the wall, etc., to the sound of (hard) rock music (1980). Also *noun* such a dance.

slasher (movie)   *noun* a type of horror film in which people, usually women or girls, are slashed with knives, etc., and the spilling of blood is a prominent feature. The term dates from the seventies but became widely known in the mid eighties, when this sort of film became generally available in video shops and attracted much criticism.

sleaze   *noun* sordid, disreputable, squalid or seedy behaviour and characteristics. Also **sleazebag, -ball** a despicable person. The informal noun *sleaze* is a fairly recent (1967) back-formation from the older adjective *sleazy*. It is specially found in *sleaze factor* (the sleazy aspect of a situation), coined in 1983 by an American journalist, Laurence Barrett, and often used in US politics to denote malpractices, scandals, attempts to smear one's political opponents, etc. – a sense now sometimes found in British political vocabulary. **Sleazebag**, originally and still chiefly US young people's slang, was also coined during the 1980s, probably on the model of SCUMBAG and *scuzzbag* (see SCUZZY).

sledging   *noun* trying to intimidate or break the concentration of a batsman by insulting or teasing him continuously while he is in play. Australian cricket slang (c.1977), but now known more widely. It is thought to be a sardonic adaptation of the phrase 'subtle as a sledgehammer' i.e. not subtle at all.

sleeping policeman   *noun* a low hump built across a road to deter speeding by vehicles (1973). *Policeman* implies law-enforcement; *sleeping* is a fanciful reference to the similarity between the hump and someone stretched out asleep across the road. The more formal name is now **speed bump** (1975), originally US.

slimline *adj.* attractively thin in style or appearance; conducive to slimness. The first meaning (1949) is applied to artefacts, such as a television set or telephone that is less bulky than others. The second (c.1973) comes from the use of the word on the labels of soft drinks to denote that the contents have less sugar and are therefore less fattening. In both cases, *line* means 'outline', 'contour' or 'shape'.

Slim (disease) *noun* The (East) African name (c.1985) for AIDS, in reference to the wasting effects of the disease.

Sloane (Ranger) *noun* young upper-class person, especially a woman, living in the vicinity of Sloane Square, London (i.e. Chelsea, Kensington, Belgravia) and perhaps in the country, or with country connections, and typically wearing expensive but informal country clothes. Also noun and adjective **Sloanie**. The name was coined by Peter York in 1975 in an article in *Harper and Queen* magazine; it was a pun on *Lone Ranger*, the well-known law-enforcing hero of western films, stories and television, and *Sloane Square*. The *Sloane* is well-bred, expensively educated, active in fashionable society, and conventional in upbringing and outlook.

slo-mo *noun* (abbreviation for) slow motion (replay); the facility for playing something in slow motion. The term has become familiar since the early eighties as a result of the general availability of the video recorder and camera, but was in specialist and spoken use before then, most notably in the US film industry where it originated.

smack *noun* heroin. Slang since c.1960, though it existed earlier in the more general sense of 'drug'. It is from the Yiddish *schmeck* (sniff).

small is beautiful *phrase.* The title of a book by EF Schumacher (1973), adopted as a catchphrase signifying opposition to the concept of large-scale institutions, bureaucratic centralisation, expansionist businesses and anything insensitive to the human scale. The phrase is actually not Schumacher's: it was devised by his publishers.

small print see FINE PRINT.

smart *adj.* (of systems) operating as if by human intelligence (e.g. by reacting differently to different circumstances) because of control by computer. *Smart*, in its predominantly US sense of 'intelligent', has been used in computer vocabulary since c.1970, with the same sense as INTELLIGENT. See SMART BOMB as an early example (1972) and for the way that their performance in the Gulf War brought the term to general attention. However, by the end of the eighties manufacturers and advertisers had already begun to use smart of almost any gadget that had an element of computerisation, so beginning a process of weakening of the term.

smart-arse *noun* an irritatingly or smugly clever person who shows off his knowledge offensively or boastfully; a clever dick. Also *adj.* **smart-arse(d)**. Derogatory slang, c.1960, originally US. *Smart* means clever and *arse* is used as a term of abuse, as in a number of vulgar expressions. The normal American usage is now *smart-ass*, but the use of *ass* as an evasion of *arse* is not native to British slang.

smart bomb or **weapon** *noun* a bomb or weapon using radar, laser and computer technology in its guidance system. The expression *smart weapons* became familiar to the general public only at the time of the Gulf War (1991), but *smart bomb* is recorded as early as 1972 at the time of the Vietnam War. See SMART.

smart card *noun* a plastic card resembling a credit card, issued by a bank etc., and containing integrated circuits capable of memorising the transactions the card is used for. Developed in France during the eighties and generally known since c.1987, the *smart card* is mainly used with a computer link that can provide services such as the automatic transfer of funds. See SMART.

smart house *noun* a house in which all the electrical systems are controlled by a single computer which itself can be activated by remote control, telephone, etc. A domestic development, originally US, late eighties, of the commercial application described for *intelligent buildings* at INTELLIGENT. See SMART.

smarty-boots *noun* a smugly or ostentatiously clever person; a know-all. Originally US slang, c.1962. A variant of the earlier *smarty-pants*. Both are elaborations of the much earlier US *smarty*, a would-be smart or witty person.

smashed *adj.* completely intoxicated with alcohol; very much under the influence of a drug. Slang, originally US, since c.1960, presumably in reference to the dislocation of the senses.

smoke-stack industry *noun* a traditional manufacturing industry (e.g. heavy engineering) as opposed to modern technology (e.g. electronics). A 1970s term originally US, and perhaps slightly deprecatory, implying the use of coal-burning with tall chimneys.

snail mail *noun* conventional or surface mail as opposed to e-mail (electronic mail). This is an eighties e-mail user's facetious term, contrasting the (sometimes) instantaneousness of their electronic communications with the snail's pace delivery of surface mail.

snake *noun* a narrow range of fluctuation in exchange rates agreed by certain member states of the EEC in 1972. So called, presumably, from the relatively slight 'fluctuation' in the motion of a snake as it moves forward. The original metaphor was 'the snake in the tunnel', where the 'tunnel' was the dollar band exercising constraint, and the 'snake' was the 'wrigglings' of the EEC range within the wider dollar band.

snarl-up *noun* a muddle, blockage, especially a traffic jam. To *snarl up* (become entangled) goes back four hundred years; *snarl-up* as an informal noun goes back only to c.1960.

snatch-squad *noun* a group of personnel trained to operate as a unit in riot control by identifying ring-leaders and arresting them. A technique first used by the army in Northern Ireland c.1970, later adopted by the police elsewhere.

snuff *adj.* (of film or video) depicting the torture and death of an actual victim, not an actor (1975). From the old slang *snuff (out)* (to kill, murder) and *snuff it* (to die), which came from an even older meaning, 'to extinguish'. No definite evidence of the use of real-life victims has ever been found, but rumours – especially involving the use of children – have circulated since the 1970s.

soca *noun* a combination soul and calypso music. The word is a blend of soul and calypso. The music originated in Trinidad during the early seventies.

Sod's Law *noun* Since the early seventies this has been the preferred term for MURPHY'S LAW, *Sod* being a facetious personfication and referring back to one of its old-established meanings: 'something difficult or a nuisance'.

soft-core *adj.* (of pornography) less explicit and obscene than the most extreme forms of pornography. Formed c.1966 as the opposite to the earlier HARD-CORE.

soft drugs *noun* non-addictive or only mildly addictive drugs, as distinct from hard drugs. Based (1959) on one of the standard meanings of *soft*, i.e. 'gentle'.

soft landing *noun* a landing by spacecraft on the moon or a planet at sufficiently low speed to prevent damage to instruments or occupants (1958). The expression is now most often heard in a figurative sense to mean the painless resolution of a (usually economic) problem (1973).

softly-softly *adj.* cautious, slow, gradual, discreet. The expression is normally found with the noun *approach*, though it can be used adverbially. These usages date from c.1967, a year after a long-running police drama series *Softly Softly* (1966–76) was first broadcast, taking its title from the motto of the Lancashire Constabulary Training School. The popularity of the series was no doubt responsible for the subsequent currency of the expression. The origin is the proverb 'Softly, softly, catchee monkee'.

soft porn (short for) SOFT-CORE pornography (1976).

software *noun* (in computer technology) the programs that are used with a particular computer system. Formed (c.1960) on the model of the earlier HARDWARE, on which *software* is run.

solarium *noun* an establishment, or part of an establishment e.g. of a health club, equipped with sun-lamps and sun-beds giving an artificial sun-tan. This has been the dominant meaning since c.1960; previously it was 'a glassed room or terrace providing exposure to the sun'. The derivative is from Latin *sol*, sun.

solid-state *adj.* (of physics) concerned with the structure and properties of solids e.g. superconductivity (1953); (of electronic devices) making use of the electronic properties of solids such as transistors and other semiconductors, rather than using valves (1959).

solvent abuse see GLUE-SNIFFING.

-something *suffix* added to *twenty, thirty, forty* etc. to denote a person of a certain age: e.g. a *fortysomething* is a person aged between 40 and 49. There is nothing new in the addition of *-something* to a number to indicate an indeterminate number somewhere between the stated number and something a little higher (just as *-odd* has a similar effect). What is new, however, is the use of the resultant - **something** word to denote a generation of people, and this can be traced to the popularity of the US television series *Thirtysomething* (1987), about a group of people in their thirties.

song, on *phrase* (of a person or thing) performing well. A colloquialism first noted in 1967. Presumably a metaphor taken from bird song; it can be used of a well-tuned engine or an on-form football team, and has in fact been widely used by sports commentators but is now more generally established.

soul *adj.* relating to Black Americans, their life and their culture. An early sixties development from the use of *soul* in SOUL MUSIC. It is exemplified in *soul brother/sister* (a fellow Black man/woman) and *soul food* (food traditionally eaten by southern US Black people), which also date from the sixties.

soul (music) *noun* the popular music of North America that arose from Black sources during the late 1950s and became a dominant form of popular music in the 1960s, particularly in the USA. It derives from blues, and includes elements of rhythm and blues, jazz, gospel and ROCK. *Soul*, originally a jazz term associated with sincerity and seriousness, seems to have been incorporated into the name *soul music* because some of that music has roots in the negro spiritual and has the intensity of expression of religious songs — the outpouring of the 'soul'.

sound bite *noun* a succinct extract, lasting perhaps 20–30 seconds, from a recorded speech, interview etc., used in a news broadcast; a short recorded comment by a politician, spokesman, etc., intended to be suitable for news broadcasts. Because of a general assumption that many of the public are too inattentive to understand or be interested in anything that lasts longer than 20–30 seconds (i.e. the length of many TV advertisements) politicians, lobbyists, public relations people, spokesmen, trades union leaders etc. are now trained to offer comments of this length for the benefit of the television cameras and radio microphones. The expression *sound bite* has been generally known only since the 1988 US presidential campaign, though it was media jargon before that: *bite* implies something small cut out of something bigger but also brings associations with information technology and BYTES; *sound* is a reference to recorded speech. Because British elections, party conferences and political life generally have, since the eighties, been increasingly perceived as being stage-managed along American lines, there have been worries about the general deterioration of political discourse into the sloganising of the sound bite, summed up in the pejorative phrase **sound bite politics**.

South, the *noun* the less developed nations of the world, mainly located in the Southern hemisphere. This term, increasingly heard since c.1975, may have originated as an attempt to avoid possible implications of 'third rate' in THIRD WORLD (which some consider to be at any rate a misnomer since the demise of the 'second world' at the end of the eighties): it is commonly used in expressions contrasting the economies and technology of *the South* and the NORTH, but is not in general use, probably because in the UK – and in a number of other countries – *the South* is already a well established expression for the Southern part of one's own country.

space   *noun* living space; one's personal environment, including emotional, spiritual or mental environment, allowing room for personal growth. Informal originally North American, in general use since c.1976; considered by some as an example of PSYCHOBABBLE, but by others as a useful concept.

spaced   *adj.* (a frequent shortening of) SPACED OUT. See also SPACEY, SPACY.

spaced out   *adj* under the influence of drugs, especially LSD; (of person) dreamy, detached, absent-minded; in a state of euphoria or disorientation as a result of a moving experience; lacking efficiency, as if under the influence of a hallucinogen. The expression emerged in the US c.1969, and appears to have been based on the notion of floating in space and being out of touch with reality. It remains in slang use but normally in the milder sense of 'in a daze or apparently dazed state'.

Space Invaders   *noun* (trademark of) a video war-game in which a player tries to defend himself against waves of enemy spaceships by obliterating them from the screen with the use of levers, buttons etc. on a console (1979).

spacelab   *noun* a scientific laboratory in space for the performance of experiments (1966). The best known were SKYLAB and (with a capital letter) *Spacelab* (1980), the latter being a small manned space station built by the European Space Agency and carried in the cargo bay of the space shuttle, where it remained throughout the outward and return flights as a working base for astronauts.

space shuttle   see SHUTTLE.

spacey, spacy   *adj* (of a person) vague, dreamy, as if under the influence of a hallucinogen. Slang, c.1969, a variant of SPACED (OUT).

spaghetti junction   *noun* a complicated junction of roads, usually including motorways and their access or exit roads, with many underpasses, overpasses, intersections etc. The name was first applied to the Gravelly Hill interchange on the M6 near Birmingham (c.1970), but the single word *spaghetti* had been used in the colloquialism of lorry drivers since at least 1963 to denote multi-level road junctions, especially on motorways. The reference is to the supposed likeness of such interchanges, viewed from the air, to plates of spaghetti.

spaghetti western   *noun* a type of cowboy film about the American West made by an Italian director, often in Spain (1969). A rather dismissive term, *spaghetti* being a reference to the nationality of the director (and sometimes of the film crew and some of the actors, though the principal performers were usually American). Critics have complained that the films were hybrids, even parodies, with more atmosphere than action, but they were very popular during the later sixties and their devotees claim that they gave a new lease of life to a stereotype that had become very tired.

-speak   An informal suffix added to a noun (usually one denoting a group, organisation or occupation) to indicate the jargon or language used by that group, organisation etc. *Computerspeak*, DOU-BLESPEAK and EUROspeak are among many coinages, many of them transient, that have appeared since c.1960, copying George Orwell's famous and deliberately ugly coinage of NEWSPEAK and *Oldspeak*. The use of *-speak* often implies vacuousness, obfuscation or pretentiousness: *educationspeak, oickspeak, radfemspeak*.

speciesism *noun* discrimination by man against other species of animals on the grounds that, being inferior, they may be used for man's benefit without regard to their suffering, etc. Formed c.1975 on the model of *racism, sexism*, etc. Also spelt **specism**, with **specist** for someone adopting these views.

speed *noun* amphetamine. Also **speed-freak** *noun* a person addicted to amphetamines. Both are slang, c.1967. *Speed* appears to be an allusion to the stimulant effects of the drug which *speeds* up mental activity, reduces fatigue etc. See FREAK.

speed bump SEE SLEEPING POLICEMAN.

sperm bank *noun* store of semen, voluntarily donated, for use in artificial insemination (1963).

spin doctor *noun* a political adviser, public relations expert, etc., employed to provide the best possible interpretation of an item of news to the media or interpret a policy, a decision or any other newsworthy event, on behalf of a client. The informal expression became public in the US in 1984, though it had previously existed in the private jargon of the public relations industry. *Spin* means 'bias', from the spin put on a ball in certain games in order to make it go in the required direction. *Doctor* as a verb means to 'repair' or 'mend', though it can also mean 'falsify, adulterate', but it seems more likely that it is a doctor who by his expertise treats, cares for and cures a patient that is in mind in this term. Certainly the alternative term **spin-meister** (*meister* is German for 'master') suggests this. Spin doctors can be found at work during electoral campaigns, party conferences and international meetings and negotiations to make sure that speeches, debates and all outcomes are favourably represented to journalists, in accordance with the current practice of stage-managing news as much as possible.

spin-meister see SPIN DOCTOR.

split *noun* to depart, leave. Slang, originally US c.1956; it seems to be a shortening of the BEATNIK *split the scene* i.e. split away from the place where one is; see SCENE.

spoiler *noun* **1.** a device fitted to the rear of a car to reduce the tendency to lift off the road at high speed; **2.** (in journalism) something published with the intention of spoiling the impact of a similar item published by a rival newspaper, magazine, etc.; **3.** an electronic device in recording equipment, for the prevention of unauthorised recording (especially from CD on to DAT). The first meaning (1963) comes from earlier use of the word in 1920s aeronautical engineering: a *spoiler* was a flap on an aircraft's wing; it increased drag by breaking up the smooth flow of air and reducing lift (it is sometimes called a 'lift destroyer'). Hence the connection

spokesperson

with *spoil*. The other two meanings more obviously derive from the normal definition of *spoiler*, 'person or thing that spoils', and belong to the eighties.

spokesperson *noun* a person authorised to speak on behalf of another person, group or organisation. One of several words invented (c.1972) to avoid the sexual discrimination allegedly implied by the previously customary use of *spokesman* to denote either a man or a woman. As the sex of a *spokesperson* is normally known, some argue the case for using either *spokeswoman* (an old and perfectly respectable word) or *spokesman* and allowing the somewhat artificial *spokesperson* to lapse. See PERSON.

sports centre *noun* a (usually public) facility where a variety of sports can be practised and played on payment of a fee (1973).

spreadsheet *noun* (in computer technology) a software system in which numerical data can be displayed on a VDU in a set format (e.g. columns and rows), providing easy access and rapid manipulation of figures (1982). Used especially for financial planning and budgeting, and now well established as a central part of business software.

spritzer *noun* a drink consisting of white wine with soda water. A German word meaning 'splash' or 'squirt' – a reference to the sound of soda being added to the wine – which has been known in English since c.1961.

Sputnik or **sputnik** *noun* the first man-made satellite to orbit the earth, launched by the USSR in 1957. The word means 'tracking companion', from the Russian *put* (journey) and Russian (and Yiddish) *-nik* (person involved in whatever precedes). Because of the sensation created by the *sputnik* series of launches (1957–61), there was a rush of *-nik* coinages, mostly humorous or perjorative (because the Russian achievement was thought to be threatening; worse, it outclassed the Americans) though only **beatnik**, **peacenik** and **refusenik** have lasted for any length of time. A recent one is **returnik** (c.1987), an emigré from an Eastern European country who returns there, usually as a result of the collapse of communism.

square *adj.* old-fashioned in views, appearance, habits, etc.; conventional, dull, law-abiding. Also noun, person (or thing) with qualities of this kind. Adopted in the UK c.1958 from Canada, though it originated in the US in the 1930s, probably in the vocabulary of jazz ('not interested in something new and lively'). *Square* has a long association with reliability and plain dealing (*square deal*, *fair and square*, *four-square*, etc.) and the modern slang use (now rather dated) is probably rooted in this, in contrast to the idea of volatile people who are *swinging*, *with it*, etc.

square-eyes *noun* someone who watches a lot of television. A rather dated slang expression (c.1964) based on the jocular notion that the addict's eyes assume the same shape as the television screen.

squeaky clean *adj.* above criticism; beyond reproach. This is thought to be a metaphorical development (c.1975) of an earlier meaning having to do with hair 'washed so clean that the wet strands squeak when rubbed'. As such, the origin is thought to be a shampoo advertisement, though no particular one has been identified. An alternative explanation is that the origin is military, perhaps from the vocabulary of sergeant majors demanding that boots should be so highly polished that they squeak as if they were new. In some contexts the expression implies a slightly contrived or unnatural degree of blamelessness that is almost too good to be true.

stagflation *noun* an economic situation combining stagnant (or falling) output and employment with inflation. Combined from 'stagnant' and 'inflation' by Ian Macleod in a House of Commons speech during 1965.

stand-alone *adj.* (of computer equipment) capable of operating independently, without having to be linked to any other equipment (1966). Now sometimes used of a person, organisation, etc., to mean 'operating independently', especially when the person or operation has previously been part of a system.

stand-by *adj.* (of airline passenger) having not reserved a seat but willing to wait until one is available, (often at a lower price than a reserved seat) (1963). The term, which is also applied to fares or seats available under the *stand-by* system, comes from the well established, originally nautical phrasal verb *stand by*, 'to hold oneself in readiness'.

starter *noun* the first course of a meal, eaten before the main dish. The traditional term is *hors d'oeuvre*. The adoption of the less forbidding *starter* (1966) coincides with a period of expansion in the popular restaurant trade in Britain.

starter home *noun* a house or flat designed to suit the requirements of a young couple or family buying their first home and likely to move to something bigger a few years later. The term has been known in the UK only since c.1980, and originated in the US a few years earlier.

Star Wars *noun* (colloquial nickname for) SDI. *Star Wars*, the title of a highly popular sci-fi film (1977), was adopted as the almost universal name for SDI as soon as the latter was announced in 1983, because SDI's weaponry appeared similar to – and as farfetched as – that of the film. It is not known whether the name was a piece of journalistic opportunism, or a reference to President Reagan's Hollywood origins, or an ironic allusion to the fact that the necessary technology was far in the future and might even be imaginary.

Stasi *noun* the secret police in communist East Germany. A colloquial German name, formed from two of the syllables of the German word for 'state security service'. It became widely known in the UK at the time of the collapse of communism (1989–90), when there were demonstrations against the Stasi and successful demands for its abolition – though its name had occasionally cropped up in spy stories before that time.

state-of-the-art *adj.* the latest – and by implication the best – of its kind. Usually applied to some product of modern technology. This meaning has, since c.1967, supplanted the much earlier definition of *the state of the art*, which was 'the current level of generally accepted and available knowledge and achievement in some practical or technological subject'. In other words, a phrase which originally indicated 'the *current* state' has been changed (colloquially, some would say) into one about 'the *most advanced* state'.

statement (as *verb*) to set out in a written statement e.g. 'If you order goods by phone, quoting a credit card number, these transactions will be statemented on your monthly account in the normal way'. Business jargon, c.1990, though the use of *statement* as a verb grew up in educational jargon a few years earlier: a child is said to be *statemented* if his or her educational needs are so acute as to justify the drawing up of an official *statement* of the provisions necessary to meet those needs: this statement is legally binding on all the parties responsible for the child's wellbeing.

Stealth *noun* (of military technology) the technology designed to make aircraft, missiles, weapons, etc. unrecognisable to enemy radar and the detection systems. Most often used attributively: **Stealth technology, Stealth bomber**. From the standard meaning of *stealth* ('furtive action, eluding observation'), first applied to US weapons technology in the late seventies but not generally known in the UK until the *Stealth bomber* (or *B2*), virtually undetectable because of its shape, instruments and the materials it is made of, became known to the public during the Gulf War of 1991.

steaming *noun* robbery by a gang in a public place. The technique is to run through a crowd (e.g. on a train or bus or at a public event), stealing by sheer force of numbers. The word, which surfaced c.1987, is said to be from fairly recent cockney slang *steam in*, 'to start or join a fight', though others attribute it to Black US slang. Also **steam** (verb) to practise steaming, and **steamer** (noun) someone who does this.

stiff *verb* to kill i.e. to turn into a *stiff*, old slang for 'corpse'. First recorded in the seventies and increasingly used figuratively for 'deal with harshly, punish' in slang use. Perhaps from the vocabulary of the Northern Ireland troubles.

stir-fry *verb* (mainly in Chinese cooking) to cook (uniformly cut pieces of meat, vegetables, etc.) rapidly by stirring them in a pan with a small amount of hot oil kept at a high temperature (1959). Stir fry cookery in a wok became fashionable in the UK in the early eighties.

stockbroker belt *noun* an area outside a city where stockbrokers and other wealthy commuters live. Originally (1960s) used of any prosperous area of the Home Counties around London, but later used of a similar area outside any city. For the US use of *belt*, see RUST BELT, though it is likely that *stockbroker belt* was modelled on the 1930's term *green belt*.

stocking mask *noun* a mask worn by a criminal, especially a thief, to disguise his/her identity, consisting of a woman's stocking worn over the head and face (1966).

stop-go *adj.* (of national economic policy) in which contraction and expansion are alternated in a way that prevents coherent long-term planning (1962). The *stop* element is normally a restraining of demand in order to curb inflation; the *go* element is an expanding of credit to reduce unemployment.

storecard *noun* form of CREDIT CARD issued by an individual shop, department store, chain, etc. for use only at that shop, etc. The established name since the late eighties for what has been variously called a '(store) option card' and a 'charge card'.

streak *verb* to run naked in a public place. Also *nouns* **streaker**, one who does this; **streaking**, the act of doing this. Although isolated instances had occurred earlier, this became a craze c.1973 as a stunt among American students, and spread rapidly to other countries. In the UK, it was mainly practised by individuals who ran across the pitch at a sporting function to amuse or shock the crowd. It still occurs from time to time, but is no longer a craze. The standard meanings of *streak* include 'move very rapidly, normally in a straight line'. The above (informal) meaning of *streak* comes from this, with the implication that one has to move like a streak of lightning in order to avoid getting caught.

street cred or **credibility** *noun* status (in the eyes of one's peers) as a result of one's personal know-how and familiarity with current fashions. *Street credibility* (abbreviated to *street cred* by the early eighties and later simply to CRED) originated in the seventies, probably in young Black urban culture, when it had to do with one's 'believability' (acceptability, reputation, knowledge, etc.) as someone who could look after oneself on the streets, i.e. who was STREETWISE. The term now has less to do with the street, more with one's conformity with (or understanding of) fashions in clothes, music, etc., and contemporary attitudes among one's peers. See CRED and STREETWISE.

streetwise *adj.* understanding, and able to survive in, an urban (especially a poor, sometimes criminal) environment. Originally US slang, c.1965. *Street* in this context – as in STREET CRED – has to do with the street as the place where modern urban life, or the urban COUNTER-CULTURE, particularly among the young and deprived, is focused. *Streetwise* implies the quickwittedness needed for survival in this environment.

stressed *adj.* (of person) subjected to stress or strain, mainly psychological (c.1973).

stretch limo *noun* an ostentatiously long limousine that looks as if it has been 'stretched' to provide extra seating or leg-room. Originally and still chiefly North American, c.1971.

strimmer *noun* a grass trimmer that rotates a stout nylon cord at high speed instead of employing a cutting blade. Formed by a blending of *string* and *trimmer* (1978). It may be powered by electricity or petrol and is used for cutting rough grass.

strippergram, strippagram see KISSAGRAM.

structuralism *noun* The word goes back to the beginning of the twentieth century, but since 1950 it has acquired the sense 'an

stun grenade

approach to a field of study in terms of the interrelation of its elements', these structures being seen as more important than the elements on their own. In anthropology and sociology, *structuralism* is particularly associated with the work of the French anthropologist Levi-Strauss. In linguistics, it is an approach that interprets language as a self-contained structure (of phonology, morphology, etc.), as distinct from studying comparative and historical aspects.

stun grenade *noun* a grenade that temporarily incapacitates by its noise and flash rather than permanently damaging those it is employed against (1977). Like the comparable **stun gas** (1968) and **stun gun** (1971) *stun grenades* can be used in riot control, though they have also played a crucial part in the freeing of hostages.

stun gun *noun* a weapon which emits a charge of high-voltage electricity (eighties). *Stun gun* originally denoted a riot control weapon firing rounds that would incapacitate rather than wound its targets (see above under STUN GRENADE). Electric *stun guns* have been illegal in Britain since 1988.

styling mousse *noun* light, foamy substance, usually sold in an aerosol, applied to the hair before styling in order to help it set in the shape of the style (usually abbreviated to MOUSSE). Developed in the seventies but not called *mousse* until the early eighties by a French firm, since when it has become the standard term for all makes; it has the advantage of being a French word, and therefore 'chic'. It has, of course, long been in use as a cookery term.

subsidiarity *noun* the principle of ensuring that decisions are taken at the lowest possible level i.e. as close as possible to the people affected by them. EURO-jargon from the vocabulary of debate about relationships between central authority and national or regional governments; in this context it often means 'the principle of ensuring that the national governments of member states in the EC retain a proper measure of sovereignty'. *Subsidiarity* shows signs of gaining a more general currency as a useful word for an important feature of delegation within any large organisation. The word has been generally known only since 1990, as a result of controversy about the speed of progress towards European union, but it had been in use in the private vocabulary of Eurocrats some years before that: in 1982 the *Times* newspaper reported that the 'principle of subsidiarity' was being discussed in the European Parliament, that it was a 'meaningless or even misleading phrase in English' and that it meant that the EC should limit itself to those activities that are best performed in common rather than by member states individually. *Subsidiarity*, however is older than that. It first occurred in English in the thirties as a translation of a German noun meaning 'the quality of being subsidiary'. The context was theological, having to do with the principle that a central authority should have a subsidiary or auxiliary function, performing only those tasks that cannot be performed better at a local level. The word remained obscurely in use, always in a theological context, usually a Roman Catholic one, until the EC gave it a new lease of life sixty years after it first saw the light of day.

sudden infant death syndrome   (technical name for) COT DEATH.

suit   *noun* a manager, executive, bureaucrat – seen as someone faceless, dull, aloof and anonymous, though important; a person in charge, as distinct from an active or productive member of an organisation. Eighties' slang, said to have originated in the advertising business where creative people dressed casually and referred to more formally dressed executives as *suits*. The term was sometimes jocular, sometimes disparaging; executives were seen as less important than creative people in the success of an agency, yet their status and rewards were often higher because they were the ones who dealt directly with clients – hence the formality of the statutory suit. In the mid eighties the term was elaborated to *men in suits*, a political term denoting a bureaucrat, civil servant or political adviser; *suits* here implies anonymity, officialdom or conventional attitudes. These implications were reinforced in the slightly later *men in grey suits* (c.1990), where greyness perhaps implies dullness, but it was these same grey-suited men of the Conservative Party who were credited with playing the decisive role in easing Mrs Thatcher from power in 1990.

Sunbelt   *noun* the southern states of the USA from California to the Carolinas (1969). For *belt* see RUST BELT.

sunrise industry   *noun* new high-technology industry such as that using electronics. Also **sunset industry**, traditional heavy industry of the kind that is on the wane. *Sunrise* implies the dawn, in this case of an era of new techniques, processes, etc. *Sunset industry*, though coined at the same time, c.1980, has not caught on to anything like the same extent.

super-   *prefix* this familiar prefix, indicating that what follows it is of greatly superior quality, size or extent, is found in numerous modern coinages, most of which are self-explanatory. The most durable include *supercomputer* (one able to process huge quantities of data very quickly, 1967), *supercontinent* (a great landmass thought to have existed in the past and to have broken up to form existing continents, 1963), *superglue* (extremely strong adhesive, 1977), *supergrass* (informant who implicates a large number of terrorists or major criminals, 1978), *superloo* (public convenience, first installed in some UK railway stations, with a more than usual range of facilities, such as showers, 1969), and *super-rat* (a breed of rat that has become immune to most poisons; originally US, 1974). *Superwoman* has, since c.1975, denoted a woman who is successful in her career as well as in her family and social life, though the word goes back to the beginning of the twentieth century in its original sense of 'female version of superman'.

superstring   *noun* (in some theories of particle physics involving supersymmetry) hypothetical sub-atomic particles, postulated as the fundamental component of matter and being one-dimensional like thin string (1982). *Supersymmetry* postulates the view that all the different particles in some sense derive from a *superparticle*.

supply-side economics *noun* (in economics) an approach that emphasises the importance of the circumstances in which goods and services are supplied to the consumer. This implies tax-cutting, reduction in government spending and economic intervention, and allowing market forces to determine levels of output, unemployment, etc. This policy, said to increase incentives to produce and invest, and to be the basis of a strong economy, was popular in the UK during the eighties. Its name comes from the US, c.1976.

surf *verb* to ride on the outside of a train, especially on its roof, for excitement (or in response to a challenge). The practice is thought to have originated in Rio de Janeiro; by the late eighties it was known in the US and the UK. *Surf* suggests the use of a train as a sort of surfboard beneath one's feet, except that the risk of serious injury or even death is far greater than it is when surfing on water.

surfing the net (or Internet) *phrase* travelling the WORLD WIDE WEB to see what is of interest to you: sampling its wares. This was an often reiterated phrase in 1995 when the general public was being told it must find out about the Internet and the *Information Superhighway*.

surgical *adj.* (of military operation) swift and precise, usually carried out from the air. A good example of US military DOUBLESPEAK, c.1965. The adjective is intended to imply minute exactness, a high degree of skill and a therapeutic intention. The results have often failed to match these claims under the actual circumstances of war.

surrogate mother *noun* a woman who agrees to undergo pregnancy to produce a child for another woman who is unable to have a child herself. Also **surrogate motherhood**. The process normally involves artificial insemination from the husband of the woman who is unable to have a child, or implantation of an embryo from this woman, though other procedures are possible, such as recourse to a SPERM BANK. The phrase is new (c.1978), though *surrogate* meaning 'substitute' is very old.

surtitles *noun* a translation or précis of an opera libretto projected on to a screen above the stage during a performance in a foreign language. Also verb **surtitle**. Subtitles have been familiar in the cinema and on television for many years; *surtitles* (from *sur-* meaning 'above' as in 'surcharge') were invented in 1983, and the usage is now well established, though many opera buffs resent the practice as intrusive.

survivalist *noun* a person whose belief (or hobby) is that he should arm himself and become accustomed to living wild so as to survive a great disaster such as a nuclear explosion. Also **survivalism**, the pastime of practising survival techniques. The word emerged c.1982, from the idea of 'outdoor *survival* skills', though the pastime had become known during the 1970s as an elaboration – some would say a dangerous one – of earlier outdoor pursuits which developed personal toughness and the capacity to respond to a challenge. By the late eighties, by which time the word *survivalism* had emerged, the activity had become associated with the collection of large quantities of weaponry and, in the USA, with groups of people taking part in paramilitary activity, some of it associated with racialism and religious fanaticism. The death by shooting of 16 people in Hungerford, Berkshire, UK in 1987 at the hands of a self-confessed *survivalist* not only brought the word and the activity to public notice for the first time but also associated them with deranged behaviour, lonely or inadequate people, and an obsessional or menacing interest in militaria.

sus, suss (abbreviation for) suspicion, suspicious, suspect. The abbreviation belongs to the earlier part of the twentieth century in criminal and police slang, but some other slang uses are newer. The *sus law* (law permitting the arrest of a person *sus*pected of loitering with criminal intent) was not generally known until the controversy leading up to its repeal in 1981. *Suss* as a verb meaning 'to suspect' and therefore 'imagine, surmise' belongs to the 1950s, and was followed by *suss out* (c.1966), 'work out, figure out, often by intuition', 'investigate or uncover the truth about (person or thing)'. As a slang adjective, *sussed* means 'socially astute'.

swap shop *noun* a place or event where people can exchange articles they no longer want for other articles; an agency which puts people into contact with each other so that they can do this. (1976). In North America sometimes called a *swap-meet*.

sweetheart deal (or **arrangement, etc.**) *noun* a secret business arrangement for mutual advantage. 'Secret' because it is corrupt, unethical or in some ill-defined area of commercial law. The use of *sweetheart* as an adjective in this sense has been common in the USA since the 1950s; it was originally used of private agreements between employers and trade-union leaders which were beneficial to them but not to the workers. Later the meaning broadened to denote other forms of corrupt transaction, and this is the sense which became known in Britain in the late eighties when American business practice gained ground as a result of governmental enthusiasm for deregulation.

swing *verb* **swinging** *adj.* As a verb, **swing** has had two new slang or informal meanings recently, though both are now dated but not obsolete. One is 'to enjoy oneself in a lively, fashionable and modern way, free from constraint' (1957); the other is 'engage in promiscuous sexual activity, especially by swapping sexual partners in a group' (1964). Both of them seem to be developments from *swing* as a technical musical term. The essence of swing in the twenties and thirties was a sense of controlled excitement stemming from a driving rhythm, repeated musical phrases and a strong jazz influence. Swing had general associations of novelty and freedom, as well as a compulsive quality, and these are the feelings that lie behind the later non-musical uses of *swing*. One of these uses is *swinging*, best known from *swinging sixties* (1967) and *swinging London* (1966). In both terms, swinging means 'uninhibited, lively, fashionable, unconventional'; sometimes it means no more than 'highly enjoyable' and sometimes implies sexual liberation. Ironically perhaps the 'swinging sixties' gave rise to radical and innovative cultural changes or 'swings' that transformed much of modern society, notably in its attitudes towards race, gender, sex, the environment, abortion and censorship, so that it really was a time of change or swings. Though this may seem a far cry from the origin of *swing* as a musical term, it is possible to trace a line of descent.

swipe   *verb* to pass a SWITCH card through an electronic till to effect payment for goods or services (late eighties). See SWITCH for an explanation of this method of payment. The cashier passes the Switch card along a groove in the till so that the information stored on the card's magnetic strip can be read electronically. One of the standard meanings of *swipe* (a variant of 'sweep') has long been 'to strike with a sweeping motion', and the cashier's rapid movement of the card along the groove of the till is a sort of 'swiping' movement.

Switch   *noun* a computerised system allowing sums of money to be electronically transferred from the bank account of a purchaser to that of a retailer. See EFTPOS. The system was launched in the UK by a number of banks in 1988, and many of their account holders now have the plastic debit card known as the *Switch card*. The name *switch* had been used of this system in the US about ten years earlier, and had probably been borrowed from existing computerese. When making a purchase from a retailer who offers a *Switch* facility, the holder of the *Switch card* may present it instead of cash, a cheque or a credit card. When the card is fed through the retailer's electronic device (see SWIPE), funds to cover the purchase are automatically and immediately transferred from the card holder's account to the credit of the retailer.

switched on   *adj.* (of person) lively, alert, efficient and up-to-date. Also **switched off**, bored, alienated. When the terms originated as mid sixties slang , they had to do with a person's awareness or ignorance of fashionable sixties trends; indeed one meaning of *switched on* was 'under the influence of drugs'. These senses are now dated, and the modern meanings, though still informal, have nothing to do with the SWINGING sixties.

synergy   *noun* the (supposed) ability of two businesses (or other organisations) to be more effective and efficient when they join forces (e.g. after a takeover bid) than either had been or could be in isolation. The word has existed since the fifties but was little used until the eighties when the increasing number of mergers and takeovers brought it to prominence in the need to justify such mergers.

system building   *noun* a building method using prefabricated components. Popular in the sixties (the term dates from c.1964) because of its speed and cheapness, but much criticised because of the resultant appearance.

t and e   (abbreviation for) TIRED AND EMOTIONAL.

tack, tackiness   *noun* although *tacky*, originally a US colloquialism for 'vulgar, cheap, shoddy, in poor taste', goes back to the middle of the nineteenth century (its derivation is unknown), the corresponding noun *tackiness* did not emerge until c.1977, since when it has been abbreviated in fashionable quarters to *tack* (slang, late eighties), permitting *high-tack* to emerge as a trendy pun on **high-tech**. These noun forms denote anything cheap, nasty and tasteless.

tad, a   *adv. phrase* a little; slightly. This sense has been known in the USA since c.1940, but filtered through to the UK only in the eighties: it is informal and has only recently entered general use. *Tad*, thought to be an abbreviation of 'tadpole', was originally a nineteenth century North American colloquialism for a small child, usually a boy – both are lively, small and quick-moving.

Taffia   *noun* a supposed network of Welsh people exercising influence and helping each other within a largely non-Welsh organisation, society, etc. or on their own ground. A facetious pun on *mafia* and *Taffy* (slang nickname for a Welshman) (1970s).

tag   *noun* a spray-painted graffito comprising a logo, word, initial or (nick)name used as a personal signature or symbol. The practice of *tagging* originated in New York in the seventies as a feature of HIP HOP culture, and spread to the UK c.1987. For a while it was something of a youth sub-culture, the aim being to leave one's *tag* in as many public places as possible, preferably in prominent and inaccessible ones. *Taggers* sometimes worked in teams, producing collective rather than individual tags, and promoting their own specialised vocabulary and etiquette. See also ELECTRONIC TAGGING.

tailback   *noun* a long queue of stationary or slow-moving traffic stretching back from some obstruction. Also *verb* **tail back** (1975).

takeaway   *noun* ready-cooked food sold for consumption away from the shop or restaurant where it is prepared (1964); an establishment cooking and selling such food (1970). The idea is not new, of course – fish and chip shops, for example, have existed for a long time. It was the widespread development of Chinese and subsequently Indian restaurants during the late 1950s that gave rise to *takeaway*. Scotland prefers *carry-out* and North America *takeout* or *to go*.

talking head   *noun* a head-and-shoulders television picture of a person talking, usually at length, in a documentary programme, studio discussion, etc. Sixties media slang, often slightly derogatory in that it implies static and therefore possibly dull television.

talk show   see CHAT SHOW.

tamper-evident   *adj.* (of the packaging of consumer goods) made in such a way that any tampering with the packaging (and therefore possible tampering with the contents) after it leaves the manufacturer is clearly evident. The development of such packaging was one of several responses to CONSUMER TERRORISM. The expression was first used in the US, c.1985.

tank top   *noun* a once popular garment consisting of a sleeveless pullover with a low, round neck, wide shoulder straps and deep armholes. It was worn by either sex, usually over a shirt or blouse. Its name (1968) comes from its resemblance to the upper part of the *tank suit*, a 1920s one-piece bathing suit worn in 'swimming tanks' (pools).

tape deck *noun*. As *deck* (platform, floor) implies, a *tape deck* (c.1949) is strictly speaking the flat surface of a tape-recorder on top of which are mounted the spools, playing head and other visible apparatus. As this sort of design has given way to cassette arrangements in which tapes are played internally, with no external machinery, the name (sometimes shortened to *deck*) has become applied to the entire tape-recorder.

TAURUS (acronym for) transfer and automated registration of uncertificated stock. A computer system planned for introduction by the London Stock Exchange in 1993 to replace share certificates as a record of shareholdings. Despite several years of development and an expenditure of over £400m, technical problems caused the system to be abandoned in 1993 before it was even operational.

tax exile *noun* a wealthy person who chooses to live abroad in order to take advantage of lower levels of taxation there (1969).

tax haven *noun* a country which has lower rates of taxation and which therefore attracts wealthy individuals (such as TAX EXILES) and companies to base themselves there (1973).

tax shelter *noun* a means of organising one's business or financial affairs in order to reduce the sum that is liable to taxation – for example, by off-setting expenses or the losses elsewhere in your business, or by donations to charity (1961).

teach-in *noun* an informal conference consisting of lectures and discussions on a specific issue. The term is said to have been invented at Harvard in 1965 as the name of a protracted free-for-all discussion-cum-demonstration in which staff and students discussed the Vietnam War. Similar events took place at other universities during the same year as a form of protest. The term has since lost these associations with political dissent or demonstration. For its formation, see -IN.

techno *noun* a type of music popular in RAVE culture. The name is an abbreviation of *technology* or *technological*, and the music, which is a derivative of synthesised electronic dance music, makes use of technology such as SAMPLING. It originated in Detroit in the late eighties.

techno- *prefix* related to technology or its use. Of many recent coinages, some of the most durable appear to include TECHNOBABBLE (see next entry), *technophobia* (fear of technology; 1965), *technostress* (stress caused by working in a technological environment, especially one dominated by computers; 1983) and *technostructure*, a word invented by JK Galbraith in 1967 to denote the hierarchy of people who control the technology of a society, e.g. administrators and managers.

technobabble *noun* the jargon of technology, especially in its computing and military applications. One of a number of 1980s -*babble* words: see PSYCHOBABBLE for an explanation.

Teenage Mutant Hero Turtles *noun*. Known in the USA, where they originated, as the Teenage Mutant Ninja Turtles, these were four children's comic-book figures invented in 1988. Their popularity developed into a craze (sometimes called *turtlemania*) associated with numerous commercial products, computer games, a TV series, etc.; it reached the UK in 1990. The turtles were also responsible for popularising a version of US children's or youngsters' slang. See NINJA.

teenybopper *noun* a young girl (occasionally boy) fond of pop music and fashionable clothes. Rather dated slang, c.1966. *Teeny* is from 'teenage', probably influenced by *teeny* meaning 'very small' (a variant of 'tiny'). *Bopper* is from 'bop', a form of jazz that originated in the 1940s; by the time that *teenybopper* was coined, *bopper* had became a young person who enjoyed dancing to popular music.

Teflon *noun* (when used attributively, as in **Teflon President**) always able to avoid blame, criticism, scandal, etc., usually by having others take responsibility. The word has been known since 1945 as the trademark for a non-stick coating, used on saucepans since c.1954. In 1983 a US Congresswoman memorably accused President Reagan of perfecting 'the Teflon-coated Presidency. He sees to it that nothing sticks to him'. Since then, this figurative use has spread from President Reagan and US politics, and has become familiar in British politics as well as, occasionally, in nonpolitical use.

tele- *prefix* related to telecommunications. This prefix comes from the Greek *tele*: 'afar, from afar', and most of the numerous new coinages are self-explanatory e.g. *telebanking* (1981), carrying out banking by electronic means rather than personal visit; *teleshopping* (1980s), the ordering of goods from shops by means of a telephone and computer link; *telemarketing* or *telesales*, the (attempted) selling of goods by making an initial, unsolicited approach by telephone – a plague of the late eighties. Less obvious is the verb *telecommute* (1974), to work from home, using datalinks to keep in contact with colleagues, clients, etc. (also known as *teleworking*) and the noun *televangelist* (1973), an evangelical preacher who, in the US, appears regularly on television. See also the following entries.

telecoms *noun* (abbreviation for) telecommunications, the science and technology of communication by any electrical means (1963). Both the abbreviation and the full word are singular. Although *telecom* (another abbreviation of 'telecommunications') is best known from *British Telecom* (1981), *telecom* is by no means restricted to the technology of the telephone; it embraces computer networking (see LAN for example), INFORMATION TECHNOLOGY and the whole field of communications technology.

telecottage *noun* a room or suite of rooms in a country area equipped with on-line computers and other communications technology so local people can TELECOMMUTE from a local base. A Swedish concept that has aroused interest and seems to promise one pattern of future work practice in the UK. Discussed in the UK from the late eighties.

Teletext *noun* a system by which adapted television sets are able to receive up-to-date information broadcast by a television station (e.g. news, weather forecasts, sports results, in printed form). Now a tradename, but originally (1974) the generic term for the two systems developed and later adopted by the major television companies in the UK. The BBC developed **Ceefax** (1972); the name was based on 'seeing' and 'facts'. The Independent Broadcasting Authority chose to call their system **Oracle** (1973), a word previously best known from its use in classical mythology; a laborious acronym – **O**(ptional) **R**(eception of) **A**(nnouncements by) **C**(oded) **L**(ine) **E**(lectronics) – was later coined.

telethon *noun* a lengthy television programme to raise funds for charity. The word has been known in the USA since 1949 but arrived in Britain only in the 1980s. In America it is sometimes also applied to a prolonged television programme used for other purposes, such as a PHONE-IN to politicians. The *-thon* part of the word, like the *-athon* found in some occasional coinages, is from *marathon*, the long Olympic run named after a messenger's famous feat of endurance in running from Athens to Sparta to seek help before the battle of Marathon in 490 BC.

Telstar *noun* a US communication satellite launched in 1962. It relayed the first live television transmissions between the USA and Europe, as well as transatlantic telephone messages. A second Telstar was launched in 1963.

temp *noun* a temporary employee, usually an office worker. Also *verb*, to work as a temporary employee. A colloquialism of c.1967. The verb is a little later.

teriyaki *noun* (in Japanese cookery) a dish of meat or, more usually, fish marinated in soy sauce and broiled on a skewer over charcoal. Known in the West since c.1962, the word is from Japanese; the first two syllables mean 'lustre', and the other two 'roast'.

TESSA, Tessa (acronym for) tax-exempt special savings account. Announced by this name in the budget of 1990 and introduced in 1991, the scheme enables a certain amount of interest to be paid tax-free if the capital paid into the account, held in a bank or building society, is not withdrawn for five years.

TGV (abbreviation for) train à grande vitesse (French, 'high-speed train'). The initials are widely used in France and have been familiar in the UK since the first high-speed service (Paris–Lyon) began in 1981 as the world's fastest rail service. The use of the TGV to connect with the Channel Tunnel further popularised the name in the nineties.

thalidomide *noun* a drug formerly used in medicine as a sedative and hypnotic. It was developed in the 1950s and prescribed for pregnant women. Between 1959 and 1962 several thousand deformed babies were born, usually lacking limbs and having fingers or toes attached to the trunk by a short stump. The drug was identified as the cause of these and other abnormalities, and withdrawn from the market.

Thatcherism *noun* the policies associated with the government of Margaret Thatcher, prime minister from 1979–1990. Also **Thatcherite**, a person supporting such policies. The policies included monetarism, privatisation, depletion of the welfare state, reductions in public expenditure, self-help, the encouragement of the entrepreneurial spirit and of the free play of market forces, the diminution of trade union power, and resistance to the development of the European Community. *Thatcherite* was coined in 1976, a year after Mrs Thatcher became leader of the Conservative Party, then in opposition. *Thatcherism* in its now familiar sense belongs to the years following 1979, the year she became prime minister, but actually first appears in print in a *Tribune* headline of 1973 ('The Blight of Thatcherism') when she was Education Secretary, though this use of *Thatcherism* had little to do with what the word later came to mean.

Theatre of the Absurd   *noun* a type of drama, mainly French, stressing absurd and futile aspects of human existence in an inexplicable world, often with illogical or incomprehensible dialogue, characterisation and plotting. This was an important development in early post-war drama, especially in the work of Ionescu, Becket (notably *Waiting for Godot*, 1954), Genet and Pinter. Its collective name emerged c.1961.

theme   *noun* (when used attributively, as in **theme park**) the unifying idea, subject or image around which a park or place of entertainment is designed. Also *adj.* **themed**, centred round a particular theme. A *theme park* (1960) is an amusement park in which the activities etc. relate to a particular subject in the way that Disneyland pioneered in the USA. Extensions of the idea include the *theme pub* and *theme restaurant* (both 1983) in which the decor and atmosphere are unified by reference to a single idea.

think-tank   *noun* a group of specialists (often brought together by government, business concerns, etc.) studying particular problems in order to find solutions, make recommendations, etc. An American term of the late 1950s, from earlier slang for 'brain' (*think* = act of thinking; *tank* = reservoir). It first became known in Britain when it was applied to the Central Policy Review Staff established by Edward Heath in 1970 to give advice to the cabinet and to government ministers. Since then it has passed into more general colloquial use.

third age, Third Age, the   *noun* older age, especially as an opportunity for enjoyment and education. A translation of the French term *troisième âge* which started to become known in Britain after 1983 when the University of the Third Age (U3A), founded in France ten years earlier, was established in the UK to provide opportunities for learning for retired people irrespective of age limits, qualifications, etc. See WOOPY.

Third Market, third market   *noun* market trading in shares in companies that are not required to provide as much information as those whose shares are traded on the main market. Established by the London Stock Exchange in 1987.

Third World, the   *noun* underdeveloped countries, especially those in Africa, Asia and South America. The term was coined by the French diplomat Georges Baladier in 1956, when he used the phrase *un 'Tiers Monde'* to describe the 29 African and Asian nations who had met at the Bandung Conference a year previously. By this he meant that they did not belong to either of the two 'blocs', one led by the USA, the other by the USSR, which dominated international politics at the time. The term subsequently shifted and enlarged its meaning; *third world* is now a polite evasion of 'poor', 'backward' or 'underdeveloped'. See also DEVELOPING COUNTRY. The terms *First World* and *Second World* emerged in the seventies; the first was generally taken to refer to the developed market economies, and the second to the communist countries. Only the first term is much used; the meaning of the second has yet to be redefined following the fragmentation of the USSR and the Eastern European communist bloc since 1988. Occasionally *First World* has been used to mean the (then) two superpowers, and *Second World* the other developed countries. *Fourth World* is another seventies term, though little used. It denotes the very poorest countries in the world and, sometimes, the poorest people in the developed world. See SOUTH.

thirtysomething see -SOMETHING.

thrash *noun* a party, especially a fairly wild one; (short for) **thrash metal**, a type of fast, hard ROCK music combining features of HEAVY METAL and PUNK. The first is slang, c.1952, though it is found in naval slang before then; the origin is probably one of the standard meanings of *thrash*, 'wild movement', 'plunging around with violence'. The second belongs to the late 1980s; its names include *thrashcore* and *speed metal*. In this sense, *thrash* seems to be a development of the jazz term THRASH meaning 'a short energetic passage', though *thrash(metal)* was often violent, shocking and morbid rather than merely 'energetic'.

ticky tacky *noun* and *adj.* (made of) cheap and inferior material. Used particularly of the materials in some modern buildings. The expression (c.1962) is probably an elaboration of *tacky*; see TACK.

tie-break(er) *noun* a method of deciding a winner when the contestants have tied scores. A fairly recent innovation (1970), found particularly in tennis, and probably introduced in response to the demands of television, which requires competitions to be of a reasonably predictable length.

tie-in *noun* a book, film or merchandise that is produced for sale to coincide with the appearance of related material in a different medium (1962). A simple example is the publication or republication of a book to take advantage of the fact that it has just been made into a film or television series, but more sophisticated marketing may include tapes, music, toys, computer games, etc.

timeframe *noun* a defined period of time in which something is planned to happen; a schedule. Originally US English, this meaning (1964) is based on the idea of a *frame* which limits the *time* available for something. Since the eighties, however, the term has been used less specifically, both inside and outside the US, to mean little more than 'a period of time'; so that 'in the 1995–96 timeframe' has come to mean 'in about 1995 or 1996'.

time-share *noun* the part ownership of a property, usually holiday accommodation, entitling one to use it for a fixed period every year. Also **time-sharing** *noun* a system of joint ownership of this kind. This meaning (1976) is now more familiar than the original one (c.1953) which had to do with the apparently simultaneous sharing of a computer by users at different terminals; something made possible because of the high speed at which the computer carries out transactions.

time-warp *noun* a distortion of space-time as a result of which a person or thing remains stationary in time or travels backwards or forwards in time. A term from science fiction (1950s), now in general – perhaps slightly informal – use to denote a state in which time appears to have stood still. For example, people with fixed, old-fashioned views may be said to be 'living in a time-warp'. A *warp* is literally a twist or a bending.

TINA (acronym for) there is no alternative. Coined c.1979 at the outset of Margaret Thatcher's premiership when monetarism was being introduced. The full expression is said to have been one of her favourite sayings; even if it was not, it certainly represents the uncompromising certainty with which she habitually expressed herself on economic as on other matters. *Tina* also figured briefly as a (temporary) nickname for Mrs Thatcher (as she then was).

tired and emotional *adj.* drunk. A euphemism usually said to have originated in the satirical magazine *Private Eye* in 1965, applied to George Brown, the then Foreign Secretary. Another version is that the phrase was used by a BBC spokesman attempting to explain the much criticised TV appearance of the same George Brown on the night of President Kennedy's assassination in 1963. Be that as it may, the phrase was certainly much used by *Private Eye* and has been much copied, either as a joke or as a journalistic device to avoid prosecution for libel.

tissue-typing *noun* the assessment of bodily tissue to determine its immunological compatibility with other tissue, especially for purposes of a transplant operation. *Typing* here means 'determining the type' (1965).

TM (abbreviation of) TRANSCENDENTAL MEDITATION (1967).

toasting *noun* a disc jockey's addition of his own lyrics or other vocal effects to a reggae record or other prerecorded track; any speaking by a disc jockey while playing a record. Also **toaster**, a person who does this, and *noun* and *verb* **toast**. Chiefly US and West Indian from c.1976. The derivation is from an earlier *toast*, a long narrative poem or story recited extempore by Black Americans or Caribbeans on street corners or at other meeting places. This in turn is probably from one of the familiar meanings of *toast*, a speech in honour of a person, institution, event, etc.

together *adj.* (of person) competent, well-organised. Slang in this sense, and often used as an adjective before a noun, e.g. 'a very together person'. The current meaning is a weakening of late sixties HIPPIE slang, in which the word was used to mean 'mentally and emotionally stable'.

toke

toke *verb* to inhale smoke from a cigarette or pipe, usually one containing marijuana (1952). The word, which is US slang, is also used as a *noun* (c.1968) meaning 'the inhalation of such fumes'. Its origin is unknown, possibly Chinese.

tokenism *noun* the practice or policy of making a minimum (or 'token') effort in order to be seen to do something, especially to comply with equal opportunities legislation or with certain expectations. Coined in the US c.1962, but now used generally, especially of the token representation of minority groups, e.g. a few Black people or women being admitted to areas of social or business life dominated by White males.

ton, the *noun* a speed of 100 mph. Also *adj.* **ton-up**, (of person) liking to travel at 100 mph or more; (of motorcycle) capable of travelling at such speeds. It seems that *ton* was first used to mean (a score of) one hundred in the vocabulary of darts in the 1930s; the origin was probably an earlier colloquialism in which *tons* meant 'lots', as it still does. The usage spread to cricket and to other areas of slang (e.g. £100 became known as a *ton*) before being applied to speed c.1954. *Ton-up* emerged c.1961.

tonepad *noun* an electronic device used for transferring data to a central computer, often via a telephone (late eighties). It resembles a remote control KEYPAD, so its name is based on that word with the substitution of *tone* for 'key' because of the electronic tone that the device uses when transmitting data.

toot *noun* any drug that is snorted, especially cocaine; a snort of cocaine; a tube for snorting. Mid seventies US slang of unknown origin, possibly criminal slang.

topless *adj.* (of person, usually woman) bare-breasted; (of place) where women do not cover their breasts (1960s).

tower block *noun* a multi-storey building (1966).

town house *noun* a terraced house, usually modern, in an urban environment and designed to facilitate certain aspects of contemporary urban life. Originally a US term c.1965, but rapidly adopted by estate agents in the UK, where 'terraced' generally implies cheap housing but *town house* suggests a smart terrace in a Belgravia square as distinct from one's country house – the sort of sense the term has had for over two centuries. The modern meaning often denotes a house with a ground-floor integral garage, a first-floor living room and second-floor bedrooms. In North America, however, a *town house* is simply a terraced house.

toyboy *noun* the young male lover of an older person, usually a wealthy (and possibly celebrated) mature woman. The word is a tabloid newspaper invention of the early eighties, and owes its catchiness to its rhyme and to its succinctness in implying that a young man may be kept as a plaything by an older – and presumably wealthier and more dominant – owner. It is an aspect of the SEXUAL REVOLUTION that women are now doing what men have always done: using their influence or money to procure sexual gratification with a young lover.

track record *noun* (of person, business, etc.) the past record of successes and failures, especially when used as a guide to likely success or failure in the future. This has been the dominant meaning since c.1965, but the primary one (c.1951) is 'the fastest time ever recorded at a particular (running) track by a horse, athlete, etc.'

traded option *noun* an option that can itself be bought and sold on a stock exchange. Stock exchange language, 1973.

trade-off *noun* an exchange, especially one made in order to achieve a compromise (1961). From the verb *trade off*, a comparatively recent elaboration of *trade*, both meaning 'to dispose of by barter'.

trainers *noun* running shoes for sports training, commonly worn as informal or leisure footwear generally. The word emerged c.1978 as an informal shortening for the slightly earlier 'training shoes' (1973). Light, rubber-soled sports shoes had previously been called 'plimsolls' or 'gym shoes'. A new term was necessary for the more elaborate – and much more expensive – footwear that was launched as part of the leisure-wear boom and the taste for gaudy informal clothing more generally.

train station *noun* a railway station. Since c.1955 this has gradually overtaken 'railroad station' as the preferred US term. There are signs, since c.1990, that it is challenging 'railway station' as the preferred British term.

trannie, tranny *noun* a transistor radio, a type of small, light, portable radio. Introduced in the late 1950s, at a time before popular music became ubiquitous in public places, it was soon being denounced as a nuisance on the streets, etc. The colloquial abbreviation became established during the sixties but is no longer used except facetiously because the transistor radio has been superseded by the GHETTO BLASTER and WALKMAN.

transcendental meditation *noun* a method of meditation and relaxation based on a type of yoga popularised by the Maharishi Mahesh Yogi. First heard of in the West c.1966, though it had been taught in India since 1955, and subsequently widely known because it attracted the Beatles. Often abbreviated to *TM*.

transputer *noun* a chip that incorporates all the functions of a microprocessor, including the memory. The word was coined in 1978 from 'transistor' and 'computer', and the first chips appeared in the mid eighties.

trash *verb* to attack or destroy, wilfully or maliciously, especially to vandalise as a means of protest. Slang, originally US c.1970. A new verbal use of the well-established noun *trash* (rubbish).

trendsetter *noun* a person, or sometimes thing, that creates a new fashion, especially a person who habitually does this (1960).

trendy *adj.* fashionable; also *noun*, a person who is (consciously) fashionable; also *noun* **trendoid** (eighties) the same. An informal term of praise when it was first used c.1962, but by the eighties it had become often derogatory, implying superficiality or ephemerality.

trip *noun* a hallucinatory experience induced by a drug. Late 1950s

triumphalism

US slang, much popularised in the sixties because of the use of LSD among hippies; the word implied a visit or tour in another realm of consciousness. The word is now a more general colloquialism for any stimulating or profound experience (i.e. unconnected with drug-abuse).

triumphalism *noun* boastfulness and ostentatious celebration of any success. The word was originally used, from c.1964, in theological contexts and meant 'sense of pride – often ostentatious – in the merits of one's church'. Since the 1970s, however, it has become increasingly familiar in its present sense.

trivia *noun* miscellaneous facts about something. Until the 1980s, *trivia* were petty details or trivialities. Since the extraordinary success of the general knowledge quiz game Trivial Pursuit (1982), the launching of similar games with similar names and the popularity of pub and computer quiz games (sometimes called *trivia* quizzes or questions), *trivia* has acquired this new, possibly short-lived meaning.

Trojan horse, **Trojan** or **trojan** *noun* (in computer technology) a bug inserted into a computer program and designed to sabotage a system. First developed in the seventies by hackers (see HACK) and later recognised as a significant hazard, capable of facilitating fraud or theft, for instance. The bug, hidden in an apparently trustworthy program, is designed to be activated after a certain period of time. In this respect it resembles the Greek soldiers who, in Homer's *Iliad*, were smuggled into Troy inside an apparently innocuous wooden statue of a horse, from which they emerged after nightfall to devastate the city.

Trot (informal abbreviation for) Trotskyite (1962).

tube *noun* a can (or bottle) of beer or lager. Originally and still chiefly Australian slang, c.1969, from the tubular shape of a can or bottle.

tube(s), (go) down the *phrase* (be) lost, finished, in difficulty. Originally US slang, probably college slang meaning 'fail an exam', c.1963. The *tube* appears to be the tube-shaped underground channel of a sewer or drain; anything which goes down such a tube is heading for trouble.

tug of love *noun* a conflict over the custody of a child. A tabloid newspaper term of the early seventies, probably based on 'tug of war'.

turn-off *noun* person or thing that repels, bores, discourages, etc. (1975). Also *verb* **turn off** to cause (a person) to experience boredom or revulsion. *Turn off* emerged in hippie slang of the sixties, presumably as the antithesis to the earlier TURN ON. The more common noun form *turn-off* is slightly later.

turn on *verb* to give pleasure to; to excite emotionally or sexually; to introduce (a person), or be introduced oneself, to drugs. Also *noun* **turn-on**, a person or thing that is pleasurable or exciting. *Turn on* was originally 1950s US drug slang, though it may have been earlier jazz slang, and was presumably based on the simple idea of turning on a tap or light to obtain a supply of what you need. The noun form *turn-on* followed in the sixties as part of hippie vocabulary, and referred to arousal by drugs or sex. Nowadays both terms have milder and more general colloquial meanings: the jocular catchphrase 'it depends what turns you on' means no more than 'it depends on what you enjoy'.

TVP (abbreviation for) textured vegetable protein. A meat substitute known since c.1968. It is a protein obtained from soya beans or other vegetables which have been made to have the texture of meat (hence the first word of the name) as well as the flavour.

tweak *verb* and *noun*. The standard meaning of *tweak* has long been 'to pinch and pull with a sudden slight jerk and twist'; as a noun, a *tweak* is the act of doing this. In the mid sixties, *tweak* developed a new informal sense of 'make fine adjustments to a mechanism'; this was clearly based on the earlier meaning, which implied small movements of the hands. The noun *tweak* had a corresponding development, and by the eighties had become 'a small enhancement or optional extra', especially on a computer. Also in the eighties, *tweak* began to be used of drug addicts in the USA as a verb meaning 'to twitch violently', in other words to twitch as though one had *been* tweaked.

twist *noun* a popular dance with vigorous movement, especially a twisting movement from the waist (1961).

twitcher *noun* a bird-watcher whose main aim is to collect sightings of rare birds. Also *verb* **twitch**, to bird watch in this way. *Twitcher* has been in use in bird-watching circles for several years (probably from the early seventies) but came into general use only in the mid eighties, and is thought to come from the way such enthusiast became *twitchy* (nervously excited) at the prospect of another sighting.

UB 40 *noun* (index number of) the registration card formerly issued by the Department of Employment to a person registering for benefit because of unemployment. The initials *UB* stand for 'Unemployment Benefit', and the card was introduced in the early seventies, replacing the UI40 (for Unemployment Insurance). Informally, unemployed people were sometimes known as UB 40s.

unban *verb* to lift a ban from. The word was unfamiliar until it was used of the *unbanning* of the African National Congress in 1990. Its use has now spread to other contexts unconnected with South African politics.

unbundling *noun* (in commerce) taking over a large business or conglomerate company with the intention of retaining its central part but selling off its subsidiary companies and assets to help pay for the take-over. The word dates from the 1980s in this sense, and some have argued that it is no more than a euphemism for ASSET STRIPPING.

underclass *noun* the lowest class in society. The term was first used in the UK in the early sixties, probably from the Swedish 'underklass' and the writings of the economist Gunnar Myrdal. It came to more general notice in the eighties as the widening gap between the prosperous and the poor became more obvious. The underclass are seen as being at the bottom of the heap, unemployed and increasingly unemployable, often poorly educated and with scant opportunity to extract themselves from their depressed condition, but condemned to pass on this deprivation to their children.

underwhelmed *adj.* less than impressed. An outwardly polite way of describing your reactions to something that is meant to impress you but does not. A humorous back-formation from overwhelmed (early nineties).

-unfriendly *adj.* harmful; unhelpful. Found in compounds such as *environment-unfriendly* or *user-unfriendly* and several others since the mid eighties, this new meaning of 'unfriendly' is based on the very popular **user-friendly** (late seventies) and subsequent *-friendly* coinages. The search for an opposite to *-friendly* produced *-hostile*, but *-unfriendly* remains the most popular in the vocabulary of the GREEN movement.

ungreen *adj.* harmful to the environment; (of person) unconcerned about the environment. Formed in the late eighties as the opposite of GREEN.

unisex *adj.* (of fashions, hairdressers etc.) designed or intended to be suitable for either sex (1968).

unleaded *adj.* (of petrol) not treated with tetraethyl lead. The adjective has been used in this sense since c1965, though it did not become generally known until the eighties when petrol of this kind first became generally available, and motorists were encouraged by price incentives to use it. Plans were made to phase out the use of leaded petrol – a process which had started in the USA in the mid seventies – because of the damage caused to health and the atmosphere by exhaust fumes. See LEAD-FREE.

unreal *adj.* **1.** too good to be true, incredibly wonderful. US, colloquial, 1965. **2.** unbelievably off-putting, incredibly NAFF US, colloquial, 1966.

unsocial hours *noun* hours of work that are socially inconvenient because they fall outside the normal working day. For example, shift work that requires people to work during evenings or nights and is therefore disruptive of social or family life. The expression (1973) is rather formal and occurs in job advertisements, pay bargaining, etc.

unwaged *adj.* (of a person) not earning wages. Also *noun* **the unwaged**, people not earning wages. An old word, but not widely used and applied to people not at work until c.1971. It is not a euphemism for 'unemployed', but rather links the unemployed with the retired and those who do not receive wages for their full-time work, as, for example, housewives and mothers.

upbeat see DOWNBEAT.

update, an *noun* up-to-date information. The noun (1967) is from the verb *update* (bring up to date, 1948); both are originally US, from the earlier 'up-to-date'.

up-front *adj.* honest, frank, outspoken; (of money) paid in advance. The first of these meanings is c.1967 and is a figurative development of the slightly earlier *up front*, i.e. 'up at the front', in a position of prominence or responsibility, standing in front of other people, where it is impossible to hide or to dodge one's obligations. This being so, it is not surprising that *upfront* has more recently come to mean 'extrovert' or 'showing leadership'. Also *noun* **up-frontness** the quality of being up-front (late eighties). The second meaning is c.1972 and largely confined to the vocabulary of commerce.

up-market   *adj.* (of products, services, etc.) expensive, of superior quality, having prestige. From the early seventies. Also used adverbially: to *go upmarket* is to deal in or buy more expensive merchandise.

upper   *noun* a drug having a stimulant effect, especially amphetamine. Informal, originally US, from c.1968, probably based on the colloquial verb *up*, 'to increase or raise' (i.e. one's feelings of well-being). Compare DOWN.

upside   *noun* an upward movement of share prices. Stock Exchange slang (c.1961), sometimes now used to mean the opposite of DOWN-SIDE.

uptight   *adj.* (of person) tense in a worried, uncommunicative or irritable way; inhibited; strait-laced. Colloquial, originally US slang. When it achieved sudden popularity in the UK during the sixties it was associated with HIPPIE jargon – denoting the antithesis of 'relaxed', the normal hippie style – but it has remained in use as a serviceable word, often now meaning 'ready to take offence'.

urban guerrilla   *noun* a guerrilla fighter, revolutionary, terrorist, etc. operating in an urban environment. Applied since c.1967 to any member of an organisation such as the Baader–Meinhof gang using hijacking, kidnap, bombing, etc. for political purposes in cities and towns.

urban legend or **myth**   *noun* a piece of modern folklore in the form of a widely known story usually of a macabre nature (early eighties). Called URBAN because they relate to modern urban society, such stories are often retold and sometimes believed. They are largely apocryphal, though they may contain elements of reality, plausibility or even truth, and consist of anecdotes told as though they had actually happened, usually to someone known to the teller. Typical is the one about the family who went on a motoring holiday abroad. During a car journey, the elderly grandmother died and was covered with a travelling rug. While the family were reporting the death at a police station, the car was stolen, together with grandmother. Neither was ever recovered.

use-by date   *noun* (on packaging of perishable goods) date by which the goods should be used and after which they will deteriorate. Familiar in the UK since the mid eighties, gradually replacing the more permissive 'best-before date' as a result of anxieties about food safety.

user   *noun* someone who uses others for their own advantage. Colloquial, originally N. American, 1982.

user-friendly   *adj.* easy to use or understand; sensitive to the customer's needs or wishes. The second is a development from the first, which was originally (c.1977) restricted to computer language and meant 'catering for the non-specialist' – a highly important attribute at a time when the use of computers was becoming part of everyday life for the first time. Such was the popularity of the term that it was taken up on all sides, with consequent shifts in its meaning. There is also a noun *user-friendliness*. See also -FRIENDLY.

user-hostile *adj*. the opposite of USER-FRIENDLY. A development (early eighties) from *user-friendly*.

U3A (abbreviation for) the University of the THIRD AGE.

U-turn *noun* a reversal in the direction of a political or other policy. When it was invented in the 1930s, this term denoted a U-shaped turn made by a vehicle, resulting in a reversal in direction. By c.1960 it was established figuratively in the above sense in the USA, and it became familiar in the UK in the seventies, particularly in politics. In the eighties, when Mrs Thatcher, the then prime minister, made a virtue of never changing her mind, the idea of making a U-turn became part of the vocabulary of political abuse, since when it has verged on cliché.

vaccine *noun* (in computer technology) a piece of software designed to detect and remove a computer *virus* or to prevent attack by one. A late eighties usage, developing the figurative use of the slightly earlier *virus* in computerese. In more familiar medical language, a vaccine is something that is administered to produce immunity to a disease. See VIRUS.

Valley girl *noun* a well off and possibly spoiled, teenage girl from the San Fernando valley, California. Known in the early eighties because of her passion for shopping and especially for her language, VALSPEAK.

Valspeak *noun* the jargon of the VALLEY GIRLS. US slang, early eighties, based on *Valley* and -SPEAK. The argot, spoken in a high-pitched staccato like a dazed schoolgirl, was a mixture of US teenage slang with surf-talk, drug vocabulary and the repetition of certain words ('like', 'totally') and set phrases.

vanilla *adj*. ordinary. Computer slang, c.1984, from the idea of vanilla ice-cream being the standard run-of-the-mill flavour.

vapourware *noun* (in computer technology) software still at the early planning or theoretical stage; computer products that are much trumpeted or long awaited but have not yet materialised. The *-ware* element is from SOFTWARE. *Vapour* can mean 'something fanciful' or, as a verb, 'to make empty boasts', though it is more familiar in the sense of 'substance suspended in air and visible as steam, smoke, etc.' i.e. something lacking solidity; any or all of these senses could lie behind *vapourware* (1987).

Vatican roulette *noun* the rhythm method of contraception as recommended by the Roman Catholic church. The expression (c.1960) is based on 'Russian roulette', a highly dangerous game of chance played with a gun which has only one bullet in its chamber: each player spins the chamber, puts the gun to the head, and pulls the trigger. The implication of dubbing the rhythm method (the only method allowed by the Vatican) as Vatican roulette is that it is as uncertain and chancy as Russian roulette, and as likely to end in grief.

VCR   (abbreviation for) **video cassette recorder** (1971). The normal term has since become VIDEO.

VDU or **vdu**   (abbreviation for) visual display unit. The television-like screen on which words, graphics etc. are displayed when a computer system is being used (1968).

veggieburger or **vegeburger**   *noun* a flat cake of vegetables and/or pulses cooked and served in a bread roll. That is to say, resembling a hamburger but with a vegetarian filling instead of meat. The word (1970s) is a compound of two familiar abbreviations, *veggie* (vegetable) and *burger* (hamburger), on the model of 'cheese-burger', 'beefburger', etc., though *veggie* is also a familiar abbreviation for 'vegetarian' and that could also lie behind its use.

venture capitalist   *noun* a person engaged in investment, finance or business that is based on risk capital, i.e. capital invested in a highly speculative enterprise. Also **venture capitalism** *noun* the sort of activity practised by a venture capitalist. Both terms (early seventies) are from *venture capital*, a 1940s term meaning the same as 'risk capital', as defined above. In the UK from the early eighties, following the example of the US from the sixties, the encouragement of small businesses produced a demand for high-risk investment in new ideas and entrepreneurs, so much so that *venture capitalism* became a full-time specialism in the financial world instead of an occasional aspect of traditional financial activity in the markets. *Venture* in the same broad sense of 'risky' is found in a number of other examples of business jargon e.g. venture buyout.

VHS   (abbreviation for) video home system. A **video cassette** recording system introduced at the beginning of the eighties, it established itself as the market leader and soon became the standard system for home recordings and playback and for commercially recorded tapes available for purchase or hire.

vibes   *noun* (abbreviation for) vibrations, intuitively understood signals about a person or thing. Slang c.1967. It became so popular that 'vibrations' itself started to seem and become colloquial, even though it had had a long and blameless history in its standard meaning of 'instinctive feelings about a person or thing' or 'emotional atmosphere communicated by a person or thing'.

Victorian values   *noun* qualities thought to have been characteristic of British society and individual behaviour during the Victorian period, especially the second half of the nineteenth century. The most frequently mentioned are hard work, initiative, self-help, free-market capitalism, rigorous budgeting, a belief in the importance of the family, and a strict moral code opposed to frivolity or extravagance. They were often referred to during the Thatcher years (the 1980s) because the then prime minister was known to admire them, though some commentators would argue that cruelty, hypocrisy, bigotry, prudery, greed and social injustice were equally *Victorian*.

video   *noun* a film recorded on a VIDEO CASSETTE and available for purchase or rental; *verb* (short for) to VIDEO RECORD (1971); *noun* (short for) VIDEO CASSETTE or VIDEO CASSETTE RECORDER; *noun* a video recording (1968); *verb* the production and use of video recordings (1970); *noun* (short for) POP VIDEO a short promotional film to accompany the release of a pop or rock record (1980).

video cassette   *noun* a cassette containing video tape, i.e. magnetic tape used for the recording and playing back of television programmes or containing a pre-recorded film (1970). The latter may be purchased, or rented from a *video store/shop* (1982).

video cassette recorder   *noun* a tape recorder used for recording and playing back television programmes or for playing pre-recorded videos (1971). Usually abbreviated to VCR or referred to as a VIDEO or VIDEO RECORDER.

videodisc, videodisk   *noun* a disc on which video material is stored in DIGITAL form and played back on a television screen. (Now also called OPTICAL DISC.) The word was first used c.1967, but the system was not ready for commercial exploitation until the early eighties. Compared with CD it has been slow to catch on in the domestic market.

video game   *noun* an electronic game involving the manipulation of graphics on a VDU screen. Available first in arcades and some pubs from c.1973, and then increasingly popular for domestic use on computers or television screens in the eighties.

video nasty   *noun* a video horror film or one depicting violence, cruelty, sadism, killing etc. Video films, available cheaply for purchase or hire, constituted an important new commercial activity from the early 1980s, and soon began to include dubious material that evaded normal censorship procedures. Soon shortened to *nasty* (a word already in established use to mean 'unpleasant thing or person'), *video nasty* was coined c.1982 in the context of public concern about the content of such videos and their effect on the people who watched them, including children whose viewing was not always supervised.

video recorder   *noun*, also *verb* **video record**. Originally (c.1951) an apparatus for making video recordings in a television studio. Since the seventies the term has been short for the domestic VIDEO CASSETTE RECORDER. It has given rise to the verb *video-record* (1961), to record (a television programme) on a video recorder. See VIDEO.

video store/shop   see VIDEO CASSETTE.

Viewdata, viewdata   *noun* any system that exchanges information between a distant computer and a domestic television set via a telephone link. The system enables shopping, ticket-booking, banking, etc. to be done from the home. Some dictionaries print the word with a capital letter, claiming that it is a trademark. According to the Oxford Dictionary, which records the first sighting of the word in 1975, it has been spelt without a capital letter since 1978, when the Post Office failed to get it registered as a trademark (because the word was thought to be too all-embracing).

The Post Office therefore chose PRESTEL, and *viewdata* is now a general term for computerised public information systems.

virtual *adj.* (in computer technology) not physically actual, but made by software to appear to be actual. Thus *virtual memory* (1959), a facility available in large computers: the programmer is not restricted to the size of the computer's memory because the computer translates the programmer's *virtual* locations into actual ones as required, using a large-capacity backing store. Also *virtual reality* (1989), a computer-generated environment that resembles reality from the point of view of the user, who is able to interact with it. Although the use of this development features most commonly in computer games, it has more important potential: it has, for example, been used by Fire Brigades to see how fires may develop in certain sorts of buildings, and by architects to find out what it would be like to walk round the interior of one of their planned buildings.

virus *noun* (in computer technology) an unauthorised program deliberately introduced into a computer system to interfere with it. A figurative use (1983) of the familiar *virus*, which can replicate itself within an organism just as the computer virus can copy itself in other parts of a computer system, often destroying data. Though some viruses have been practical jokes, the possibility of fraud, blackmail or expensive loss of information clearly exists.

visitor centre *noun* an information centre at a tourist site, sometimes combining booking office, shop, toilet facilities, etc., and often providing a slide-show, film or lecture as an introduction to the site. Originally US c.1964, the concept has been familiar in the UK since the eighties with the growth of the HERITAGE INDUSTRY.

vogueing *noun* a type of dance of the late 1980s. The dance is based on imitating the movements of fashion models on the catwalk of a fashion show and caricaturing their (often exaggerated) poses for the camera. Hence the name, based on that of the fashion magazine *Vogue*. The origins appear to have been in the gay clubs of New York, but the dance has been more generally known as a club entertainment in Europe since c.1988.

voiceprint *noun* the graphic representation, electronically constructed, of a person's voice. A tape recording of the voice is fed through a machine – a sound spectrograph – which converts some distinctive features of the voice into a visual pattern, said to be unique to each individual and therefore useful for identification purposes in police work. The name of the technique (1962) is modelled on 'fingerprint', a similarly unique feature that is used in police work.

vox pop *noun* interviews, surveys, etc. conducted with ordinary members of the public, usually in the street by television and radio reporters recording material for news broadcasts, documentary programmes, etc.; public opinion sampled by this method. Media jargon since c.1964, an abbreviation of the well known Latin maxim 'Vox populi vox Dei': the voice of the people is the voice of God.

wack

wack *adj.* harmful, bad, useless. Originally and still chiefly US HIP HOP slang (late eighties), often used of the dangers of CRACK. The word seems to be a variant of WACKO.

wacko *adj.* crazy; *noun* madman, crackpot. Slang, originally and chiefly US, c.1977, from the much earlier US slang *wack* (eccentric person) and *wacky* (crazy). The origin seems to be *whack*, to strike (over the head, causing eccentric behaviour).

walkabout *noun* an informal stroll by royalty, a politician or a celebrity, with a view to meeting the general public. Also **go walkabout** take such a stroll. First used in this sense in 1970 in New Zealand when the Queen left her planned route in order to greet people. The word is originally Australian English ('a periodic journey into the bush by an Aborigine') and its application to the Queen was probably lighthearted, though it is now so familiar that it has lost that particular tone, though it still has the feel of pidgin English, especially in *go walkabout*, which is now sometimes used (e.g. of misappropriated funds) to mean 'go missing'.

Walkman *noun* (trademark for) a small battery-operated personal stereo or portable hi-fi listened to through light headphones. So called because it can be used while walking, it was introduced in the West by Sony in 1979 and became so popular that the name shows signs of losing its capital letter and becoming a generic term for any make of personal stereo.

wall-to-wall *adj.* widespread, impossible to avoid, all-encompassing, ubiquitous, stretching as far as the eye can see. A colloquial figurative use, c.1967, of the earlier literal *wall-to-wall* carpet (1953), i.e. carpet fitted so as to cover the whole of the floor.

wally *noun* stupid, incompetent, unsophisticated person. British slang, possibly working-class London, coined c.1969 and very popular by the late seventies. It is thought to be the familiar form of the forename *Walter*, used in something of the same way that *Charlie* is.

WAN (abbreviation or acronym for) WIDE AREA NETWORK.

wannabe *noun* a person who hero-worships and imitates someone else, often a pop star; person who wants to be someone else or aspires to a way of life that is beyond them; (adjective) behaving in this way; emulous or envious. Originally US slang, mid eighties, formed from the informal pronunciation of 'want to be'. Among the first to be given this name were wannabe surfers, longing to be accepted, and more recently there was a glut of Madonna lookalikes.

-ware In computerese, a popular combining form; see LIVEWARE, SHAREWARE, VAPOURWARE, WETWARE. It is borrowed from the second syllable of SOFTWARE (*ware* meaning 'articles' as in 'glassware'), and has been used in numerous coinages since the early seventies. Many of them are short-lived or restricted to specialist contexts in computing.

warehouse party *noun* large, commercially organised party for young people, where they can dance to very loud popular music and have ready access to drugs. The numbers attending are usually so great that only a *warehouse* or a building of similar size, such as an aircraft hangar, can accommodate them. Another feature of such parties is that they are normally advertised by word of mouth, often at the last moment, so as to avoid detection by the police: many parties are illicit, and the police are additionally concerned with drug traffic. The *warehouse party* originated in the UK in the early 1980s, and developed a particular association with HOUSE music and the ACID HOUSE party as these crazes reached the UK from America in the mid eighties. See also ORBITAL.

WASP or **Wasp** (acronym for) White Anglo-Saxon Protestant i.e. a member of the US middle or upper class descended from the first N. European settlers. This group is often thought to be the most powerful and privileged in American society. The acronym, often used derogatively, was coined in 1962.

wasted *adj.* seriously damaged by drug abuse. Sometimes also used of alcohol abuse. Slang, c.1968, mainly US.

Watergate see -GATE.

weenybopper *noun* a child, especially a girl, aged approximately 8–12, who enjoys pop music and other fashions. A seventies colloquialism based on the slightly earlier TEENYBOPPER. The *weeny-* element is from 'teeny-weeny', meaning 'very small', and implies that a *weenybopper* is younger than a teenybopper, though the two terms may seem interchangeable.

Weight Watchers, weight-watcher *nouns* the first is a tradename (1964) for an organisation, originally US, formed to promote slimming by diet-control, though the singular *Weight Watcher* had been patented in 1960 as an adjective for foodstuffs said to be good for slimmers. The second (1966) is the general term for anyone who is trying to lose weight, especially by dieting.

well woman *noun* a woman who attends a clinic for preventive monitoring, screening tests, etc. to make sure she is healthy, not because she is ill. Most often found used attributively in **well-woman clinic** (late seventies). Based on the much earlier *well-baby clinics*, such clinics reflect the growing interest in preventive medicine as well as the feeling that in the past women's medical problems have sometimes been overlooked by what has been a male-dominated profession. **Well man** and **well person clinics** are now beginning to appear.

welly or **wellie** *noun* a kick or forceful effort. Most often found in the phrase **give it some welly** – an invitation to try harder or go faster. The underlying idea is of a wellie (wellington boot) being put to good use, as, for example, pressing down on the accelerator.

wet *adj.* (of Conservative politician or policy) not taking a hard line, especially in economic matters; liberal. In its familiar colloquial sense of 'ineffectual, foolish, soppy', this is said to have been one of Margaret Thatcher's favourite adjectives for those political colleagues thought to lack her own toughness. After this became known (1980), it was common for certain Tory politicians to be described as *wet* or one of *the wets* (and for others to be called *dry*). This terminology – which some politicians use of themselves with

wet look

pride – appears to have survived Mrs Thatcher's demise and continues to denote different political emphases within the Tory party.

wet look   *noun* and *adj.* (of) shiny appearance as if glistening with wetness. Originally (1968) used of leather or synthetic materials used for clothing and footwear, but later applied to lipstick, hairstyle, etc.

wetware   *noun* (in computing) the human operator of any computer. Modelled on SOFTWARE, this seventies coinage is a reminder that any computer depends on the human *brain* (the *wet*ware) for its effective operation.

whammy   *noun* blow or setback causing a serious problem or upset. Al Cap's comic strip *Li'l Abner* was responsible for popularising this term in 1951: his character Eagle Eye Feeney could put people in an unnerving trance by looking at them: his stare with one eye was called a *whammy*; in emergencies he used both eyes, giving the *double whammy*. The word thus meant 'the evil eye' or 'evil influence', and soon came into wider use as 'burden, jinx, bad luck'. Al Cap did not invent the word, however, though he must be credited with *double whammy* which made a surprising appearance on Conservative Party election posters in 1992 – the first time most British people had come across it. *Whammy* existed earlier in US colloquialism in the sense of 'paralysing blow' and in such expressions as *put the whammy on* (overpower). It appears to come from the colloquial and echoic *wham*, used variously since the twenties as a noun, verb and interjection denoting the use of a heavy blow. This sense of 'knockout blow' is now the dominant one, and the one likely to pass into British colloquialism. Since the 1992 election there have been many examples of *whammy* being used, rather colloquially, to mean 'severe shock', 'worrying event', 'bombshell', etc., and of *double whammy* meaning two such blows in quick succession. The popularity of the term has led to the emergence of a verb *whammy* ('he was whammied by the news' i.e. stunned, dumbfounded).

wheel and deal   *verb* to engage in bargaining and scheming. Also **wheeler-dealer** *noun* a person who does this, usually quick-wittedly. Originally US slang, now colloquialism (c.1960) frequently with derogatory overtones. Although *wheel* implies turning – and perhaps twisting – or manoeuvring, these are not the senses here. *Wheel* means 'act as a leader, innovator, entrepreneur' from US slang *big wheel*, a big shot or important person.

wheelchair games   (same as) **Paralympic Games**. An inaccurate colloquialism (1972) as competitors are not necessarily confined to wheelchairs.

wheel clamp   *noun* a clamp designed to immobilise an illegally parked vehicle by being locked to one of its wheels. Also a *verb* to immobilise a vehicle in this way; and, by extension, the owner of the vehicle may be said to have been clamped. The term dates from the eighties when **wheelclamping** came into general use in the UK. Before that the device had been known as a DENVER BOOT.

wheeler-dealer   see WHEEL AND DEAL.

wheelie *noun* a stunt on a bicycle or motorcycle in which the front wheel is raised off the ground and the rider balances on the rear wheel; a stunt in a motor-car in which the vehicle is driven, usually by a stunt driver, while balanced on two wheels on the same side (1966).

wheelie bin *noun* a large refuse bin with wheels. Introduced in the UK c.1986. The slightly playful name (*wheelie* is informal, and previously unknown in the sense of 'wheeled') was perhaps intended to make the bin sound like a toy and thus improve its acceptability. It is in fact unpopular, because the wheels are there so that the householder can push the bin to the pavement and refuse-collectors can more easily (and cheaply because more quickly) do their work. The bins are large and difficult to manoeuvre when full, and there are even reports of pensioners attempting to clean them out who have tumbled right in – but this may be an URBAN LEGEND.

whistle-blower *noun* a person who informs on someone or something in order to draw attention to a malpractice, often in government or big business. The *whistle-blower* (1970) is normally an insider and is often punished by dismissal. The term comes from 'blow the whistle on', i.e. expose an irregularity as a referee does when blowing a whistle to signal a foul. Earlier the phrase simply meant 'put an end to', as a referee does when blowing a whistle for the end of a match.

white goods *noun* electrical household appliances which are normally white, such as refrigerators, washing machines and freezers. The term is found only in the language of merchandising (1960).

white knight *noun* a hero, rescuer, or champion; (in Stock Exchange slang) a company or person who rescues a company from an unwelcome takeover bid or from financial problems, etc. The first of these meanings is from the early seventies; the second is from c.1981. The origin of the expression appears to be Lewis Carroll's *Alice Through the Looking Glass* (1865) in which there is a character called the White Knight, an enthusiastic but ineffectual person. The origin of the meaning, however, appears to be the more general, romantic and traditional notion of the 'knight in shining armour' – riding on a white charger and dedicated to the rescue of damsels in distress – and the associations of 'white', the colour of purity, honesty and hope. The emergence of *white knight* with a new meaning in the latter part of the twentieth century is one of the curiosities of modern English.

white-knuckle *adj.* causing terror and/or tension; nail-biting. The reference is to the way that certain experiences cause us to grip something with our hands until the knuckles turn white – as on a **white-knuckle ride** at a fun-fair (late eighties).

whiz(z) kid *noun* a young person who is very successful, active, brilliant and innovative in his or her particular field. The term was coined as 'Whiz Kids' to denote a team of clever young people got together in the USA by General Motors. It became generally known in 1960. It may be based on 'wizard' but is more likely to come from the well-established verb *whiz(z)*, an echoic word meaning 'to make a buzzing sound, or move with a buzzing sound, as of a body rushing through the air'. Whiz kids therefore whizz around, busily skilful, or whiz along rapidly.

wholefood   *noun* food containing no artificial additives and eaten in its natural state, having been processed as little as possible. For example, wholemeal bread is made from flour containing the whole grain, not from white flour which has had the bran removed and has usually been refined in other ways as well. The word is first found c.1960; by the end of the decade it was well known and *wholefood* products were generally available, initially in specialist shops but later quite widely.

wicked   *adj.* very good. Young people's slang, originally US, since the early eighties. It may originate in earlier US slang or in Black colloquialism: see BAD for another example of the reversal of normal meaning.

wide area network   *noun* (in computer technology) the linking over a wide area of a number of different computers or LANS by cable or phone. An extension (early eighties) of the function of the LOCAL AREA NETWORK. Frequently shortened to WAN. It may involve a multi-sited organisation linking its LANs, or it might mean setting up a system whereby one organisation's computers talk to those of other organisations. The INTERNET is a public access WAN open to anyone who can afford a telephone and modem.

wilding   *noun* a group rampage with the intention of terrorising, thieving, assaulting, etc. US youth slang, mainly Black, apparently from the title of *Wild Thing*, a pop song. The word was first reported in 1989 in connection with a gang attack on a woman in Central Park, New York.

wimmin   *noun* women. A late seventies non-sexist spelling which avoids the syllable *men* and was preferred by some feminists because it signalled their independence from men. Because it became associated with aggressive feminism, it has never caught on in the way that other attempts to avoid sexist usage have, and if met at all now is likely to be being used facetiously.

wimp   *noun* a feeble, insipid, ineffectual person. This meaning became established in the late sixties or early seventies, though the word goes back to the beginning of the twentieth century with other meanings. The derivation is probably from 'whimper'. Mr Wimpy, the cowardly character in the US cartoon *Popeye*, is more likely to have been named after *wimp* than be the source of it, as some have suggested. In the eighties, the popularity of the word gave rise to *wimpish* and *wimpishness* and to a slang verb *wimp out* (1986), to fail to do something because of cowardice.

WIMP, Wimp   (acronym for) WINDOWS, ICONS, MENUS (or mice: see MOUSE) and pointers (or PULL-DOWN). Computerese for a type of screen-display designed to simplify the use of small computers. The basic feature was the use of a mouse to select from options represented by icons and menus displayed in windows on the computer screen. This type of computer, developed during the seventies, became commercially available during the early eighties and proved to be very popular into the following decade.

Winchester disk (drive) *noun* (in computer technology) type of hard disk memory of large capacity. So called (1973) because its IBM number was 3030, the same as that of the famous Winchester rifle.

wind of change *noun* a new current of opinion. The phrase was popularised as a result of its use by Harold Macmillan, the then prime minister, when addressing the South African parliament in 1960; he was referring to the development of African national consciousness, and his reference was bold and controversial in the political context of the time. It is not known whether the image of the *wind of change* was invented by the diplomat who wrote the speech, David Hunt, or was inserted by Macmillan, who revised it, or by some other reviser.

window *noun* (in computer technology) any rectangular area of a VDU screen that can be operated separately from the rest of the display; (in politics) a period of time during which certain action is possible. The first (mid seventies) belongs to an important development in computer technology that became widely known in the eighties and continued into the nineties: the use of *windows* permits different files to be displayed simultaneously on the screen and manipulated. The popularity of this technique has given rise to *window* as a verb meaning 'to divide into windows' or 'to use windows'; the form *windowed* and *windowing* also exist. The word is often found with a capital letter either to distinguish it from the every day sense of 'window' or because it exists as a trademark. The origin of all these usages is the similarity between the shape of windows in a wall and that of rectangular areas on a screen. The second goes back to LAUNCH WINDOW and subsequent US official jargon such as *window of opportunity* (1980); initially used by US military strategists and negotiators in arms talks, this soon became an eighties catch-phrase for any opportunity capable of being turned to one's advantage. During the late eighties, busy executives, especially YUPPIES, were fond of looking for *windows* rather than 'spaces' or 'spare time' in their appointments diaries. This sense of 'period of unbooked time in a schedule, timetable, etc.' is presently the dominant one.

wind surfing *noun* a sport in which the participant stands on a SAILBOARD in order to sail. Officially known as 'boardsailing', and sufficiently well established to have been an Olympic demonstration sport in 1984, *windsurfing* (1969) is still best known by this name. It comes from *Windsurfer*, trademark of a sailboard introduced in 1969 at the very beginning of the new sport; the name is a simple combination of *surfing* with the power of the *wind* in the sail.

wind up *verb* to irritate, make (a person) tense (1979). Also *noun* **wind-up**, an instance of such teasing or infuriating (1984). Slang, from the idea of winding up a mechanism, such as a toy or watch, so that its spring is in a state of tension and ready to be activated.

wine lake

wine lake   see CAP.

winkle-pickers   *noun* shoes or boots with prominent, elongated, narrow, pointed toes. Slang, c.1960, describing a teenage fashion of the day; it recurred briefly in the eighties. The term implies that the shoes are so long and sharp that they could be used for extracting winkles from their shells.

winter of discontent   *noun* the winter of 1978–9, marked by serious strikes in the UK. The strikes of the 1978–9 winter are thought to have been a determining factor in the fall of the Labour government and the election of Margaret Thatcher's first administration in May 1979. These consequences, and the subsequent anti-union legislation, are said to have brought to an end the period of attempted partnership between governments and unions that had been an important feature of post-war politics, and to have replaced it with a more aggressive form of government that marginalised union power. *Winter of discontent* has become almost a historical term for the cause of this termination of consensus politics. It was first used by Peter Jenkins, a political journalist, in January 1979; he borrowed it from the opening lines of Shakespeare's *Richard III*, in which it refers to the reign of the Lancastrian King Henry VI, brought to an end by his murder and the accession of the Yorkist Edward IV, in the Wars of the Roses.

-wise   It is common to add this combining form to a noun in order to avoid using a longer phrase meaning 'as far as ... is concerned': thus *pricewise* means 'as far as the price is concerned'. This colloquial habit grew up in the US during the 1940s and has continued to the present, producing new formations every year to join such established forms as *timewise*, or *profitwise*. Some purists consider such coinages as ugly and unnecessary.

with-it   *adj.* fashionable, trendy, up-to-date; understanding what is happening, being said, etc. In this adjectival form, the term was popular sixties slang; it is still sometimes heard, though it is rather dated. The phrases *to be/get with it* (to be/become fashionable or alert to what is going on) are earlier US slang, possibly from Black musicians' vocabulary.

wobbly, throw a   *phrase* to lose one's temper or self-control, become suddenly angry, agitated or unstable; act in an unexpected way, causing consternation. Slang, c.1977. *Throw* can mean 'perform' or 'execute', notably in *throw a fit* which may be the basis for the present expression: it is close to it in meaning as well as form. *Wobbly* is best known as an adjective meaning 'unsteady' or 'shaky'; *a wobbly* is therefore 'an unsteady piece of behaviour'. More recently **wobbler** has emerged as a variant of *wobbly*.

wok   *noun* a large bowl-shaped metal pan used in Chinese cookery. The word, from Cantonese, has been known in Britain since the early 1950s, though it became generally known only in the early eighties. Since then, as a result of the popularity of Chinese cooking – especially among the more cosmopolitan younger generation – the *wok* has become a familiar item of kitchen equipment.

womanist   *noun* a Black feminist; a supporter of the **women's**

movement who is opposed to the aggression and exclusive emphasis of radical feminism. Coined in 1983 by the US writer Alice Walker, who felt that the feminist movement in the USA was racist and divisive. She wished to popularise a term which linked the rights of womanhood and the community as a whole. *Womanist*, however, is not much heard outside the USA.

women's liberation (movement) *noun* the movement for the removal of practices and attitudes based on the assumption that men are superior to women, for the equal treatment of women, and for their social and psychological emancipation. The term was coined c.1966, closely followed by the more colloquial *women's lib* (1969). A supporter of the movement then became popularly known as a *women's libber* (1971), though the term is not liked by the supporters themselves. The older terms 'feminism' and 'feminist' are now preferred, together with the WOMEN'S MOVEMENT, while 'liberation' is reserved to denote an earlier, more militant phase in a struggle against oppression which many think has now been largely won. See LIBBER and POST-FEMINIST.

women's movement *noun* now preferred term (c.1969) for the slightly earlier and more explicit **women's liberation (movement)**. It also implies a grass-roots movement as distinct from that of the more militant liberationists.

women's studies *noun* academic courses in history, literature, etc. concerning themselves with the role, experience, emancipation etc. of women. Virtually unknown before 1970, they suddenly became popular in the US as a result of the rapid development of WOMEN'S LIBERATION in the late sixties.

wonk *noun* an excessively and tediously studious or hard-working person. Originally and chiefly US c.1962. It is a disparaging term, implying that a *wonk* is boring, pedantic, obsessive, and full of specialist knowledge and facts rather than high intelligence. The origin is unknown: it may be *know* spelt backwards, but is more likely to be an invented nonsense word, perhaps from student slang. The *-onk* sound is rare in Standard English but common in colloquialism e.g. *honk* (vomit), BONK, YONKS, ZONKED, and is perhaps thought to be inherently funny. Chaplin, for example, used *schtonk* as an invented word when lampooning Hitler's oratory in *The Great Dictator* (1940).

woopie or **-y** *noun* an elderly, often retired person who is comfortably or well off. The word (late eighties) is formed from the initials of 'well-off older person' and the diminutive -y or -ie, on the model of YUPPIE. It is one of several jocular coinages that followed the success of that word, and has the additional advantage of echoing *whoopee* (a cry of joy) and *make whoopee* (have an exuberantly joyful time), not to mention the *whoopee cushion* (1960), something which looks like a cushion but which, when sat on, makes a farting sound.

word processor *noun* a computer used for the preparation and production of letters, reports, documents, etc. (1970). Also **word processing**, the use of a computer for this purpose. It typically

word(-) wrap(ping)

combines a keyboard, microprocessor, VDU and printer, and can handle corrections, justified margins, hyphenation, varieties of typefaces and graphics, the movement of paragraphs, the numbering of pages, alphabetisation and the checking of spelling or even grammar. Material may be stored, or dispatched by ELECTRONIC MAIL to another computer for storage or reading.

word(-) wrap(ping) *noun* (in computer technology) the automatic transfer of a partially typed word from the end of one line to the beginning of the next so that the word can be completed without going beyond the pre-set margin. Also called **wraparound**. A term in **word processing** since c.1977.

workaholic *noun* a person addicted to work. Also **workaholism** *noun* compulsion to work incessantly. Coined by the American WE Oates, who popularised them in his *Confessions of a Workaholic* (1971) though he had used them three years earlier in an article and they had become current very rapidly. *Workaholic*, the more popular of the two, is based on the earlier *alcoholic*, and has given rise to several *-aholic* imitations, such as CHOCAHOLIC or *chocoholic* (a person who eats a lot of chocolate), and jokey SHOPA-HOLIC.

workfare *noun* a scheme under which unemployed people must work (e.g. by doing unpaid community work) or undertake training in exchange for their social security (i.e. welfare) payments. Chiefly and originally US, first heard c.1968 and still an important political issue during the presidential election of 1992. The word is based on 'welfare', as in 'welfare state', a system in which government provides for the wellbeing of the population by financially supporting the old, the sick and the unemployed. In the free-market economy, however, such official Governmental altruism has to be matched by the individual recipient's willingness to do his or her bit by working. Thus 'welfare' (assistance given to the needy) must give way to *workfare* (assistance which is earned).

work station *noun* (in computer technology) (a desk with) a computer terminal comprising keyboard and VDU linked to a mainframe computer (1977). The user has access to the database of the company, organisation, etc. to which the mainframe belongs. The keyboard may be used to send messages to other terminals or to the mainframe. Incoming messages may be stored until an appropriate time. Increasingly, a *work station* does not have to be in a conventional office; it could be at home, or be carried about.

world music *noun* a genre of popular music marketed in the UK and US and combining conventional Western mainstream (i.e. ROCK) music with music of various ethnic origins and styles. In practice this often means a mingling of commercial rock with African folk music. *World music* (c.1988) is also used adjectivally to denote a performer or group with an interest in this sort of music.

World Wide Web *noun* the interactive exchange of information and commerce over the Internet. The **Web** is a global (hence *World Wide*) hypertext system – i.e. capable of interrogation and interactive use – a cross between a magazine, an encyclopedia and an art form. Its system of hypertext links allows you to jump from computer to computer – hence 'WEB'. The term became widely known in the early nineties, at a time of growing interest in the INTERNET.

worm *noun* a form of computer VIRUS. The term was invented in 1975 though not generally known until 1988 when a substantial network of US computers was temporarily sabotaged. The name is based on well established definitions of *worm*, e.g. a parasite, or anything that corrupts, gnaws or torments.

WORM (acronym for) write once, read many times (1985). In computer technology, this is an optical memory or storage device consisting of a disk on which large quantities of data are written once by laser and which then is ROM.

worst-case *adj.* having to do with the worst possible combination of circumstances. Although not responsible for its coinage (c.1964), military bureaucrats popularised this term, especially in the cliché 'worst-case SCENARIO' when discussing the possibilities of nuclear warfare during the Cold War.

wraparound *adj.* (of sunglasses) having lenses extending around the side of the head. Also *noun* such sunglasses. From c.1966. See also WORD-WRAP.

wrecked *adj.* drunk; under the influence of drugs. Slang, originally US, c.1967.

wrinklie or **-y** *noun* a middle-aged or elderly person. Strictly speaking, younger than a CRUMBLY, though also used in the same general sense. British slang of the early seventies, used mainly by young people, and sometimes thought to be derogatory because of its reference to facial wrinkles. However, the term is usually jocular.

write-in *noun* a form of organised mass protest by the sending of a large number of letters of complaint to a person in authority, MP, organisations, etc. See PHONE-IN for the probable model for this term (1972).

WYSIWYG (acronym for) what you see is what you get. A computing term meaning that what is displayed on the VDU is exactly the same as what will appear on the printout. Pronounced 'wizi-wig', the jargon (1982) was generated by the introduction of high-resolution screen-display and the rapid development of desktop publishing offering a variety of typography, etc. Increasingly *wysiwyg* is being used more generally in a variety of claims to UP-FRONTNESS in many different contexts.

yah *noun* (another term for) SLOANE RANGER. An affectation of Sloanes, and, to a lesser extent, YUPPIES, is or was to pronounce 'yes' as *yah*, frequently and loudly. In the early eighties the word was therefore used as an alternative name for them.

Yardie, yardie *noun* a member of a Black, mainly or exclusively Jamaican, criminal gang or syndicate dealing in international organised crime, especially drug-trafficking. Also **the Yardies**, these gangs or their members as a whole. The organisation has been generally known since the late eighties, but *yardie* is older as Jamaican slang for any Jamaican (or West Indian). It comes from

yellow card

Jamaican English *yard*, meaning 'home' or 'house'; *Yard* with a capital letter is therefore another word for Jamaica and a *Yardie* is someone from the home country.

yellow card see RED CARD.

yellow rain *noun* in S.E. Asia, a form of chemical pollution falling as rain, causing injuries to people, and alleged by some to be produced by chemical warfare (1979).

yesterday's men *noun* men with outmoded ideas; men whose achievements are behind them. Used especially of politicians and particularly by the Labour party of the Tory leaders in a poster slogan in the election campaign of May 1970. Later the phrase was turned against them as the title of a TV programme about Labour screened by the BBC in June 1971.

Y-fronts *noun* men's underpants with a front seam in the shape of an inverted Y, part of which forms an opening. From *Y-front*, the trademark of a tight-fitting style of men's vests and underpants introduced by Lyle and Scott in 1953. The style became so popular that *Y-fronts* was virtually synonymous with 'underpants' until the 1980s, when fashions changed.

Yippie *noun* a politically active HIPPIE. From the initials of Youth International Party, an anarchic organisation which is now only of historical interest. US slang, 1968.

yips, the *noun* (in sport) nervous tension or twitching that spoils concentration and performance. First used (c.1963) in golf, but later in other sports requiring steadiness and control of hand and arm. The origin of the term is unknown.

yo *interjection* an expression of greeting, or to attract someone's attention, or to express excitement. Originally US Black slang of the second half of the seventies, it spread by way of RAP and became a cult greeting among young people in the UK during the eighties. *Yo, yoho* and *yo-heave-ho* have existed for centuries as exclamations used to call attention or to warn, but the current use seems unrelated.

yomp *verb* to march across difficult terrain with a full army pack as part of a military operation. Also *noun*, a march of this kind. The word was unknown to the general public until it emerged as Royal Marine's slang during the Falklands War of 1982. Its origin is unknown, though it has been tenuously linked with two Scandinavian terms, one from car-rallying, the other from cross-country skiing. Attempts have been made to incorporate it into civilian use meaning 'go for a long and arduous walk', but these have not caught on.

yonks *adv. phrase* for a very long time. Popular slang, originally upper-class, since c.1968. The derivation is unknown.

young fogey (or **fogy**) *noun* a young or youngish man (below forty, say) with the dress, manners and views of the previous generation. Typically, he is middle-class, traditional, Conservative, prematurely middle-aged and opposed to 'anything new'. The term is a parody of the familiar 'old fogey' – a fussy, old-fashioned, reactionary, jingoistic elderly man – and has been much used since the early eighties, mainly as a result of the installation of a distinctively Conservative government in the UK. The expression had cropped up in literature a couple of times before then, as an occasional witticism based on 'old fogey', but did not become common until the appearance of a recognisable type in the eighties.

YTS (abbreviation for) Youth Training Scheme. A government scheme to provide vocational training for unemployed school leavers and other 16–17-year-olds, introduced in 1983.

yuck or **yuk** *interjection* an exclamation expressing disgust or dislike (1966). Also *adj.* **yucky** or **yukky** nasty, disgusting (1970). Both are slang. *Yuck* probably originated as an imitation of the sound made by children when expressing strong distaste. *Yucky* followed a little later and has the subsidiary meaning of 'messy', 'sticky', 'gooey', 'oversweet', even 'sentimental'.

yuppie or **-y** *noun* a young, ambitious, cash-conscious executive, especially one working in business, finance, etc. An acronym for 'young urban (upwardly mobile) professional person' plus the common **ie** ending as in *hippie*, etc. It was coined in the US and became one of the best known colloquialisms of the period, inspiring many jocular imitations denoting lifestyle: see WOOPIE, WRINKLIE, CRUMBLIE, for example. The rapidity with which it spread to the UK, established itself, and immediately produced a rash of formations such as **yuppiedom**, **yuppified**, etc., shows the extent to which it answered the need for a word to denote the cocky, materialistic, self-absorbed money-makers of the Thatcherite eighties, and the ostentatious, consumerist lifestyle they followed. *Yuppie* soon took on pejorative overtones. The deepening of the recession in 1990, and the political demise of Margaret Thatcher towards the end of the same year, were among the factors that helped to change the climate.

yuppie flu or **disease** *noun* (informal name for) ME and some other long-lasting viral disorders associated with stress. The name (c.1986) reflects the fact that such disorders are associated with high achievers such as YUPPIES, though its informality also reflects the lack of seriousness with which the medical profession regarded **ME** until c.1990. *Yuppie flu* is the more common term because the condition has debilitating effects similar to those caused by flu, and sometimes follows an attack of flu. See ME.

zap *verb* to use a remote controller to channel hop or fast forward when watching live or recorded TV, especially so as to avoid the adverts. **Zap** began as an echoic word in American comic strips to represent the impact of bullets or the firing of ray guns. In the Vietnam War US troops used it to mean 'kill' or 'strike', as in 'Zap the Cong' and it then passed into computerese in the sense of 'erase'. *Zap* also means 'to move quickly', and these various meanings come together in this latest use, when the remote control device (see ZAPPER) is aimed at the set to erase one set of pictures and move on to another.

zapper *noun* the remote control device for a television set. Slang, late eighties, from ZAP. Also someone who habitually channel hops using the remote control (mid eighties).

zero option   *noun* (in international arms negotiations) a proposal by one side to reduce the number of, or not to deploy, nuclear missiles if the other side will do the same. The expression originated in 1981, perhaps as a translation of a German phrase. *Zero* implies reduction to nothing; this option was never realistically on offer at the time, and *zero* therefore smacks of propaganda. The *zero option* proposed was made by the USA to the Soviet Union at the INF talks, 1981–3, but came to nothing at the time. The *zero-zero* (or *double zero*) *option* (1984) was a later proposal by the Soviet Union for the withdrawal by both the Soviets and the Americans of all short and long range nuclear weapons from Europe.

zero-rated   *adj.* (of goods and services) on which no value-added tax is chargeable (1971).

ZIFT or **Zift**   (acronym for) zygote intra-fallopian transfer, a technique for helping infertile couples to conceive. The egg is fertilised with the partner's sperm outside the body (thus becoming a *zygote*) and is then re-implanted in a *Fallopian* tube. The technique belongs to the second half of the eighties.

zilch   *noun* nothing. US slang, c.1966. Its origin is uncertain though it may be from Yiddish 'nich' (nothing) with a mixture of 'zero' and 'nil'. Or it may be simply a borrowing from Zilch, the invented surname of a family of characters in a US comic magazine from 1931.

zit   *noun* a pimple, especially one caused by acne. Originally US slang, c.1966, but well known in the UK by the 1980s. The derivation is unknown.

zonked   *adj.* utterly exhausted. This slang meaning (c.1972) grew out of an earlier one, 'intoxicated from drugs or alcohol' (1959). This in turn developed from an earlier echoic word *zonk* (c.1949–50) suggestive of the sound of a blow or heavy impact, and *zonked* still suggests the effects of having been knocked out by such a blow.

zouk   *noun* a style of dance music with African and Latin American elements, using some electronic instruments and technology. Originating in the French Antilles, this became known in Paris in the late seventies, and in the UK in the late eighties. It is joyful in style; its name seems to come from a Guadeloupean word.